BRUTAL CATALYST

WHAT UKRAINE'S CITIES TELL US ABOUT RECOVERY FROM WAR

Russell W. Glenn

KEYPOINTPRESS
BOULDER, COLORADO

An AUSA Book

AUSA
ASSOCIATION OF THE
UNITED STATES ARMY

Copyright © 2024 by Russell W. Glenn
All rights reserved. No portion of this book may be reproduced in any form without written permission from the publisher or author except as permitted by U.S. copyright law.

KeyPoint Press
Boulder, Colorado
keypointpress.com

Edited by Penny Brucker
Cover design by William Kelley

Cover image of tattered Ukrainian flag used with permission of photographer Mykhaylo Palinchak https://palinchak.com.ua

Layout/Typesetting by Michael Mysik

"Language Geography of Ukraine" map used with permission of Translators without Borders/CLEAR Global

ISBN 979-8-9909158-4-8 (Ebook)
ISBN 979-8-9909158-5-5 (Paperback)
ISBN 979-8-9909158-7-9 (Hardcover)
www.ukrainecities.com

To those—soldier and civilian—who defend their freedom in the face of unwarranted aggression and all who assist their recovery from its depredations

TESTIMONIALS

"Dr. Russ Glenn in his latest work, *Brutal Catalyst*, has proven himself to be the foremost authority on urban recovery from war. This seminal work that captures innumerable lessons learned from recent history is now and will continue to be biblically indispensable for Ukrainian and all civil authorities in providing an essential blueprint for recovery from the devastations of war. This splendid tome also has broad applicability for those urban areas recovering from the severe impact of natural disasters. Meticulously researched and brilliantly written, *Brutal Catalyst* is another magnificent and invaluable achievement from one of the most distinguished scholars in the areas of warfare and recovery from it."

—*Lieutenant Colonel Daniel T. Miltenberger (US Army, retired), former faculty and staff, US Army War College, co-author,* Guide to IGOs, NGOs, and the Military in Peace and Relief Operations

"Urban warfare is brutal and disruptive, damaging both physical and social systems. Corruption, crime, and ethnic conflict are among the consequences of this disruption. Dr. Glenn, one of the world's premier scholars of urban operations, examines the situation in Ukraine in light of historical context to inform civil and military leaders alike on the perils and promise of post-war recovery in cities. This is an essential read for those seeking to learn how to plan and implement urban recovery efforts."

—*Dr. John P. Sullivan, Research Fellow, Arizona State University Future Security Initiative; Instructor, Safe Communities Institute, University of Southern California*

TESTIMONIALS

"*Brutal Catalyst* fills a significant gap in the professional libraries of soldiers and diplomats alike. As the commander of multiple urban battles in Iraq and Syria, I found that if the operation's purpose is anything other than a Carthaginian outcome, reconstruction planning is at least as complex and important as planning for the battle itself. Most of the world's population is now urbanized so that city fighting will be unavoidable in future wars. Russ Glenn's examination of the impact of war on Ukraine's cities is exactly what future post-conflict planners will need to help them understand their task."

—*Lieutenant General Sean MacFarland (US Army, retired),
former Deputy Commanding General of US Forces in Afghanistan*

"In *Brutal Catalyst,* soldier-historian Russ Glenn delivers a clear, well-argued, well-documented study of the man-made disasters that befall cities at war, post-war, and even by accident, as in the case of the Halifax explosion. Brutal Catalyst is neither a military nor an urban history but takes each as context. Accessible to the general public, this book is of particular interest to soldiers, historians, and political scientists who need to understand the complex systems that constitute cities today. After the fall of Aachen eighty years ago this fall, the 1st Infantry Division sent Lieutenant Robert G. Botsford, a one-time writer for *The New Yorker*, into the city to assess the condition of its facilities. Botsford's report concluded, "the city is as dead as a Roman ruin, but unlike a ruin, it has none of the grace of gradual decay." Such is the fate of most cities in which modern armies fight. *Brutal Catalyst* promotes understanding of that and what recovery will be like. Like

TESTIMONIALS

Aachen, Ukraine's cities will recover, but the road ahead will be long and hard."

—*Colonel Gregory Fontenot (US Army, retired), Commander, 1st Brigade, 1st (US) Armored Division in Bosnia-Herzegovina, 1995-1996*

"Dr. Glenn's *Brutal Catalyst* strikes the key chords on the spectrum of considerations vital to the ongoing and future recovery of Ukraine's cities. The deadly material and human costs of war being inflicted upon a liberal democracy by an authoritarian Russia haunt us daily in the news and social media. Yet history tells us that cities and peoples devastated in war can rebuild and come back even stronger than before. The analysis and policy guidance found in this important new work is indispensable reading for governmental and private donors who provide the lifeblood funding which supports international urban recovery efforts."

—*Dr. Robert J. Bunker, Director of Research and Analysis, C/O Futures, LLC and past Minerva Chair, US Army War College*

"At last compelling proof that widely applicable lessons from the ongoing conflict in Ukraine go way beyond both the tactical and the military. Nothing brings to life the concept of cities as finely woven and finely balanced "systems of systems" as starkly as the compelling, hyper-contemporary examples in Russell Glenn's *Brutal Catalyst*. What is clear is that repairing such systems after shock or crisis requires a comprehensive and coordinated approach balanced in both the short and long terms. Glenn's insights clearly signpost the nature of urban recovery from this war and other conflicts yet to come. This book deserves, and needs, to be widely read."

—*Lieutenant Colonel Ben Baker MBE (British Army, retired), former British Foreign Office Urban Conflict and Security Advisor*

"An expert in how wars are waged and the destructive impact of conflict in urban areas, Russell W. Glenn's historically informed analysis is a must-read for any town planner, government official, economist, or private donor contemplating how Ukraine rebuilds and recovers from the present war."

—*Dr. Rhys Crawley, University of New South Wales Canberra, author of the Official History of Australian Operations in Afghanistan, 2005-10*

"Dr. Russell Glenn has produced a well-researched and historically contextualized study of war-torn Ukrainian urban spaces. His observations and conclusions inform a traditional audience of military professionals and provide exceptional insights for organizations addressing war's influence in cities. *Brutal Catalyst* is a uniquely informative volume that will empower these responding agencies with practical, actionable solutions, instilling a profound sense of hope and optimism for the future in themselves and the people they are helping, inspiring and motivating them in their crucial work."

—*Dr. Howard G. Coombs, Director of the Queen's University Centre for International and Defence Policy, Kingston, Ontario, Canada*

"Cities are complex ecosystems made even more so by conflict. This compelling study of urban populations devastated by military force—from Tokyo to Mariupol—

explores the myriad challenges of successful recovery. It is an essential starting point for anyone hoping to bring such cities back to life."

—*Lieutenant General J.J. Frewen AO DSC (Australian Army, retired)*

"When I first walked the high ground in Frankfurt, Germany, my warrior-historian father shared pre-WWII pictures of the city, devastation from the war, and how the city was rebuilt. He noted that we were standing on rubble delivered by human chains and looking at a new city rebuilt largely with US help. Russell Glenn's book captures the idea that we know how to do this, brilliantly, and why we must close out the war in Ukraine properly to avoid recurrence."

—*Major General Paul D. Eaton (US Army, retired)*

"Having an effective and executable recovery plan after a major conflict is foundational to the long-term success of any war-torn nation. Dr. Glenn's solid historical research and astute pragmatic analysis identify key trends that policymakers should consider as they grapple with what to do in Ukraine now and postwar. Truly appreciating these trends allows critical leaders to set the conditions for recovery and renewed growth as Ukraine rises from the ashes. This book is valuable to both military and civilian professionals as well as the informed and interested public."

—*Major General Anthony Funkhouser (US Army, retired), former Commander, Afghanistan Engineer District–South, 2010-2011*

OTHER BOOKS BY DR. RUSSELL W. GLENN

NONFICTION

- *Come Hell or High Fever: Readying the World's Megacities for Disaster, 2023.* Available for free download at https://press.anu.edu.au/publications/come-hell-or-high-fever

    "The time to prepare for the inevitable is now. Dr. Glenn has written a book that should be read by all leaders, planners, and responders who may be called upon in an urban disaster, whether natural or man-made."
    — Lieutenant General (US Army, retired) Sean MacFarland

    "This excellently researched book frames the discourse on megacities in the *all-hazards* perspective, namely exploring disasters along the natural, technological, and man-made (to include war conflict) continuum. It maintains perfect balance in straddling topics and cases across emergency management, national defense, civil defense/civil protection, and as such is unique as an offering to Homeland Security and Emergency Management (HSEM) scholarship."
    — Dr. Magdalena A. Denham

- *Trust and Leadership: The Australian Army Approach to Mission Command, 2020*

    "An essential addition to every leader's library."
    — General (US Marine Corps, retired) James N. Mattis, 26th US Secretary of Defense

ACKNOWLEDGMENTS

"An important and insightful exploration of what it takes to nurture mission command."

– *General (Australian Army) Angus J. Campbell, AO, DSC, Chief of Defense Force, Australia*

New Directions in Strategic Thinking 2.0: Proceedings of the Strategic and Defense Studies Centre's Golden Anniversary Conference, 2018

"Never before has the call for reasoned innovative security studies thinking been more pronounced. Rarely has a group so able to offer that thought come together.... This book encapsulates the essence of this cutting-edge thinking and is a must-read for those concerned with emerging strategic challenges facing Australia and its security partners."

– *Book is available for free download at http://doi.org/10.22459/NDST.07.2018.*

Rethinking Western Approaches to Counterinsurgency: Lessons from post-colonial conflict, 2015

"A much-needed corrective, analyzing modern variations of insurgency and the range of innovative responses to it.... Should be required reading for all students and practitioners of this complex and constantly-evolving form of war."

– *Dr. David J. Kilcullen*

Counterinsurgency "isn't dead; we just need to do it better.... Essential reading."

– *Nicholas P. Warner, Director-General, Australian Secret Intelligence Service*

OTHER BOOKS BY DR. RUSSELL W. GLENN

■ *Reading Athena's Dance Card:*
Men Against Fire in Vietnam, 2000

"A superbly researched book that digs deep into all the controversial subjects dealing with grunts in that tragic war…. A great book for students of why and how men fought in Vietnam at the bayonet level."
– *Lieutenant General (US Army, retired) Harold G. Moore*

"This book is a must-read for the true military professional."
– *Lieutenant General (US Marine Corps, retired) George R. Christmas*

FICTION

■ *Gods' War (an American Civil War novel), 2023*

"In God's War, Lee's prescient strategic genius at the command of the more powerful Union Army of the Potomac manages to avoid the historical butchery and mass casualties of Ulysses Grant's 'human sledge-hammer' 1864-5 Virginia Campaign…. God's War is a 5-star novel that appeals to a wide range of readers—from Civil War buffs to casual readers seeking a well-informed account of what might have been."
– *Dr. Jerry D. Morelock, Senior Historian/Senior Editor,*
America's Civil War magazine

"For those who like to speculate what might have been with a President Robert E. Lee, this book will certainly be of interest."
– *Lieutenant Colonel (US Army, retired) Edwin L. Kennedy*

CONTENTS

Testimonials iv
Other Books by Dr. Russell W. Glenn vi
Acknowledgments xv

CHAPTER 1
INTRODUCTION 1
- The Pages Ahead 7
- A Momentary Aside Regarding
  Statistics and a Look Ahead 14

CHAPTER 2
UKRAINIAN CITIES AT WAR 19
- Disaster as Opportunity 30

CHAPTER 3
**THE PAST SPEAKS—DRAWING ON PREVIOUS
URBAN WARTIME DISASTERS** 37
- Post-WWII Tokyo and Nagasaki 40
  - Tokyo 41
  - Nagasaki 57
- Berlin 58
  - Architecture as Competition 75
- Manila 79
  - Manila in the Immediate Aftermath 82
  - Ties That Bound, Ties That Hindered 86

CHAPTER 4
RECOVERY IN AN ETHNICALLY STRIDENT CAPITAL (SARAJEVO) . 93
- The Ethnicization of Sarajevo 105
  - The Costs of Ethnicization 115

CHAPTER 5

THREE CITIES, THREE FATES — RECOVERY IN KHARKIV, KHERSON, AND MARIUPOL 121

- Occupation Touches but Lightly;
  Not so Bombardment: Kharkiv 122
   - *Kharkiv's First Steps Toward Recovery* 131
   - *What Funds Can't Buy: Soft Challenges to Kharkiv's Recovery* 135
- Occupations Heavier Hand: Kherson 147
- Propaganda's Front Lines:
  The Enduring Occupation of Mariupol 155
   - *Occupied Mariupol* 161

CHAPTER 6

MORE ON CHALLENGES FOR CITIES RECOVERING FROM WAR . 173

- International Cooperation and Assistance 180
   - *Orchestrating Aid: Improving Effectiveness,
     Enhancing Efficiency, and More* 188
- Plans and Planning Considerations 195
- Leadership and Management 210
   - *A Brief Further Look at Funding* 223
   - *A Closing Thought on Centralized Orchestration* 225
- Housing, Building, and Employment 226
   - *Approaches to Housing and Other
     Infrastructure Recovery in Ukraine's Cities* 230
- Health Care 236
- Millions in Debris, Billions of Dollars:
  Disposing of Unexploded Ordnance in Ukraine 240
   - *The Demining and Unexploded Ordnance Disposal Burden* . . . 241
   - *Unexploded Ordnance in Cities:
     War's Dangerous Lingering Legacy* 245
   - *Further Specifics Regarding Clearance
     of Unexploded Ordnance in Ukraine* 252
   - *Closing Thoughts on Unexploded
     Ordnance Neutralization* 258
- The Mire of Collaboration 263
- The Other Mire: Corruption 270
- The Specter of Ethnic Conflict 283

CONTENTS

- Education and Information Campaigns in
  Previously Occupied Cities 290
    - *Education and Re-Education in Post-WWII Japan* 291
    - *Enter the Occupiers* 293
    - *Education and Re-Education in Germany* 298
    - *Education Insights for Ukraine* 304

CHAPTER 7
CONCLUSION 311
- Adapting for Today, Readying for Tomorrow 313
- Recovery Can't Wait 321
- Monitoring, Measuring, and Managing
  Urban Recovery 327
- Black Markets and Ukraine's Urban Recovery 347
    - *Once Again: Tokyo, Berlin,
      Manila, and Sarajevo* 349
    - *The Arizona Market* 357
    - *Further Thoughts on Controlling Black Markets* 367
- Closing the Ethnicity Gap in Ukraine's
  Information Operations Armor 374
- Preparing for the No Longer Unthinkable: The Nuclear Threat to
  Ukraine's Cities 376
- Closing Thoughts 384

Notes 393
About the Author 455
Bibliography 457
Index 495

TABLE OF IMAGES

IMAGE 1. MAP OF UKRAINE SHOWING SELECT CITIES 20

IMAGE 2. MAP OF POST-WWII ALLIED SECTORS IN BERLIN 64

IMAGE 3. MAP BOSNIA-HERZEGOVINA WITH BRCKO AT UPPER RIGHT 97

IMAGE 4. WELL-CONSIDERED MIXED ARCHITECTURE (VIENNA) 175

IMAGE 5. RUSSIAN POM-3 ANTI-PERSONNEL MINE 244

IMAGE 6. LANGUAGE GEOGRAPHY OF UKRAINE 286

ACKNOWLEDGMENTS

The individual meriting first recognition in these acknowledgments remains unknown to me. Having submitted an article to the *Journal of Strategic Security* for consideration, one peer reviewer recommended to journal editor Jay Tamsett that he ask me to expand the shorter piece into a book.[1] Jay, in turn, asked whether I might put my now thirty years of urban-related research toward such a venture in support of his newly created KeyPoint Press. Another nod of thanks in his direction for a willingness to support what will hopefully prove an offering of some value to a country seeking to free itself from the most recent miseries born of living next to one of history's worst neighbors.

Four gentlemen make recurring appearances in my various books' acknowledgments. Rusty Rafferty at the US Army's Combined Arms Research Library is an army civilian whose dedication to country matches that of serving military members, past and present. If one were to need a human exemplar of "reliable," it is Rusty. Greg Fontenot evolved from being a former boss to good friend and intellectual sparring partner. A superb historian and gentleman, he is also among those whose interview input added substance to the following pages. Longtime colleague Dr. Luc Pigeon offered his ever-pithy insights, valuable nuggets from one of Canada's most innovative minds. Chris North, thanks for sharing thoughts over the years and a contact for this book.

ACKNOWLEDGMENTS

The staff of the Williamsburg (Virginia) Regional Library are unfailingly helpful in running down hard-to-get articles and books. Allison, Avery, and Dwight are but three among many whose efforts helped me add depth and breadth to the chapters below.

Those interviewed or who provided understanding otherwise unavailable include Damir, Tony Funkhouser, Paul Heslop, Karl Jensen, Erik Kramer, David McMahon, Laurie Venter, and several others who remain anonymous at their request. Special recognition is due to interviewee Pehr Lodhammar. He not only agreed to be interviewed again after supporting my research for *Come Hell or High Fever: Readying the World's Megacities for Disaster* but kindly responded to email queries addressing issues needing clarification.

And, of course, thanks to my wife Dee, who persists in sticking with someone who will never run short of subjects on which to write.

CHAPTER 1

INTRODUCTION

> Military men, while skillfully planning their intricate operations and coordinating complicated maneuvers, remain curiously blind in failing to perceive that it is the outcome of the war, not the outcome of the campaigns within it, that determines how well their plans serve the nation's interests.[1]
> — Fred Charles Ikle, *Every War Must End*

> It is an easier task to convert from peace to war than war to peace.[2]
> — Bernard M. Baruch and John M. Hancock, "Report on War and Post-War Adjustment"

Warsaw was 80 percent destroyed. The city had lost 800,000 of its pre-war 1.3 million residents. Germany had crushed uprisings during its 1939 invasion, those in the Jewish ghetto in 1943, and a third time as Soviet forces approached in 1944. Slaughter during the last alone numbered an estimated 150,000 civilian deaths. Another 650,000 suffered deportation to labor camps. Warsaw, in the words of historian Maciej Siekierski, was "a vast desert of hollow-shelled buildings and rubble" when the Soviet army belatedly arrived toward the end of World War II.[3] It would take until the end of 1947 to remove roughly one million cubic meters of rubble and neutralize some 100,000 pieces of unexploded ordnance.[4] Half a world away, Manila's pre-battle population of one million had seen 100,000 killed and tens of thousands wounded after Americans reseized the city from Japanese occupiers in 1945. Tokyo, Berlin, Hamburg, Coventry, Hiroshima, and Nanking were among so many other cities visited by the same conflict's devastation. Some recoveries were little short of miraculous. Tokyo rose to become the world's most populated urban area. Manila ranks sixth today.

War inflicts terrible suffering on those living in cities and the environment in which they live, work, love, and raise families. Wartime destruction suffered by 21st-century cities has too little diminished despite improvements in weapons technology.[5] There is nevertheless room for optimism when considering urban areas' post-war recovery. Construction equipment, materials, techniques, and technologies all have undergone dramatic advances since the mid-20th century. Ukraine too—the focus of this book—experienced several enviable improvements in the years just prior to Russia's most recent intrusion. The number of citizens living below the nationally defined subsistence income level more than halved between 2015 and 2019, improvements particularly notable in the country's urban areas. Internet usage nearly tripled during the decade ending in 2020.[6]

CHAPTER 1

War imposes cruelties of its own, but disasters share many lessons regardless of cause. "We need to think of Russia as a natural disaster, like they do a tsunami or earthquake in Japan," concluded Valentyna Poliakova of Ukraine's State Agency for Restoration and Infrastructure Development during a 2023 visit to Tokyo. Fellow team member Igor Korkhovyi requested copies of national regulations regarding disposal of post-earthquake rubble, recognizing their applicability to his own country's war-ravaged cities.[7] Korkhovyi remarked on the security advantages of placing electrical substations underground…though we will see such placement can bring risks of its own.

Urban recovery entails far more than repairing or replacing buildings. Authorities in Nice, France grasped this in the aftermath of its tragic July 2016 terrorist attack during which a truck plowed through over a mile of Bastille Day celebrants. City leaders saw opportunity in disaster. The event inspired construction of new streetcar lines, reducing traffic along the city promenade by 20,000 vehicles daily. Protected pedestrian and bicycle lanes sprouted along streets. The longtime haven for retirees became a draw for France's younger as well. Residents and officials alike came to recognize the importance of psychiatric support to address maladies that, zombie-like, can rise again months or years later. In Nice, it was the runup to the trial of eight individuals accused of involvement in the attack that generated a renewed spike in post-traumatic stress symptoms. Nice also validates the seemingly unavoidable truth that some urban residents will find what most see as progress undesirable. Vehicle drivers complained new bike lanes too greatly narrowed those left for cars. Others were unhappy with plans to expand the city's urban forest.[8]

Ukraine will confront similar tensions as cities recover from its struggle with Russia. Unlike in Nice, however, theirs is not a single, short duration event. Punishment continues even as recovery proceeds. It is a learning recovery, one simultaneously addressing both damage done and ways to reduce that yet to come. Infrastructure repairs benefit from clever thinking no less than military equipment adapted to new challenges. Strikes on generators and other power equipment magnify costs when the original installation ignores vulnerabilities. Urban engineers now disperse key infrastructure components around the country...and beyond.[9]

It is notable that though the examples on which this book draws are primarily urban, most of what follows can inform wartime recovery regardless of the environment. Among the obvious (yet sometimes overlooked) insights: War is a brutal catalyst. Its end does not mark the return to a previous norm. Some will champion a return to the familiar. Others see a chance to introduce greener and safer progressive designs. (We will see that movement toward no-emissions energy and away from easier-to-target larger power generation facilities are already in progress.)[10] History tells us neither is likely to seize the day. Officials' desires, public input, and economic reality are but three factors driving an end in which a blend of alternatives all but inevitably proves both desirable and unavoidable. History likewise informs us that physical rebuilding tends to dominate initial thinking. Focus on the material alone, however, ignores the many other ways in which a city will evolve during and in war's aftermath.

Russia's targeting of energy, education, medical, and other social support infrastructure demonstrates that waiting for peace is not an option.[11] Five waves of attacks between March and June 2024 reportedly "completely destroyed" power stations owned by Ukraine's DTEK private energy provider, the output of which was 20 percent of that in Ukraine. Countrywide losses totaled approximately eight gigawatts of production, nearly half of what is needed to meet the country's demand during peak periods.[12] Such deficiencies force the kinds of decisions Kyiv's leaders confront across all sectors during national recovery. As we will see was the case in Tokyo, Berlin, and elsewhere after World War II, attempting to balance immediate housing, food, and other of a suffering population's needs with demands to restart the economy and thereby provide jobs and a quicker return to economic normalcy leaves no good options, only those less bad. These tough decisions cannot wait. Ukraine's leadership and international aid providers already recognize this truth. It has not always been so. Franklin Delano Roosevelt disliked "making detailed plans for a country we do not yet occupy.... I cannot agree at this moment as to what kind of Germany we want in every detail."[13] Delay created confusion when Europe's war ceased in May 1945. Consequences of similar procrastination in 2003 Iraq, nearly sixty years later, proved more severe, spawning years of misery after short but brutal combat operations there.

Iraq's and broader regional stability continues to suffer the consequences today.

Nation states are by far the largest funders of postwar recovery. They are not the only parties taking on the challenge. As evident in the ruins of Gaza as I write, nongovernmental organizations and intergovernmental organizations (NGOs and IGOs, respectively) often brave affected areas even as bombs fall, shells detonate, and soldiers battle on city streets. Many of their personnel are present before combat's start. Those members' consequent knowledge of real-time conditions and understanding of local populations can be a valuable resource for any willing to ask and listen. Understanding local populations offers dramatic benefits. Too often city government authorities and architects dominate early recovery planning, overlooking the myriad of individuals and interest groups who should have a say. They are the ones who will live with the results day-to-day. (It says much when politicians adept at soliciting support during elections ignore the electorate when recovery is at hand.) NGO and IGO aid providers can identify individuals legitimately representative of resident communities. These same men and women can later be conduits for officials explaining the reasoning behind recovery decisions, thereby promoting acceptance and mollifying those less enamored with decisions. Wise governmental and intergovernmental representatives vet anyone purporting to speak for a community. Many such people are sincere and wish to assist the mending process. Others are less so. Pursuit of personal economic advantage and power is sure to lurk within some purporting selflessness. Of this, more later.

CHAPTER 1

▌ The Pages Ahead

> Braving rain and snow, hundreds of Ukrainians gathered last week outside the Kyiv City Council with signs reading, "I don't want a park" and "Why do I need paving stones?" They chanted, jumped, and clapped as they called for an end to road repairs and a freeze on the construction of a new subway depot. Protesting the renovation of one's city may seem highly unusual, especially in a country whose president was elected four years ago on a promise to repair roads. But protesters said a more urgent cause demands funding today—the war effort.[14]
> — Constant Méheut, "More Drones, Fewer Parks."

> The emergence of a large group of people with a new set of values represents a fundamental change in the history of Ukraine. We can call them the new urban middle class.... Ukraine now has a large sector that is less dependent on government influence and less riddled with corruption. To successfully survive and compete, the owners and employees of this sector need to know everyone is playing by the same rules. This makes them potential change agents.[15]
> — Yaroslav Hrytsak, *Ukraine: The Forging of a Nation*

The pages to follow take much from history. Other authors have of late briefly looked over their shoulders at the topic of recovery from war, most often to call for something akin to the post-WWII Marshall Plan. The past might offer insights in that regard, but differences between conditions then and what confronts Ukraine now outnumber similarities by a fair margin. The Marshall Plan had a single, overarching fund source, for example: the United States. Ukraine is instead already benefiting from (and suffering bureaucracies of) many. Each funder has its own motivations. Constraints accompanying assistance vary in equal measure. It is unrealistic to believe Ukraine can ignore these motives without consequences. Yet, there will be a need to restrain funders seeking to influence recovery in ways counter to legitimate Ukrainian objectives.

Were Ukraine's urban recovery not difficult enough *within* the arenas of economics, social interactions, architecture, and politics, those responsible for planning and turning plans into reality must also orchestrate legitimate considerations *across* these functions. Looming over their efforts is the darkness of ethnic division—the use of ethnicity as a latent or deliberately politically-manipulated weapon in the service of self-interest. We will consider the unfortunate lessons of Sarajevo in this regard, knowing not dissimilar antipathies lurk in Ukrainian communities, antipathies Russia is and will continue to exploit.

Descriptions of urban areas as systems and parts of larger systems might strike those familiar with urban studies as trite. Yet planning and implementing recovery operations without acknowledging these ties that bind would result in funds being misspent, inefficiencies tolerated, and recovery delayed. Alternatively, recognizing the interrelationships means acknowledging the existence of second and higher-order effects resulting from every decision and action taken. Making the effort to identify and understand these links increases synergies and seizure of opportunities otherwise surely overlooked. If those familiar with my previous work will indulge me, the following representation is one some have found helpful:

CHAPTER 1

> Imagine a pool table. It's a good metaphor for explaining urban relationships given their complexity. Let's say that three numbered balls on the table represent the population in a rural environment, or maybe a few market towns tied to each other economically. We might hit one, two, or maybe all three of that trio after striking the cue ball. Each could in turn impact others. Regardless, the consequences of our strike are easy to guess beforehand. Now let one rack of numbered balls represent 1 million people in a population. Tokyo's population of nearly 38 million becomes 38 racks of balls dispersed across the table's felt surface (that's 15 x 38 = 570 balls, for those wondering). Manila is 25 racks (375 balls), Kyiv 3 (45). Strike that cue ball now. Determining just the second-order effects (the secondary collisions of any initial balls impacted by the cue ball) begins to boggle the mind. Figuring out third, fourth, or higher-order effects would send you fleeing the room.[16]

The larger the urban area, the broader its influence. There are exceptions. A particularly notable cultural center, economic niche filler, or location on a hyper-strategic piece of land inflates impact. But for our purposes, the lesson is clear: Planning and managing recovery won't be easy for any city. Leaders in larger urban areas will find it less easy yet. Nonetheless, keeping a systems perspective in mind during recovery should help those responsible from repeating an already-mentioned frequent stumble from past undertakings: too great a focus on the physical to the detriment of the whole. Typical recovery retellings tend to contemplate whether a city sought to return to its previous architecture or replace its fabric with something new where war's tearing presented a tabula rasa. A systems approach should protect us from these too narrow assessments, forcing recognition that recovery includes not only physical infrastructure but any others that are relevant. This wider reflection should preclude egregious errors resulting from not recognizing the totality of roles cities play in the many systems of which they are a part.

Urban recoveries can be reactionary, progressive, or revolutionary. They are likely to integrate elements of all three. This means decisions facing Ukrainian urban leaders require them to know of their city's past, what adaptations will likely prove wise, and when risks offer benefits sufficiently great as to make them other than gambles. The key lies in finding the right balance. Solomon would be bamboozled. That other cities have trod similar paths offers rich food for thought. That experts aplenty offer their advice is at once irreplaceable and cautionary as their expertise is essential to effective recovery but often lacks local savvy. There is thus a need for balance within the pursuit of the larger balance.

Man does not wage war in the military arena alone. Unfortunately, the arrival of peace in Ukraine will not mark the end of conflict. Russia will perpetuate its war via incursions in economic, informational, social, cyber, and other domains. The evolution from hot to warm war will present challenges unlike those at the end of WWII. Yes, recoveries in the aftermath of that and other earlier confrontations can inform these pages, but Russia's continued malice will preclude the cooling from reaching the status of cold.

Russia is the aggressor in the war underpinning the reason for this book. Yet these pages do not linger on apportioning blame. Nor do they waste readers' time speculating on how a war waged by a more civilized government in Moscow might have spared Ukraine's people and properties. The interest here is how Ukraine's cities might more effectively recover by drawing on lessons from the past when addressing the phenomenon of urban disaster.

The Swedish Defence University's Kristin Ljungkvist posits, "it is only in the last few decades that military thinkers and strategists have seriously started to consider urban warfare as imperative—that cities have become unavoidable in war." She goes on to consider "what appear to be mismatches between these urban battles and the type of urban wars anticipated and planned for by Western military organizations and strategic thinkers."[17] That anticipating future urban combat has proven difficult is no surprise. A far from comprehensive list of examples in this century alone spans the use of firepower from what would have been familiar to many World War II veterans (Fallujah, Iraq, and the Israel Defense Forces in 2024 Gaza), others pitting national militaries against insurgent forces (Marawi, Philippines and Mosul, Iraq), and yet further examples revealing weapons virtually unknown several years ago. Another fly in the forecasting ointment is the size of current urban areas' populations and geographic expanses, both tending to be dramatically larger than all but their largest WWII counterparts.[18] The population of the 2022 Kyiv urban area was a hair's breadth over 2.9 million. Kharkiv sat at just under 1.5 million.[19] US large-city ground combat experiences in WWII maxed out at one million in Manila (1945).[20] Five years later its armed forces retook Seoul, population 1.1 million. Even the largest city in which ground forces competed in World War II (Berlin) had a population of only 2.8 million at the time of Russian capture in 1945.[21] [Note: An "urban area" includes the political entity of its eponymic city and other urban features in the immediate vicinity. Countries use a variety of often very different definitions for urban areas. One I have found consistently useful and with the advantage of being easily envisioned: an urban area is "a continuously built-up landmass of urban development containing no rural land—one best thought of as the lighted area that can be observed from an airplane (or satellite) on a clear night."[22] Interestingly, the Romans viewed urban areas similarly, using the term *extrema tectorum*, meaning the expanse of a contiguous built-up area.]

Yes, the focus herein is unapologetically urban. That might risk some thinking the book suffers from what political scientist Stathis Kalyvas calls "urban bias," too-great a focus on cities to the neglect of rural or small built-up areas.[23] I trust I avoided the pitfall. A reviewer might instead accuse me of covering much with application well beyond urban considerations alone. To that I plead guilty. One of my doctoral advisers, the unfortunately now passed Dr. Roger Spiller, once told me a person can't understand history if they only focus on one of its disciplines. A military historian who reads only of battles cannot understand the forces motivating conflict, the political decisions behind a country going to war, or the diplomacy that either sought to prevent or manipulated war's declaration. Thinking one can be an expert in American history without delving into

CHAPTER 1

Great Britain's past would make understanding the American Revolution or either of the world wars virtually impossible. (Some have not recognized Spiller's wisdom. When taking a history course spanning American history from the late 1700s to the later 19th century, I asked an instructor why we completely neglected the American Civil War. Putting it nicely, the response "War is only a series of battles" cast doubt on the individual's credentials as a historian.)

This is not to say Kalyvas's concern doesn't merit consideration. Those reporting or studying overseas tend to live in or travel primarily to cities. That is where they are more likely to find needed life support broadly available, quality of life higher, and internet and phone coverage more reliable. The consequences can include mistaking urban experience as representative of a country or people as a whole. That misconception can be skewed further if the city in question is a capital. (Few would consider Washington, DC as remotely representative of United States urban life generally.) That Ukraine's cities are at once systems themselves and parts of other systems means that, in keeping with Dr. Spiller's insight, one cannot understand how the country's urban areas recover from war without understanding how they are inextricably interconnected with the rest of Ukraine and beyond.

Irony has a particularly hard edge when considered in light of Russian leaders' behavior in Ukraine:

> During the brief but violent France-Prussian War of 1870-71, the city of Paris and its civilian population had come under indiscriminate bombardment resulting in the death of hundreds of Parisians…. Nations bristled with

new weapons of destruction, each striving for superiority in a 19th-century arms race. In an attempt to defuse tension, Russian Czar Alexander II convened a conference in Brussels in 1874 to discuss, of all things, proper behavior during times of war. There had already been a conference in 1868—also convened at Russian invitation—in Saint Petersburg, Russia, to "humanize" warfare.... At the 1874 Brussels meeting, the international delegates who attended displayed surprising benevolence by forging restrictions on state power. Violence to civilians was a strict violation of their "new" order of warfare. Total war and reprisals against innocents were condemned.... Then, in a move tailored to embellish the humanitarian works of his grandfather, Alexander II's grandson, Nicolas II, convened another session in May 1899, inviting participants of the 1868 and 1874 meetings. This would be known as the First Hague Peace Conference.[24]

A Momentary Aside Regarding Statistics and a Look Ahead

> Hospital beds were limited in number and far below demand. Medical supplies were scarce and many of the hospitals were completely out of narcotics.... In the borough of Steglitz it was estimated that out of 14,000 homes, 3,260 had been destroyed, 3,200 were uninhabitable, and in the remaining 7,500 which were considered habitable, 10,000 out of 43,000 rooms were seriously damaged, and only 5 per cent undamaged.[25]
>
> — Lucius D. Clay, *Decision in Germany*

Facts are a historian's bricks. Some are stronger and more reliable than others. War's perpetrators and their apologists have less regard for facts than might be the case in less conflicted times. The former compete on many fields other than those military. Economic, social, informational, and diplomatic are but a few. The latter employ misinformation and disinformation to induce favorable views of those they support. Wartime bricks are therefore often of lesser quality than those formed during peacetime. Such has ever been the case as kings and warriors, dictators and sycophants, presidents and media inflate *raison d'être*, tales of heroism, magnitude of victories, and punishment inflicted on an adversary. One would have hoped the invention and rise of the internet would have strengthened the stuff of which bricks are made. Its offerings have proved otherwise, introducing another form of Clausewitz's fog of war. It is increasingly difficult to determine whether a source is reliable, fabrication, or even whether it is human.

War is fertile soil for distortion. Deceivers have raised deception and falsehoods to fine art, fine in the sense of sophistication rather than merit. Armed conflict promotes the cultivation of hatred to motivate soldier and civilian alike. Enemies become vermin, beasts, automatons, or barbarians. Such constructions are easier when longstanding ethnic frictions provide fuel awaiting a spark. They are easier yet when the distorters have a talent for inventiveness.

Statistics are among the types of information suffering. The turmoil consequent of war means validity is at risk even when there is no deliberate effort to deceive. Sometimes the deluge of numbers acts to confuse despite that not being the intention. (Though I will provide statistics when thought helpful, I aspire to restrain the flow a bit more than did Lucius Clay in the quote above...but admit I don't always succeed.) Further, armed conflict can render false once authentic values. Estimating a city's wartime population becomes something of a guessing game as casualties, refugees, and influxes of combatants enter or leave. All this is to say statistics appearing in these pages are unavoidably sometimes approximations. Population, casualty, and military force numbers are amongst the most dynamic of values when war visits a city. Nor are statistics the only dubious bricks with which to build analysis. First-hand accounts are subject to bias depending on the interviewee, interviewer, authors' or editors' word choices, or—in the worst cases—the imagination of alleged rapporteurs with little interest in the truth other than its value as a facade. Add to this the unavoidable reality that historians are imperfect beings (as much as it pains me to admit). Most of us, unlike some politicians, will readily admit such is the case. The conscientious historian seeks to avoid falsehood or partiality to the extent possible, including by seeking out multiple sources when available (they often are not); by gauging the likelihood of assertions given past events of similar kind; by constantly searching for inconsistencies; by evaluating the reliability, reputation, expertise, and experience of a source; by turning to others known to be more familiar with the events under consideration; and by doing all possible to suppress their own inherent and frustratingly unavoidable subjectivity. I have written these pages with the ambitious end of accuracy always in mind. Ultimately, that is a mark on a wall unattainable despite unquestionably being worthy of the pursuit. I share the view of Ukraine as the violated country in the ongoing war. I have striven to avoid that bias showing in what appears below.

And now I take bricks of varied strength to complete this offering. The following chapter briefly reviews how Ukraine arrived in its current state due to Russia's renewed incursions on its sovereign territory. (I do not, by the way, hold this war began on February 24, 2022. It is at a minimum a continuation of that begun in 2014 with the usurpations in Crimea and Donbas.) Chapter 3 draws on four historical cases of cities ravaged by war and their subsequent recovery, all victims of World War II fighting: Tokyo, Nagasaki (briefly), Berlin, and Manila. Thereafter we consider an instance in which ethnic divides intensified the agonies of war and hindered—and continue to hinder—recovery of both the city in question (Sarajevo) and the country of which it is the capital. In Chapter 5 we again turn our attention to Ukraine. The focus is on three cities, each representing varying extents of Russian occupation. Kharkiv was violated by enemy ground forces only on its periphery and in its suburbs, though that did not, does not, spare it from air and artillery attacks. Kherson bears the scars of Russian capture and several months of occupation before returning to its rightful fold. The third case, Mariupol, is one of loss and continued occupation at the time of writing. Each of this trio offers lessons unique to its individuality as a city and extent of occupation. Drawing on the more distant historical discussions of Chapters 3 and 4 and those of the three Ukrainian urban areas, Chapter 6 views collective insights these several cases offer in the following areas:

- International cooperation and assistance
- Plans and planning considerations
- Leadership and management
- Housing, building, and employment
- Health care
- Unexploded ordnance disposal
- Collaboration with the enemy
- Corruption
- The specter of ethnic conflict
- Education and information campaigns in previously occupied cities

A concluding chapter gives particular attention to factors less recognized in disaster literature. Included are challenges inherent in measuring recovery effectiveness, the benefits and dis-benefits of black markets, further discussion of difficulties posed for officials when addressing some of the issues considered in Chapter 6, and a brief reflection on the nuclear weapons threat to Ukraine.

CHAPTER 2

UKRAINIAN CITIES AT WAR

> Bombing is serious and sensational. It makes headlines, kills people, and smashes property; but it doesn't win wars.[1]
> — Edward R. Murrow, *This is London*

> There could be no more crushing demonstration of Germany's abject condition after VE-Day than this. It was, as the Germans themselves called it, *die Stunde Null*, hour zero: the moment of the hiatus when the people of a nation that had ceased to exist touched rock-bottom, when the hands of the stopwatch were reset to zero and began to tick toward an unthinkable future.[2]
> — Douglas Botting, *From the Ruins of the Reich: Germany 1945-1949*

Russian forces advanced on four main fronts during their February 24, 2022, continued invasion of Ukraine. Key cities were the primary objectives. The invader pushed toward Kyiv from Belarus in the north as did other forces from the northeast. Kharkiv was the target for incursions from the Donbas in the east while Kherson, Odesa, and Mariupol were among the foci of Russia's Southern Front forces.[3] Kyiv: symbolic because it is

Ukraine's capital city, desirable as Russia envisioned its capture marking the collapse of resistance and return of Ukraine to Russian control.

Image 1. Map of Ukraine Showing Select Cities[4]

Kyiv remained free two months later. Irpin, a suburb, had fallen along with other outlying areas during the initial assaults. It was retaken by Ukrainian forces in late March. Kharkiv's city center escaped occupation. Less fortunate edges and suburbs would return to Ukrainian control in September. Kherson fell, and the invaders soon introduced policies to Russify the city. It would remain under occupation until November when it too was again free. Defenders in Mariupol held out until mid-May, although they were, by that time, well behind enemy lines. Roughly 130,000 of the city's original 430,000 population remained trapped with Ukrainian fighters as Russian forces continued west. Estimates of Ukrainian noncombatants killed in the city ranged as high as 21,000.[5] Thousands of mines strewn by the two sides denied farmers use of their land and killed soldiers and civilians indiscriminately. Trenches scarred landscapes across Ukraine's east and south. In Kherson, Mariupol, and elsewhere, the invader's ultimate goal was evident as its officials ordered the replacement of Ukrainian hryvnia with the ruble. Occupying authorities rerouted internet traffic through Russia. Reminiscent of the Soviets in World War II, soldiers plundered factories, stores, and homes; seized control of power plants and industrial facilities; raised Russian flags on Ukrainian government buildings; purged Ukrainian symbols from city squares and walls; and introduced re-education programs in schools and communities.[6] The adjective was Russian rather than Soviet, but residents in Warsaw, Berlin, Vienna, and other cities occupied in 1945 would have readily recognized the depredations.

The term "urbicide" increasingly appeared in Western descriptions of the invaders' approach to the war in 2022. Russian urbicide meant disproportionate casualties among noncombatants, in particular, what one author labeled "definitive civilians": "women, children, the elderly and infirm, and persons who were not just noncombatants but [were] mainly involved in continuance of, and dependence on, civil life." He further cited the deliberate targeting of civilian housing, historical and culturally-significant buildings, and civil support infrastructure such as hospitals, schools, and religious sites.[7]

Cities are the merit badges of war. Each taken marks an accomplishment proudly displayed as a measure of progress. The bigger or more prominent the city, the more important the achievement, thus the significance of Ukraine repulsing Russia's attacks on Kyiv and Kharkiv. But propaganda value is not the only reason major urban areas receive attackers' attentions. Cities are transportation hubs through which reinforcements and other of war's sustainment flow. Control means ensuring the movement of your forces and denying the enemy theirs. Cities are often themselves sources of sustaining supplies. Loss of larger cities has a disproportionate impact on perceptions of progress, morale of those in the victor's (and often defeated's) ranks, and international support. Russia's own histories of WWII celebrate Moscow and Leningrad's defense, Stalingrad's recapture, and seizure of Berlin as a symbol of ultimate victory. In Ukraine's cities, Vladimir Putin imposes his political and economic facades most publicly although they are no more legitimately Russian than Potemkin's villages were real.

Whether attacked by ground forces, bombarded by air, or left untouched by military aggression, few if any of Ukraine's cities have escaped war's effects. Even those in the relatively safe west have and continue to occasionally taste war firsthand. Cruise missiles struck Lviv in western Ukraine on July 6, 2022, killing ten and wounding forty-eight.[8] Despite this and other attacks, the city has been a conduit for those moving to other locations. An estimated 5 million had transited Lviv as of October 2023. Some stayed. The city's population increased by approximately 150,000.[9] Ukraine as a country has seen over one-quarter of the national population leave their homes.

More than 7.7 million were internally displaced while estimates of those becoming international refugees vary from nearly 5.6 to 6.2 million as of 2023.¹⁰

Mined farmland, or that otherwise contaminated with unexploded ordnance, is impossible to work safely. While aid organizations assist some farmers in transitioning to new products (e.g., from crop farming to chicken raising, which is less constrained by the danger of unexploded ordnance), others find it difficult or impossible to sustain a viable living. The consequences for Ukraine are twofold. First, there is the loss of essential produce for public consumption or export. Second, the inability to work incites movement adding to the internally displaced person (IDP) or refugee numbers. Cities over 100,000 residents housed 35.5 percent of the country's population in the opening months of 2020. These larger cities were recipients of nearly half of post-February 2022 IDPs (45.5 percent). Distribution varied considerably. Several cities received over 200 IDPs per 1,000 residents [Sieverodonetsk (491), Sloviansk (381), Kramatorsk (321), and Mariupol (227)]. Four others experienced an influx of more than 50 IDPs per 1,000 (Berdiansk, Brovary, Kyiv, and Kharkiv) followed by six with over 20 per 1,000 (Pavlohrad, Dnipro, Zaporizhzhia, Odesa, Kherson, and Poltava). Together, the fourteen cities accounted for 21.1 percent of the country's population but 41.1 percent of its IDPs.¹¹ Difficulties in housing and otherwise supporting these individuals were complicated by mid-June 2022 damage to nearly 13,000 apartment buildings and an additional over 107,000 private structures countrywide.¹² The former number is particularly notable. Ukraine is 70 percent urbanized; 79 percent of its larger city residents are apartment dwellers. Continued aerial and artillery attacks add to the damage. Housing accounted for 17 percent of an estimated $486 billion in recovery costs as of early 2024, the largest of any economic sector.[13]

If these dark clouds have any silver lining, it is that many of Ukraine's apartment buildings are aged and were showing signs of wear well before the war. Only 12 percent are reported to have been built after 1991.[14] Repairs and replacement to modern standards would not only upgrade the quality of apartment living. It would also provide an opportunity to incorporate energy efficiencies and other improvements in a country where the rate of buildings' thermal modernization greatly lags most other European countries.[15] There is an inevitable tension between rapid recovery and such enhancements, however. "Temporary solutions often become permanent," creators of the Prague Charter noted in 2022 when meeting to discuss Ukraine's recovery.[16] Interruptions in recovery funding and ease of leaving quick fixes in place rather than dealing with the turmoil of re-replacement are two causes. Unfortunately, the quick and cheap "temporary" solutions hinder more effective development. They can in the long run be more expensive than getting it right the first time as maintenance and utility costs mount.

Vitally, both Ukraine's government and its partners recognize the benefits of planning for recovery even as the war continues, aspects of which were being put into effect within weeks of the February 2022 incursions. The government created a National Recovery Plan as early as mid-2022, a mix of broad-scope ambitions, detailed goals, proposed initiatives, and hopes. Elements include:

- ▶ Recognition that even pre-war, Ukraine was "lagging Central European peers in terms of economic performance." The country's gross national product was growing at less than 2 percent a year. The plan optimistically notes that recovery provides "a unique opportunity not just to recover war-related damages, but to leap-frog economic growth and quality of living in Ukraine."[17]
- ▶ The plan wisely acknowledges conflict with Russia is likely at least a semi-permanent condition even after the current war's end, a situation prosaically noted as Ukraine being "unlikely to have a 'clean victory,' 'clean peace,' or clear milestones to transition from 'recovery' to 'modernization.'" Recovery must therefore incorporate "resilience and agility for the economy to function under continuous security threats and provide the foundation to win the war."[18]
- ▶ Other aspects of the National Recovery Plan ambitiously address green and climate change initiatives, improving sustainability (and presumably resilience) of war-damaged infrastructure, mental health capabilities able to attend to what are sure to be extensive psychological well-being demands, information and other campaigns supporting smooth integration of returnees and veterans, and financing and promoting new housing best practices.[19]

Other planning initiatives recognize the centrality of urban areas to national recovery. ReStart Ukraine, for example, is "an open-source collective of researchers and practitioners who are collaborating on strategies for the postwar recovery of Ukrainian cities, [that actively seeks] collaborations with international partners."[20] It is but one of many cooperative efforts bringing together Ukrainians and outsiders.[21] These efforts tend to share several characteristics:

- Recognition that recovery should not await the end of the war
- Acknowledgment of financing's key role
- Confirming the necessity of incorporating Ukrainian citizens' views during decision-making
- Large numbers of participants, domestic and international, public and private
- Encouraging perception of recovery as an opportunity to modernize Ukrainian society and ready the country for future challenges, to include incorporation into the European Union
- The need to tackle corruption
- Affirmation that Ukrainians must lead the recovery.

The last point is repeatedly emphasized by Ukrainians themselves. They are aware of the drawbacks of international partners wielding too much influence. Concerns include issues that "can arise when supporters outside of the country seek to impose solutions upon communities with which they lack familiarity."[22] The inconsistency of US support due to its internal political struggles has also clearly made another vital point: Words spoken during well-intentioned recovery gatherings are only relevant if speakers follow through. An additional concern: the form of support can determine the pace of recovery. As of this writing, around 60 percent of the funding reaching Ukraine comes as loans rather than grants.[23] The country's recovery will be hamstrung if the burden of repayment is too great.

Government or otherwise, Ukraine's officials demonstrate a firm understanding when it comes to the value of recovery fast-tracking alongside wartime operations. Unfortunately, participants failed to directly involve the leadership of the cities involved in at least one case bringing together potential donors to the country's urban areas. Unlike in Tokyo and Berlin eighty years ago, Ukraine and most of its city governments remain free of occupiers. They, not outsiders, retain responsibility for recovery. The benefits cannot be overstated. Ukrainian contracting practices and its construction environment pose conditions that are unfamiliar to many. Better those most familiar are able to provide the continuity key to coherent recovery locally and, ideally, countrywide. (This is not to overlook the considerable challenge of corruption and bureaucratic lethargy, which will be discussed later). As the German Marshall Fund's Henri-Paul Normandin observes, "international cooperation has demonstrated time and time again that resources and good intentions do not necessarily make for good and effective development."[24] Yet, partnership is and will continue to be essential. Ukraine was in a period of transition from years of Soviet domination to a functioning and mature capitalist economy prior to the most recent invasion. Writing in the summer of 2022, the Organization for Economic Cooperation and Development (OECD) noted,

> Ukraine's economic transition to a competitive market economy is not yet complete. For example, competitive procurement legislation and procedures are in place, but "competition" takes place between state-owned enterprises, and many private suppliers own local resources or other capabilities that limit market entry.[25]

Knowledge of both the macro and nuanced implications of such an environment can underpin better recovery efforts. International assistance from those with experience in urban disaster recovery is unquestionably desirable.[26] The key is to avoid the imbalance that has too often resulted when underappreciating local knowledge. Yes, incorporating residents' views on their needs and wants is fundamental to effective urban recovery. Contrarily, doing otherwise courts inefficiencies at best and failure, rejection, and alienation of local populations at worst.

The above international support constitutes the first steps. When funding clears the hurdle marking the leap from promise to aid in hand, determining how best to allocate support presents one equally high. Urban recovery requires years. Some aspects will take decades (though not, hopefully, a half-century as was the case in Berlin). Year-to-year aid financing risks termination mid-project. Disruption introduces inefficiencies avoidable when guaranteed funding streams allow start-to-finish backing. Responsible design and engineering practices benefit from longer funding streams. (Even less common than longer funding guarantees: funding incorporating life cycle sustainment considerations.) Ideally, all plans and funding programs can turn to guidance provided by an overarching national urban master recovery plan prepared by Ukrainian officials (one linked to a master plan for all aspects of recovery nationwide, urban and otherwise). These would orchestrate individual city efforts such that urban recovery countrywide is synergistic rather than merely locally optimized. External donors merit seats at the table throughout the recovery process to make their requirements for continued support known (for example, in terms of acceptable levels of corruption). This participation is fundamental to both initiating and maintaining funding streams but should not overly impinge on Ukrainian management.

Multiple OECD, International Monetary Fund, European Union, and World Bank reviews continue to provide analysis of Ukrainian government activities and suggest reforms. Topics addressed advise recovery operations and approaches to acquisition of the aid necessary to turn concept into reality. Among them are government decentralization and administrative procedures, infrastructure needs, and funding policies, all of which directly impact urban recovery efforts. Funding partners are interested in the pace of physical infrastructure recovery in addition to having concerns regarding corruption and country-wide planning coherency. Attempting too much in too little time could overheat Ukraine's construction sector, leading to inflation and additional fiscal requirements. Conversely, over-reliance on international contractors could speed rebuilding but inhibit recovery of the local construction sector. That sector's recuperation will ideally include maturation as a capitalist force. It has previously been one among several lacking healthy competition.[27]

The above is but a minuscule list of EU, US, other individual countries, IGO, NGO, and other recovery initiatives ongoing at the time of this writing. The focus of this book is not to summarize these efforts. It is instead to consider how these and other, yet-to-come recovery efforts might benefit from reviewing historical cases and management practices of proven worth. Every war is a vehicle for innovation. As Elliot Cohen and John Gooch made clear in their classic *Military Misfortunes*, there is a risk for competitors failing to learn, anticipate, or adapt when combating an adversary. The degree of risk increases considerably if that "or" is instead an "and," i.e., if the failure encompasses two or all three of that trio. The same is true when the undertaking is recovery from war. The past offers much value in reducing costs, turbulence, and pain in war's aftermath.

■ Disaster as Opportunity

> Enjoy the war—The peace is going to be terrible.[28]
> — Scrawl on Berlin Wall, March 1945

> What turned out to be particularly important for those associated with town planning was to call for more positive and comprehensive state intervention, i.e., national planning…. It was now keenly realized that town planning should be part and parcel of national planning and not a local matter as it had been.[29]
> — Junichi Hasegawa, *Replanning the blitzed city centre: A comparative study of Bristol, Coventry and Southampton 1941-1950*

CHAPTER 2

Ukraine's future should seem much less dark than was the case for Berliners in the spring of 1945. The path will be long, but entry into the European Union is one of many encouraging lights at tunnels' ends for Ukrainians confronting rebuilding wounded cities, displacement of so many in their population, war-driven economic woes, related unemployment, and—according to a 2022 United Nations Development Programme (UNDP) assessment— eighteen years of lost socioeconomic progress.[30] However, the technological savvy shown by many supporting the war effort (e.g., advances in unmanned aerial and marine vehicle capabilities) suggests new avenues could speed recovery in the economic sector. The "opportunity" to redesign components of the power grid fits well in this regard. A tech-progressive Ukraine will be a power-hungry Ukraine. (Electronics manufacturing in Taiwan consumes 37 percent of the country's power according to one estimate.)[31] Redesign and rebuilding can incorporate newer power generation technologies in addition to characteristics increasing the system's survivability during any future Russian aggression.

Ukraine shared several of its European neighbors' demographic challenges even before Russia's invasion. Population outflow was in progress before 2022 as those of working age pursued promise elsewhere. These losses aggravated the burden of an aging population in a country where deaths have outnumbered births since 2013. A January 2022 population of just over 41 million was 4.2 million fewer than in that year of 2013.[32] This was *before* Russia's invasion of the following month after which another up to 6.2 million left the country.[33] Further challenging Ukraine and its urban areas: It is the young who tend to live and work in cities but are less likely to return once combat ceases. To these social challenges we must add others involving physical infrastructure. In July 2022, only two-thirds of the country's population had access to modern drinking water supply systems and less than half to sewerage systems. A third of the country's sewage went directly into water bodies without treatment.[34] In short, opportunity for improvement abounds thanks to war even as war complicates the way ahead.

Fast-tracking recovery before fighting ends is wise, essential, commendable, and already a source of debate regarding its direction. How ecologically progressive recovery should be is among the primary issues. Just what comprises legitimate green programs and what role they should play are no less objects of discussion than elsewhere around the world. The transportation arena is a notable focus while also being one over which national-level responsibility is poorly defined. Control therefore falls largely on cities. It is a positive in the sense projects can more effectively address local needs. Less beneficially: Urban governing capacity and financing are often not up to the challenge of what is among an urban area's most costly enterprises.[35] While decentralization is commendable for addressing local needs, the lack of a single coordinating body at the national level and high demand for resources such as steel, power, vehicles, and other system components risks counterproductive competition akin to the struggle for low-density COVID supplies given poor management in the 2020 United States.

Such lack of sufficient centralized guidance ensures system inefficiencies, lost economies of scale, and generally exacerbates decentralization's shortcomings. Historical failures to standardize key infrastructure components include countries having incompatible recharging connectors for electric vehicles, mismatched rail ticketing systems (and rail gauges for that matter), and inconsistent standards for meeting the needs of the handicapped. Lack of standardization can be life-threatening. Over one hundred years after a disastrous fire in 1904 Baltimore, only eighteen of the United States' largest cities had fire hydrants meeting the recommended national standard. Among those with non-compliant hydrant threading or other disparities were New York, Chicago, Phoenix, and San Francisco.[36] While the damage to Ukrainian cities will generally not be such that complete replacement of transportation, information, water, sewage, and other fundamental infrastructures will be necessary, destruction provides an opportunity either to establish nationwide standards where lacking or transition to those existing. Example cities could provide the basis for national standards or voluntary adoption by other urban areas. Lviv, for example, developed an urban mobility plan in 2018 prioritizing pedestrian and public transportation movement. As in parts of New York City, separate lanes now exist for public transportation vehicles.[37]

The recent proliferation of traffic congestion in Ukrainian cities means immediate urban needs include addressing parking and public transportation shortfalls. Automobile proliferation has also resulted in high numbers of on-road and pedestrian fatalities.[38] Emerging international trends are another potential source of inspiration for inclusion in recovery planning. Growth of interest in electric vehicles suggests a reevaluation of current zoning based on fossil fuel-powered vehicles. Emerging acceptance of driverless taxis in Western countries prompts some to question the future need for current levels of parking spaces in downtown areas. Together these several issues suggest efforts to address congestion and safety challenges should integrate flexibility when repairing, replacing, or planning buildings, streets, bike lanes, and pedestrian ways to smooth future urban transport evolutions.

Vehicle-related issues are but one of many areas presenting recovery challenges. Another is the displacement of commercial enterprises to Ukraine's west and the consequent economic and employment issues for eastern cities.[39] Tackling these equitably should include acknowledging the perceptions of eastern oblast residents that Kyiv neglected them in the pre-2022 period. There will be artistry called for here. The westward movement of many commercial enterprises will prove to be permanent. The pull of employment opportunities and need to house IDPs choosing to remain in the West will demand economic support from Kyiv even as the loss of jobs and population add further misfortune to oblasts suffering the bulk of wartime damage given their proximity to Russia.

CHAPTER 2

    Innovation is a good thing. Spreading the costs of innovation and avoiding local redundancy when testing new approaches are better yet. Kyiv can promote recovery by identifying and circulating successful local approaches. Similarly, effective national-level legislation should reduce the local legal challenges often accompanying recovery, thereby avoiding delays as suffered by some British cities as they rebuilt after WWII.

CHAPTER 3

THE PAST SPEAKS— DRAWING ON PREVIOUS URBAN WARTIME DISASTERS

> The then preeminent political leader President Beirut went further, declaring in 1949 that: "Our Party must express itself not only regarding what and how much will be built in Warsaw but also what, where, and for whom.... This 'new form' would entail both rebuilding in a politically correct architectural and urban design style and the simultaneous rejection of those styles perceived to be associated with capitalism."[1]
>
> — Lawrence J. Vale and Thomas J. Campanella, "Warsaw: Reconstruction as Propaganda"

Kharkiv's mayor, Ihor Terekhov, also received Moscow's offers of collaboration in exchange for generous financial benefits under a future Russian regime. The Russians had reasons to be hopeful he would accept. Terekhov was far from a Ukrainian radical. He spoke only Russian, including when performing official functions that in theory should only be carried out in Ukrainian. Appealing to older residents still in thrall of Soviet nostalgia, he had spent the previous year opposing attempts to remove a monument to

Marshal Georgiy Zhukov, the Soviet commander in World War II, and to rename Zhukov Avenue in the city.... But all of that had been peacetime politics.... Terekhov rejected the Russian proposals.[2]

— Yaroslav Trofimov, *Our Enemies Will Vanish*

To state Ukrainians suffering war's punishment are in any way fortunate seems absurd, even cruel. Yet there is truth therein if only in the sense that residents of past cities have suffered much worse. Plague ravaged European cities in the mid-13th century. London, Paris, and Hamburg lost over half their residents to death or societal collapse due to the disease. Recent work estimates Italy's Florence saw four of every five die within four months. Dubrovnik's authorities ordered every resident to complete a will.[3]

But it is to the more recent past we will turn for insights into urban disasters. What follows is a review of wartime destruction suffered by four WWII cities (Tokyo, Nagasaki, Berlin, and Manila) and a fifth besieged for nearly four years from 1992 to early 1996 (Sarajevo). The five provide context as we consider Ukrainian cities' recovery generally and via our three illuminating examples (Kharkiv, Kherson, and Mariupol).

For some idea of how our historical examples compare with cities in Ukraine today, we recall Kyiv's population was just under 2.9 million in 2021, the year prior to Russia's renewed incursions. That is roughly equal to Berlin's May 1945 2.8 million residents but less than a third of Tokyo-Yokohama's during World War II's last year. Kharkiv, the second most populous city in Ukraine, was just short of 1.5 million in 2021, nearly half again that of Manila's February 1945 approximately one million.[4] Mariupol stood at 436,644 in 2021, Kherson an estimated 279,000.[5] Sarajevo's population in 1991 was 340,746, that being the year before the four-year siege began.[6] Irpin, a suburb of Kyiv to which we will give a bit more attention, was home to a pre-2022 population of less than 100,000. Estimates of Nagasaki's pre-atomic bomb attack population vary. Its mayor at the time estimated 270,000, a value with which British mathematician I. Bronowsky agreed during his work with the United States Strategic Bombing Survey.[7] Most estimates of the number killed range between 40,000 and 70,000.

As touched on above, Ukraine's cities have experienced a gamut of challenges during the ongoing war. Most have remained under Kyiv's unbroken government control throughout. Kharkiv is one such despite portions briefly falling under Russian control early in 2022. Others, Kherson and Irpin among them, were lost but later liberated by the Ukrainian military. Then there are those remaining subjugated, Mariupol being that from our trio of examples remaining in that status as I write. Threats from Russian forces and the damage they inflict are among the continued challenges. Another: portions of Ukraine's population remain sympathetic to Russia. That others are passionately nationalist provides a social fault line Russia will surely seek to exploit (as is evident from the second quotation at the opening of this chapter). Those sympathetic span much of Ukraine's social spectrum. Some from Ukraine's intelligence service in Kherson provided attacking Russians information on Ukrainian defensive positions, then welcomed the attackers when they reached the city. One of the city's previous mayors stood ready to assist a Russian regime.[8] To this brief list of concerns, we remind ourselves of another. Resolving the variety of views on what a city's recovery should look like and then bringing those ambitions in line with available funding has so often plagued past urban (and national) leaders as to comprise a rule. Fortunately, the past has much to say of value when confronting these and other challenges sure to come.[9]

■ Post-WWII Tokyo and Nagasaki

> On the night of November 29-30 [1944], the sirens sounded: the first night raid…. Feudal Tokyo was called Edo, and the people there had always been terrified by the frequent accidental fires they euphemistically called "flowers of Edo." That night, all Tokyo began to blossom.[10]
>
> — Robert Guillain, *I Saw Tokyo Burning*

> "Japan offers an ideal target for air operations…. [Its] towns, built largely of wood and paper, form the greatest aerial targets the world has ever seen…. Incendiary projectiles would burn the cities to the ground in short order."[11]
>
> — General Billy Mitchell, *Liberty* magazine, January 1932

Occupiers did expect to find significant war damage when they entered Japan. Some, especially those who had served with MacArthur in the newly liberated Philippines that summer, were familiar with urban postcombat areas. A member of MacArthur's staff wrote in his diary that he expected to find "a city considerably devasted by war with the remaining population under poor control, the public parks filled with homeless, and all suburban areas jammed with refugees." These assumptions were soon confirmed. An early situation report from Tokyo noted that the machinery that had produced goods for export, and even basic items like telephones, had been converted into scrap for war production. Huge quantities of food would be needed to maintain the barest subsistence of the population. Given the current conditions, MacArthur warned that the Japanese could become an albatross around the neck of the United States.[12]

— Dayna L. Barnes, *Architects of Occupation*

Tokyo

As summarized in the *United States Strategic Bombing Survey,* "by the time the air attack was seriously undertaken against the Japanese home islands in November 1944, Japan had been conducting military campaigns in China for seven years…. The Pacific phase of World War II had been under way for three years."[13] Tokyo's residents accordingly felt themselves safe from the worst of war's brutality for much of the Second World War, Billy Mitchell's April 1942 bombing raid notwithstanding. Those aware of the Allies' progress northward as the conflict progressed knew the capital's longtime status as sanctuary would soon come to an end. Tokyo's punishment would largely follow that dealt Germany, the latter having merited Allied first-priority status.

The capital's residents were already intimately familiar with major disasters. Mother Nature wedded an earthquake and strong winds as many were preparing lunch just before noon on September 1, 1923. Tremors scattered embers, igniting the city's houses by the thousands:

The quake shattered Tokyo's wood and shoji-paper structures, creating a plentiful surface area for the slightest spark to find a home. Five of the city's 15 wards lost 90 percent of their buildings; a sixth suffered but a fraction less. Only one was untouched, sheltered as it was in the western hills. Accounts from the period suggest three-quarters of Tokyo's buildings were destroyed or badly damaged in the aftermath, with two-thirds of the total falling victim to fire.[14]

Over 100,000 died, the vast majority due to those flames.

Unlike the grinding destruction experienced in bombing raids on Berlin, Hamburg, London, and elsewhere in Europe, the introduction of the B-29 Superfortress into the Pacific theater took aerial-delivered destructiveness to a new level. Tokyo experienced some ninety raids in the last year of the war. Eight accounted for ninety-nine percent of civilian casualties and areas burned. Of the eight, none could compare to the three-hour long March 9-10, 1945 nighttime visit by 334 B-29s.[15] The focus was the Asakusa District, the city's most densely occupied and a major industrial concentration. The means were flame-inducing napalm munitions. Most air raid shelters were of little help. Some were nothing more than holes dug in yards. Occupants died of extreme heat, burns, carbon monoxide poisoning, or asphyxiation as firestorms sucked oxygen from the air. Casualty estimates vary widely. Japanese official numbers for the night are 83,793 killed and 40,918 injured. Other estimates cite 200,000 total casualties, a number equating to 90 percent of all Tokyo's deaths due to bombings during the war. (The *US Strategic Bombing Survey* puts the total number of casualties—killed plus injured—during the March 9-10 attack at approximately 185,000. The same document concludes total civilian casualties in Japan for the war probably exceeded the war's combat casualties in the country's armed forces, though not all of the former were attributable to aerial bombing.)[16] Estimates of those made homeless likewise vary, ranging as they do from 644,000 to over a million.[17] Again regarding the March 9-10 raids, the US Army Air Force official WWII history notes, "The physical destruction and loss of life at Tokyo exceeded that...of any of the great conflagrations of the Western world.... No other air attack of the war, either in Japan or Europe, was so destructive of life and property."[18] Every one of the area's fifty-four major factories suffered at least major damage. So too did many smaller industrial producers. Only the Seiko watch factory, making artillery fuses at the time, escaped without significant devastation.[19] Immediate response and recovery were handicapped by the extent of ruin. The Tokyo Metropolitan Government's offices were destroyed, crippling coordination. Hundreds of sites that had been designated as first aid stations were gone, making it virtually impossible for many with injuries to find treatment.[20]

The similarity to the 1923 earthquake disaster was not a coincidence. The earlier event made clear the fire susceptibility of the city's residential areas and magnifying effect of its March and September winds. Allied planners drew on that knowledge in preparing for the attack.[21] One author pointedly stated, "the objective, indeed, was to create a calamity."[22] The mass flight from Tokyo in the attack's aftermath meant none to follow would ever match the slaughter of that early March night.²³ Authors would report bombers destroyed 1,066,000 of the city's 1,650,000 residences—65 percent of houses and apartment buildings—by war's end. Over half the city was rubble or ash. Four of five factories and other industries were gone by that point.²⁴ Tens of thousands would for weeks or months have no alternative to living in hovels pieced together with stone and metal scraps remaining after the devastation.²⁵ Citing the Strategic Bombing Survey's brutally frank but understated appraisal: "If the mass incendiary raids against Japanese cities were intended to disrupt the economic life of the communities, destroy their industrial potential, and thereby weaken the will and the ability of the people to support the military operations of its leaders, these attacks may be said to have been highly successful."²⁶ Further providing evidence of the extent of desolation: More than half of Tokyo's hospitals and nearly 75 percent of its clinics fell victim to the bombings. Ruptured waterpipes disrupted delivery to seven in ten houses, meaning they could receive water for only two hours in the morning and two additional in the evenings.²⁷ Despite the extent of ruin, the bombing had less effect on some capabilities than might be thought. Focus on residential areas and industry left other key infrastructure less ravaged, railways being one sector escaping worse crippling, as did most utilities outside of the worst hit areas.²⁸ (The focus on dwellings was in considerable part due to their being thought key both in the sense of housing workers and labor for small industry. A summary report by the US Strategic Bombing Survey concluded, "by 1944 the Japanese had almost eliminated home industry in their war economy. They still relied, however, on plants employing less than 250 workers for subcontracted parts and equipment. Many of these smaller plants were concentrated in Tokyo and accounted for 50 percent of the total industrial output of the city.")[29] Nevertheless, a Japanese postwar study estimated that 24.5 percent of Japan's physical plant and related assets had been destroyed. Industrial output in 1945 and 1946 was less than a third of its pre-WWII peak. Physical devastation was significant though the drop was at that point due more to lack of production materials than capacity.[30] The effects of bombing were noteworthy in terms of economic impact, but arguably it was the interruption of shipping from outlying areas of the once-empire that had a greater effect. Again citing the *Strategic Bombing Survey*,

> physical damage...cannot be used as a measure of the total economic loss due to air attacks.... Area raids, and to some extent precision attacks, did reduce the total industrial potential, [but] remaining plant facilities were in general still adequate for the ever diminishing support of fuel, raw materials, and component parts brought into the area.[31]

The same was true of manpower losses due to fatalities, injury, or flight from the Tokyo urban area. While regional factory employment decreased by only 44 percent, these losses combined with the effects of food shortages, mismanagement of manpower, failure to repair factory damage, and noted material deficits drove industrial productive hours down by 70 percent.[32]

Japanese plans for the capital's postwar recovery ranged from practical to near fantasy. Any such undertakings would be made under the overseeing eyes of Allied occupiers, though admittedly Douglas MacArthur and his subordinates were more concerned with political, economic, and social changes than physical rebuilding. Planners envisioned a city fireproofed and rezoned with business districts decentralized, separated by green belts, linked by new highways, and served by subways replacing surface or elevated trains. Cost played a limited role during planning, notable as no significant reconstruction funding would be forthcoming until some three years after 1945. Nor would the homeless and ambitious wait. What funds and materials that were available found their way into the pockets, trucks, and storehouses of corrupt black marketeers and other criminal elements. These included military men, politicians, bureaucrats, and established enterprises.[33] The military officers, those politicians, and the already rich were among the many who made killings on the black market while by the end of 1939, over two million of the less connected or protected had already suffered arrest for participating in its exchanges.

Even before the war's end, in the autumn of 1944, the Institute for the Science of Labor reported factory workers turned to the black market for 69 percent of their vegetables and over a third of fish purchases.[34] While many suffered arrest, others operating or buying from these markets showed great initiative in side-stepping relevant laws. As Owen Griffiths wrote in his study of the phenomenon:

> In his 1940 study of black market transactions, [Inomata Keizo] identified more than a dozen separate types of transactions ranging from simple barter (*butsubutsu kôkan*)

and pawning (*daki awase*) to extracting fees for paying off loans (*fusai no katagawari*) and overdrafts (*karikoshi no kaisai*).... Many Japanese also adapted the time-honoured tradition of gift-giving (*omiyage*) to circumvent the price ceilings. Through a clever reinvention of tradition, buyers would purchase a good or service at the official price and then give a gift or small payment of cash to the seller, which effectively raised the price of the item in question to its black market level. Another tradition adopted and modified by buyer and seller alike was the payment of thank-you money (*shareikin torihiki*).[35]

The attractiveness of the market was in part due to its relatively low markups prior to the July 1944 fall of Saipan from which the United States Army Air Force could more regularly bomb Japan's cities. Previously less a matter of avoiding starvation than supplementing diets, the ensuing destruction to infrastructure meant decreases in food availability to the point of starvation if one relied solely on ration allocations.[36] The black market economy was Tokyo's—and much of Japan's—*de facto* primary civilian economy by the August 15, 1945 surrender. Within several months, approximately 45,000 open-air stalls employed some 80,000 people in Tokyo alone...and breathed life into criminal gangs' ambitions. One estimate concluded some 90 percent of Tokyo's street stalls were under the control of *yakuza* gangs working through the auspices of the Street Stall Tradesmen's Cooperative Union.[37] Efforts to avoid arrest or paying inflated black market prices saw tens of thousands travel to the countryside around the capital to buy or barter for food directly from farmers. Others were fortunate enough to get handouts from private providers such as the Mahayana or Higashi Honganji Buddhist temples.[38]

In the weeks and months following the surrender, a significant portion of black market goods came from items stored by the military in preparation for defense against an Allied ground invasion. Senior armed forces officers, politicians, those controlling some of Japan's largest companies, and criminal organizations were again prominent in spiriting away these stores before the occupiers could take control.[39] Hoarding of food and other vital materials and their manipulation as black market goods drove inflation while large conglomerates (*zaibatsu*) created unemployment by closing factories, essential materials instead being routed to more lucrative black market sales and building more profitable structures than housing. Cafés, brothels, movie theaters, and additional quick money-generating construction that might lure the relatively wealthy monied occupiers took precedence over structures better suited to restimulating the broader economy.[40] What the occupiers might deem desirable in the latter regard received little attention as MacArthur and his subordinates largely left the day-to-day running of the country to the Japanese as long as they toed the line in terms of headquarters directives.[41] The commercial area of Ginza notably benefited from the waylaying of building materials from legitimate construction.[42]

Further driving the closure of factories was the first two postwar Japanese governments' wrong-headed policy of paying large indemnity disbursements to Japanese companies that had supported the war effort, arguing the money was necessary to renew production. MacArthur's

General Headquarters quashed the policy, but payments had already been made before the occupiers firmly grasped control. Such massive government, commercial, and criminally-supported corruption—combined with gross misjudgments such as dramatically increasing the money supply—drove unemployment to new heights and undermined industrial output such that by autumn 1945 it was less than 10 percent of that in 1935-1937. This was at a time when prices of services also jumped multifold. Water prices increased fifty-fold, rail transport thirty-five, and electricity twenty-two.[43]

Black marketeering did not account for all corruption and criminality. One of every thirty Tokyo residents was robbed during the 1945-1946 period. Many of the perpetrators caught claimed to be war orphans. The same was the case for those arrested for prostitution.[44] City assemblymen, police, and other government employees also numbered among the lawbreakers.[45] Starvation stalked a population also experiencing diseases spreading even before surrender, providing new opportunities for the corrupt. Officials charged individuals living in Shinagawa ward for spraying homes with DDT that was actually little more than water when encephalitis came to visit.[46]

Tokyo established an office to encourage use of any available open land—public or private—for planting and required landowners with over 165 square meters to allow sowing unused space.[47] Officials offered "How to eat weeds" instruction during the summer of 1945. Some practiced what the government preached. Writer Iwakami Shinichi spotted a skinny boy who had scavenged chickweed from around a forlorn government building, "certainly to be eaten later."[48]

Some refused to compromise principles despite the impossibility of surviving on government ration rates. After sentencing individuals to mandatory jail time for black market activity, thirty-three-year-old judge Yamaguchi Yoshitada decided to refuse food other than his designated ration intake. It was a self-imposed death sentence. He died in October 1947.[49] So too did teacher Kameo Hideshirô who had likewise chosen to protest government food rationing policies.[50] Food shortages during and in the immediate aftermath of the war are evident in average height and weight statistics for Japanese sixth-grade boys. In 1946, they had respectively decreased by 1.89 inches (4.8 centimeters) and 5.07 pounds (2.3 kilograms) since 1936.[51]

High black market prices undermined efforts to stabilize the economy. One rather draconian February 1946 counter-policy established by the Monetary Emergency Measures Ordinance required all money be deposited in banks with withdrawals being allowed only in amounts required to live on, these being specified as 330 yen monthly for the head of a household and 100 per additional family member. The result was 70 percent of deposits being effectively frozen and disruption of economic exchanges necessary for daily business functions such as purchasing inventory and, some claimed, even paying taxes, the latter reportedly requiring the sale of personal goods to provide what was owed the government. Economist Yoshikawa Hiroshi wrote that the resulting economic chaos saw inflation rise seventy-fold between 1945 and 1950 in terms of official prices.⁵² Tokyoites described their existence during this time as "bamboo shoot life." To buy food, residents sold what they could piece by piece just as they peeled layer after layer when eating bamboo.⁵³ The occupiers did prevent mass Japanese starvation by importing large amounts of staple food beginning in the spring of 1946. Shipments were doubly vital given the previous year's rice harvest was the worst in forty-two years. What starvation did occur would have been worse had the local availability of potatoes and sweet potatoes not filled some of the caloric gaps.⁵⁴

There were Japanese who contemplated recovery even before the war's end. Okita Saburo and Goto Yonosuke, electrical engineers in China, created a group dedicated to the task. The pair eventually gained official status after returning to Tokyo, providing an interim report by the end of 1945 and completing a slightly modified version by September of the following year. Emphases included technology development; an agile trade structure; and maintaining a comprehensive, overarching strategy the core of which would be industrialization. Other significant points emphasized the pragmatic: being able to compete with foreign competition, avoiding large amounts of international debt by stressing the need to be content with minimum standards of living in lieu of consumerism, and firm control over the economy rather than tolerating the inefficiencies of a laissez-faire approach in the private sector.⁵⁵ Saburo and Yonosuke influenced Japan's postwar economic policies, but their report's recommendations were not formally adopted.⁵⁶ Other economic recovery planning continued after the war, a recognition that preparations could not be "one and done." Factors necessitating economic adaptability included delays in receipt of significant US funding until 1948 (though the beginnings of what would eventually total nearly two billion dollars in humanitarian and economic aid by 1950 began in 1946). The unpredictable demands of having to finance housing and other support for the occupying military further hampered planning. These obligations constituted a third of the country's budget in the immediate postwar years.[57] The result was a struggle between controlling inflation and building economic capacity.

The resulting recovery path was a dynamic one, sometimes dramatically so. Were funding constraints, obligations to occupiers, crop failures, and black marketeering not sufficient challenges, Mother Nature again stepped forward. Age caused Tokyo's surviving buildings to crumble, further burdening demands on construction materials and labor. Floods, fires, and typhoons visited regularly. Over one million additional houses were lost nationwide before the 1952 end of occupation. The country's population grew by six million over the same period, further stressing resources. Other buildings were temporarily "lost" to the occupiers. This was especially the case after April 1946 when MacArthur's headquarters directed all houses of Western design be turned over to accommodate occupier families.[58] Tokyo's burden was significantly greater than elsewhere. The city and neighboring Kanagawa Prefecture together housed a third of the country's 117,580 occupation troops.[59] The Japanese government also had to build and furnish housing for American families of the occupying force, this beyond what was already available. The requirement included manufacturing Western necessities such as appliances.[60] These occupier demands accounted for over half of all cement, a quarter of plate glass, and nearly 90 percent of iron pipe available over months spanning 1946-1947.[61] The requirements further deprived Tokyo of needed materials, reinforcing black market reliance and additionally spurring inflation.[62] June 1946 brought yet another occupier demand: Provide gas service to all US facilities in the capital. Meeting it became the largest project in Tokyo Gas history as occupier gas consumption constituted 40 percent of output by 1948. The same group was also consuming a fifth of all electricity in Tokyo by 1950.[63] A report by the Allied General Headquarters Economics and Science Section concluded the dependent housing program was collectively "the single largest factor in the Japanese currency inflation." Little wonder when one considers the details:

> The Japanese government not only had to supply the materials and labor to build the houses. GHQ expected it to make almost every item deemed necessary for a middle-class home, from heating units, electric stoves, and refrigerators to clothes pins, magazine racks and ice buckets. In a March 1946 procurement order, GHQ sent the Japanese government a very long list of required items meant to give a sense of "the scope of the production involved in order that immediate action may be taken to initiate production." The first half of the list involved those components required to build the housing units, including

massive amounts of lumber, cement, nails, screws, galvanized steel, asphalt, glass, paint, insulated wire, transformers, and circuit breakers. The second half of the list contained all of the items—20,000 of each to be manufactured—meant to go inside of the house. A critical aspect of the above situation is that Japanese manufacturers had never made many of the items on the list, which required GHQ to supply them with working samples and manufacturing instructions.[64]

A burden at the time, the longer-term consequences of these requirements kickstarted the expansion of Japan's domestic goods manufacturing for which it became well-known worldwide.[65] On the other hand, a poor decision by Tokyo's governor and the city's planning bureau to build poor quality houses with a short lifespan hindered longer-term housing needs, another of history's examples demonstrating the costs of "temporary" solutions.[66]

Japan's capital also suffered housing challenges more than most other regions because returning soldiers and civilians who had earlier evacuated the capital quickly overwhelmed availability. Estimates of when and how many returnees made their way to the capital vary. One source reports just short of one million returning in the four months from September through December 1945. What is not debatable is that most homes housed two or even three families. Tokyo began restricting returnees in January the following year. March 1946 brought a federal mandate denying ration books to returnees unable to provide a transfer authorization from their point of origin. Only those needed to meet immediate demands were to move into major cities, carpenters, translators, and utility and transportation workers among them. Though food shortages caused some to leave Tokyo in hopes of better accessing sustenance, the capital's population was again over four million by July 1946.[67] Construction proceeded very slowly despite low availability. Severe inflation meant construction costs were 200 percent higher than before the war while rental rates increased but 50 percent over the same period. Seventy percent of Tokyo's population was renting before and during the war, meaning there was considerable disincentive for new housing construction.[68] Streets and public transportation were overwhelmed, repairs and expansion were unable to keep pace with demand. Further resident and authorities' headaches arose two years later when capital water consumption increased so greatly as to require rationing.[69] Malnutrition or hypothermia killed six people a day at Tokyo's Ueno railway station, a location where the homeless, prostitutes, and other downtrodden gathered for shelter. Economic and social problems were such that "Tokyo's mental asylums brimmed."[70]

Not all parts of the city struggled with growth. The Honjô ward in what was the industrial Kôtô region of the city's east had few standing buildings as the war ended. Only 13,000 from a 1944 population of 241,000 persons remained in the autumn of 1945. The fire bombings of March had destroyed ward residency records. Copies were fortunately available from the central government; the documents were necessary for obtaining food rations. Yet, reflective of the human catastrophe visited from the air, 40 percent of residency documents went unclaimed after a year's passage.[71]

That construction proceeded despite obstacles and lack of incentives was more due to private enterprise than government programs. Poor workmanship; ignoring zoning dictates; and flouting fire regulations, safety considerations, and aspirations for relieving traffic congestion were among the consequences.[72] The occupiers might have initially done little to spur recovery in the civilian housing sector. They incited change nonetheless. Tokyo had for centuries found no need for street names. A combination of neighborhood and ward designations had sufficed. The occupiers would have none of it. Streets received names. New civil codes all but eliminated the family system that had for centuries underpinned Japanese social structure. Widespread purging of officials thought to have been too close to wartime authorities removed some whose ties should have been recognized as insufficient to merit depriving local governments of needed expertise (though many others were fortunately allowed to retain their positions.)[73] Public health, other medical services, and diet saw improvement.[74] The Americans required that chlorination of city water meet US Army standards. Other directives mandated creation of vaccination and insect control teams. Tokyo became a model for nationwide health improvements. The same was true of the program establishing standards for school children's diets. Students in the Tokyo-Yokohama region were soon growing taller and weighing more than those elsewhere in Japan.[75]

CHAPTER 3

Nagasaki

As with Tokyo, and as noted above, estimates of Nagasaki's pre-attack population and number of casualties due to the dropping of the atomic bomb range widely. However, sources coalesce around approximations that one in three of the city's residents either died or suffered injury.[76] Recovery was unsurprisingly slow to start given these numbers, numbers exacerbated by many evacuating the city in the attack's aftermath. Malnutrition disrupted revitalization as damage to transportation networks, distribution infrastructure, and administrative functions precipitated food shortages. Crippled physical and social networks, poor harvests, corruption, and interruption of food flows from once occupied countries further upset social networks and led to similar deficiencies nationwide.

Cholera, meningitis, polio, tuberculosis, smallpox, and scarlet fever were among the ailments affecting 650,000 in Nagasaki and throughout Japan, 100,000 of whom died. Added to these were psychological injuries. Causes included survivors' guilt and social marginalization of individuals bearing scars or otherwise physically harmed in bombing attacks. Children could be particularly cruel. Burned or crippled suffered taunts of "monster," "chicken leg," "baldy," or "tempura," the last referring to Japanese dishes featuring deep-fried foods.[77] Adults could find themselves spurned as possible spouses, potential mates being concerned radiation might affect yet-to-be conceived or newly-born children. Others shunned fell into categories traditionally outside socially acceptable bounds:

crippled war veterans, war orphans, widows, homeless, and any showing signs of mental illness, including soldiers with post-traumatic stress disorder (PTSD).[78] Actual or perceived mental and emotional maladies were sufficiently common that victims of sustained despair were labeled as suffering the "*kyodatsu* condition" from what had previously been employed only as a technical psychological term.[79]

Despite the witch's brew of physical devastation, bodily injuries, mental turmoil, other social damage, and economic tribulation, public housing replaced much of the blackened ground and debris within four years. Teachers, parents, and students came together to rebuild schools and find ways to furnish classrooms. Food supplies increased. Authorities brought inflation under control.[80] As in Tokyo, much of Nagasaki's recovery was thanks less to the occupiers or government officials than to individual men and women surviving wartime ruin.

■ Berlin

> For the extent of devastation, Berlin was unique. Willy Brandt, a future mayor of Berlin and West German chancellor, called the city "a no-man's land on the edge of the world with every little garden a graveyard, and above this, like an unmovable cloud, the stink of putrefaction.... In the streets [the icy cold] attacked the people like a wild beast, drove them into their houses, but there they found no protection either. The windows had no panes; they were nailed up with planks and plasterboard. The walls and ceilings were full of cracks and holes—one covered them with

CHAPTER 3

paper and rags. People heated their rooms with benches from the public parks…. The old and sick froze to death in their beds by the hundreds."[81]

— Barry Turner, *The Berlin Airlift*

Our featherbeds were our lifesaving possessions.[82]

— Inge E. Stanneck Gross,
Memories of World War II and Its Aftermath, 1940-1954

Germany's capital was spared the B-29 Superfortress. It was not spared catastrophe. Berlin had suffered bombing in 1940 and 1941. As with Tokyo, there was something of a hiatus between earlier raids and intensification. The next year saw only a single visit, one by British aircraft. It was not until the evening of March 1, 1943—a full two years before Tokyo's most damaging aerial bombardment—that the British returned in earnest.[83] The "Battle for Berlin" began on November 18, 1943, when over four hundred Royal Air Force (RAF) Lancaster bombers struck the city, albeit to little effect due to poor visibility. The reprieve was short. More than 750 bombers struck four nights later. Attacks continued. Some half a million residents were homeless in just over a week. By month's end, one resident wrote he "could hardly breathe in the city for the smoke. When the sun came out on Wednesday, you just couldn't see it. We had to have a light on all day as the sky was a dirty yellow." Bombing would continue until the war in Europe approached its end, the RAF bombing by night, the US Army Air Force by day.[84] As was the case for Tokyo, estimates of Berlin's demised varied widely. The leader of the Civil Defense Police quoted 49,600. Other reports cited 80,000. One author leans toward these higher numbers, his writing the official estimate of 18,019 is thought "much too low."[85] The capital's more open layout meant it was not amenable to firestorms such as those consuming Dresden and ravaging Hamburg. Nevertheless, a third of city housing was badly damaged or entirely destroyed. A member of the United States Strategic Bombing Survey Berlin team arriving on July 19, 1945, wrote, "the place is uniquely devastated…. The city is a living corpse."[86] Individual remains were plentiful. Historian Roger Moorhouse observed,

> initially, any unidentified corpses would be laid out in the street so that a name might be provided by neighbours and passers-by. After the larger raids, however, the potential shock caused by leaving large numbers of corpses on public display was such that the dead were laid out…in school halls and gymnasiums.[87]

The closing days of the war brought further horrors, these from the ground rather than the air. Soviet soldiers swept onto Berlin's streets and, too often and too intimately, into what remained of homes. An official US Army source states "it would not be until 1947, when Soviet commanders confined soldiers to strictly guarded posts and restricted almost all contact with the civilian population, that the rampage against German civilians subsided."[88]

Some residents resisted official offers to relocate, choosing to rough it in the remnants of their homes and rebuilding to the extent possible. Many did what they could to repair damage even as fighting continued despite the risk of their work again falling victim to future bombs. Resident Ruth Andreas-Friedrich recalled, if our living room goes, we move into the kitchen. If the kitchen is smashed, we transfer to the hall. If the hall is in ruins, we set up in the cellar. Anything so long as we can stay at home. The most dismal scrap of home is better than any palace somewhere else. That's why they all come back someday—the people whom the bombs have driven out of the city…. They go to work with shovel and broom, hammer, tongs and pickaxe, until one day a new home rises out of the charred foundation—a Robinson Crusoe stockade, perhaps, but a home nonetheless. You can't live if you don't belong anywhere.[89]

And so it was even if it meant living without heat and little more than a canvas over ruins of what was still home.

Food shortages joined the shells of once houses as a source of suffering. These were not alone. Again as amongst Tokyo's hungry, public health had declined as wartime months passed. Interrupted sleep joined with hunger to weaken bodies. Flu and colds were commonplace. Cases of scarlet fever, typhus, and dysentery rose in numbers, little wonder given the dreadful living conditions and piles of garbage and human waste on which flies swarmed.[90] Lack of medical supplies and hospital beds constrained the ability to address ailments.[91] Stress also weakened systems—the stress of daily living, British and American bombing, and, as the Luftwaffe became little more than a memory, strafing Soviet aircraft routinely targeting civilians.[92] Once they arrived, those Soviets stripped Berlin of anything they thought might be of value. Theft ranged from individual possessions—watches running up the arms of soldiers became synonymous with looting—to disassembly of entire factories.

Stealing took precedence over governing. Boundaries with the American, British, and French occupation sectors were no protection against Soviet incursions. Berlin's power was put at risk by their attempt to remove equipment from the city's only modern generation plant, that in the British sector.[93] Lucius D. Clay; first US Deputy Military Governor, later commanding general of the Office of Military Government for Germany; wrote to the Soviet Deputy Commander-in-Chief of the Soviet Zone of Occupation in Germany on April 20, 1946, informing him US soldiers had been instructed to prevent further removal of railway tracks from the American sector.[94] Soviet documents would later confirm the dismantling of 605 plants in West Berlin. In the words of the US Army's *The City Becomes a Symbol*, such pillaging "severely compounded the difficulties of restarting Berlin's economic life and permanently darkened the mood against the Soviet Union."

Not all Soviet behavior was destructive. There were improvements in restoring order and public services in the two months between their capture of the city and arrival of the Western Allies.[95] (Ukrainians returning to their cities occupied by Russians for lengthy periods will likely find a similar combination of both widespread theft and improvements, the latter to convince residents life under Russia is preferable to that governed by Kyiv. As was the case in 1945 Berlin, it is unlikely Ukrainians—other than those predisposed to viewing Moscow favorably—will forgive Russian depredations despite efforts to sway hearts and minds.)

Food became a weapon in the struggle for influence between the occupying powers. Marshal Gregory Zhukov was the senior Russian in Berlin immediately following the city's fall. He initially refused to supply Western sectors with food or coal.[96] Zhukov eventually agreed to provide support until the Allies could put logistical systems in place to supply their charges.[97] It was not from the goodness of his heart. The US Army Office of the Chief Historian recorded,

> the Soviet Union...would receive from the western zones, in exchange for an equivalent value of food and other commodities later to be agreed upon, 15 percent of such usable capital equipment from the metallurgical, chemical, and machine manufacturing industries as was not necessary for the German peace economy.[98]

As Berlin was surrounded by the Soviet zone, Western occupiers had to transport life-sustaining supplies over the miles between their sectors and Berlin...or from even farther. Transport of food from the United States began in January 1946.[99] Logistics for feeding the capital were always more difficult for the Americans, British, and French given Berlin was an island within the Soviet sector.

Germans in the Soviet sector did receive more generous food allocations than did residents in the British sector throughout most of the occupation, unsurprising given Great Britain too was suffering food shortages and, as a democracy, its government could not afford to be equally laissez-faire about allocations to its citizens at home. As one author put it, "the Soviets had their own long history of rationing and understood its importance better

Image 2. Map of Post-WWII Allied Sectors in Berlin[100]

as an important social control measure, so much so they diverted foodstuffs from the Red Army's stocks to fund the rationing system in Berlin."[101] Berliners in the Soviet sector benefited from additional favoritism. The Soviets granted residents in Germany's larger cities higher ration entitlements than those living elsewhere (as was also the case with Moscow). The difference was particularly significant for those who worked. Heavy industrial laborers in Berlin were authorized 2593 and a half calories daily while those in the same status in smaller Dresden were to receive only 2026 and a half.[102]

Making both the food and housing situations worse, by July 1945, only three months after the end of war in Europe, Berlin alone housed over half a million expellees (those forced out of other countries or regions) in forty-eight transit camps. By year's end the number of returning German former prisoners of war, refugees, and those expelled from elsewhere exceeded one and a half-million.[103] As in Tokyo, housing these numbers was more difficult as dwellings allocated to the occupiers reduced the number available for locals. It was a situation soon mitigated by the dramatic drawdown of forces that saw 1,622,000 US soldiers Germany-wide in May 1945 diminished by ninety percent to 162,000 by the end of 1946, a reduction meaning all enlisted soldiers were housed in barracks rather than homes or other properties.[104] The first winter after the war was fortunately a mild one. Increases in ration standards further helped the population avoid widespread starvation.[105]

As Berlin-wide elections approached in October 1946, the Russians ordered the mayor to bolster their claims of superior life in the Soviet sector (and thereby, they hoped, for the success of their chosen political party, the SED) by distributing food only in their sector. The citizenry was not duped, wise as they were to Soviet manipulations and depredations by that point.[106] The Americans were not without means to influence voters in the West's favor. The Cooperative for American Remittances to Europe (CARE) program allowed individuals in the United States to send a $15 food parcel to persons of their choosing in Germany regardless of the sector in which they lived. Recipients tended to be relatives or notable personalities such as church officials. The program never constituted more than a drop in the Berlin food bucket, but the impact reverberated well beyond the limited numbers actually receiving its packages. Run not by the US. government but by a humanitarian organization, CARE was nonetheless a propaganda coup all the more important as its introduction came just two months before the 1946 elections.[107] (In 1953, after the 1948-1949 Berlin blockade, the US would again successfully employ food as a propaganda tool, distributing parcels as Berlin and German Democratic Republic labor protests challenged Communist Germany's government.)[108]

Soviet efforts to win support suffered from more than the atrocities committed in the opening months after the city's fall and inept attempts to garner votes for food. Other maneuvers included filling important education system and other positions with Communists.[109] Berliners' perceptions were reinforced when Moscow's harsher hand again revealed itself in the days immediately after the election. On October 21, 1946, the evening following that event, secret police knocked on the doors of Germans living in the Soviet sector who possessed technical skills Moscow coveted. The visitors confronted their targets with the choice of having their families accompany them to Russia or leaving alone. It was kidnapping, plain and simple.[110]

The second occupation winter proved much different from that before. German Inge E. Stanneck Gross recalled:

> The winter of 1946 and 1947 will remain in our memory forever. Not only was it the coldest winter so far this century, but it was so much worse because of circumstances. Most people's apartments had a number of broken windows. Glass was not available. We had repaired our

windows with cardboard, wood, or rags to keep the wind, rain and some of the cold out. With none of the materials available we had to make do with whatever we had among our belongings. Wood panels could be taken out of certain pieces of furniture, such as a back wall of a China cabinet or a wardrobe. While none of the substitutes insulated as well as glass, we were grateful for the protection we did have.[111]

Another Berliner's December 21, 1946 diary entry recorded,

it's twenty degrees below zero outside, one degree below zero in the kitchen and four degrees below zero in the bathroom. Twice it has happened that during the night the water in Heike's hot-water bottle froze in her bed.... More than seventy pipes have burst, claims the superintendent.... In the British sector these days the lights are on only for twenty minutes a day—no water, no way to cook, and no possibility to use the bathroom or take a bath. In little packages people in Berlin carry their bodily waste out of the house and discreetly bury it in the nearest pile of rubble.[112]

Authorities initiated several measures to help city residents survive. They designated air raid shelters, hospitals, and other heated facilities as public warming halls. The city's food department provided the ill or elderly a free warm meal at municipal cafeterias. Police officers checked the houses of those thought to be at risk. Despite these and other measures, 1,142 persons reportedly froze to death, three-quarters of whom were older than sixty.[113]

Only eleven of January 1947's days saw temperatures above zero. February remained below freezing both day and night. Frozen pipes deprived many areas of water.[114] Suicides spiked. Unsurprisingly, black markets multiplied and expanded; they had existed during the war. Railway stations were popular locations. Berlin and Vienna were notable for their black market operations. The German capital's best known was also its largest: that in the *Tiergarten*, a large park not distant from the Reichstag and Brandenburg Gate. As a source of food and other necessities for many Germans, these were a boon to occupiers looking to make a profit. Occupiers and locals alike were buyers and sellers, though generally for different reasons. Russians were especially avid. Having served for years without pay, their leaders took advantage of an American decision to provide them the plates for printing Allied occupation marks. The Russians printed freely, using the bills to pay their soldiers in a currency they were not allowed to return to Russia. The black market would have been a source of inflation without such prolific printing, but the combination of money in Russian soldiers' pockets and limited places to spend made it an accelerant. Western occupier soldiers were also paid in the currency. They augmented their incomes by selling goods on the black market or via exchanges with flush Russians. This explains why the US garrison in Berlin, which received only $1 million in pay in July 1945, could remit three times that to the United States after exchanging occupation marks for dollars.[115] Limiting remittances only to the maximum amounts one could obtain via legal sources was thwarted by initiatives such as that developed by the Mackay Radio Corporation with its "flowers by cable" ploy. The company set up a scheme for soldiers to order flowers for addresses in the United States. What was actually delivered was dollars.[116] Historian Kevin Conley

CHAPTER 3

Ruffner wrote inflated prices for goods and services in Berlin cost the US Army an estimated extra $300 million during its occupation.[117]

Open day and night, those operating black markets were often criminals, petty and otherwise, who scammed the needy by selling sealed goods buyers found on return home to be filled with inedible waste.[118] Nonetheless, those hungry—and many, many Berliners were hungry—sought additional calories amidst the corrupt, criminal, and hopefully, reasonably candid. As halfway around the world in Tokyo, the black market was fundamental to survival for some. This was true from the earliest days after the war's end. Refugees in the city's Soviet sector, for example, were denied ration cards until October 1945, leaving the black market as one of their few remaining options. (Some turned to theft and other illicit means of acquisition.) These refugees in particular needed alternatives to rationed amounts; they were authorized only a children's ration when cards became available.[119] Concerns regarding drains on limited food supplies saw the British deny refugees entry into their sector. Nor did they provide support to those already there. This denial of ration cards was made formal policy throughout Berlin on December 21, 1945...then reversed a week later. British policy remained unfriendly to those displaced, however, and the Soviets attempted to remove some 2,000 to a location outside of Berlin. All but thirty fled to the American and French sectors before removal. The refugee problem increasingly became an American one as the French themselves relied on American support.[120]

As early as May 1945, concerns regarding the ability to feed Berlin's population led city authorities to propose or employ various policies to reduce the number of mouths they would have to feed. That month they threatened to repossess ration cards for any—Berliner or otherwise—who did not register with the police for compulsory labor. Berlin's administrators issued a formal decree the following October dictating that anyone failing to show up for work without a valid excuse risked reduced rations. A number of factors initially forestalled a food crisis, pushing it back into the winter of 1945-46. The Allies had yet to release most former German soldiers from prisoner-of-war camps. Resident raiding of Berlin's food stockpiles meant for the Wehrmacht's defense of the city, access to the 1945 harvest, and that first winter being a mild one combined to hold the worst of starvation at bay.[121] US authorities officially introduced the Berlin Barter Center on January 1, 1947. Officials hoped it would reduce the attractiveness of black markets, which they admitted "could not be controlled."[122] Other efforts to contain the negative effects of black markets included outlawing cigarettes as tender and arresting counterfeiting ring members reported to have printed and been on the verge of circulating two million phony Allied Military Marks. Outstanding because of the amount involved, it was just one of numerous cases involving forged currency. Replacing the script in use did little to thwart the criminality. Revised currency appeared in bogus form less than a month after the introduction of new notes.[123]

US authorities were less troubled by Berlin's black markets being a source of food than they were a disrupter of the city economy, a black eye for the Americans' reputation and a destination for goods from American military post exchanges. (These were—and remain today—stores designated for use only by US soldiers, their families, and select other authorized personnel.) Black markets were where an estimated third of all goods traded in Berlin exchanged hands, an environment in which "food and other commodities in very short supply were traded most often."[124] When the Berlin Barter Center opened

> in August 1946. German "sellers" brought in durable objects—silverware, crystal, paintings, porcelain figurines, stoves, radios, carpets, and clothing. Appraisers evaluated the objects on the basis of prewar prices, adjusted for depreciation, and issued certificates in the amount of "barter units." Americans brought in consumables—usually coffee, toiletries, cigarettes, and food—that appraisers also valued in barter units. The two sides then spent their certificates in the official barter store, which was soon stocked with "a fine quality of merchandise" in "new or in excellent condition."[125]

The Berlin Barter Center was considered a necessary evil among senior US leaders from the beginning. In the words of Lucius D. Clay, the "barter market was started in Berlin as an experiment to reduce barter in downtown stores which frequently led to black market operations which could not be controlled. This office has always viewed the barter market with some misgivings and accepted it as the lesser of two ills which it has proved to be." Both Germans and Americans living in Germany found value in the barter market (the latter having difficulty acquiring "essential articles for reasonable household comfort" given the destruction suffered by the city). Clay wrote, despite "certain undesirable features [the market] does provide a controlled medium of exchange between Germans and Americans which appears to be desired by both, which has contributed to morale, and which has reduced much more undesirable methods of trading."[126] German views of the Barter Market are less well documented, but their views on the black market share Tokyoites anger that individuals in need were arrested while the real criminals escaped unscathed. The Berlin Barter Center likely shared some of this ill-will given the complexity of rules regarding what could or could not be traded, where something might be exchanged safely while elsewhere it was prohibited, and gap in living conditions between those making financial killings and others facing daily hunger. An author for the newspaper *Telegraf* posed the question "What is permitted?" in a January 1947 piece, pondering whether

> the dear mother who attempts on Brunnenstrasse to sell the old top hat of her dead husband for 25 or 30 marks in order to pay the rent; the diabetic who buys a small package of sweetener for 25 marks; the transportation worker who is not able to satiate his hungry flock of children and "obtained" a sack of potatoes from the farmers: have they committed a crime? Many would say: no. And yet it is so. This shows how wide the gap has become between what the law says is criminal and what in the minds of most people is just.[127]

The "working population," according to a summer 1946 radio broadcast, "was demanding 'the strongest possible measures against extortioners, hustlers, and freeloaders, who have become a genuine plague.'" Undesirable to many, markets—black or barter—were nonetheless a necessity for others. Reasons for ire differed depending on perspective; the issue for those threatened with starvation was not the markets but rather prices so high they worsened the suffering of the needy.[128]

Clay's comments make clear senior US leaders' lack of enthusiasm for the Berlin Barter Center. It is therefore not surprising its existence was a short one. Black marketing became more difficult in the wake of the barter market's demise and soon notably declined as its departure left those participating in illicit exchanges without an excuse for holding large amounts of tradeable goods:

> Previously personnel receiving unreasonably large amounts of such barterable items as coffee, fat, and sugar from mail order houses in the United States had found it easy to explain that they had received these articles for exchange at the officially established barter centers. Since this alibi had been eliminated, occupation personnel intent on continuing black market activities were forced to find other excuses to allay the suspicions of postal authorities, law enforcement agencies, and co-workers when importing sizeable amounts of food-stuffs and other scarcities into the US Zone of Germany. From the time of the closing of the barter marts, the report concluded, such shipments could reasonably be considered as intended for the black market.[129]

Despite American participation in supplying the black market (or, perhaps, in part because of it), US soldiers and civilians compared very favorably with their Soviet counterparts in the eyes of Berliners. Though the method of data collection might be frowned upon by some today, the results did give US authorities a sense of resident perspectives and, thereby, a basis for interdicting disgruntlement that could have caused the occupiers problems:

> For numerous other Germans, however, the sole firsthand criterion by which they could judge "the American way of life" was the conduct of the soldiers whom they met upon the streets, in stores and shops, or at other public places. That their attitudes were on the whole favorable was indicated in an unpublished study prepared at Berlin early in 1946 from censored German mail…. Based on 21,306 opinions as expressed in 16,048 letters read by Berlin censors between December 1945 and March 1946, the study portrayed the sentiments of the Germans toward each of the occupying powers. Approximately 75 percent of the comments on the American forces expressed satisfaction whereas a full 80 percent of the remarks on the Russian forces were unfavorable.[130]

The Americans' greater popularity despite Soviet efforts to sway those in their sector is in part explained by the esteem granted the individual US soldier. A habit of generosity with chocolate and cigarettes reinforced favorable resident views while higher ration allocations in the East sector carried less goodwill than authorities hoped for. The Wehrmacht's plundering of Soviet Union produce during the war meant Germans had not suffered the same food shortages as did much of Europe elsewhere. Relative food wealth thus meant Soviet ration levels failed to impress East Berliners though their intake was roughly equivalent to that of the average Soviet citizen.[131] Further, the greater allocations were not evenly distributed. Russians better fed individuals filling key political and security positions (police, administrators, and party members, for example). This left others with less, especially those thought not to be as valuable to Soviet interests.[132]

The American occupiers' formal efforts sought to underpin Berlin's economic growth and stability through means more traditional than control of black markets alone. The separation of Berlin from the US Western sectors by approximately 200 air miles and 275 road miles tasked logistics for even the most routine of activities. In late 1949, America's occupying authorities logically turned to local means to meet basic needs such as replacement vehicle repair parts. Resultant purchases totaled over 8.4 million Deutschmarks in 1950, most from small manufacturers, with the belief increases would be forthcoming once Berlin prices became more competitive with those to the West.[133]

Architecture as Competition

> [In Warsaw,] all reconstructed buildings tended to invoke a progressive architectural style from the pre-1830 period regardless of the appearance prior to being damaged or destroyed during the war. Hence the Old Town was reconstructed entirely in an idealized seventeenth-and eighteenth-century form; nineteenth-century modifications and additions were removed…. Even the details of individual buildings were altered. In several buildings in the Old Town, religious elements were removed in favor of supposedly neutral decorations. On one building in the Old Town, surviving statues on its facade of the Agnus Dei and St. Mary were destroyed and replaced with a wild boar and the goddess Diana with a dog.[134]
>
> — Lawrence J. Vale and Thomas J. Campanella, "Warsaw: Reconstruction as Propaganda"

> Planning and design in Ukraine are still strongly influenced by the "old school" approach that does not reflect best EU practices. For instance, the cities still develop and update so-called Genplans, and those are developed by one of several "research institutes" based in Kyiv even for small cities somewhere in the country—reflecting planning approaches from 40-50 years ago.[135]
>
> — Marta Pastukh, Mathias Merforth, Viktor Zabreba, and Armin Wagner, "Anchoring green recovery of urban mobility in Ukraine: Eight building blocks"

Just as the Communist regime in Warsaw sought to employ the city's rebuilding as propaganda, so too did Berlin's occupiers recognize the power of architecture as an influencer. Both the Soviets and the Western powers agreed a break with Germany's past was essential in the architectural choices made. How they sought to make that break differed considerably.[136]

Blaming Berlin's devastation first on Hitler and his Nazi regime and later the "Anglo-American terror bombers," an early Soviet citywide plan for physical infrastructure recovery favored new buildings rather than repair of the thousands of damaged structures. The change of tone reflects the cause behind the demise of a city-wide reconstruction plan. The soon-recognized east-west division of the city joined rising objections to ignoring existing property lines (especially in the western sectors) to put a stake through such ambitions. Residents and officials also recognized that much of what was damaged could be repaired and some physical infrastructure was little disrupted despite the extent of devastation. This was markedly true of underground infrastructure such as water pipes (something also found to be true in Hiroshima and Nagasaki), subways, and foundation material of streets estimated to be 90 percent intact.[137] More exposed conduits fared less well. Some suspended beneath bridges broke and spilled sewage into city canals, providing plentiful sustenance for flies and other potential disease carriers.[138]

In East Berlin, decentralized, low-rise housing featuring individual properties was thought antithetical to the socialist way. Showpieces were therefore rows of towering apartments lining the broad Stalinalle, architecture that would become associated with Soviet and Eastern European buildings during the Cold War (and is familiar in Russian construction in occupied Mariupol today). The West unsurprisingly chose otherwise. Early housing developments were small in size and often not facing a street. A later, larger showcase apartment neighborhood mixed low-rise and high-rise while maintaining this separation and avoidance of lockstep lining of vehicle traveled ways, the result touted as featuring "individual achievements embodying the decentralized, unregimented order of democracy and the free market."[139] Ironically, however, the celebration of democracy "had been made possible by expropriating all of the private land of the old Hansa quarter and giving planners the power to redraw the streets and property lines, which they were not able to do elsewhere."[140] The very different approaches of Berlin's east and west shared the characteristic of being prohibitively expensive. (Flair, tasteful or not, comes with a cost.) Thus both projects were "one-offs" not repeated elsewhere in the city. In the Soviet case, the long stretch along Stalinalle also failed to provide sufficient housing for the numbers in need.[141]

Large-scale modernist buildings in the West struck many as insufficiently different from the Nazi style. Architecture in the capital therefore took a new turn. Prewar maps and photographs served as the basis for designs as architects sought to replicate or restore the pre-Nazi character of Berlin (just as Communist architects in Warsaw similarly relied on Venetian Bernardo Bellotto's paintings from the 18th century).[142] And, lest we forget, all this building could take place only after disposing of the thousands of tons of rubble resulting from months of bombing and destruction wrought by Soviet ground forces. Much of the debris went into the new Berlin thanks in no small part to the city's *Trümmerfrauen* (rubble women) whose tasks included moving debris and determining what was salvageable for reuse. It was brutal work: cleaning mortar from the recyclable, loading heavy material into carts, then hauling it to centralized collection points where they transferred loads to a *Trümmerbahnlokomotive* (rubble train) for further processing. The same work had been done by individuals from concentration camps and other slave labor while the war was still ongoing. Some of the material became part of new runways at the three airports of Tempelhof, Tegel, and Gatow. Other became hills atop of which appeared new parks. Among Berlin's highest points today is the Teufelsberg (Devil's Mountain), constructed by piling WWII rubble atop an existing building.[143]

Recovering Ukrainian cities will fortunately not have the aggravation of dealing with four occupying governments, but they will be unable to escape the tensions inherent in deciding how to rebuild. "Reconstruction had to happen," historian Brian Ladd wrote in summarizing Berlin's rebuilding, "and reconstruction, like all action, entails selective remembrance and selective forgetting."[144] Despite the unique challenges inherent in Berlin's recovery, the city benefited from a vital truth soon after the war's end: "That America would help out financially was never seriously in doubt."[145]

■ Manila

> Twenty people might live together in a most intimate fashion in one-room shacks; no toilet facilities, even in outhouse form. The odor of human excreta permeated the air in vast areas of [Manila]. Then there was the sour odor of filthy bodies and rancid, cheap food. Naked children ran through graveled streets, seemingly without control…. During the Japanese occupation, schools were closed for three years. Children were taught to deceive the occupiers and, therefore, deceit has become a virtue.[146]
>
> — George Sharpe, *Brothers in Blood*

> A disaster affecting a capital city carries an especially heavy burden since any city that is host to many national institutions is swiftly equated with the nation-state as a whole.[147]
>
> — Lawrence J. Vale and Thomas J. Campanella, "Conclusion: Axioms of Resilience"

Though hell for the soldier, the WWII battle to retake Manila reinforced only too clearly the reality that victims of urban combat's ferocity and its aftermath are rarely the province of combatants alone.[148] Its noncombatants—the innocent, the civilians—are all too often caught up in the fighting that invades their neighborhoods or depredations of a combatant bent on punishment, destruction, and sacrificing residents' lives. The number of attacking Americans killed during the 1945 retaking of the Philippine capital totaled 1,010. Some 14,000-17,000 Japanese defenders lost their lives. Terrible numbers, but nothing like the 100,000 Filipinos perishing during those days of fighting in early 1945, one in ten from a population of an estimated one million as the battle began. Many others were physically injured, widowed, orphaned, or psychologically scarred.

Japanese forces occupied Manila after General Douglas MacArthur declared it an open city in December 1941. Much of the pre-war population remained during the interim years. Others joined them as months went by, some involuntarily as prisoners of the occupiers, others seeking shelter, food, or the work making the formers' acquisition possible. An idea of how hard it was to survive in the countryside is evident in Manila having achieved the urban area's largest wartime population in early 1944 despite the oppressive policies of the Japanese. Only with the beginning of Allied bombing in the autumn of that year did numbers start to lessen, though not so much as to reduce the population level to that seen prior to the occupiers' arrival. Manila's 1945 defenders had no intention of declaring the Philippine capital an open city a second time. Manileños would see no repeat of the earlier reprieve from combat's devastation.[149]

CHAPTER 3

It was exchanges of artillery fire that caused the greatest loss of civilian life in 1945. Originally prohibited by MacArthur in hopes of preserving the city in which he had lived before the war, growing US casualties caused a change of mind. Destruction could have been worse. Despite the loss of life to attacking soldiers, their general constrained aerial bombardment to the city's outskirts.

Such limitations can subdue but not eliminate the effects of war's wrath. Urban combat is inherently destructive even when decisions curb the use of bombs and bigger guns. American soldiers in Manila were unfamiliar with city fighting after years of seizing Pacific islands, defeating enemies in tropical jungles, and maneuvering across Philippine plains. They learned quickly: how to minimize their exposure in open areas by avoiding broad boulevards and moving between and within buildings only after hacking a hole through a wall rather than entering by door or window where the enemy might await in ambush. Even then there was no assurance someone wasn't lurking within the room on the other side of a newly-made gap. A grenade or blast from a flamethrower was the answer, munition or flame making first entry through these just-hewn "mouse holes"…unless it was known civilians dwelled within. Americans also found firing their weapons when moving into rooms helped seize the initiative and cause any surviving defenders to open fire prematurely, aiding detection of where a foe waited in ambuscade. The tactics reduced US casualties; the approach was far less helpful in sparing Manila's buildings or preserving the lives of unfortunate Filipinos caught between opposing forces. Japanese defenders visited yet more punishment on physical infrastructure and population alike by setting fire to neighborhoods. Fighting destroyed an estimated 11,000 of Manila's buildings. The result was 200,000 Filipino homeless in addition to the 100,000 killed. The capital's industry had already suffered from its machinery being sent to Japan; fighting further depleted remaining stocks.[150] A.V.H. Hartendorp was interned at the Santo Tomas University prisoner camp during the Japanese occupation. He described the Manila he found after liberation:

> At least four-fifths of Greater Manila was razed to the ground...stinking with the thousands of dead of massacre as well as battle. It had lost its piers, docks, and bridges, its electric light and power and gas plants, its telephone exchanges, radio-stations, and newspaper plants, its factories and warehouses and office-buildings, its schools and universities, libraries, museums, churches, and theaters, its hotels and apartment houses, nine-tenths of its private homes, even its parks and avenues and streets. A great city, of a million inhabitants, a metropolis, three hundred years in building, was gone.[151]

Manila in the Immediate Aftermath

> It was miraculous...that we hadn't seen epidemics of cholera ravaging the population.... [Then there are the children, homeless] and without parents. The shortage of food, other items, the temptation to steal army property, the black market, and the Fagins taking advantage of the situation all complicate the situation.[152]
>
> — Dr. George Sharpe, US Army

CHAPTER 3

> Neither Poe with his raven, nor Dumas with his dungeons...could capture in words this immense picture of desolation. For one who had not seen this, it is impossible to believe or imagine it.... Everyone, soldier or civilian, who as visited this place, repeated the same refrain: "I never could imagine anything like this. It is horrible."[153]
>
> — Juan Labrador, *A Diary of the Japanese Occupation*

Death and the spread of disease were both possibilities if the Americans could not maintain the flow of potable water. Survivors at first had none, nor did they have electricity or sewage treatment. Garbage services had broken down. Rats thrived while humans suffered. Dispensaries reportedly served an average of 87,540 patients daily once the worst of the fighting ceased.[154] Civilians continued to die. Dangers lurked on streets and within buildings. Many fell victim to not-yet-removed enemy mines, booby traps, and munitions that had failed to burst. Thousands of unexploded artillery rounds required disarming, detonation in place, or movement to locations where soldiers could safely neutralize them. Over fifty tons of unexploded munitions were piled near the Manila Hotel alone.[155] Morality and, surely, emotional stability suffered as well. Wrote author James M. Scott, "the city's social fabric had begun to unravel during the latter stages of Japanese occupation, but post-battle it totally disintegrated". Quoting the above Dr. Sharpe once again, "morals and convention had been completely set aside.... Children of six and seven ran up to soldiers and openly pandered for prostitutes.... It was really appalling to even the most unthinking person as to what the effect of war had on these people."[156]

Then there were those ready to take advantage of neighbors in need: Unsavory property owners capitalized on the misery of fellow residents by charging extortionate rents, the result being multiple families squeezing into spaces so they could afford the shelter (thereby increasing the threat of communicating diseases). Those who could not afford rents or find sturdier structures amidst Manila's destruction constructed their own of scrap metal and wood.

It took four weeks to clear Manila of its Japanese occupiers. Recovery would take much longer. The War Damage Corporation stepped in to cover property losses insurance would not.[157] Efforts to relieve suffering included civil affairs units hiring over 27,000 Manileños to provide some form of income. Unemployment lingered nevertheless. The US Army stepped in, hiring 116,492 from Manila's depleted population. American military representatives set up employment offices throughout the devastated city.[158]

The line between civilized behavior and anarchy was sometimes knife-edge thin. Aircraft sprayed insecticide to subdue mosquitoes feasting on the weakened population and a fly population gorging on carcasses, corpses, and untreated waste. Malaria, tuberculosis, and venereal disease spread. Leprosy—previously limited to those in leper colonies—appeared in the general population. Confronted with extensive wartime destruction of laboratories and other public health facilities, US and Philippine authorities tailored recovery to the funds available, both agreeing not to establish a medical program the country would be unable to sustain once American aid ended. That program wisely relied primarily on Filipinos the better to establish a foundation of trained personnel and thereby ease the coming transition. Successful, by January 1948 only three of approximately 1,100 public health employees were not Filipino. Education in disease control, nutrition, and sanitation accompanied treatment, medical personnel understanding that lack of awareness sustained spread of disease. Support from the United Nations initially underpinned feeding, clothing, medical care, and reestablishment of farming. That ended with Philippine independence in 1946.[159] Termination of US funds was fortunately more gradual, another reflection that while transition was coming, it was essential to avoid breaks in health coverage. The apparent benevolence came with a price. Recovery funding for war damages gained approval only after Philippine authorities agreed to US control of trade. Sustaining disproportionate reliance on US products undermined the Philippine government's ability to compete with other countries, impeded development of industrial capabilities, and generally hindered the speed of recovery.[160] Linking the peso to the US dollar also burdened Filipinos by linking their cost of living to that in the United States. Compared to a 1937 value of 100, by 1949 it was at an overall index value of 385. Food stood at 405 (though it varied depending on the product). Wage levels, unlinked to prices for American consumer goods, could not keep pace.[161] The situation tended to be worse in Manila than elsewhere in the country. Based on a 1941 index of 100, the average price level in November 1946 was 379 Philippines-wide but 492 in the capital.[162]

Ties That Bound, Ties That Hindered

> It was accepted in the Philippines, and initially in the United States, that the major responsibility...for the restoration of the economy of the Islands rested on the United States. This obligation went beyond that of compensating for direct war damage to include that of rehabilitation and reconstruction. The discharge of the responsibility for reconstruction also presented a real opportunity for more imaginative planning of an economy suited to the needs of independence. So approached, the problem was not that of restoration of the pre-war status but was rather one of financing the development of economic activity which was divorced from dependence on the American tariff system.... This type of planning and assistance in reconstruction and rehabilitation did not materialize.[163]
>
> — Harold M. Vinacke,
> "Post-War Government and Politics of the Philippines"

The capital, and country as a whole, suffered badly during the occupation by the Japanese and fighting to retake the Philippines. One gauge is the country's balance of trade in 1945. The Philippines benefited from a favorable balance of trade in the ten years before the war. From June-December of the war's last year, however, imports outpaced exports by a factor of forty-three. The US accounted for 87 percent of imports during the same six months.[164]

Two months before Philippine independence, the US Congress passed the Philippine Rehabilitation Act authorizing some $620 million for war damage reparations, rebuilding public property, and aiding the reestablishment of services. Coordinated by the US Department of State, it—as did the public health program—emphasized the training of Filipinos in the interest of the country being able to sustain itself once American support ended, an end scheduled for June 1950. Funding overwhelmingly favored education (62.2 percent nationwide), followed by restoration or replacement of national government buildings, medical facilities, municipal and provincial government buildings, water supply and irrigation, and other projects.[165] All well and good…aside from the act's focus being on *public* properties and services while the vast majority of damage was to *private* assets. "The war has left the Philippine economic system entirely prostrate," stated a Philippine Bureau of Census and Statistics report. "The major industries which used to be the bulwark of the national economy have been almost completely wrecked. The banks and other sources of credit have been sacked by the Japanese invaders who left them all bankrupt."[166]

Efforts by citizens to maintain a reasonable standard of living, much less restore their properties to pre-destruction conditions, were made more difficult given that wage rates only doubled by the end of 1945 while the cost of living had increased six and a half times.[167] Inflation's rise was neither constant nor linear. One must consider the ebb and flow of economic cycles even during times of disaster and they exercised their vagaries as Filipinos worked to recover. Poultry prices spiked as Christmas approached, then fell after the holiday.

Families compensated for the wage-price imbalance in several ways. Some heads of households worked multiple jobs while other family members also took positions. Less popular but cheaper sources of food replaced more desirable ones, e.g., canned goods found their way to tables in lieu of fresh produce. "Payment in-kind" exchanges sometimes helped.[168] Potentially further skewing longer-term recovery was the aforementioned number of greater Manila's residents who were employed by the American armed forces—the in excess of 115,000 individuals hired constituted over 10 percent of the city's population.[169] One official study noted, "it may be safely estimated that at least one-half of the entire working population of the City of Manila are making a living fully or in part from businesses which owe their existence to the presence of the US armed forces." Direct employment by United States representatives remained popular despite the failure of the Americans to align wages with inflation. Access to products helps explain the apparent dichotomy. Again quoting the Bureau of Census and Statistics, "The US Army, in adopting standards of wages which do not conform to changes in cost of living, in effect has invited pilferage and theft of its stores."[170]

Adding to Filipinos' troubles was the occupiers' wartime printing of their own currency. Japanese authorities began issuing their version of the peso as they established themselves in January 1942. This was forced on the citizenry at par with legitimate Philippine pesos. Inflation was inevitable when printing became rampant. P8,747,000 were in circulation by the end of that first month. The *monthly* release of Japanese pesos was P250,000,000 by July 1945 at which time a total of P7,959,542,000 was in circulation.[171] Given this mismanagement's effect on inflation, Japanese authorities found it necessary to limit the amount of currency available to Filipinos by restricting their bank withdrawals to P500 per month after earlier forcing them to deposit funds.[172] Post-occupation outlawing of the Japanese military peso had a significant effect on both individual and commercial wealth as some had been hoarding notes. An idea of the losses absorbed in those tumultuous times is evident in the total amount of Commonwealth (legitimate) currency in circulation being less than one billion pesos even after import of over 700 million pesos by the US government on its retaking the Philippines.[173]

Just under a third of Manila's buildings bore some extent of ruin, but of that nearly one-third, 96 percent was listed as being in a state of "full damage." Here too, the vast majority of properties harmed were private, constituting 97 percent of structures damaged.[174] Burdens on housing were made worse by increases in household size; those without shelter joined relatives as did many of the large number of orphaned children.[175] Rents in the months following the end of fighting more than doubled as compared to 1938.[176] The capital attracted individuals from elsewhere nonetheless. Based on the estimated pre-battle Manila population of one million and 100,000 civilian deaths during that catastrophe leaves a population of approximately 900,000 in mid-1945 (excluding the American military and other outsiders). By the end of 1949, the city was home to 1.2 million, an increase of 33 percent in four and a half years, a period when housing was at a premium and unemployment or its threat was a constant challenge.[177]

The honest suffered most as the less ethical set up rackets to capitalize on shortages and others turned to theft in the face of possible starvation.[178] The United States further handicapped recovery by hastening Philippine independence in the interest of reducing its obligations to the soon-to-be-former colony. Hurriedness undermined an effective transition and sowed seeds that created support for an evolving Hukbalahap (Huk) insurgency, one continuing to plague both city and country in evolved form today. In the words of the official US Army history for this period,

> by mid-1945, 200 million pounds of food were shipped to Manila to relieve shortages caused by the near total breakdown of Philippine agriculture. However promising the effort, emergency programs suffered from a lack of American supervision once the aid reached the Philippines. Once unloaded, the distribution of aid was mismanaged by inept, usually corrupt, Filipino officials. These problems were aggravated by the release of several thousand Filipino collaborators by United States and Philippine authorities when their skills were needed by the Osmena government. However, as often is the case involving large sums of money and materiel flooding into an impoverished nation, many local officials took the opportunity to become wealthy through corruption and the black market at the expense of their countrymen.[179]

As in Tokyo and Berlin, corruption in its many forms provided plentiful potholes on Manila's road to recovery. Philippine presidents came to recognize it was a significant factor in support for the Huk insurgency. The primary social friction was a Manila-elsewhere one rather than ethically based, a gap between Manila's elite and other citizens throughout the country (though some Chinese Filipinos, Moros, mountain tribesmen, and other groups felt themselves particularly marginalized by the country's rulers).[180] The federal government actively sought to address this divide by promoting community development, building on President Manuel L. Quezon's 1939 declaration that Tagalog would henceforth be the country's national language.[181] President Manuel A. Roxas (1946-48) promoted decentralization, with communities outside Manila being allowed to make decisions regarding taxation, goods licensing, and local appointments.[182] It was not a policy without risks, and risks came to roost when local leaders sought to pull away from Manila's control in part due to pressures from Hukbalahap insurgents and their political arm, the Filipino Communist Party. Central Luzon suffered outbreaks of violence as corruption amongst the capital's elite continued uninterrupted.[183]

The growing threat of rebellion motivated Ramon Magsaysay's appointment as Minister of National Defense in 1950. His approach in dealing with Huk influence blended force with programs bringing social services to those outside of Manila regardless of race or geography. The military became a nation-building force while also confronting the insurgent threat with armed might.[184] The choice of Tagalog as a national language had also proved a wise one in that regard. Tristan Miguel Santos Osteria's extensive research on Philippine integration concluded Tagalog "became a major vehicle for unification since not only were Manila and the surrounding areas Tagalog-speaking, but all the other dialects across the archipelago had a lot more in common with Tagalog than with one another."[185] Magsaysay's influence as Defense Minister and later as President was fundamental to the significant progress made in subduing the insurgency by the early 1950s. His premature death in a plane crash was a significant setback not only in counterinsurgency but also counter-corruption terms. As with the *yakuza* in Tokyo, corruption continues to undermine Philippine quality of life and governance eighty years later.

CHAPTER 4

RECOVERY IN AN ETHNICALLY STRIDENT CAPITAL (SARAJEVO)[1]

The siege of Sarajevo by the Yugoslav People's Army and the Army of Republika Srpska during the Bosnian War is the most prolonged city blockade in modern history. It lasted almost four years (from 1992 to 1996) and cost the city its historical development and infrastructure. The post-war reconstruction of Bosnia and Herzegovina's capital did little to improve the situation. Sarajevo city authorities burned through the international organizations' money, flooding the city with chaotic development.[2]
— Kateryna Kozlova, "A Facelift Worth Billions"

Reconstruction in Sarajevo occurred in a situation defined by the threefold challenge of post-war cities: a destroyed built environment, a traumatized population, and a number of displaced people who are there to stay as a result of post-war political settlements.[3]
— Gruia Bădescu, "Dwelling in the Post-War City: Urban Reconstruction and Home-Making in Sarajevo"

One of the first things Russian forces do when they occupy a town is to purge libraries of "harmful" books and dismantle any monument to Soviet-era crimes, such as those marking Stalin's starvation of millions of Ukrainians in the 1930s. As Mr. Mykhed puts it, "My faith in the power of literature is being restored by the...occupiers' fear of our books."[4]

— "Your land is my land: Imperialism then and now," *The Economist*

Disasters too often scrape away the facade of civility to reveal latent prejudices. Tokyo's 1923 earthquake roused Japanese distrust; they blamed Koreans living among them for fabricated post-event poisonings of wells and even the tremors themselves.[5] Halifax, Nova Scotia's December 1917 munitions ship explosion led to accusations against residents of German descent, including claims one family concealed a gun emplacement under its lawn awaiting invaders from their ancestral country. The police would soon after arrest every German citizen in the city.[6] European Jewish communities were burned in retribution for bringing the scourge of plague during the Middle Ages, the fact those communities similarly suffered the Black Death notwithstanding.[7] We have observed that the end of (or pause in) Ukraine's war will not be the cessation of conflict with Russia. The latter's propaganda fabrications and gullibility of both Russians at home and sympathizers in Ukraine guarantee quarrels will continue to fuel tensions between Ukrainians, stoking rifts in their social structure and complicating Kyiv's efforts to build unity in the war's aftermath. It therefore makes sense to consider a historical case in which war shattered social bonds at least as much as it did a city's—and country's—physical infrastructure.

CHAPTER 4

Created at the end of World War I, Yugoslavia was birthed by the union of Bosnian, Croat, and Slovenian territories from within what was once the Austro-Hungarian Empire.[8] Partially fragmented by the Nazis during WWII when they spun off an allied Croat state, the whole was remade under Josip Broz Tito when his Communist-dominated partisans defeated German and local opposition forces. Tito's death in 1980 and a combination of domestic and international influences dissolved the adhesive that had bonded the country's several ethnicities for a generation. Regional leaders saw an opportunity. First, Serbian Slobodan Milosevic ended the autonomous status of two provinces within Serbia (Vojvodina and Kosovo) while also replacing neighboring Montenegro's leadership with allies. These 1989 events preceded Croatian, Slovenian, and Bosnian declarations of sovereignty soon thereafter. Macedonia likewise declared independence in September 1991. The province's Serb minority boycotted a referendum on independence in March 1992.

An incursion into Slovenia by what was effectively a Serbian Yugoslav People's Army (JNA) force lasted but ten days, the result being the country's independence. The JNA later intervened in Croatia when its Serbian minority declared independence and requested unification with Serbia. Tens of thousands died in the ensuing war. The conflict left hundreds of thousands displaced. Croatia remained independent. Later fighting between Serbian, Croat, Bosniak (generally Muslim), and JNA forces in Bosnia and Herzegovina (hereafter referred to as Bosnia-Herzegovina or BiH) was an order of magnitude more costly with deaths in the hundreds of thousands and displaced in the millions, Bosniaks being the primary victims of Serb and Croat ethnic cleansing. Though the collective Yugoslav presidency ordered the JNA to depart Bosnia-Herzegovina in early May 1992, roughly 90 percent of the 100,000-strong force remained in the country. Milosevic had, in December of the year before, presciently directed that those serving in JNA forces operating in the country be primarily Bosnian born. Units transitioned from the JNA to the Army of Republika Srpska (VRS) and continued the siege. Organization names changed. Their soldiers and equipment did not.[9] The war ended only after NATO involvement and economic sanctions forced Milosevic to accept an international peacekeeping force. Placed under a United Nations mandate, the country remained internally fragmented, the whole containing two autonomous entities: (1) The Federation of Bosnia and Herzegovina and (2) Republika Srpska. A third entity, the self-governed Brcko District, would remain under UN auspices given its strategic location between two segments of the Republika Srpska as well as bordering Croatia to its immediate north. (See Image 3.) The BiH capital of Sarajevo remained badly fractured along Bosniak, Croat, and Serb lines.

Tokyo, Berlin, and Manila all had cultural divides of some sort as WWII came to a close. Tokyo's Japanese, Korean, and Chinese gangs competed for black market turf, sometimes in engagements involving machine guns.[10] Berlin struggled with displaced persons brought in by the Nazi regime to serve as slave labor. We recall Manila's divisions were less ethnic than urban-rural in character (or Manila-

CHAPTER 4

Image 3. Map Bosnia-Herzegovina with Brcko at Upper Right[11]

rest of the country), these serving as a basis for continued Hukbalahap support. Such scapegoating can provide an excuse to avoid acknowledging one's own shortcomings. Researcher Alice Weinreb found that post-WWII Germans readily acknowledged their own participation in the black market but blamed its existence and food-related crimes on "foreigners" and Jews presumed to be in control of the markets. This illusory "they" meant accusers did not have to confront the reality of corrupt German officials responsible for food collection and distribution, fellow citizens taking advantage of others via black market operations, outright thieves, or farmers whose hoarding to increase prices kept sustenance from the mouths of the malnourished and starving.[12]

The above problems were problematic, but none were sufficient to tear Tokyo, Berlin, or Manila apart as was the case in Sarajevo when Serb and Bosniak communities separated in the face of genocidal threats and violence. Opposing factions targeted historically significant buildings, seeking to destroy cultural touchstones.[13] Once compatible, groups suffered rifts crafted by politicians bent on creating and securing power bases at the cost of unity. (Politicians also promoted their agendas at the expense of Croats and other groups, but Serb-Bosniak was—and remains—the primary rift in Sarajevo.) As one author put it, "Nationalist leadership on all sides made sure that no intact empty homes were waiting for their rightful prewar inhabitants."[14] Urban planner Dr. Haris Piplas succinctly described the opening of the city's crisis that foretold of this unfortunate outcome:

> Approximately 100,000 protesters gathered in [the Sarajevo neighborhood of] Marijin Dvor on April 6th, 1992, demanding a new revolution: the resignation of the ethnonationalist government coalition whom they held responsible for the political fragmentation of Sarajevo and BiH…. Shots from snipers sitting on the Olympic Holiday Inn Hotel [the Serbian Democratic Party's (SDS) informal headquarters] were fired at the protesters, killing six. These were considered the first casualties of the war in Sarajevo….

According to Biljana Plavšić, a high-profile member of the SDS, the Serb paramilitary forces aimed to divide Sarajevo into two ethnic zones. Marijin Dvor, as the geographical and political center of the city, represented, in their opinion, the most convenient area to halve the city. "Everything west of the Holiday Inn" was supposed to belong to the future ethnically clean Serb territory.[15]

From whence had Serb motivations to besiege and divide come? The president of Republika Srpska, Radovan Karadžić, and his fellow Bosnian Serb leaders had no intention of allowing Sarajevo to retain its character as the symbol of a multi-ethnic, open, and welcoming Balkan city, a character established when it served as host of the 1984 Winter Olympics. In Karadžić's view,

> the battle of Sarajevo would decide the war, with the city being either divided or destroyed…. Warren Zimmermann, then US ambassador to Yugoslavia, recalled from an interview he had with Karadžić his plan to ethnically divide Sarajevo into two parts by erecting walls…. "We will have the Serbian area, and that will be part of the Serbian Republic. We will have a Muslim area, and we will have a Croatian area, so nobody will have to live next to another ethnic group. There will be divisions…. We are going to build walls that will separate all of these areas." After fruitless demands for the division of Sarajevo…the SDS leadership placed Sarajevo…under a military siege.[16]

Opposing forces confronted each other at short range on Sarajevan streets, but snipers and artillery fire were the primary killers. An August 1992 visitor from the United Nations Human Rights Commission recalled, the city is shelled on a regular basis in what appears to be a deliberate attempt to spread terror among the population. Snipers shoot civilians. The mission visited the hospital and was able to see many civilian victims. It was also able to see the damage done to the hospital itself, which has been deliberately shelled on several occasions despite the proper display of the internationally recognized Red Cross symbol.[17]

Serbs seized control of the city's water supply. In response, an international aid worker designed and installed an innovative system to filter and pump water to denied areas, turning it on surreptitiously after Bosniak officials tried to block its use. (Author Peter Andreas speculated its production would have reduced black market income.) Not all outside assistance was as helpful. United Nations organizations repeatedly granted Serb besiegers concessions allowing them to impede residents' freedom of movement, deny supplies, and interrupt services including mail delivery for almost four years.[18] The 350,000 residents within saw over 35,000 buildings destroyed, 13,952 fellow residents killed, and another 70,000 wounded or otherwise injured.[19]

Misfortune compounded miseries that would have been familiar to Tokyoites, Berliners, and Manileños fifty years before. Author Peter Lippman described life in Sarajevo once a ceasefire went into effect:

> Thousands of windows in Sarajevo were covered only by a sheet of plastic…. Gas for heating was…not turned on until well after the cold season had started. The lack of fuel and a shortage of electricity meant people bundled up and lived by candlelight at night. In the first few years after the war, people in Sarajevo were saying that "the only difference

between now and the war days is that there are no bombs falling."[20]

Food joined electricity, gas, mail, and water as commodities in short supply before war's end. Bosniak leader Alija Izetbegovic made restoration of services one of the conditions for a ceasefire. It was an accomplishment hindered by Serbian-laid mines and the fact the gas provider was the Russian state-controlled Gazprom that refused to restore delivery until the country paid long overdue debts. Only after external pressures did Gazprom restore service, the ceasefire following a few hours later.[21] Factories in Sarajevo and elsewhere stood idle in the aftermath, victims of looters, lack of management, and an absence of skilled labor and materials among other causes. It would be several years before production climbed much above 20 percent of that prewar. Postwar unemployment was rife. Many who did find jobs worked for international aid groups rather than establishments that would better underpin long-term economic revival. Income for numerous families was meager nevertheless. Conditions could be especially difficult for persons displaced due to ethnic cleansing elsewhere as they had no one to turn to for support nor any home to which they could return, their former abodes now being in the "wrong" communities.[22] One man, his home usurped by another, commiserated, "I have a key and no house."[23]

A ceasefire existed, but ethnically-riven Sarajevo's status remained a prominent obstacle to signing of a final settlement. US President Bill Clinton proposed a solution, believing "it would be a mistake to divide the city. We don't want another Berlin. If you can't unify it, internationalize it."[24] Others agreed, proposing it become a city administered by the United Nations. Another option was a "federal" or "DC model" in which Sarajevo was neither part of the Federation of Bosnia-Herzegovina nor Republika Srpska but rather an independent enclave in which all three primary ethnic groups cooperatively governed.[25] Neither course of action saw realization. The former fell short in part given the UN's none-too-enthusiastic receipt of the idea, the latter because Serbian President Slobodan Milosevic refused to grant his support to the plan. The Bosnian Serb Assembly's formal strategic goal of May 12, 1992, to see "the division of the city of Sarajevo into Serb and Muslim parts and the establishment in each of an effective state authority," continued to motivate that leadership segment.[26] Milosevic would eventually withdraw his refusal to allow Sarajevo to become part of Bosnia-Herzegovina apparently out of frustration with Bosnian Serb leaders with whom he had been previously aligned.[27]

Sarajevo's unification remained elusive. Bosnian Serb leaders demanded fellow Serbs leave Bosniak-controlled areas rather than live intermixed. Any refusing were forced out. Removals at times included rapes and beatings. Some departing saw their apartments burned by Serb forces with all belongings therein.[28] These losses were of less consequence for Serbs displaced from elsewhere during the civil war and who therefore had few belongings. Not so for most who had long called a neighborhood home. Others who had managed to avoid Bosnian Serb purges fell victim to Bosniak forces set on killing any Serb who remained in Bosniak neighborhoods. Victims and observers alike were appalled when members of the North Atlantic Treaty Organization's (NATO) Implementation Force (IFOR) stood by during such atrocities, a spokesman stating the actions were "unfortunate" but asserting IFOR "is not a police force and will not undertake police duties." International disgust was widespread.[29]

In the WWII days of March 1942, President Franklin D. Roosevelt spoke to an American Library Association convention audience. "Books cannot be killed by fire," he pronounced. "People die, but books never die."[30] Yet the value of books as purveyors of truths and opposing viewpoints threatens those with no interest in any but their own agendas. Efforts to erase cultural landmarks from the ground, and thereby minds, included burning almost two hundred libraries and destroying 90 percent of the books and other collections in the National Library of Sarajevo.[31] Piplas thought it, "the most books in human history destroyed at one time."[32] The importance of libraries as sources of knowledge and cultural pride is evident in the United Nations 1949 Public Library Manifesto recognizing "the library is a prerequisite to let citizens make use of their right to information and freedom of speech...necessary...for open debate and creation of public opinion."[33] Libraries were not alone in being targeted by Serbian military forces. Other cultural sites included a Habsburg-period villa housing the Olympic Museum and Oriental Institute with its irreplaceable Ottoman-era manuscripts.[34]

Restoration of culturally-significant structures has through the ages brought forth a multitude of conflicting approaches. In Sarajevo's case, American architect Lebbeus Woods suggested devastated landmarks be partially restored while other parts remain as testimony to war's damage done. Critics countered that such daily reminders would unsettle residents. For them, repairs should be less a source of remembrance than what should be.[35] Perhaps these critics also believed repairs made to buildings better healed and tamped ethnic tensions than would unmended sores.

A report supporting the International Criminal Tribunal for the Former Yugoslavia's case against Slobodan Milosevic concluded that 9,502 individuals died as a direct result of the Sarajevo siege. Over half of these (4,954) were civilians.[36] Estimates of wounded ran to approximately three times the number of deceased.[37] Death and wounds continued to ravage the innocent after the siege. In addition to dangers due to remaining mines and other unexploded ordnance, building safety features had deteriorated or been damaged during the fighting. The former included elevator cables so corroded they gave way, occupants plummeting to their demise. Jury-rigged gas lines exploded. Though Sarajevo was disproportionately favored in the distribution of $5 billion in international recovery aid to address these problems, much was lost to corruption. Individuals with political or criminal connections (in many cases both) pocketed what should have served public welfare.[38]

Sarajevo experienced Bosnia-Herzegovina's challenges in microcosm much as might be the case in Ukrainian cities when those with conflicting loyalties find each other at odds. Russia already seeks to culturally cleanse, monuments and other structures meaningful to Ukraine's population being among the targets. As in Sarajevo, libraries are eminent among them. In December 2023, the British publication *Labour Hub* reported,

> In the occupied territories, Russians are deliberately seizing and destroying Ukrainian literature that they consider "extremist." Such literature includes school textbooks on the history of Ukraine, scientific, and popular historical literature.... The destruction of Ukrainian literature is part of a broader programme of cultural erasure, which includes the looting and destruction of museums. It is aimed at suppressing any sense of Ukrainian cultural identity.[39]

The threat of ethnic division is very much pertinent to Ukrainian urban areas given what have previously been largely latent differences in perceptions of Russia and Russian influence, differences on which occupiers of Ukrainian cities have already seized.

▪ The Ethnicization of Sarajevo

> Beirut had the reputation of the Paris of the Middle East, a sophisticated, thriving city at the edge of the Mediterranean, while Sarajevo was a celebrated symbol of urban coexistence, especially after the 1984 Winter Olympics which portrayed it to the world as a confident place of harmonious relations between a diverse population. In fact, both cities were hailed as examples of harmonious, pluralistic urban societies.[40]
>
> — Gruia Bădescu,
> "Post-War Reconstruction in Contested Cities"

> During the war, over two million people were displaced or made refugees [from Bosnia-Herzegovina's prewar population of 4 million]. Somewhat over a million of those people returned home from abroad or from internal displacement, but the return movement was not successful in recreating a multiethnic population in any part of the country. In the places where there was significant return...the different ethnicities have lived alongside each other rather than with each other.... Corruption and the accompanying economic stalemate prompt both an economic and emotional depression, conditions that drive people to leave Bosnia in ever greater numbers.[41]
>
> — Peter Lippman, *Surviving the Peace*

Thousands dead, millions displaced. The first would never return home. The second might find homes occupied by others and a local government unwilling to restore their properties. Some governments created a veneer of legitimacy, specifying return conditions but making them all but impossible to meet. These authorities dictated previous occupants had to return in timeframes unrealistic even should owners receive word: fifteen days for those no longer in the country, seven days for internally displaced persons.[42] This was merely perpetuating behaviors such as Bosnian Serb initiatives to oust other ethnic groups from most of Sarajevo. Representatives of one side or another had posted sentries to block entry into the city's various ethnic areas as early as April 1992.[43] Yet there were several obstacles even when a government sought to return properties to their rightful owners. How to identify those owners when ownership records were destroyed? What of properties when the status of absent owners or renters is unknown, when they have not returned within a legitimately prescribed time for claiming ownership, or when housing is in short supply?

Sarajevo was fortunate most of its housing was still habitable after the worst of hostilities ceased. That did not mean all needing housing were properly sheltered, however. Individuals and families displaced from elsewhere lived in dwellings of various fabrications along hillsides, the city having spilled beyond its prewar bounds. Ethnic cleansing made it risky for any who might consider occupying a property where the status of previous occupants was unknown or debated. Resolution could take years to establish even when governments were supportive. The situation was at times one in which housing was plentiful yet many lacked proper places to live. A problem for residents, but also a conundrum for city leaders as they needed to decide whether to build new properties and infrastructure despite the availability of structures some of which had owners who would never return.[44]

Threats and actual acts of ethnic violence did not cease with the end of the shooting war. Bosnia-Herzegovina's government created a Return and Reconstruction Task Force in 1999 that sought to address recovery issues via a three-part strategy of space, sustainability, and, still necessary, security:

> Creating space for return involved evacuating usurped homes and reconstructing houses. Establishing security required ending the low-level terrorism practiced against returnees…. Sustainability…referred to the most difficult aspect of return: reestablishing life and livelihood for returnees in their prewar home.[45]

Some actions were long overdue. Prior to the war, for example, license plates depicted an owner's municipality, a means that had been used to identify victims for ethnic cleansing. A new policy eliminated this overt display.[46] Antipathies between Serbs, Croats, and Bosniaks were not the only challenges to reestablishing security and rebuilding communities. Differences within the three groups presented potential frictions of their own. Sarajevo Muslims tended to lead relatively secular lives. Those displaced from other locations were more religiously conservative. They could also pose an economic threat. Muslims from the Serbian province of Sandžak tended to fall into this category, causing concern among some in the capital when considerable numbers chose to settle there. Researcher Gruia Bădescu quoted one long-time resident:

> People look the same, but there is animosity between Sarajevans and Sandžak people. It is not that they did something to us. It is just that with their coming here, they brought new sets of beliefs, even a new language.... They are more traditional, more religious than us. There is a large population of Sarajevans with a socialist mentality and then these 100,000 who come in from Sandžak with religious beliefs.... As foreigners, they took the jobs, diminishing opportunities for the local people. People look at them as a threat, for this reason they are not welcome.[47]

Were these many divides not obstacle enough to Sarajevan unity, the city suffered an urban-formerly rural divide similar to that found in Manila. This was seen by some as a cultured versus uncultured rift, those considering themselves the former believing the latter, newer arrivals were tainting the city's character. While this attitude was found among homegrown Sarajevans and others considering themselves urbanites, concerns by those with rural backgrounds were more economic, creating another element of potential factionalism: the haves-have nots divide common in many urban areas.[48]

Sarajevo effectively became two cities in the months after the war much like the country of which it was a part. Both the country and city have a considerable Croat minority and a small Jewish community that estimates its number at roughly one thousand, most in Sarajevo. Protestant and other small religious communities similarly have their greatest numbers in the BiH capital or Banja Luka (effectively capital of the Republika Srpska).[49] That portion of Sarajevo in the Federation was over 87 percent Bosniak with the remainder being primarily Croat after the opposing sides purged neighborhoods.[50] Istočno Sarajevo (East Sarajevo) in Republika Srpska was overwhelmingly Serb. Architects there made a point of replicating familiar features found in downtown (Bosniak) Sarajevo. Economics sometimes softened the "hard" boundary between the two cities. Serbs found jobs in Sarajevo proper while Muslims desiring pork found the product easier to come by in Istočno Sarajevo. Politics—or more accurately politicians—were less flexible with their policies. Taxis registered in one city were not to cross the boundary with passengers. Public transportation offered no routes spanning the pair.[51] As one author described the situation,

> in Bosnia-Herzegovina…multiethnicity still lives mainly at the level of the three ethnonationalist profiteering leaderships. There is tacit cooperation, even amid apparently

rancorous election campaigns, to ensure that the elite confound the public and retain their positions.... These leaders tacitly worked together as if they were a three-way protection racket, effectively collaborating with their "enemies" to keep their flocks separate.[52]

Such manipulation of public perspectives goes far toward explaining why Sarajevo, a multicultural city the population of which was 50 percent Muslim, 30 percent Serb, 8 percent Croat, and 10 percent self-declared Yugoslavs had devolved into its fractured state.

Failure to collectively contemplate the city's future as a whole meant each side addressed recovery without consideration of their approach's consequences elsewhere. A Sarajevo architect noted how expansion of the greater urban area failed to account for an eventual need to expand its airport, condemning the facility to a too-limited capacity as the population grew.[53]

History is replete with demonstrations of ethnicization fomenting ill-will (or worse). It can also undermine an urban area's long-term health. Singapore continues to struggle with a tendency for Chinese, Malay, and other ethnicities to view themselves less as national citizens than members of their demographic group. Sustained divisions can, often do, reinforce economic differences. The same is true socially. Echoing Gruia Bădescu, author Peter Lippman observed,

> to walk down the street in Sarajevo after the war was to notice contrasts between the newcomers, who were mostly villagers, and the city folk.... Those who were of the city felt not only outnumbered but also endangered.... They mistrusted the *papci*, a disparaging word for villagers.[54]

CHAPTER 4

Many intellectuals, Lippman went on to note, chose to leave their country altogether. They were among the almost two-thirds of the city's population that was displaced, this in addition to the estimated nearly 14,000 killed during the siege.[55]

Many are the ways ethnic divides cripple urban recovery. The experiences of Tokyo, Berlin, and Manila make it clear that post-disaster physical infrastructure recovery is fertile ground for competing views amongst architects, city planners, politicians, budget managers, and (hopefully) resident viewpoints. Add the yawning social gaps present in Bosnia-Herzegovina and the planning landscape becomes an emotional minefield. Shying away from tough negotiations and difficult decisions invites increased costs, inefficiencies, and delays. Eyesores are another threat. Failures to cooperate during planning and funding can lead to building on the cheap and architectural fragmentation. Dr. Linda Kinstler described post-siege Sarajevo initiatives as spurred by "an outpouring of concern and support." Those initiatives included designs for an art museum, proposals by world-renowned architects, and the Massachusetts Institute of Technology dispatching students in hopes of spawning creative building concepts. Kinstler instead found lack of an overarching central plan

> led to an ad hoc reconstruction that was corrupted and uncoordinated. Refugees who had their homes destroyed were pushed into temporary shelters on the mountain slopes outside the city center while international aid groups pursued their own plans for rebuilding individual

structures. The outcome...was a chaotic race to reconstruct Sarajevo in the image of its varied benefactors.[56]

Despite faction leaders loudly touting their separatist and even ethnic cleansing messages, we know money proved sufficient motivation for inter-ethnic connections. Public meetings were forums for posturing and condemning the "other" as behind-closed-door sessions saw city faction leaders conducting business while "drinking and smoking together like old friends."[57] These leaders were among those profiting from surreptitious black marketing operations. Some at the highest levels allegedly blocked the development of Sarajevo-based arms manufacturing even as their own Bosniak supplies ran short.[58]

The city's black market exchanges might not have been as fundamental to survival as those in our WWII examples, but they could be an important way to supplement shortages of food, fuel, or medicine.[59] As a half-century before, they also served to meet the needs of internationals residing in the city. These included journalists and members of the UN mission during the siege, the latter both selling and buying goods while the former were more likely purchasers. Fuel was a hot commodity. Journalists needed it to power their vehicles. Residents needed it for heating and cooking. (Sarajevo was, after all, host to a *Winter* Olympics.) Select United Nations Protection Force (UNPROFOR, the military presence responsible for keeping the airport open and delivering aid among other functions) representatives were notorious for their black market participation, Ukrainian units among those foremost. A Ukrainian corps commander lost his position in the autumn of 1992 for selling oil, liquor, and cigarettes; nineteen more Ukrainian and three French soldiers were likewise removed from the country a year later.[60] Non-governmental aid organization representatives likewise participated in black marketeering, some of their organizations being nothing more than fronts for criminality.[61] (Effective vetting of NGOs remains an unmet challenge. Two decades after the end of war in Bosnia-Herzegovina, an unknown number of alleged medical and other organizations were little more than vehicles for thrill-seekers during the 2016-17 liberation of Mosul, Iraq.)[62]

Sarajevo's black market had more facets than the most intricately-cut diamond. Exchanges of stolen goods and services for money were a significant part, but products waylaid from their humanitarian aid purposes were routinely given to one or another combatant side as bribes to allow the remainder to hopefully reach the needy.[63] These costs of doing business made a direct line to black markets, profits filling the pockets of local criminals, military faction leaders, or city politicians (all often one in the same group or individual as was the case in Tokyo). That the siege was a realm of varying grays rather than black or white is evident in the end states: Though a good number of these profiteers are among the capital's most wealthy today, the money made from the illicitly procured goods arguably allowed Sarajevo to survive as capital and BiH as a country rather than fall to the better equipped and supplied Serb besiegers. Author Peter Andreas concurs, concluding, "Bosnia as a state would probably not exist (or certainly not in its present form) without the assistance of criminal combatants, black market traders, and arms embargo busters." Yet he provides a second perspective in addition: The siege of Sarajevo could have ended considerably earlier had United Nations forces not supported various combatants with bribes and otherwise buckled to demands that made war an attractive business venture.[64] Mark Cutts provides a comparison to the aid provided by the 1948 Berlin airlift:

> The Allies would certainly not have succeeded in delivering such large quantities to Berlin, and in eventually forcing Stalin to back down and lift the blockade, if they had started off with an agreement which allowed the East Germans to dictate the terms of the airlift, to inspect all arriving cargo, to receive a pay-off of one quarter of all arriving supplies, and to have the remainder pass through an East German road checkpoint before being allowed into the city.[65]

It was, admittedly, criminal elements that were Sarajevo's most capable defenders given BiH's lack of an effective army in the opening months of the country's existence. One notorious Bosniak criminal faction leader held several government titles bestowed as thanks for the proficiency of his force.[66] We must also not overlook another side to Sarajevo's black market: its value to factions' recruiting. Andreas continues, noting, "irregular fighters from Serbia were wooed to Bosnia by the prospects of looting and selling stolen goods on the black market. Indeed, many of the irregulars were common criminals" who had recently been forced out of Western Europe by police pressure or tightened immigration policies.[67]

CHAPTER 4

The Costs of Ethnicization

> Many were shocked because people were dying and suffering in a part of Europe where most believed ethnic slaughter would never again be countenanced.[68]
>
> — Robert J. Donia, *Sarajevo: A Biography*

> Now we won't ever live as well as we did, nor will the next generation.[69]
>
> — A Sarajevo landlord

Competition during rebuilding extended to that for the resources needed to build. The failure to cooperate and orchestrate recovery led to other failures as well. Economies of scale were lost. Coherency and efficiency—and Sarajevo's architectural beauty—gave way to waste and a visual fragmentation painful to the eye. In Sarajevo's case, parks and other once public open spaces lost out to buildings. Once again demonstrating the inescapable consequences of a city being a system, the resultant traffic congestion compounded an already unfortunate air pollution problem thanks in part to Sarajevo being nestled in low ground surrounded by mountains.[70] Bădescu suggests such unplanned urban recovery also risks further deepening social rifts as perceptions view new structures as favoring one group over others.[71] That certainly came to be in Sarajevo given the divide between predominantly Bosniak Sarajevo and its East Sarajevo suburb, one physically clear in the change of script, religious architecture, and monuments. It could have been worse. Despite earlier declarations, the urban area escaped division by the physical wall favored by Serb leaders.[72]

Recovery is no freer of entropy's forces than any other physical process. Guidance and some measure of management are essential not only in the face of residents, politicians, and ambitious architects. In Sarajevo's case, additional influences with little interest in urban coherency included monied sources with their own agendas and a disregard for playing a unifying role at a time when such was notable by its absence. Bădescu recorded how there were Sarajevo residents who regretted involvement by external influences that might impose unwanted change both architecturally and socially. One interviewee blamed

> a "new line of badly behaved architects" [who] keep introducing grand un-Bosnian elements in mosque architecture. Many Sarajevans of diverse backgrounds decry in particular the influence of Saudi capital in erecting grand new mosques and education centres which also act as a place of propagating Salafi (Wahhabi) radical Islam perceptions. In their accounts, these mosques are "foreign," as Bosnian Islam is "different," echoing the geopolitical musings of Bosnia as a Western state with a Western type of Islam distinctive from Arab conservative versions.[73]

Bădescu went on to express further concerns regarding the unique impact memorials can have when they glorify but one group's history.

Those overseeing urban recovery are ideally honest brokers serving residents' interests both immediate and longer term. Lippman observes criminals and faction leaders in Bosnian Sarajevo instead used intimidation and acts of violence against non-Muslims to appropriate homes for profit.[74] Money, corruption, violence, vested interests, politics, and simple differences of opinion: The almost inevitable presence of these influences during urban recovery makes it clear that success demands exceptional individuals possessing exceptional powers if the worst of ethnic divisions are to be kept at bay. Dr. Piplas offered several observations for those embarking on Ukraine's urban recovery during a mid-2022 interview:

> Post-war Sarajevo authorities made a mistake when they didn't coordinate with the international organizations willing to help the city. Hopefully, Ukrainian cities will pay more attention to this…. Your first step should be establishing a platform to coordinate all initiatives. Second, I suggest you stop thinking that international partners will rebuild your cities by themselves. It's Ukrainians who should decide what their cities would look like. You have been scattered all over the world now, and you are seeing new things. This experience must be leveraged during reconstruction.[75]

Physical recovery proceeded quite quickly in Sarajevo. The majority of its housing was restored to something approximating normality within three years. As in Ukrainian cities, it was multi-unit housing rather than single-family units that made up most of the building. Transportation networks, including roads, were likewise repaired within this timeframe.[76] The story was far less positive in terms of social recovery. Professor Robert D. Putnam sees the importance of social capital—the personal and group relationship networks allowing a society to function effectively—as having three primary components. It (1) provides a structure for residents to resolve collective problems more easily, (2) facilitates community progress, and (3) demonstrates how the fates of society are linked.[77] The once metropolitan exemplar of greater Sarajevo remains as splintered socially as it is fractured visually. For each step toward the reasonable, there has been another canceling the progress. A 2016 US State Department report noted Sarajevo students could choose between religious or ethics courses or opt out altogether. The Sarajevo Canton Ministry of Education provided instruction in Orthodox, Protestant, Catholic, and Muslim religious practices. Yet in October of that year, the Sarajevo Canton Assembly named both an elementary school and street after a WWII-era pro-Hitler anti-Semite. The names remained unchanged after protests by a Jewish community leader.[78] In 2019, Human Rights Watch (HRW) estimated that 12 percent of the country's population—400,000 persons—were barred from running for the presidency or national parliament's upper chamber due to their ethnicity, religion, or residence location.[79] Four years later, more than a quarter-century after the end of Sarajevo's siege, a senior European court ruled Bosnia-Herzegovina's political system "amplifies ethnic divisions and undermines the Balkan country's democratic elections." The ruling concluded, "power-sharing arrangements have turned the country into an 'ethnocracy' in which ethnicity, and not citizenship, is the key to securing power and resources."[80] The court's findings reinforced those of HRW, concluding BiH's political system denied individuals not affiliated with one of the country's three primary ethnic groups from voting for their preferred candidates.

CHAPTER 4

Demonstrating the passage of time is no guarantee of social healing, Bosniaks raised a giant wartime banner near Sarajevo's boundary with the Republika Srpska in 2023. The response: a telecoms tower above the city is nightly lit in Serbian colors. In November of that year, Bosnian Serb leader Milorad Dodik reemphasized a belief that all Serbs should reside in a single state.[81] It is the social recovery of Sarajevo that is proving the greater challenge.

CHAPTER 5

THREE CITIES, THREE FATES – RECOVERY IN KHARKIV, KHERSON, AND MARIUPOL

> In wars to win land, the dead fill the fields. In wars to seize cities, the dead fill their streets.[1]
> — Confucian scholar Mengzi (or Mencius), 372–289 BC

> Russian-speaking Ukrainian patriotism is no weaker than the Ukrainian-speaking Ukrainian patriotism.[2]
> — Okeksandr Vilkul, Mayor of Kryvyi Rih

Occupation does not burden all equally, whether within a single city or across several. Some, like Kyiv and Kharkiv, suffered only outlying neighborhoods falling to Russian control, and that but briefly. Those residing in others knew invaders' oppression more broadly and longer before being, in a phrase popular when describing Ukraine's war, de-occupied. Kherson is such a city, its inhabitants less fortunate than peers in Kyiv and Kharkiv but more so than those residing in Mariupol who continue to suffer occupation as I write these words. Yet "fortunate" can be a deceiving word. Freedom from occupation in Ukraine's war is no guarantee of relief from bombardment and death.

Occupation Touches but Lightly; Not so Bombardment: Kharkiv

> I did not see, did not feel the Ukrainian people in Kharkiv, did not see a Ukrainian community. There everything is smeared with, trampled by the Muscovite spirit, Muscovite tastes.... Everything is foreign, not our own.[3]
> — Mykola Lysenko, Ukrainian musician and composer (1842-1912)

> Before Vladimir Putin's invasion in February 2022, almost everyone in Kharkiv dismissed the idea that Russia would attack this predominantly Russian-speaking city, 40km south of the border. "Would your brother attack you? No, he would not" yelled an angry woman…. Ten days later Russian troops entered Kharkiv, only to be beaten back by Ukrainian forces. They then spent six months shelling it from the outskirts.[4]
> — "Within range," *The Economist*

Putin may have reasoned Kharkiv's strong ties with Russia meant it would accept a hostile military takeover. The city was Russian-speaking. It was just forty-two kilometers from the Russian border. Many residents had close family living in Saint Petersburg, Moscow, and other Russian cities…. Early on Sunday, February 27, the Russians tried to seize Kharkiv. Light military vehicles penetrated the northern suburbs and headed toward the center…. Ukrainian troops counterattacked, hitting them with small-arms fire and grenade launchers…. By evening, the assault had been repulsed. The city was under local government control again.⁵

— Luke Harding, *Invasion*

Kharkiv's history is one of identity crisis. Briefly capital of Ukraine (from 1920-1934), Mykola Lysenko's comments above reflect Russia's longtime influence on its population and culture. It is an influence that should not surprise given the city's being less than thirty miles from Ukraine's border with its bigger neighbor. Yet Lysenko's commiserations from over a century ago are at best a snapshot in time. Kharkiv's population would by and large come to consider itself as much Ukrainian as Russian in the aftermath of World War I. The change was less due to any influx or flight of individuals than self-identification: That Kharkivites came to consider themselves Ukrainian rather than Russian was perhaps a form of resistance to the country's new designation as the Ukrainian Soviet Socialist Republic and its incorporation into the Soviet Union. This political change drove Russification. Names of Kharkiv streets and other features evolved, becoming more Russian and reflective of the recent revolutionary overthrow of the tsar.⁶ It was the beginning of a trend that would see the naming and renaming of Kharkiv's infrastructure echo the waxing and waning of Moscow's influence.⁷ Social ties to Russia remained strong. The city's mayor since late 2021, Ihor Terekov, stated one in every four Kharkivites had relatives east of the border.⁸ They were among many from the city who routinely crossed the dividing line to shop or partake in other activities in Russia.

And Russians surely traveled in the other direction to take advantage of Kharkiv's considerable offerings, for the city was Ukraine's second largest and closest major urban area. Size and location helped make it cosmopolitan, a mix of old districts with serpentine streets and ruler-straight broad avenues whose buildings covered several blocks. The city hosted the oldest permanent opera company in the country, Ukraine's largest plaza (Freedom Square), and what residents liked to claim was Eastern Europe's largest market, Barabashovo.[9] Kharkiv was also the choice for former Ukrainian president Viktor F. Yanukovych in 2014 when he fled Kyiv and the protests that removed him from the presidency during the Maidan Revolution.

Most in Kharkiv steered a middle path between overt declarations of pro-Russian or pro-Ukrainian commitment. Latent tensions did sometimes heat from simmer to boil, making themselves known in the form of demonstrations, riots, and violence. University of Alberta's Professor Volodymyr Kravchenko cites a 2013 event during which pro-Russian city government authorities mounted 117 memorial plaques on buildings where Heroes of the Soviet Union once lived. Persons acting on behalf of those authorities removed and smashed another plaque installed by pro-Ukrainian activists two days before the official dedication of the 117 plates. In the face of protests, Kharkiv's Administrative Court of Appeal ruled the single plaque's installation had been legal and granted permission for its replacement, though as of 2022 no action had been taken to do so. Prior to Russia's 2014 incursion into Crimea and Donbas, one writer noted, "Kharkiv appeared to be the ideal place to mount political opposition to Kyiv-based nationalism.... No other Ukrainian city outside of Crimea looked to be quite as firmly rooted in the 'Russian World.'"[10] Those invasions in the winter and spring of that year triggered months of protests by both pro-Ukrainian and pro-Russian groups, the latter seeking separation from Kyiv. Russian leaders reportedly sent "thousands of so-called volunteers...to Kharkiv from Belgorod oblast and other Russian territories to mix with the local population and take initiatives in its name," hoping to obtain control.[11] Police supportive of pro-Russian factions stood by as those favoring separation beat Ukrainian nationalist activists. The situation stabilized only with the arrival of a federal Jaguar special forces unit dispatched to the city from the 700 kilometers-distant village of Kalynivka. Kharkiv police withdrew in the face of the new arrivals, the pro-Russian faction's efforts collapsing as nearly 300 separatists were arrested and others fled to the Donbas. Kravchenko reported that pro-Russian terrorist groups continued to operate in the city, committing murders and acts of terrorism.[12] It is from this period some of the most recent and outrageous fabrications made themselves known, including claims Ukraine's Russians were endangered, neo-Nazis had seized control in Kyiv, and the country existed only thanks to foreign powers' support.[13]

Kharkiv's pro-Kyiv governors confronted a series of problems consequent to renewed hostilities and continued bombardment in the aftermath of Russia's 2022 invasion. Once a regional center in terms of industry, trade, and transportation, fractured links with Russia dealt a blow to local commerce. Surprisingly, however, the decrease in industrial production was roughly only half of that for Ukraine at large, a situation author Volodymyr Kravchenko credits in part to Kharkiv's commercial sector never having suffered the same domination by Ukrainian oligarchs as experienced elsewhere.[14] The city and its surrounding area also benefited from wartime contracts granted to local factories and growth of the information technology (IT) sector. Labor transitioned from reliance on jobs in Russia to those elsewhere as 130,000 to 150,000 persons displaced from Russian-occupied territory moved to the city in the period following the 2014 invasions of Crimea and Donbas. Many of these displaced continue to hold pro-Russian sympathies, a factor to be considered as Kharkiv continues to adapt to its new state of affairs. Forty percent of city residents expressed nostalgia for the Soviet Union and 80 percent had pro-Russian leanings as recently as 2018 (this includes just over 70 percent feeling similarly positive regarding the leadership in Moscow). Despite the related reelection of pro-Russia politicians—including Hennadiy Adolfovych Kernes who refused to recognize Russia as the aggressor in the Donbas and was reelected as late as 2020 with over 60 percent of the vote—feelings on the street have gradually undergone a transition to a more pro-Ukrainian stance. Nothing is straightforward, however. The complexity of inter-ethnic leanings, overlapping political ideologies, and secular-religious tensions were apparent even in 2014 with monuments again being the screen for their display. A statue of Lenin in Freedom Square was a magnet for pro-Soviet and pro-Russian factions (the two not being equivalent) and Ukrainian nationalists. Sensing changes in Kyiv-Moscow relations, Kharkiv's government authorities failed to follow up on a promise to replace the statue when pro-Ukrainian demonstrators pulled it down, instead erecting a column topped by an angel holding an Orthodox cross. It was a misread of resident inclinations. Just as pro-Russia and pro-Soviet are not coincident, pro-Ukrainian is not equivalent to pro-Orthodox. Local activists protested against the "clericalization" of the previously secular plaza. A fountain eventually filled the spot. The waxing and waning of Soviet and Russian influence on street names, monuments, and symbols underwent another evolution after 2015 with Ukrainian personalities and representations again coming to the fore. Many residents expressed regret, not because of a desire to preserve what was replaced but rather in hopes of the city's return to a straddling of the fence marking compromise. Journalist Peter Pomerantsev astutely summarized the situation: "Kharkiv is not so much a place of bipolar dividing lines and 'simmering historical resentment' as a do-as-you-please, disinterested mess of mini-movements."[15] Nevertheless, on July 27, 2023, a Ukrainian law directing "the decolonization of toponymy" went into effect. It was the date by which replacement, removal, or renaming of Russian, Soviet, or Communist-related plaques, statues, places, and street names was to occur. Transparency International-Ukraine described the reasoning behind the law:

> Three hundred years of Russia's domination over Ukrainian lands aimed to erase the national identity of Ukrainians. The streets of our cities and villages have

become "pantheons" honoring the memory of those who had no connection to Ukraine, or even were hostile towards it and its people.[16]

In reality, leanings could differ for economic and other as well as political reasons.[17]

Remaining pro-Russian sympathies have proved less robust in the aftermath of the February 24, 2022 invasion in which Kharkiv was an objective. By then hosting a population of 1.4 million and holding status as the capital of Kharkiv Oblast, the city watched as Ukrainian forces held off the invaders for several days. Elements of the 1st Guards Tank Army then broke through Ukrainian defenses, briefly occupying parts of the urban area before a counterattack ousted them hours later.[18] Residents assisted Ukrainian soldiers, posting Russian troop locations online as the intruders advanced. Over seven hundred locals volunteered to join the local territorial defense unit.[19] Russian forces turned to shelling the city from afar, attacks that included use of cluster munitions. These scattered explosive submunitions can linger, unexploded, long after delivery. Soldiers continued to die, as did civilians, both as immediate casualties of incoming rounds or victims of these residual dangers. Power substations suffered damage.[20] Destruction initially outpaced repairs. Some parts of Kharkiv suffered shortages of medical care and supplies. Daily bombardments continued until the middle of May when Ukrainian forces pushed the Russians sufficiently far that only the latter's heaviest artillery and rocket systems could reach the city.[21] An investigation by Amnesty International found Ukrainian forces were not without fault. Artillery units sometimes positioned guns too closely to residential structures, attracting enemy fire. The investigators concluded, however, that this positioning "in no way justifies the relentless indiscriminate shelling of the city by Russian forces."[22] Over six hundred noncombatants fell to enemy fire in the initial weeks while 600,000 fled the city. Russians employed their heavy weapons to strike Kharkiv's power and water infrastructure as cold weather threatened in September 2022. Viewing Karkivite life from the perspective of its garbage collectors provides some idea of the onslaught's extent:

> For a while, the binmen were the only city staff left working above ground. Decked out in flak jackets and helmets, they collected rubbish as fast as they could between curfews. They quickly spotted a pattern: the Russian gunners took breakfast, lunch, and dinner breaks. So the binmen did not…. There were many close calls. Fully 30% of the city's standing rubbish containers were damaged.[23]

Occupation but lightly touched Kharkiv. Russian bludgeons have not. Bombardment in the spring of 2024 reached levels seen only in the opening days of the war as enemy ground forces again crept toward the city.[24] Some thought the motivation was in part to bring artillery close enough that it, in lieu of more expensive rockets and missiles, could again strike the city.[25] As in 2022, the attack faltered.

As was the case with Kharkiv, Tokyo, Berlin, Manila, and Sarajevo, cities are often havens in times of disaster. They offer shelter even when damaged. They are hubs in which aid organizations coalesce, easing access to food, fuel, medical care, and other essentials that may be less available in rural or smaller urban areas. The diversity of economic activities means cities are sources of opportunities more difficult to find elsewhere, jobs in particular. Many stay once calamity passes.

Kharkiv reportedly suffered its first glide bomb attack on March 27, 2024. (The system is an aircraft-launched weapon capable of being released tens of kilometers from its target and thereafter proving difficult to intercept. Other attacks followed with larger forms of the munition. Flight time for releases nearest Kharkiv is only 40 seconds.) Kharkiv's residents refuse to allow these and other bombardments to ruin their lives. Restaurants and cafés conduct good business. The once and now again popular zoo has many visitors who pay little attention when air raid sirens warn of attack and speakers encourage movement to shelters. That is not to imply the population has thrown caution to the wind. Mayor Terekhov ordered the construction of underground facilities to support delivery of public services. These include a school and a depot for metro trains. The school opened in April 2024, all 900 seats having already been reserved.[26] Evenings see underground plays and concerts. Officials hold public meetings in basements. Schools and universities conduct classes online, a sometimes-problem when attacks interrupt internet service. Yet any ambivalence comes with risks. October 6, 2023, saw thirty residents wounded. Two, a grandmother and her ten-year-old grandson, were killed. By that time the number of residents displaced from elsewhere had risen to an estimated half-million. Power interruptions pause industrial output, leading to fears the city's economic base will suffer as the war drags on and companies seek safer locations in the country's west. The IT sector has thus far proven robust, however. Though most of its 50,000 software engineers opted to leave, the city's some 500 technology companies reportedly continue to thrive. The mixed news has consequences for other sectors of the economy as the loss of those engineers means their spending no longer sustains Kharkiv businesses. For Ukraine more generally, there are fears skilled workers who have left the country will find permanent employment elsewhere in Europe. There is also hesitation on the part of some NGOs that fear spending in Kharkiv will see recovery funds wasted should the war and its destruction continue. Fortunately, officials in Kyiv join Kharkiv's mayor in understanding the importance of initiating recovery before war's end. Up to $5,000 is available to Ukrainians needing to repair war-damaged properties. Kharkiv residents applied in greater numbers than those in any other city. The more unfortunate whose homes have been destroyed or severely damaged can request up to $40,000. The money in part comes from seized Russian assets.[27]

Kharkiv's First Steps Toward Recovery

> It has been a few days since a 250kg Russian glide bomb landed in Iryna Tymokhyna's courtyard on 23rd August Street, and it is fair to say she is not happy.... "If it was up to me, I would shoot the bastards...and I'd wipe Belgorod (the closest Russian city) off the face of the Earth."... Ms. Tymokhyna's sharp language is striking for the

fact she was born in Russia, and most of her relatives still live there. But her outrage is far from unique in a 1.3m-person city now living through an airborne terror mostly originating from the region just across the border.[28]

— "The race to save Kharkiv," *The Economist*

Many here dream that after the war, Kharkiv will not only be rebuilt but reimagined for the 21st century, to shake off the last shackles of the Soviet Union.[29]

— Adam Taylor, Anastacia Galouchka, and Kostiantyn Khudov, "Ukraine dreams of rebuilding but Russian destruction continues"

It would be naive to assume there remains no risk of ethnic tensions as Kharkiv continues recovering from its brush with Russian occupation. Yet Kharkivite historian Anton Bondarev concludes, "probably no one in Kharkiv has done as much to promote Ukrainization as Putin." Kharkiv's IT sector co-founder Eduard Rubin believes the city is now all but devoid of "outsiders" and "those who...expressed feeble hopes of peaceful relations with [Russia] have seen the light," cutting off relations with family and friends to the east. Still, long-held biases seem sure to reassert themselves as war's threats fade.[30] Failing to plan for a reemergence of previous tensions would be unwise. So too, the specter of collaboration with Russians seeking to promote such sympathies looms.

Planning for the city's recovery began early. The Norman Foster Foundation volunteered to take on the creation of a master plan for rehabilitation of physical structures in the spring of 2023, bringing together local urban planners and architects who were joined by the

Advisory Council of International Experts. In the words of its mayor, the goal is to make Kharkiv the "ideal city of the future."[31] A year before, mere weeks after Russia's attacks, the United National Economic Commission for Europe (UNECE) brought together Ukrainian federal officials, Kharkiv authorities, and Norman Foster representatives in the April 12, 2022, initial UN4Kharkiv task force meeting. Weekly online gatherings and additional consultations with local and international architects supporting creation of the master plan followed. The Ministry for Communities, Territories Development, and Infrastructure of Ukraine simultaneously put together a framework including support for immediate urban reconstruction. Kharkiv is the pilot project, one the ministry hopes will provide a blueprint for all of Ukraine. Sought-after ends include providing a vision for the master rebuilding plan and an integrated national rehabilitation plan, to include mechanisms for coordinating donor and other financing. UN4Ukraine is part of this broad initiative, the task force eventually coming to incorporate sixteen UN and other international organizations for which the UNECE acts as a matchmaker for planners, engineers, architects, city authorities, and other relevant parties.[32]

Aid and assistance are both helpful, vital even, but the sustainment of long-term recovery needs commercial financial commitments to complement those public. As with NGOs' hesitation, private investors might hold on to their cash in the belief that "a return to economic growth will need a definitive end to the war, not a stalemate."[33] Others will forgo committing funds until there is reasonable assurance another Russian incursion is unlikely. War may help fuel the economies of countries supporting a conflict; it is rarely so kind to those of the combatants on whose land fighting takes place. Previous pages demonstrate black marketeers—and authorities linked to them—can profit grandly...the national economies they undermine not so much. This is all the truer when aid comes not as grants but rather loans as continues to be the case for most from the EU. Such funding feeds essential needs now while eroding soil underlying future recovery. (A June 2023 *Washington Post* article reported, "while the United States has provided billions of dollars in nonrepayable grants, almost 95 percent of the money coming from the European Union and other partners is in the form of loans." More recent US funding, however, has in part come as loans, though these have specifically been designated as potentially forgivable in future years.)[34] Little wonder some reviewing the Norman Foster plan view it as unlikely to see fruition.[35]

Reminiscent of post-WWII Tokyo (and post-Great Fire in 1666 London for that matter), not all will await plans' guidance. Owners are already undertaking repairs and rebuilding in a city where some have had to replace windows repeatedly or turn to plywood rather than expose themselves to the vagaries of Ukrainian weather. Such initiatives challenge authorities in several ways. Damaged structures might seem stable when actually otherwise. Repairs not done to code present both immediate safety and other concerns even where structural integrity exists (assuming such standards exist). They also create down-the-road issues when owners want to sell properties with code violations. The opportunity for sellers to mislead buyers and corruption by building inspectors and realtors is obvious. Arguing against waiting to repair: the severity of Kharkiv winters. The city has sought a middle ground. Late 2023 saw structural engineers asking property owners to allow inspection of questionable buildings and advising how to address issues. These and other experts' charters extend beyond individual properties to include analysis of damage to infrastructure and ways repairs might promote local business recovery.[36]

What Funds Can't Buy: Soft Challenges to Kharkiv's Recovery

> It is one of the traumatic features of civil war that even after the enemy is defeated he remains in place; and with him the memory of the conflict.... Many men and women were accused of Fascist felonies when their major crime was membership of the wrong national or social group, association with an inconvenient religious community or political party, or simply an awkward visibility or popularity in the local community.[37]
>
> — Tony Judt, *Postwar: A History of Europe Since 1945*

The most obvious cases are those in which a person took up arms against Ukrainian forces or was involved in spying or sabotage to aid the Russian war effort. But assessing culpability can get murky at the level of local governance. "We're looking for people who worked for the benefit of the Russian occupation," Kravchenko told me. "But does that apply to a welder or carpenter who maintained buildings or equipment for the occupiers? Or people responsible for critical infrastructure?"[38]

— Joshua Yaffa,
"The Hunt for Russian Collaborators in Ukraine"

Not all the remains had been recovered from the rubble. This was not for want of purpose; the firefighters and the police and other civic workers remained dedicated.... There were instances when ideology dissolved amid destruction.[39]

— Sinclair McKay, *Berlin*

Ukraine's war is mercifully not a civil war, though Kharkiv residents' diverse stands on Russia tell us some of such wars' tensions exist. Yes, statues of Russian figures have been removed from downtown Kharkiv. They now sit in a bland loading area roughly two miles distant from their former locations. Yes, the removal reflects many residents' attitudes regarding the former master. But not all. Proximity, aforementioned family ties, and commercial benefits still link no few to Russia. The city's population is a mix of long-time residents and some from the half-million who migrated in the aftermath of the 2014 seizures of Crimea, Donetsk, Luhansk, or were displaced more recently by incursions during 2022.[40]

The fighting in 2022 left the Kharkiv region's power infrastructure badly damaged. Recovery was made further difficult as Russia had connected occupied territories to its grid. Ousting of its forces meant termination of those links. This left many Ukrainians devoid not only of heat during the fortunately mild winter of 2022-23, but also lacking water, internet, and other communications.

Generators met shortages to some extent. However, as was the case in early 2000s Iraq, turning to these alternative power sources depleted diesel and gasoline supplies. Mobile post offices and banking stepped in to ensure pensioners and others received services. Those were only partial solutions.[41] Aid provided by charities, foundations, and other supporters met additional requirements by providing goods and services closing other gaps.[42]

Russia's partial occupation of Kharkiv environs was short enough that residents were spared the worst of Russian impositions. The same was not true of the oblast's smaller city of Izyum (also spelled Izium) 125 kilometers (just under 80 miles) northwest of Kharkiv. Many of its government personnel left for Kharkiv proper. Some collaborated and departed with the Russians once it was retaken. Others continuing in their positions once the occupiers put a replacement government in place stayed once the city was de-occupied. There were also those who for a variety of reasons took other employment under the new authority. One author described the situation as "those who fled the occupation" and "those who were under occupation."[43] The choice was often not an easy one. Some teachers left. Others stayed and resumed teaching using curricula modified by the occupiers while obeying an imposed prohibition against Ukrainian language instruction. Reasons for continuing in teaching and other government positions included "fear, pro-Russian sympathies, opportunism, [and] the hope of doing something productive for the city."[44] Other reasons common to Izyum and historical occupations include the need to secure an income, protect property, maintain access to pension payments, coercion by occupier authorities or those working for them, and a desire to get back at locals against whom one has a grudge. Regardless, cooperating with occupiers in any way risked condemnation by neighbors and formal charges of collaboration once Ukrainian authorities regained control.

What, then, is a collaborator? The answer is rarely clear cut. Those who flee before an occupier's arrival because they can afford to do so or have connections ensuring support elsewhere often harshly judge others less able to flee. These wealthier and better connected frequently include officials who reassume positions giving them authority to deal with stay-behinds now open to accusations of collaboration. They frequently do so with a sense of moral superiority. Others who remained and continued to work in their positions are likely to have had fewer options to support themselves or their families if they departed.

Policies regarding collaboration will have significant, even life or death, implications. Universally damning any who had an affiliation with now-departed occupiers creates unjustified ill-will and undermines a reinstalled government's legitimacy. Failing to act against others who actively sought to abet occupier objectives or betrayed neighbors sows similar seeds, albeit of a different variety. Ever present is the danger of enflaming ethnic tensions if residents perceive collaboration policies align with social divides. Such pitfalls have unfortunately characterized select early Ukrainian government approaches on retaking once occupied areas.

CHAPTER 5

Laws adopted in March 2022 defined collaboration as

> such activities performed by a Ukrainian citizen as public denial of the existence of armed aggression against Ukraine and of the temporary occupation of part of its territory; public calls for support of decisions and actions of the aggressor state; cooperation with the aggressor state, its armed formations, or its occupation administration; and the refusal to recognize Ukraine's state sovereignty over the temporarily occupied territories.[45]

Some of these stipulations identify what would be perceived as collaboration in virtually any reasonable context, as would be actively assisting occupiers by helping to keep neighbors in line (though post-WWII France included those who believed even this was acceptable if it kept neighbors from suffering worse occupier deprivations). The waters grow murky when they universally include "cooperation with the aggressor state...or its occupation administration," collaboration's scope becoming so broad as to include activities that would reasonably fall into acceptable for reasons of survival or maintaining basic community services. Should teachers refuse to instruct even when doing so deprives students of education in virtually unaltered topics (as is reportedly the case with engineering, science, mathematics, and related subjects in Ukraine)? Should city administrators walk away from responsibilities to provide power, fuel, or otherwise support their charges as winter's cold threatens? Is refusal to police communities preferable to rampant crime?

Ukraine has previously, and painfully, dealt with collaboration. German occupation began in 1941. The Devil himself could not have better designed the resulting conundrum: join the fight against the invader or support the Germans in hopes of throwing off the Soviet yoke. (There was, of course, the third option, that inevitably adopted by the majority of virtually any population finding itself victimized by armed conflict: attempting to remain neutral. It is not always an option an occupier or circumstances allow.) History tends to denigrate any collaboration with Nazis during WWII. (The term "Quisling" lives on thanks to Norwegian Vidkun Quisling who collaborated with the Nazis.) The simplistic perspective fails to acknowledge one side's evil does not bestow the halo of goodness on its adversaries. Ukraine suffered the Holodomor (Great Famine) less than a decade before Germany's battlefield arrival in 1941. Detailed studies estimate Stalin's engineered starvation killed 3.9 million between 1932 and 1933. Other estimates opt for seven million dead.[46] Given the passage of less than a decade, collaboration with the newcomer become considerably easier to understand.

Honest judgments are no easier four score years later. Joshua Yaffa's quote at the opening of this section poses the conundrum. He later goes on to relate the case of a man who worked with a team to recover and bury the bodies of Izyum residents killed during fighting for the city in 2022. Ukrainian police detained and manhandled the individual after Ukraine retook Izyum. The value of giving neighbors a proper burial, suppressing disease, and eliminating the stench of decaying bodies was apparently not considered a legitimate reason for his work while occupiers were in control. Accusations of collaboration are more justified in the case of another alleged to have provided directions to approaching Russian forces. A third reportedly carried munitions to the enemy in his private automobile.[47]

A perhaps less obvious benefit of obtaining local assistance (from an occupier's perspective) is that of relieving the outsider of having to commit greater resources to governing tasks.[48] Historian Tony Judt points out that German occupiers in WWII Norway were able to rule with only 806 administrative personnel, France with 1,500 supported by 6,000 military or civil police, while in the Netherlands "not 10 percent of the German occupation tasks would have been fulfilled" were it not for the cooperation of Dutch police. In Yugoslavia, on the other hand, defiance was of such magnitude the Germans had to commit multiple divisions and still failed to suppress resistance. This would imply even seemingly justified cooperation is unacceptable as it de facto releases occupier resources for use elsewhere. Yet, further deepening the morass, collaboration can benefit post-occupation recovery. Mayors, police, and other officials who remain in place stand ready to continue their duties during the tumultuous months and years once an occupier departs. Recovery was stunted when the Allies had to assume greater responsibility for governing after WWII due to a lack of experienced in-place authorities.

It is clear that dealing with collaboration poses a tangled web of thorns for Ukrainian officials. Cooperation including activities going beyond the pale such as supporting the deportation of select group members during WWII is certainly more deserving of condemnation and prosecution than continuing to support a population's vital services. The situation is not as clear when behaviors are less definitive. Here context plays a role, but what seems context is no less open to misinterpretation—or manipulation—than is determining what constitutes legitimate accusations of collaboration. In the case of the above individual assisting in recovering community members' corpses, a staged photo in which he appeared with individuals whose actions more clearly constituted collaboration made his culpability further difficult to assess.[49] Does appearance in a photograph, voluntary or otherwise, constitute guilt? In another instance, the village of Shevchenkove fifty-two miles (83 kilometers) southeast of Kharkiv was torn asunder once Ukrainian forces returned. Journalist Yaroslav Trofimov relates both the resulting tensions and behavior of a local authority whose actions reinforce the difficulty of defining what amounts to collaboration rather than legitimate public service:

> What I found on Shevchenkove's main square was a gaggle of schoolteachers who had refused to collaborate with the Russians and who were outraged that their colleagues who did collaborate hadn't been fired, let alone detained. "Why are our boys dying out there? Why has my grandson not seen his father for seven months? So that we forgive all these people as if nothing had happened?," wondered Olha Usyk, whose son-in-law was fighting in the military. While Shevchenkove's mayor had fled to Kharkiv in April, unwilling to submit to the Russians, his second-in-command, the municipality's executive secretary, Nadiya Shelub, had stayed on. She had urged teachers to reopen schools under the Russian

curriculum. Shelub had been interrogated by Ukraine's security services but let go…. She had gotten the Russians to demine the local garbage dump, which had become a health hazard, and had arranged for a gravel road to be built…. I ran into an SBU [Security Service of Ukraine] investigator…. He said [he] had no choice but to be lenient to everyone except the most egregious collaborators…. Rounding up everyone tainted by collaboration, he said, would be impossible. "There are just too many. We can't behave like Stalin, pack trains with everyone who worked with the enemy, and send them away."[50]

Many are the historical examples in which inflated or fabricated accusations of collaboration were used to settle longstanding antipathies, secure coveted but otherwise unattainable property, gain economic advantage, or simply curry favor with the now-returned authorities.[51] History is on the other hand also replete with instances in which individuals or groups collaborated to obtain favors thought essential to survival. Sleeping with the enemy might be the epitomic example. Is later condemnation and punishment justified when the only alternative would have been allowing oneself or family to starve? The answer to Julian Jackson's question in *France on Trial: The Case of Marshal Petain*—"Are there times when the immediate wellbeing of the people of a nation can conflict with that nation's higher interests?"—seems clear once conditions on the ground are taken into account.[52]

That justly addressing collaboration will be difficult is clear. So too is a central government's responsibility to provide unambiguous and fair guidance regarding what represents collaboration and what punishments are appropriate. Local officials must have criteria to ensure at least a semblance of uniform judgments and as a shield to ward off popular efforts to take matters into one's own hands. Punishments for collaboration meeting or exceeding a specified threshold should require mandatory review by unbiased reviewers (convictions mandating a set number of years imprisonment or death, for example). To do otherwise is to ensure inconsistency and expose local leader judgments to community pressure. Europe's post-WWII record is not commendable in this regard. Treatment for equivalent behaviors varied broadly. Too many were unjustly punished while others deserving escaped unscathed. Reasons included the influence of location, the accused's connections, and corruption. Passage of time also played a role. Punishments meted out in the immediate aftermath of an occupation tended to be considerably harsher than those handed down later.[53] Initial collaboration trials tend to address more straightforward cases requiring less investigation. These often involve individuals at lower echelons of government or society where nuance is less important and relationships straightforward. Senior officials' involvement can be more complicated. As pressures to deal with collaborators tend to exhaust themselves over time, punishments are disproportionately felt by those whose crimes were less heinous and thus judged earlier. Such was certainly the case in France where individuals tried early were disproportionately journalists "whose commitment to collaboration was easy to prove because it had been so public. The only evidence needed was newspaper clippings."[54]

Leaders in Kyiv might be wise to reconsider their initial collaboration guidance. Addressing "those officials who did not hold their noses at entering into a dialogue with the occupiers" merits more detached judgment than is apparent in Volodymyr Zelensky's March 2022 statement that "if any of you are tempted by their offer, you are signing your own sentence."[55] Such vagueness in both statements and current collaboration policy—and the physical abuse reportedly suffered at the hands of security force representatives by some merely suspected of collaboration—requires immediate attention.[56] Abuses smack far more of behaviors expected of Russian occupiers than a country seeking entrance into the European Union. Historian Franziska Exeler described how "Stalin regarded [WWII] as a 'test that revealed people's true loyalties' [and] showed no understanding for the moral gray zones of occupation."[57] Mishandling collaboration risks exacerbating ethnic divisions and inhibiting national recovery. One need not be an apologist for collaborators. One does need to address difficult questions such as where the line between acceptable and unacceptable behavior lies when the choice is acting in the presumed best interests of those to whom you are sworn to serve or adhering to national dictates by those demonstrating ignorance regarding local conditions.

In "Challenges after Russian Withdrawals in Ukraine," Sam Harshbarger notes,

> From the start of the full-scale invasion until May 2023, Ukrainian authorities convicted 142 individuals in Kharkiv of collaboration with the Russian occupation.

The sentences ranged from fines to, in the case of a Balakliia judge who in April 2022 joined the legal department of the Russian occupation administration of Kharkiv Oblast in Kupiansk, life imprisonment.[58]

Many accused of collaboration held and still hold government positions in occupied cities. Some are jobs critical to providing essential services. Mayors, city bureaucrats, engineers, infrastructure maintainers, law enforcement personnel, teachers, doctors, nurses, firefighters, and others face the choice of continuing to serve or refusing and putting community members at risk. The line between legitimate service to city residents and overzealous occupier support is filled with intertwined shades of white, gray, and black. Kharkiv all but escaped occupation. As we have noted, not all of Kharkiv Oblast's cities, towns, and other communities were so fortunate. Tensions in smaller urban areas such as Izyum have torn fabric now badly in need of mending. Ukrainian cities elsewhere have experienced longer Russian occupations, Kherson and Mariupol among them. Should collaboration be defined identically regardless of occupation's duration and scope, or should regional conditions be granted consideration just as should the circumstances of individuals?

Knowing some in Belgium's Flemish-speaking community bristled at domination by a French-speaking majority, prisoners of war taken in the opening months of WWII were freed in 1940 if Flemish was their native tongue. Walloons who spoke French remained imprisoned for the conflict's duration, an obvious attempt to recruit collaborative support from a minority population segment.[59]

CHAPTER 5

Russian occupiers will seek to similarly infect Ukrainian cities by cultivating ethnic differences no less than did Nazis in WWII Belgium. Kyiv's policies should prioritize mending rather than punishment without excusing extremes of collaboration.

▋ Occupations Heavier Hand: Kherson

> The city of Kherson in southern Ukraine has been occupied since 2 March 2022. Mayor Ihor Kolyhayev and local councillors did not leave the city and refused to collaborate with the Russian army. Instead, the mayor and city council continued to perform their duties in line with the law of Ukraine until 26 April 2022. In an interview with the Ukrainian media, Kolyhayev stated that the local authorities ensured that communal services, hospitals and public transport continued to operate; there were no shortages of water, gas and electricity. In March 2022, the Russian military attempted to appoint its own authorities in Kherson; however, it did not work out. Unfortunately, on 25 April 2022, they announced the takeover of power and removed the Ukrainian flag from the City Hall.[60]
>
> — Valentyna Romanova, "Ukraine's resilience to Russia's military invasion in the context of the decentralization reform"

[November 19, 2022] A week since the southern Ukrainian city of Kherson was liberated, residents can't escape reminders of the terrifying eight months they spent under Russian occupation. People are missing. There are mines everywhere, closed shops and restaurants, a scarcity of electricity and water, and explosions day and night as Russian and Ukrainian forces battle just across the Dnieper River.... Kherson's population has dwindled to around 80,000 from its prewar level near 300,000.... While people were euphoric immediately after the Russian retreat, Kherson remains a city on hold.[61]

— Hanna Arhirova, "'We survived': Kherson comes alive after Russian withdrawal"

Kherson sits along the Dnieper River roughly 25 kilometers (15 miles) from where it empties into the Black Sea. That location has special significance for Russia. Control means being able to open the flow of fresh water to Crimea along the North Crimean Canal without which the peninsula suffers significant shortages.[62] It was therefore no surprise Kherson and the province by the same name for which it is capital were on Russia's agenda when it attacked on February 24, 2022. Occupation began six days later when the city fell on March 2nd. As evident in the first quotation above, Kherson's Ukrainian government was initially allowed to remain in power.[63] The occupiers were tolerant when thousands demonstrated on March 5th chanting, "Kherson is Ukraine." One woman reportedly presented a Russian soldier with a small package. "Take these seeds," she said, "so sunflowers grow when you die here."[64]

The protests continued for weeks. Patience eventually ran thin, however. Russian forces used gunfire and stun grenades to disperse crowds on March 21st. Despite Mayor Kolykhayev's rosy description, the Ukrainian foreign ministry reported food and medical shortages began to make themselves known by that date.[65] (Note, Kolykhayev is a frequent alternative spelling of Kolyhayev) The occupiers eventually forced the replacement of Kherson's administrators with others more malleable as an initial step in support of Russia's propaganda program. The new officials petitioned for Russian annexation. Russia publicly insisted residents be allowed to decide, a move Kyiv quickly condemned as window dressing prior to holding of a mock referendum. Dictates informed teachers they were to teach in Russian using occupier-dictated curricula. Russia blocked Ukrainian television channels, imposing its own media feeds and internet services. Ukraine's +380 phone prefix disappeared in favor of Russia's +7. A previously removed statue of Lenin reappeared in the city's main square. Vladimir Putin offered to fast-track applications for Russian citizenship. A May 1st announcement dictated the replacement of Ukraine's hryvnia with the ruble within four months.[66] Pensioners soon found payments were in Russian currency. These efforts to completely replace the local currency failed, however. "Socialist Store" replaced "ABT" as the name for the city's largest grocery store; locals continued to pay in hryvnia despite the official announcement "only rubles would be acceptable." Even pro-Russian political parties, including "Opposition Platform—For Life" headed by oligarch and Vladimir Putin friend Viktor Medvedchuk failed to collaborate with occupying authorities. The delay in replacing Kherson's original government appears to have been at least in part due to a lack of individuals willing to accept proffered positions. Kolykhayev's April 25th replacement was his former chauffeur, Oleksandr Kobets. Volodymyr Saldo, who had served as the city's mayor from 2002 to 2012, was arguably the best known of those eventually supporting the Russians, assuming leadership of a newly formed regional civil-military administration. Additional forces imported from Russia and detention of protesters in "filtration camps" proved insufficient to halt anti-occupation demonstrations. Stun grenades were again used on May 20th in an effort to disperse protests against a referendum calling for creation of a Kherson People's Republic. (When Russia eventually held referenda in four occupied regions, the support for annexation ranged from 99 percent in the Donetsk region to a similarly unlikely 87 percent in Kherson.)[67] Perhaps in a failed effort to win actual popular support (and reminiscent of the Soviet sector in Berlin), cities occupied by the Russians reportedly received priority for food delivery, power, and other life-sustaining services while ongoing fighting and mined farmland challenged those in rural areas. A measure of the limited success is evident in forty percent of city residents having fled by mid-May.[68] The occupiers began issuing Russian passports to Kherson residents in mid-June.[69] Moscow announced babies born in Kherson would automatically be granted Russian citizenship.[70] On June 24th, assassins killed a senior member of the occupation administration.[71] Kherson's was one of four regions declared annexed on September 30th.[72]

Increased exchanges of artillery, rocket, and mortar fire at the end of October seemed to signal a pending Ukrainian offensive to regain Kherson. Russian claims they had moved 70,000 residents out of the city strengthened expectations. On November 3rd, the Ukrainian Main Military Intelligence Directorate (GUR) posted that

Russian authorities were relocating children from Kherson city to territories in occupied Crimea. An image from the same day shows Russian military personnel removing items from the Kherson Art Museum. A Ukrainian ground force advance followed on November 5th. Russia's regional administration announced loss of power and water in Kherson city on November 6th.[73] Additional reports of looting and destruction of city infrastructure followed on November 8th. Russian Defence Minister Sergei Shoigu ordered withdrawal from the city the next day. Residents celebrated the return of their army on November 11, 2022.[74] Eight months of occupation were over, but Kherson was a far different city than that prior to Russia's arrival. One author recalled,

> Life under enemy rule was grueling. Food was scarce and expensive, and four locations containing alleged torture chambers have been discovered by prosecutors in the city…. Liberated Kherson is thought to be among the most heavily mined regions in Ukraine, with 5,000 explosives, including mines and unexploded projectiles, found and destroyed in the first five days of Ukrainian control…. The long hard road to recovery includes reinstalling electricity, gas, and water supplies as Ukraine's winter turns bitterly cold.[75]

Hanna Arhirova further described the situation in a November 19th Associated Press article:

> Russian soldiers left a city devoid of basic infrastructure—water, electricity, transportation, and communications. Many shops, restaurants, and hotels are still closed and many people are out of work. Residents were

drawn downtown this past week by truckloads of food that arrived from Ukrainian supermarket chains or to take advantage of internet hotspots that were set up. Russian products can still be found in small shops that survived through occupation. And the city is still adorned with banners touting Russian propaganda like "Ukrainians and Russians are a single nation," or that encourage Ukrainians to get a Russian passport…. Firefighters said the Russians stole firetrucks and ambulances as they retreated, leaving local authorities scrambling for resources to respond to attacks…. A major obstacle to bringing people back to Kherson, and to the rebuilding effort, will be clearing all the mines the Russians placed inside offices and around critical infrastructure, according to the Ukrainian Ministry of Internal Affairs. "Demining is needed here to bring life back," Mary Akopian, the deputy internal affairs minister, said. Kherson has a bigger problem with mines than any of the other cities Ukraine reclaimed from the Russians because it had been under occupation for the longest period, she said. Akopian estimated it would take years to completely clear mines from the city and the surrounding province. Already, 25 people have died clearing mines and other explosives left behind. Before retreating, Russian soldiers looted from stores and businesses—and even museums. The Ukrainian government estimates that 15,000 artifacts have been stolen from museums in the Kherson region and taken to Crimea, which itself was illegally annexed by Russia in 2014.[76]

Russian minelaying in many cases seemed to have little purpose other than to kill civilians or delay repair of damaged structures and infrastructure. The occupiers had destroyed Kherson's main television tower, water supply system, and several electrical substations as they withdrew, leaving many residents without communications, heat, or clean water. Mined areas included pumping and water treatment facilities. Ukrainians managed to achieve partial restoration of electricity on November 26th, but difficulty in accessing water infrastructure due to mining meant water was not yet flowing in taps.

Ukrainians began to tally the costs of Russian occupation. Foodstuff prices spiked as the Russians had stopped food deliveries in late October. Humanitarian aid was quick to arrive, however, meaning shop owner efforts to gouge residents for what remained on shelves often failed. Human Rights Watch reported thefts from two Kherson museums and the Kherson Regional National Archive in addition to items taken from the cathedral. HRW's Belkis Wille summarized the losses as "systematic looting" and part of "an organized operation to rob Ukrainians of their national heritage."[77] Another source described thefts as including ancient weaponry, jewelry, and 18th-century religious items. The Russians admitted having stolen the bone fragments of Grigory Potemkin from St. Catherine's Cathedral in late October, a military commander who is a favorite of Putin (as he was of Catherine the Great).[78]

Mines and other unexploded ordnance left as Russian forces withdrew are not the only obstacles to Kherson's recovery. As in Kharkiv, Russians continued to shell the oblast capital. Over 3,000 shells fell within the city limits in the three months preceding the last days of February 2023. Zelensky appointed politician and former school teacher Halyna Luhova to oversee Kherson's rebuilding. Luhova said only about 60,000 of the city's prewar 300,000 population remained by then. Over eighty had been killed by Russian shelling. Key infrastructure damage included medical facilities that were lost to fire.[79]

Mines and other munitions are not the occupation's only residuals. Dealing with accused collaborators saw a total of 152 cases sent to Ukrainian courts with fourteen persons initially convicted. Among them were doctors, business personnel, police, and local politicians. Some of the pitfalls in attempting to identify and prosecute collaboration are evident in Elizabeth Piper's "Traitor next door? Fear stalks Kherson after Russian occupation ends":

> Cases of collaboration can point to the tough choices people have to make when trying to survive under occupation. For instance, some farmers could face prosecution because they registered their farms according to Russian rules under occupation just to keep their businesses going, according to the All-Ukrainian Agrarian Council lobby group.[80]

Others stand accused of encouraging fellow residents to vote in the annexation referendum. The challenges confronting Ukrainian authorities are similar to those confronted in Kharkiv Oblast, though the length of occupation and more strident Russian efforts to influence city residents might make decisions regarding collaboration even more difficult. Mayor Ihor Kolykhayev's decision to remain rather than flee makes him suspect in some minds despite his subsequent removal and abduction.[81] The International Committee of the Red Cross reportedly confirmed his status as a Russian prisoner on September 13, 2023.[82]

Kherson suffered much during eight months of occupation, a suffering extended by deliberate actions perpetrated to achieve that end. Ukrainians elsewhere endured Russian despoliation as well. Others continue to do so. In Mariupol, Russian occupying forces reportedly stole paintings and other items from the city's Museum of Folk Life, Kuindzhi Art Museum, and the Mariupol Museum of Local Lore and History, carting them away in trucks to destinations unknown.[83] Mariupol remains under occupation as these words are written. Kherson residents' experiences in "only" those eight months do not bode well for fellow Ukrainians in Mariupol.

Propaganda's Front Lines: The Enduring Occupation of Mariupol

> Between February and the end of April [2022], Mariupol was likely the deadliest place in Ukraine. The intensity and extent of hostilities, destruction and death and injury strongly suggest that serious violations of international humanitarian law and gross violations of international human rights law have occurred…. The removal of explosive remnants of war from the city; and recovery, identification, and decent burial of all mortal remains; must be immediately prioritized…. The city can eventually be rebuilt, but the horrors inflicted on the civilian population will leave their indelible mark, including on generations to come.[84]
>
> — Michelle Bachelet,
> UN High Commissioner for Human Rights

> The Battle of Mariupol is over and Russia is busy proclaiming the liberation of the city. In reality, Mariupol has been murdered. This formerly bustling metropolis of almost half a million people now lies on the brink of extinction, pummeled into submission by a vicious campaign of Russian annihilation. The estimated 100,000 remaining residents of Mariupol find themselves reduced to living among the rubble without medicines, running water, or electricity.[85]
>
> — Paul Niland, "Putin's Mariupol Massacre is one of the 21st century's worst war crimes"

> The power of Russian propaganda exceeded that of the Russian Army.[86]
>
> — Yaroslav Trofimov, *Our Enemies Will Vanish*

Mariupol, 35 miles (55 kilometers) from the Russian border, managed to resist occupation until the later days of May 2022. It remains under occupation at the time of this writing. The struggle for the city was brutal. Mariupol was besieged as other Russian forces continued their move farther west and north. Bombardments continued for weeks before the city fell. Ninety percent of its buildings and other infrastructure had suffered damage by then. Hosting a population of over 400,000 before the war, nearly 300,000 have left. Most are IDPs in Ukraine.[87] Human Rights Watch reports an estimated 8,000 military and civilian personnel died as a direct result of the fight for the city, a number it considers conservative given those hastily buried, under rubble, or otherwise unaccounted for.[88]

Putin's excuses for targeting Mariupol included liberating its Russian speakers from Ukrainians he claimed were

Nazis. There was unfortunately a micron of truth to the claim. The city was home to the Azoz Battalion, a unit with neo-Nazi origins. The battalion formed around a far-right volunteer militia in the aftermath of Russia's two month-long occupation of the city during the 2014 incursion into the Donbas region. The unit assisted in ousting the invaders and was later incorporated into the National Guard of Ukraine, this after pressure from Kyiv caused it to distance itself from professing right-wing leanings (though member actions at times belied claims of casting bigotry aside).[89] More importantly from political and economic standpoints, controlling Mariupol links Russian-supported separatist forces in eastern Ukraine with those in Crimea while also providing access to its industrial output, road and rail networks, and Sea of Azov port facilities.[90]

On February 24, 2022, the same day Russia launched its offensive into Ukraine, Mariupol's city council belatedly released a list of 1,033 "basement and other underground premises" it deemed could shelter residents. Many stayed, believing the attackers would be stopped short of the city center. The numbers fleeing increased as the situation worsened, some climbing aboard trains until Russian shelling shattered tracks on the 27th. Enemy forces completed their encirclement of the city on March 2nd. Some 60,000 had reportedly escaped as March ended. Roughly the same number left in April. Only approximately 150,000 residents remained by mid-June.[91] Some had

> remained in the city because they did not have their own cars, or their cars had been damaged in the fighting. Others had no information about when, where, and how they

might be able to leave, since the fighting was intense and communications were down. It was still harder for the sick or injured, older people, and people with disabilities and their caregivers to make the perilous journey, and so many of them stayed behind. Others were afraid they would not make it past the checkpoints because they had links to the Ukrainian military or had publicly expressed anti-Russian sentiments. And some, including many older people, chose to stay because Mariupol was their home. By March 22, it became even more difficult for people to leave Mariupol for Ukrainian controlled territory as Russian and DNR [Donetskaya Narodnaya Respublika or Donetsk People's Republic] forces cemented their control over more of the city. They forced or coerced some residents who wanted to go to Ukrainian-controlled territory onto buses that took them to Russian and DNR-held villages and towns, where they underwent an abusive security screening process called "filtration."[92]

The second of March also marked the day most remaining power, gas supplies, and waste treatment fell victim to shelling. Many found it necessary to find alternative shelter. Volunteers delivered water, food, blankets, medicine, batteries, and other necessities to many suffering exposure to cold temperatures, though deliveries became increasingly dangerous and sometimes impossible as fighting continued. The same day would come to mark Mariupol's complete blockading. Local authorities reported Russians were using loudspeakers to falsely claim the fall of Odesa, the abandonment of Mariupol's population by Kyiv, and that the Ukrainian city of Zaporizhia to the northwest was refusing to accept refugees. A temporary ceasefire broke down within hours, the result being continued bombardment and delayed establishment of an escape corridor. Social order likewise wavered as some took advantage of the chaos to loot. On March 21st, Moscow demanded the surrender of Ukrainian forces still holding out, this after an air attack on Mariupol's Donetsk Regional Drama Theater on the 16th had killed on the order of 600 civilians despite Ukrainians marking the location with signage stating "children" visible from above. The Ukrainians refused. (Russia claimed it entered the city center as early as March 18th. Other sources gave the date as March 24th or later.) Reports of food and water shortages continued as did those of residents being forcibly relocated to Russia. The nature of and reasons for the last varied. Some were children. Others were suspected of affiliation with the Ukrainian military. Many were attempting to escape Mariupol to other locations in Ukraine, the only routes being through Russia. As reported in the quote above, those taking this last option were processed through filtration camps. Officials collected biometric and other personal data while also conducting what could be hours-long interrogations at those sites.[93] The opposing parties made claims and counterclaims regarding the fall of the city center and extent of Russian control. Lack of power, medical supplies, and destruction rendered hospitals ineffective by the end of March. A week into April, attention turned to the Azovstal steel plant located in Mariupol's east and additional holdouts in the port area as Russian forces reduced remaining defenses elsewhere. Fighting in the city had drawn over one-tenth of all Russian forces in Ukraine by that time.[94]

From mid-April to mid-May, Mariupol mayor advisor Petro Andryushchenko reported that Russian authorities were consolidating control of the city even as defenders continued to hold the steel plant. The occupiers were said to be screening residents at filtration centers established throughout the area, *New Yorker* author David Kortava describing the procedure "as a process by which a wartime government or a non-state actor identifies and sequesters individuals it deems a threat."[95] The US Department of State responded to the practice as follows:

> The United States condemns Russia's "filtration" operations, forced deportations, and disappearances in Russia-controlled areas of Ukraine in which Russia's forces and proxies have interrogated, detained, and forcibly deported...according to a broad range of sources, between 900,000 and 1.6 million Ukrainian citizens including thousands of children. Ukrainian citizens are being taken to filtration camps in a concerted effort to suppress their resistance. Many Ukrainian citizens are facing forced deportations, arbitrary detentions, and torture and other abuses. While at filtration camps, Ukrainian citizens are often strip-searched for "nationalistic" tattoos, photographed, and have their fingerprints taken. Ukrainian citizens have had their passports confiscated and their cell phones searched, with Russia's forces sometimes downloading their contact lists.[96]

Filtration was a procedure familiar to some in Mariupol, the same having taken place when Russians briefly held the city in 2014. Other sources confirm that filtration as administered by the Russians in Chechnya, in both 2014 and 2022 Mariupol, and elsewhere can include threats and physical abuse. Andryushchenko stated Denis

Pushilin, head of the DNR, had opened an office in Mariupol on April 15th and that the occupiers might hold a referendum on the city's joining Russia on May 15th, reflecting Russia's apparent intentions of usurping the city and its surrounds into the DNR similar to what was planned in Kherson.[97]

May 15th passed with no referendum, but Pushilin took further steps demonstrating Russia's ambitions to bring Mariupol under its control. He stated DNR officials planned to destroy the Azovstal steel facility once resistance there ceased. The move was to be part of remaking Mariupol into a "resort city." The employment fate of the plant's 10,000 prewar employees merited no mention.[98] Russian authorities stepped up direct control of city administration as effective resistance at the plant drew to a close in the third week of May, marginalizing DNR's direct involvement.[99]

Occupied Mariupol

> It's a place I've described as a center of hell.[100]
> — Martin Griffiths, Under-Secretary-General for Humanitarian Affairs and Emergency Relief Coordinator

War first came to Mariupol in spring 2014.... The city was taken over by Russian forces but this occupation proved mercifully brief. Following liberation, Mariupol gained in significance as the largest city in the Donbas still under Ukrainian control. Located just a few kilometers from the front lines of the simmering conflict with Russia, it became an administrative and economic focus as well as a showcase for the higher living standards and greater personal freedoms offered by Ukraine. While regions of eastern Ukraine under Russian occupation withered and stagnated, Mariupol flourished. This city was a mirror providing a stark contrast to the atrophy of the Russian-controlled parts of the Donbas.... Mariupol was also a beneficiary of Ukraine's successful decentralization reforms. The move towards giving local communities more say over how they live their lives and spend their budgets created genuine political competition between people who wanted to serve their communities and not just plunder them. This was strikingly different to the authoritarian model of paternalism promoted in Russia and Russian-occupied eastern Ukraine.[101]

— Paul Niland,
"Putin's Mariupol Massacre is one of the 21st century's worst war crimes"

We need to start [planning for] rebuilding Mariupol now, without waiting for the end of hostilities. After de-occupation, there will be no time to prepare: we will have to utilize whatever plans and resources we have. To rebuild better than before, we need to define what "better" means by engaging citizens and holding discussions, a process that will take at least a year. Furthermore, reconstruction requires partners, investments, and grants—it's not an easy task, so we need to start now. Additionally, the Russians must pay reparations for the destruction of Mariupol. The sooner we begin assessing damages and filing lawsuits in international courts, the closer we get to making the Russians pay for the losses.[102]

— Natalia Yemchenko, Supervisory Board of Mariupol Reborn

Only in the second half of 2022 would the roughly 150,000 remaining Mariupol residents gradually regain access to power and other infrastructure services. Many had in the meantime survived in damaged apartment buildings, basements, or other makeshift shelters. As is ever the case with urban systems, lack of power meant lack of pumped water, access to working elevators, sewage treatment, most information sources, and heat. Navigating to a working medical facility, visiting a source of water, or scavenging for food meant risking death or maiming due to shelling or, later, mines and other unexploded ordnance.[103] Mariupol also proved no exception to its new rulers renaming streets, replacing monuments, redesigning children's curricula, and experiencing other Russian-imposed changes. The once Avenue of Peace became Lenin Avenue. Signs denoting entry into the city displayed Moscow's preferred spelling and the red, white, and blue of Russia's flag. Putin signed a decree declaring Mariupol a "City of Military Glory." Here again the occupiers sought to have the hryvnia give way to the ruble. The city now operates in the Russian capital's time zone. Challenges to come should Ukraine retake Mariupol are evident in continued pro-Russia sympathies amongst no few residents even in the aftermath of devastation.[104]

A September 2023 survey found that, Ukraine-wide, 82 percent favored independence. Only 5 percent expressed willingness to cede any territory to Russia but 18 percent favored not joining the North Atlantic Treaty Organization (NATO).[105] That this 18 percent choosing to forgo NATO membership matched the percentage not favoring independence hardly seems a coincidence. It also makes sense these numbers would vary across the country. A logical man or woman would suppose those closer to the Russian border are overrepresented in the

18 percent. That nearly a fifth of countryfolk do not prefer independence or closer defensive ties with the West over a year post-invasion should concern Kyiv. That it should spur a Ukrainian information campaign given continued mis- and disinformation efforts by Moscow seems a given.

Such a campaign would have at least three primary audiences. The first is obvious: those supportive of Russia and therefore more vulnerable to collaboration incentives and both ongoing and postwar propaganda. The challenge here may be an unfamiliar one to politicians and military leaders alike. It is normally a waste of resources to win over those staunchly committed to one's political opponent or military adversary. Funds and effort are better spent on swaying the undecided or reinforcing backing by the already supportive. That is not an option when the wayward are your own citizens and mending war-torn ties is indispensable. Ukrainian leaders ignore the hundreds of thousands who retain strong positive feelings for Russia at the country's peril. Civil war and insurgency are unlikely in postwar Ukraine. Neither is impossible. This is especially true when one's neighbor will assuredly promote one or both, perhaps to cultivate a sympathetic base for further incursions to come.

The second audience is perhaps less obvious: the remaining four-fifths who need to understand Kyiv's policies toward collaborators and the essentiality of not taking retribution into their own hands as the country seeks to address its social divisions. An information strategy can also not afford to ignore some seven million

CHAPTER 5

Ukrainians—nearly 20 percent of the country's prewar population—who now live outside its borders. Over two-thirds of these are women (men of fighting age being proscribed from departing). Many hesitant to return are those who have found gainful employment elsewhere, a function of their also being among Ukraine's most talented, another element any information campaign must incorporate.[106]

Russia will rebuild—has already started rebuilding—portions of Mariupol. The call of propaganda ensures construction will receive plentiful media attention. Though on a much smaller scale, the US was victimized by its foe's savvy in this regard during operations in Afghanistan several years ago. A secretive special operations raid to capture a high-profile enemy combatant destroyed the door of the home in which the sought-after individual was thought to reside. Having worked to gain local support, personnel in the US unit responsible for the area were displeased the raiders had not coordinated the operation with them. Its commander dispatched a team to repair the damage in hopes of restoring goodwill. They found the destroyed door repaired and a sign crediting the local Taliban.

The struggle for popular support is a never-ending one. Recall Soviet efforts to influence popular sympathies in Berlin via providing extra rations to those in its sector and the benefits US forces garnered thanks to the unofficial but still propaganda-effective CARE program. Berliners were too wise to fall for the Russians' transparent attempt to sway their vote in 1946. Those Ukrainians already well-disposed to Moscow, however, may be more amenable after Russia rebuilds portions of war-damaged Mariupol, the builders being the source of the damage notwithstanding.

Encouragingly, as elsewhere, neither Ukrainians nor the international community are waiting for Mariupol's retaking to begin recovery planning. Mariupol Reborn links architects, urbanists, and funders from around the world to develop a "spatial development plan" for once the city returns to the Ukrainian fold. The initiative, the brainchild of Mariupol's exiled city council, kicked off in November 2022. Its Fast Recovery Plan component seeks to restore essential public services, housing, and municipal capabilities for up to 250,000 residents within two years from initiation. Early participants and funding sources include the Union of Polish Metropolises (an association of a dozen of that country's largest cities) and other European Union urban areas in addition to the United States Agency for International Development's (USAID) Economic Support for Ukraine Project and various Ukrainian commercial enterprises. The approach is broad in scope, one wisely seeking to take advantage of insights gained through others' experiences:

> Currently, the Mariupol municipality team is adopting the experience of the Dutch city of Rotterdam, which was destroyed in World War II, in terms of the optimal model of water supply and sewage. They will use the experience of the city of Le Havre to plan the development of port infrastructure, recreational areas, and tourism. In Gdańsk and Utrecht, Ukrainian experts are studying the experience of collecting, sorting, and recycling waste and creating a

new city economy. Wrocław will help with its experience in developing an innovative technology park, IT cluster, universities, and building a road infrastructure management model. Brussels will provide expertise in creating high-quality medical infrastructure and services.[107]

Strategies inherent in Mariupol Reborn seek to capitalize on insights from at least four focus areas. First, obvious in the above, is the knowledge gained by European countries during their post-WWII recoveries. Second are more modern approaches that will separate the city's efforts from those employed by Soviet planners. Incorporation of commercial capabilities and expert input in training, design, and project execution comprises a third. Last is incorporating material and equipment support. Preliminary estimates put Mariupol's recovery at US$14.5 billion and a minimum of twenty years after removal of the Russians.[108]

Recovery will not begin from a clean slate either in terms of physical infrastructure or the city's social fabric. Moscow sees Mariupol as a chance to demonstrate how Russian control benefits those falling under its sway. No fewer than twenty-five organizations from St. Petersburg are funding construction. (St. Petersburg is Putin's hometown and that with which the occupiers have twinned Mariupol.) Russia has built showcase apartments in a new neighborhood named Nevsky after the river flowing through St. Petersburg. Individuals from throughout Russia and representing a large number of ethnicities have moved to the city. According to Petro Andryushchenko, exiled adviser to the city's now-displaced mayor, new arrivals are part of a rebuilding workforce attracted by salaries exceeding what they could get in their own country. Other sources cite favorable home loans as an attraction. Andryushchenko estimates that the number of newcomers matches that of residents remaining from before the occupation: 80,000 as of June 2024. These arrivals have displaced former Mariupol residents from construction positions. They will very likely also be among those benefiting from a Russian policy dictating that properties whose owners fail to re-register them with the occupiers be declared ownerless and put up for sale. The number of usurped properties will be considerable number given that 350,000 of the city's original 430,000 population have departed.[109] Importation of the 80,000 poses additional challenges for "re-Ukrainization" should Russian forces be removed. The presence of so many Russian citizens will leave Ukrainian authorities with tough decisions, including the disposition of these foreigners who may have been sold or given properties, meaning they will be rendered homeless if removed. Collaboration too is sure to raise its ugly head once again. Some choosing to remain under occupation will hold Russian sympathies. Others having no desire to support the invaders have legitimate reasons for staying. As elsewhere in Ukraine, medical care, many jobs (including teacher, police officer, and doctor), permission to open a business, obtaining compensation for destroyed property, access to newly constructed apartments, and other benefits are available only to those possessing a Russian passport. Those refusing to exchange their Ukrainian passport for one Russian find basic services denied and experience other forms of discrimination. (A Russian passport also reportedly allows possessors to bypass filtration camps should one want to visit Russia.) Other sources report occupier-forced changes to school curricula promoting Russification and denigrating Ukraine as a "neo-Nazi state" found elsewhere. Food prices have risen, reportedly due to corruption and price gouging. Yet some benefit from the occupation. Pensions for many are higher than what Ukraine provided, an additional stimulus for the elderly to get a passport should possession be tied to receipt.[110] "Voluntarily" requesting passports reportedly gave way to more coercive measures, including possible deportation, detention, and loss of children (including newborns). On the other hand, demonstrating interest in becoming a Russian citizen can increase the chances of being dispatched to a unit fighting Ukraine.[111]

While a city councilor commiserated, "Ukraine is losing the hearts and minds of people in Mariupol," Ukrainian journalist Denys Kazansky

> argues that Russia uses the new houses it has been building in Mariupol to distract attention from all the destruction it caused in the city and elsewhere in his native Donetsk region. "If they destroyed 10 hospitals and then rebuilt one - this isn't reconstruction. It's not something they can be thanked for," he said. "You can be happy as much as you like about a school being rebuilt, but what do you do with the thousands of people Russia has killed?" he said.[112]

Kazansky's comments recall Berliners' recognizing the hollowness of Soviet acts of apparent benevolence in the aftermath of the Red Army's atrocities on taking the city.

An international Global Rights Compliance group report found "reasonable grounds to believe that Russian and affiliated forces intentionally used starvation of civilians in Mariupol as a method of warfare, to both accelerate the surrender of Ukrainian armed forces and capture the city of Mariupol and its environs," this in addition to deliberately targeting energy, water, and medical facilities and denying access to humanitarian assistance.[113]

Some will nonetheless want to believe in Russian goodwill. Yet evocative of Soviet "one step forward, two steps back" behavior in Berlin, multiple sources cite coercion and other forms of repression acting to counter Russia's propaganda. Expulsions of Ukrainian residents and a January raiding of a Jehovah's Witnesses office by Russia's Federal Security Service (FSB) number among actions reported. According to Russian media sources, "the FSB and military counterintelligence have uncovered a location in Mariupol that was used by the Jehovah's Witnesses to promote extremist ideology."[114] The source went on:

> Russia's state-run news agency RIA Novosti reported that documents were also found "showing that the extremist organization Jehovah's Witnesses, which is banned in Russia, is involved in the financing of Ukrainian militants." An investigation was underway to identify "those involved in the financing of Ukrainian neo-Nazis."[115]

Retaking Mariupol will be bittersweet. Additional challenges confronting Ukrainian administrators will include identifying the dead and addressing thousands of requests by relatives and friends wanting to know the fate of those with status unknown. Procedures from cities suffering earthquakes, floods, tropical storms, or other catastrophes can inform in this regard. Presuming no access to occupier files, many will have to turn to social media in their searches. Human Rights Watch highlights efforts underway even before Kyiv regains control:

> The website Victims.Memorial has also collected the names, photos, and stories of some of the people who died in Mariupol. According to a chief editor of the site, the website allows people who have information about civilians and military personnel who were killed or died in Mariupol to complete a questionnaire that staff verify, sometimes contacting the person to obtain further details. Once approved, the information is posted on the website. The website coordinators also review other sources and post information once verified. As of June 1, 2023, Victims.Memorial had published stories and photos relating to 1,364 civilians.[116]

CHAPTER 6

MORE ON CHALLENGES FOR CITIES RECOVERING FROM WAR

"The Russian Communist Party [had] undertaken a systematic and through removal of heavy equipment used by industry and the public utilities throughout the city. Although strictly against the agreements reached at Yalta, the technical efficiency of the process gained the unwilling admiration of British Military Government officers."[1]
— F.S.V. Donnison, *Civil Affairs and Military Government North-West Europe, 1944-1946*

Things [in Kyiv] were certainly touch-and-go at times. The initial Russian operation was clinical, targeting hundreds of high-voltage transformers, the house-size workhorses of the national power grid. No electricity meant no gas, no water, no sewage, no heating. Some predicted frozen cities and a humanitarian crisis with millions of refugees. That this didn't happen is down to preparation, luck, quick thinking, and new air defence systems that began to arrive just in time. More than 100 energy workers have lost their lives in the battle.... There was talk that the city would have to drain water from its heating system over fears pipes would freeze over and crack.... [Electricity provider] Ukrenergo's

> Mr. Kudrytsky says [his] company had deliberately kept back-up stock of high-voltage equipment when refurbishing substations in the years before the war.[2]
> — "Winning the Electricity War," *The Economist*

Nearly a fifth of Ukraine was under enemy occupation as of September 2023.[3] Cities that had been retaken or never fallen to Russian domination were badly damaged. That recovery from war will be difficult is the height of understatement. Decisions will span economic, social, security, political, and physical infrastructure considerations and more. Looking at physical infrastructure alone, members of the public, politicians, historians, psychologists, architects, urban planners, and a good many beyond will want to be heard, no few from outside Ukraine. Which buildings merit restoration? Replacement? Relegation to the dustbin of history? What style from which era should dictate? Should cities permit heterogeneous mixing of architecture or is architectural uniformity preferable? Does each building's fate merit broad contemplation or only the most preeminent, and who defines what's preeminent?[4] History informs us there will be plenty who disagree regardless of the decisions made. Bulldozing buildings will be necessary. Bulldozing over the opinions of city residents, on the other hand, is ill-advised. Soliciting input takes time. The sooner started, the better. The later started, the more on-the-ground conditions complicate planning. Soliciting public input while the war continues also gives those suffering a sense it will not always be so.

Incorporating city resident views should be helped by Kyiv's 2020 delegation of greater authority to local governments. Efforts at solicitation will also be more efficient thanks to the same year's consolidation of the country's *hromadas* (political divisions akin to a municipality) from 11,694 to 1,469, four hundred and nine of which are urban. A complementary and no less forward-looking July 2021 law expanded hromadas' planning, expropriation, and compensation authorities for land required for public purposes. As was the case in Tokyo, this could prove key for areas ravaged by war's destruction on which on-site rebuilding is impractical, impossible, or cities seek to enhance public value.[5] (Though it was already in the public domain, one such example is a local police headquarters in Kherson boobytrapped so extensively by Russian forces that Ukrainian Army engineers deemed it impossible to demine. The building was subsequently destroyed.)[6] Kyiv can assist local decision-makers by providing early recovery guidance based on past wars' lessons and best practices revealed as individual cities move forward.

Image 4. Well-Considered Mixed Architecture (Vienna)[7]

Government or private, Ukrainian resilience has proven robust to date. US Special Representative for Ukraine's Economic Recovery Penny Pritzker provided examples of this heartiness in a February 2024 speech, emphasizing the collective nature of its accomplishments:

> GDP growth is up 5%. Investment is up 17%. State revenue up $4.4 billion, exceeding expectations for 2023. But the story of this war and Ukraine's economic recovery can't only be about statistics. It's first and foremost about the brave, resilient, creative Ukrainian people backed by the United States, the American private sector, our allies and our partners; the Ukrainian people who are defending their country from the frontline to the assembly line.
>
> Look at Cola-Cola. They have a 12 thousand square meter bottling plant in the village of Velyka Dymerka just 30 miles outside of Kyiv. The plant was shelled, then occupied by the Russians in March 2022. Many of the plant's 1600 workers fought to liberate their home village and that Coca Cola plant. By summer, it was back up and running. That plant—still the largest in Europe—produced 690 million bottles of Coke and other products in 2023.... Coca Cola is not a single example. 84% of American companies in Ukraine are back up and running.[8]

Pritzker went on to cite other companies continuing to expand in Ukraine (McDonald's), assisting with recovery tasks such as demining (Palantir), supporting maintenance of agricultural capacity (Cargill and ADM), or otherwise acting to sustain or promote various national functions. Ukraine's finance minister, however, points to darker concerns, ones that will act to mire recovery in red tape, criminality, and other self-imposed quagmires:

When it was part of the Soviet Union, Ukraine had a vast defence industry. Some 1.5m Ukrainians laboured in 700 military enterprises…. Leonid Kuchma, Ukraine's second president, ran the world's biggest rocket plant in the city of Dnipro in Soviet times. A flagship factory in Kharkiv produced 900 tanks a year. But corruption and neglect after the break-up of the Soviet Union in 1991 gradually killed these businesses. Now Ukraine is rebuilding its arms industry almost from scratch…. "We will not have one Soviet-style hypergiant plant but many smaller plants spread across the country," says [Oleksandr Kamyshin, former head of the state railway company. Serhiy Marchenko, the country's finance minister believes] the main concern for investors is not physical security but the unreliable legal system, a problem that predates the war. Similarly, it is corruption rather than the damage done by the war to Ukraine's infrastructure that most Ukrainian see as the main obstacle to recovery.[9]

Pritzker lends credence to optimism regarding timely recovery. Kamyshin and Marchenko, on the other hand, give one pause. Actuality lies between. There is light at the end of the tunnel, but it is gray, hazy, and flickering. The distance to the tunnel's end depends on many factors considered in the following pages. There is what appears to be sincere interest in addressing Ukraine's legendary corruption at the government's highest echelons. Evidence suggests initiatives such as digitizing day-to-day government activities and public intolerance of corruption are making a difference.[10] Yet whether future governments will prove as dedicated to suppression is unknown. Permanence in such progressive adaptations is essential if Ukraine's cities (and the country as a whole by extension) are to approach their potential. Changing minds amongst bureaucrats will be as important as changing policies. Any progress will be ephemeral if improvement is limited to the government sector alone.

World War II Londoners gained world admiration and lasting respect. Bombings ravaged their city as they do in Ukraine, but newspapers continued to appear on doorsteps every morning alongside bottles of milk. Rubble disappeared from the streets. Lights came on when one pressed the switch. Neighbors queued at still-functioning post offices.[11] Ukrainians in Kyiv, Kharkiv, Kherson, Dnipro, and elsewhere can still find restaurants at which to dine and stores in which to shop despite missile, artillery, and drone attacks. The country's housing sector had seen well over 150,000 private homes, apartments, or dormitories damaged or destroyed by September 2023. Replacement costs then ran to an estimated $151.2 billion. Housing, public infrastructure, industry, educational and health facilities, and other sectors continue to suffer losses.[12] Yet, as in London eight decades before, lights still illuminated and water ran from most taps. Heat warmed. Western nations provide recovery aid even as war continues. Some countries are more reliable than others. The United States has ranged from being an international leader to a notable laggard. The unfortunate tendency dates back at least to FDR's presidency when he refused to provide detailed guidance needed to plan for Europe's revitalization.[13] Today, Ukrainians act as Washington dithers. Patrick Christian, an American living in Kyiv, reported city residents' willingness to assist recovery, a habit maintained from before the war:

CHAPTER 6

> Older men and women volunteer as helpers to the many park maintenance workers. For every yellow orange vested city worker cleaning, repairing, parks and monuments, they are trailed by 2-4 unpaid civilians each who plant, clean, paint, remove graffiti, [or provide other services]. I began noticing that last year and was puzzled. I asked them if they were getting paid or if their apartments looked over the gardens and parks. They said no. They just liked helping.[14]

He went on to describe other charitable acts and an urban-rural relationship representing a longstanding tradition:

> People of all ages, genders, and socioeconomic statuses leave clothing, food, and other essential items near public garbage locations (they are everywhere) for the poor. There are no catholic charities, and only a sprinkling of NGOs that collect clothes and items for cleaning, repairing, and redistribution. I also find that everyone who has a dacha or family living in the surrounding countryside of Lviv, Kyiv, Odesa, etc. provides a sort of a time-honored lifeline from the big cities to the smaller towns and villages. This involves furniture, building supplies, wholesale foodstuffs, animals, and collected items such as gallon-sized glass jars. Even today, I have one entire closet in my apartment filled with empty jars, clothes, and appliances that we don't need waiting for the monthly run from the city to the villages. No government involvement. My wife's father (a former Army captain and civil engineer) and his friend manage this distribution line for the three villages [near] his own dacha. I tried to investigate their motives, but that seemed to be taboo as if I was disparaging its goodness.[15]

So it is with these demographic, political, economic, and diplomatic backdrops that we take into consideration several select areas of concern as Ukrainian cities pursue recovery even as war continues. Drawing on our above recent and more distant historical discussions, and as promised in the introduction, these are:

- International cooperation and assistance
- Plans and planning considerations
- Leadership and management
- Housing, building, and employment
- Health care
- Unexploded ordnance disposal
- Collaboration with the enemy
- Corruption
- The specter of ethnic conflict
- Education and information campaigns in previously occupied cities

■ International Cooperation and Assistance

> Tens of thousands more refugees, mainly Bosniaks, were pressured to leave Germany, where nearly 350,000 had sought refuge during the war. The arrival of hundreds of thousands of returnees, overwhelmingly to places that were not their prewar homes, compounded the problem of return and recovery.[16]
>
> — Peter Lippman, *Surviving the Peace: The Struggle for Postwar Recovery in Bosnia-Herzegovina*

Fewer than half of Irpin's citizens came back in the first month after the Russians left. Sapon said that the city still feels empty; the sporadic street life that has returned only seemed to underscore the extent of the damage. Around virtually every corner, civilians can be seen patching their own roofs, securing their windows, and carting out rubble in wheelbarrows. But as Iryna Matsevko, a historian and deputy vice chancellor at the Kharkiv School of Architecture, explained to me, the rebuilding of Ukrainian cities has become an industry unto itself, attracting high-profile architects from all over the world. The attention is a blessing and a curse: It can bring investment and international airtime, but it also risks diminishing the role Ukrainians play in the reconstruction. In Irpin, Sapon and Yarmolenko are trying to ensure that their city reaps the benefits of international attention without getting lost in a swirl of good will.[17]

— Linda Kinstler, "Architects Plan a City for the Future in Ukraine, While Bombs Still Fall"

International recovery assistance—and interference—comes in more than economic form. It can be of a positive or negative variety. Not forcing the hasty return of Ukrainians displaced from their homeland provides Kyiv assistance by not overburdening cities already short on housing, power, and other amenities. As was the case with Bosnia-Herzegovina in the lead quote above, the immediate post-war months will be a particularly vulnerable time. What we might call "soft aid" will be especially impactful, e.g., working with Kyiv on timings for refugee returns or lessening the constraints on assistance. Some aid is fundamentally altruistic. Most instances come with a provider's agenda. US government aid frequently has caveats requiring it to be linked with contracts with or purchases from American commercial organizations. The post-WWII Marshall Plan was much more beneficial to the US economy than many realize...and not by accident. The same was true of funding approved for Ukraine, Israel, and Pacific defense in April 2024. Approximately 60 percent was to go to US arms manufacturers with additional portions directly or indirectly supporting other US economy sectors or the military.[18]

Architects and urban planners relish assisting recovery post-disaster. Their advice will be plentiful, sometimes helpful, and occasionally free. Some NGOs have niche interests; they seek to support specific groups or provide particular services. Female education, at-risk young males, single mothers, addressing one or more diseases: These and others are legitimate causes, all requiring someone to locate prospective aid recipients of the sort sought. Most NGOs are legitimate. Not all, unfortunately. Some consist of nothing more than marginally-if-at-all-skilled thrill seekers as was the case in 2016-17 Iraq. It seems almost (but not quite) too obvious to mention Ukraine will be "assisted" by alleged aid groups (or providers within those groups) with motivations counterproductive to recovery (Russian intelligence collectors, propagandists, and corrupt or criminal enterprises as found in Sarajevo, for example). That those with unfriendly intentions so easily find their way into crisis zones is unsurprising given the turmoil characterizing unsettled times. If already hyper-busy host nation officials do not or cannot vet, chances are the task goes unfulfilled. There are exceptions. United Nations-sponsored deminers undergo well-defined vetting before receiving funding.[19] David McMahon, head of the UN's Mine Action Project Unit in Ukraine, observed one can go on the Ukraine Ministry of Defense website and see there that there are, I believe, thirty-five demining organizations certified to work in Ukraine. That number has grown exponentially since November of 2023. The United Nations Office for Project Services has its own pre-qualification system where we independently vet the credibility of organizations that work with the UN. We would...first make sure any organization working with us in the field of mine action has Ukrainian certification and then ensure that they have UN pre-qualification, because there are organizations that have absolutely no experience in the field. [Interviewer question: Are there organizations that somehow avoid certification?] There is humanitarian demining and military demining. There are probably former combat engineers who are part of volunteer battalions or volunteer units. In humanitarian demining, I have no evidence of it, but I have heard of farmers who are using uncertified and uninsured organizations to demine. You do have uncertified people who will go do demining with metal detectors. I have no evidence of that, but I know it exists.[20]

The sheer number and variety of NGOs and other aid organizations complicates the task of ensuring providers are legitimate. There are those whose charter permits only short-term involvement; they might be designed to arrive during the response phase of a crisis and depart once operations turn to recovery or sustainment. Some have so few members or limited an administrative structure they can function for only days or a few weeks before having to depart. Others employ thousands, have robust support staff and logistical infrastructure, and—important when considering which organizations to rely on for long-term recovery needs—possess sufficiently robust funding to permit multi-year mission sustainment.[21] Robust administrative support from home offices is also important. UN military missions such as that to Cambodia in the early 1990s heard only an endlessly ringing telephone when calling the New York headquarters during non-business hours. It is a situation now remedied. Other-than-military operations such as those under the auspices of the World Food Program, UNICEF, and United Nations High Commissioner for Refugees (UNHCR) also have 24/7 communications centers.[22]

Potential benefits from another sort of international "aid" remain to be fully realized. Seized Russian assets exceeding an estimated $282 billion as of early 2024 could be a significant part of Ukraine's eventual recovery bill. (The World Bank estimated that bill as having reached $411 billion in mid-2023.) Ukraine has begun using such funds under its control. The international community has been hesitant, fearing precedent setting and possible effects on the world financial system. (The reticence is ironic given Russia's flaunting its disregard for international standards.) There is precedent. The US, Britain, and France put Iraqi state funds into an escrow fund in 1990 to pay for damages after that country invaded Kuwait. There is some movement in this regard as my fingers strike keys. Prominent among them: use of interest from the Russian billions, the principal remaining untouched. The addition of such funds to aid coffers would magnify centralized oversight challenges severalfold, but there is need for timely decisions on the disposition of these funds given the extent of damage inflicted on Ukraine and lag time between plan creation and execution. That planning ought to include consideration of how best to mitigate misdirection of the monies post-release.[23]

Pages above have touched on the value of orchestrating aid efforts. Doing so offers synergies and efficiencies otherwise foregone. There are initial steps underway in this direction. The Ukraine-Netherlands Urban Network (UNUN) links Ukrainians in the Netherlands with Dutch organizations and specialists to contemplate Ukraine's physical reconstruction. The initiative seeks to find firms willing to allow such employees to dedicate a portion of their time to the country's rebuilding.[24] Small in scale compared to aid behemoths, the cooperative nevertheless bonds educational, employment, urban planning, and additional aspects of recovery into a less fragmented whole. Such efforts ease Kyiv's coordination burden.

The Cities 4 Cities United 4 Ukraine initiative alternatively operates at the city level, bringing over forty municipalities from Germany, Poland, Sweden, and France together in a relationship linking them with one hundred-plus Ukrainian urban areas. Early benefits include providing first responder vehicles, online instruction, and twinning programs, e.g., linking Kherson with Norrköping, Sweden.[25] An online platform provides a forum for cities to share needs and receive assistance.[26] Cybersecurity, communications, and technical support are among the commercial relationships benefiting Ukrainian cities. Companies involved include Microsoft and SpaceX.[27] These intergovernmental and commercial links represent further opportunities to bring participants under an orchestrating umbrella. This umbrella would less need to be one dictating policy than a mechanism for compiling information of common interest and cultivating additional relationships.

Such macro-level management entities are an outstanding need during many crisis response and recovery contingencies. For example, the UNHCR, the UN's refugee agency, lacks both charter and capacity to coordinate all aspects of Ukraine's massive internally displaced persons and international refugee support. Authors Jeff Crisp, Tim Morris, and Hilde Refstie validate the need as it applies specifically to urban challenges, an important but only one of many components of recovery needing better overarching administration:

> Rebuilding and recovery from conflict, as well as the provision of basic services, also should be, ideally, a government-led process supported by civil society and development agencies. Frequently there are problems of coordination of (often large numbers of) development agencies and government ministries/agencies in urban areas, especially in capital cities. UNHCR may have a series of relationships with implementing partners but it has no regular forum in which to bring them together. UNHCR and other humanitarian agencies must find a way therefore to build such partnerships and to make sure that the needs of urban IDPs and refugees are included in overall urban planning. What is evident is that the challenges displaced people bring to urban planning are enormous, and no actor alone will be able to address them.[28]

Deficiencies in providing support to and protecting the displaced can have heinous consequences. The unscrupulous too often find those in unfamiliar environments easy prey. Being forced to pay inflated prices for shelter or pay bribes with the hope of securing support is the most significant expense for many. Women are especially vulnerable. Being forced into unwanted sexual relationships for survival purposes is not unusual.[29] Displaced can also be targets of longer-term residents who fear new arrivals might compete for jobs, housing, and other resources. Unfortunately, Crisp, Morris, and Refstie note, "The voices of urban IDPs and refugees are rarely heard by policymakers."[30]

Previous recovery experiences provide possible funding and management solutions. That Ukraine pursues recovery while the war continues, however, complicates matters as foreign commercial investors are understandably hesitant when outcomes are unknown. Contrasting with Pritzker's optimistic February 2024 "Investment is up 17%" quoted above, a November 2022 *Economist* article found "foreign investment into Ukraine is barely 1% of its level in 2021," the last words making clear the importance of stating "since when" when dealing with statistics during tumultuous times.[31] American and European track records in Iraq and Afghanistan cast doubt on the longer-term effectiveness of their assistance. Kyiv's maintaining a functioning government offers a degree of optimism not extant in those two cases, though corruption and residual Soviet-era political and economic practices are concerns. That Europe offers significant assistance is encouraging given the vagaries of US aid (though Germany's July 2024 announcement that it is halving aid to

Ukraine demonstrates that US fickleness is not unique).[32] It is a fundamental difference between the Marshall Plan and the present situation. Another is Ukraine's status as the primary European recipient of aid vice the Marshall Plan's broadly distributed funding. The potential of drawing on frozen Russian assets in some form constitutes a third. The question of whether major providers should continue to distribute aid through Kyiv merits monitoring given its anti-corruption initiatives are adolescent. Their depth, robustness, and ability to survive beyond the current administration have yet to be proven. The possibility of stumbles suggests it would be prudent to plan for pinpoint aid distribution despite the increased management burden that approach entails.[33]

Orchestrating Aid: Improving Effectiveness, Enhancing Efficiency, and More

> In cities, however, the humanitarian community is outside of its comfort zone.... Donors often prefer to fund rural rather than urban interventions.... In urban areas, it is generally harder to observe assets and thus more difficult to cope with fraudulent claims for assistance.... Assisting IDPs in an urban context requires building new strategic partnerships both to tap into existing strategies, processes, and programmes, and to include them in disaster preparedness interventions. Humanitarian actors can no longer liaise only with national governments; they must also develop urgently closer working relationships with mayors and municipal authorities, service providers, urban police forces, and, most importantly, the representatives of both displaced and resident communities.

> This requires linking up with those development actors that have established such partnerships already.³⁴
>
> — Jeff Crisp, Tim Morris, and Hilde Refstie, "Displacement in urban areas: new challenges, new partnerships"

> The humanitarians persist in brandishing their Red Cross principles and accept no responsibility for the abuse of their aid.³⁵
>
> — Linda Polman, *The Crisis Caravan: What's Wrong with Humanitarian Aid?*

> There were many tools in the Russian's disinformation arsenal…. Sometimes a Russian surrogate would establish a GONGO, an Orwellian acronym for a government-organized nongovernmental organization…. Sometimes the GONGOs knew they were a Russian front and sometimes they were unwilling dupes, but the cutouts allowed the Russian government to plausibly deny that any of it was their doing.³⁶
>
> — Marie Yovanovitch, *Lessons from the Edge*

Aid providers as a group are regrettably no freer of fraudsters than any other calling. We have addressed the thrill-seeking posers, spies, dis-informers, criminals, and corrupt. These less scrupulous can share a propensity for illicit funding practices. The European Union looked into thirty-two NGOs suspected of massive corruption in June 2005. Among the concerns was double billing: receiving EU funding then billing USAID or the World Bank for the same work.³⁷ Bosnia received tens of millions of dollars from Croatia for over a half-decade following the war's termination. The extent of graft remains unknown given the lack of transparency, but the amount never reaching intended recipients is acknowledged to be in the millions.³⁸

The constant evolution of crisis environments further complicates related challenges. Today's needs may be those of tomorrow. If so, they are nevertheless likely to have evolved in character. If not, aid providers have to adapt or give way to other organizations better accomplished at meeting the new requirements. How much better to have one or more macro-managers skilled in orchestrating not only ongoing activities but also in forecasting those prospective. Two examples would seem to have the potential to meet these dual demands. The American-run Ukraine Defense Contact Group coordinates *weapons deliveries* from approximately fifty countries. In early July 2024, NATO's thirty-two member nations announced a mission that will operate out of Germany to orchestrate *all types of aid* over the long term with major benefits being its broader charter in terms of types of aid overseen and management capable of maintaining commitment regardless of whether Washington's proves steadfast or wavering after the November 2024 elections.[39]

Similarly, consolidated management of funding is necessary at lower echelons via organizations funded and overseen by those above. Providing care, training, job placement, family reintegration, and other support for veterans will unquestionably continue to be essential during Ukraine's recovery. The extent to which EU countries allow Ukrainian refugees to stay beyond the three-year limit imposed in 2022, in contrast, remains unknown. Macro-managers' charters at each level would include addressing knowns and providing sufficiently flexible guidance to address contingencies whether ongoing, predictable, or merely forecastable across a range of probabilities.

Better meeting the end of improved aid orchestration would do more than enhance effectiveness and efficiency. Orchestration would logically include arranging for the vetting of participants. It would thereby reduce the number of those who would otherwise be victims of fraud or bodily harm. Management would promote aid synergies and seek opportunities to enhance economic and social healing. Closer relationships between international aid providers and governments provide opportunities to better design and market controversial but necessary recovery initiatives. Denying rebuilding (or new building) in areas at climate change risk will be no more popular in Ukraine than has proved the case elsewhere. External supporters' refusing to fund dubious recovery proposals could serve as an incentive for potential aid recipients to adapt their expectations while also shielding Kyiv from pressures to proceed with unwise alternatives.

Such relationships also provide a chance for the more experienced to pass on hard-learned lessons. For example,

> it is widely accepted that charging even a small amount rather than giving something for free often leads to better use of the resource received; recipients rightly feel they have something invested, giving the good or service value…. The form of aid can also influence perceptions favorably or otherwise. When the state of a local economy and availability of essentials allow, some NGOs prefer providing cash or replenishable cash cards rather than delivering food, diapers, medicines and other [material] forms of assistance. The benefits include cash delivery being

cheaper and less logistically demanding; a US government estimate figures transport and other costs consume up to 65 per cent of emergency food assistance funds. The same study concluded that almost 20 per cent more people can receive aid when it comes in the form of cash. As long as a functioning economy remains, cash will tend to go towards purchases needed by the urban resident, who is very likely the individual best able to determine what they most require. Cash distributions will therefore in many circumstances have a better means-meets-needs rate than one-size-fits-all distributions of select foods or services chosen by an outsider. Cash can also be given directly to the individual requiring assistance, helping to hold disaster's close kin of corruption at bay by avoiding one or more middlemen who might skim. If mobile phone towers are working, dispensing aid in the form of electronic cash transfers similarly reduces the dangers of loss from theft as recipients depart distribution points.[40]

There are firm foundation stones in place for broadening coordination of what might otherwise be disparate efforts. In mid-2023, United Kingdom Prime Minister Rishi Sunak noted more than 400 companies representing thirty-eight countries were backing $3 billion in World Bank loan guarantees for Ukraine. Early examples of medical response and recovery resourcefulness in Ukraine provide insights regarding what cooperative efforts can achieve as well as the nature of the challenges. Russian attacks struck over 1,000 health care facilities during the first sixteen months of the war causing an estimated $2.5 billion in damage. Thanks to the mobilization of international public and private sector support, even the ten regions worst hit by the conflict had just short of

90 percent of those facilities functioning by June 2023. Some were commercial entities self-funding recovery and adapting in ways offering lessons for others in the medical field. A national pharmacy chain, Apteka 911, funded recovery of its Kharkiv region facilities, 30 percent of which were either destroyed or damaged. These included operations reopened only a few weeks after areas were retaken from Russian forces. Adaptations included delivering medicines by mail, providing online consultations where physical facilities lie wasted, and offering mobile deliveries to remote areas. The Kyiv School of Economics KSE Foundation responded to the annihilation of a health care center that had served 28,000 prior to the invasion by organizing fundraising events bringing in $800,000 for rebuilding. Elsewhere, Ukrainian NGO Patients of Ukraine obtained funding from an international donor and restored over twenty-five facilities in cooperation with the Ministry of Health that provided information regarding local security, health worker availability, and the nature of demand for medical services. Significantly, this interaction also covered the sometimes overlooked post-reparation life cycle costs of maintaining services. In this case, a contract with the National Health Service of Ukraine addressed future expenses.[41]

A final management and orchestration issue merits mentioning. Assistance afforded by international providers is undoubtably valuable. Recovery costs can stretch if not break all but the wealthiest in the family of nations. Yet IGOs, NGOs, state representatives, and others would be well advised to monitor their own internal performance.

A repeated theme from the over one thousand interviews I have conducted in support of thirty-odd years of research identifies aid representatives' sometimes questionable commitment to focusing on the matter at hand. Whether in East Timor in the months immediately following Indonesia's departure, Iraq during operations to retake Mosul from the Islamic State of Iraq and Syria (ISIS), or ongoing operations in Ukraine, too many aid organization representatives focus less on aid provision than finding their next job or other self-serving matters. In East Timor, it was UN representatives who were cited in this negative light. An NGO representative with lengthy service in Ukraine similarly found "too many NGOs are going through the motions of providing aid while their representatives are spending time on getting funding and the next job." (This individual did note the Norwegian Refugee Council, Danish Refugee Council, *Médecins* Sans Frontières, and the International Committee of the Red Cross as notable exceptions.)[42] This suggests the above called-for macro-management entity should perhaps include an objective component responsible for completing "report cards" on aid provider representatives when concerns dictate. An obvious choice for the role would be whatever organization(s) are responsible for vetting NGOs prior to their being allowed into a crisis region. The commitment issue is often fleeting, being a matter not of organizational culture but of an individual or cadre during a specific rotation in a disaster area. The goal should not be to punish nor, certainly, to turn away willing providers, but rather to assist in better serving the interests of needy recipients and general recovery.

CHAPTER 6

■ Plans and Planning Considerations

> Climate variability, harvest failure, dependence on long-distance trade, intense warfare, and a shifting disease environment created conditions that decimated communities across three continents—but often also served as a catalyst to long-term growth. This was especially true in Europe.[43]
> — Peter Frankopan, *The Earth Transformed: An Untold History*

> Ukrainians want to reignite their economy via their cities.[44]
> — Karl Jensen comment during interview with the author

Most of Ukraine's urban recovery planning to date focuses on reparation of physical infrastructure damage (buildings, utilities, transportation, and communications, for example). Reinforcement of previous links to the West and creation of others new is an additional benefit of these planning initiatives given the reduction or termination of many Russian and other ties. As the quotes above make clear, plans made today will be the propellants for tomorrow's progress, meaning recovery considerations should encompass both immediate and longer-term implications. Including the formation of one or more organizations providing the overarching orchestration called for above will facilitate many aspects of recovery in both the immediate and more distant terms. Establishing nationwide contracting and vetting standards, developing and disseminating reparations policies, providing guidance regarding teaching students in previously occupied areas, and clearly articulating guidance for the treatment of collaborators is a small sample of the services these organizations should provide.⁴⁵ The god's-eye view available to their representatives would provide them with the knowledge to facilitate the handover of responsibilities from aid providers initially on location and their eventual government or other replacements. The same representatives would also be in a better position to ascertain levels of corruption or other misuse of aid than individual organizations. The orchestrator would therefore best be positioned to recommend when all or some aid providers should consider terminating their support given it may be doing less good than harm, e.g., when it begins to act as a brake on local economic development. Its perspective would in addition ideally allow steering of aid providers toward recipients most in need.

Material in the previous chapters provides some illumination for the way ahead. Manila, with its one-third-again population increase between the end of the war and 1949 warns housing and employment shortages are not a static challenge. Initial progress may be insufficient to keep pace with the rate of returnees. Kherson, whose some 80,000 of a once 300,000 population continue to undergo Russian bombardment, is among the candidates whose fate could be challenged in this regard. So also Mariupol, the destruction of whose Azovstal steel plant means 10,000 pre-war jobs are among those no longer available should the city return to its rightful government.⁴⁶ The loss of the plant—and the MMK plant, also in Mariupol—goes far to explain why Ukraine's steel production dropped by 71 percent in 2022.⁴⁷ It is a problem made further difficult given the occupiers' importation of workers from around

Russia following Mariupol's fall. Recovery ambitions will inevitably confront the actuality of funding limits and property constraints. Urban planners' awareness of these limitations is best treated as a caution rather than a check. Promoting moderation by not trying to do too much too quickly should keep public expectations and expenditures in rein. There will be other brakes on ambitions. The need to spend on shelters, infrastructure protection, and additional defensive features will draw on funds better spent otherwise were Ukraine not to have to consider Russia's warped sense of revanchism. This unfortunate redirection of resources might be mitigated by clever multi-purpose design features such as capitalizing on rivers, roadways, and other features to support a defense in depth, foregoing riverfront residential sales to maintain fields of fire. Moving facilities underground is already part of Ukrainian cities' recovery. Should Russia attack yet again in future years, the time saved by adapting West Germany's Cold War concept of pre-chambering bridges and other defensive features in existing and new construction would reduce the high costs of maintaining defensive forces on high alert (and amount of explosives stored).

Yes, planners must balance ambitions and costs. Yet they should not allow the shadow of cost to too-greatly dim spending that readies a city for over-the-horizon challenges. Climate change merits attention in terms of (to include where *not* to build), building standards, and energy efficiency. The same applies to risk due to earthquakes and other natural threats. (Though few of Ukraine's earthquakes exceed magnitude 5.0, smaller quakes are fairly commonplace.)[48] The payoffs are hard to see, harder yet when war dominates attention, but planning with an eye to future crises offers considerable benefits down the temporal road. Australia offers a telling example. The country

> is estimated to have spent almost 50 times as much responding to disasters in the past couple of decades as on building more resilient houses and other infrastructure.... According to the Climate Council...about one in 25 Australian homes could be uninsurable due to excessive flood risk by 2030.... Even as New South Wales and other states are trying to nudge people out of some high-risk areas, they are funneling them into others. Thus, for examples, the intensive development taking place on the floodplains west of Sydney.[49]

Wise planners will make their products increasingly agile as the timeframe increases. Promises of recovery funding have been impressive, but promises and money-in-hand are two very different circumstances. Future support in terms of who will provide it and in what forms and amounts it will present itself becomes increasingly unpredictable as one looks deeper into the future. Administrations change. National economies slow and quicken. Other contingencies compete for resources. Agility in a plan—the ability to shift priorities, obtain support in fungible forms, and otherwise adapt to changing conditions—is fundamental. Forward-looking, dynamic, realistic, representative, and agile: These are desirable plan characteristics suggested by historical and more recent considerations. Planners further need to avoid the danger of tunnel vision. Just as the threat of epidemic disease has proven war's fellow rider, other compound disasters deserve a spot in planners' minds as they picture recovery. Six weeks after being struck by the atomic bomb, Hiroshima suffered extensive flooding, leading a city official to commiserate, "The city looked like a huge lake…. I felt as though this was the final burial!"[50] But for a favorable wind carrying radioactive contamination into the Pacific Ocean, Tokyo could have experienced a catastrophe of unprecedented proportions after the trifecta of earthquake, tsunami, and failure of reactors at the Fukushima Daiichi nuclear power plant struck in September 2011. As we will see, Mother Nature had no compassion for Halifax, Nova Scotia after a December 1917 ammunition ship explosion devastated the city.

Our post-WWII examples point to yet another challenge. Orphans are a tragic but inevitable consequence of war. Tens of thousands of Ukrainian children have lost at least one parent. Their futures are often in the hands of governments, primarily those local. Prostitution and criminality were the fate of many in Tokyo, Berlin, and Manila. Cities' recovery operations have in the past tended to overlook these unfortunates. The omission is yet more severe given cases of "orphaned elderly," older adults lacking the support of family or friends. Improved awareness can have nuanced implications. Halifax, Canada's explosion left nearly 2,000 dead and 9,000 injured. It also left young Haligonian Edith O'Connor unconscious for a fateful few days:

> As soon as news of the disaster reached the Royal Flying Corps squadron in which Edith's father, Arthur O'Connell, was serving, he was granted compassionate leave. When he arrived in Halifax he hurried to the house on Campbell Road only to find that it no longer existed and in the Chebucto Road mortuary he identified the bodies of his mother, his three brothers, his two sisters, his wife, and his two younger children. He was told that, although her body had not been recovered, it was almost certain that Edith, too, had been killed and that only by a miracle could she have survived. When he had buried his family, Arthur O'Connell went away from Halifax and the seven-year-old girl, then lying unconscious and unidentified in hospital, was never to see him again.[51]

Establishing online or physical information boards can help reestablish these broken links. As with Edith or others similarly incapacitated, further measures will be called for. Once again from Halifax:

> The blast left thousands of children orphaned. Others had lost one parent, while the other parent was still in the hospital or in recovery, leaving the children effectively orphaned for at least a few weeks or more. The problems specific to children started with the registration process, with babies who couldn't speak, children with no documents, and many faces hard to recognize due to stubborn soot or disfiguring wounds. They were also susceptible to being mis-identified by desperate parents or even uncles, aunts, or cousins convinced that this was their child, and if they didn't claim them immediately, they might never see them again.[52]

The dangers did not end with failures to locate kith or kin, nor with misidentification. Many offerings to adopt are sincere. Then there are the less kind-hearted. As in any time of chaos and confusion, society's bottom feeders sought to take advantage in the wake of Halifax's blast. One prospective adopter suggested any child with red hair, a weak chin, or an upturned nose was undesirable. Halifax authorities turned down an official from a US "Deep South" state who requested "fifty colored girls" be sent "at once."[53] Even well-intentioned efforts sometimes went astray, with siblings being separated if one or more's behavior was difficult and others' not, this though, as one author suggests, those kin might be "the only people who might understand what they were going through."[54]

Planners can fall victim to overzealousness that forsakes opportunity due to too great a focus on immediate needs. Well-considered guidance regarding contract awards provides a means of retraining and employing returning soldiers (to include war-wounded with permanent disabilities) and civilians displaced due to mined farm properties or other job losses. Government contracts can include clauses requiring training and hiring veterans—or Ukrainians generally—rather than over-reliance on imported workers. On-the-job training reduces delays if demands for labor are time-sensitive. Such contracts are also an opportunity to address social imbalances such as gender, ethnic, or other biases. Bosnia-Herzegovina provides a warning of the dangers in toothless good intentions. The Dayton Accords mandated the Office of the High Representative (OHR) provide direction for the country's recovery from war. Yet OHR lacked sufficient coercive powers to enforce its guidance, instead having to rely on "hope that in peacetime there would be a strong desire among

Bosnian leaders to re-create a unified nation."[55] BiH today demonstrates it was misguided hope.

Good plans, like good measures of effectiveness (of which more later), inspire innovation and positive behaviors. As after WWII, housing shortages will challenge Ukraine's urban leaders. Those contingencies tell us plans should provide for equitable exercise of eminent domain. This might mean taking land outright (for which fair compensation is forthcoming). It might instead involve involuntary limited-term surrender of second properties or others unoccupied but suitable for temporary housing. Owners voluntarily offering space could receive tax breaks or other financial incentives, more so if they modify or furnish the properties. Those failing to do so might be less, if at all, compensated when their properties are "leased" in the name of public service. Opportunities for evasion and corruption in such schemes would be many, meaning relevant plans and policies should (again) be dynamic, flexible, overwatched, and routinely revised as necessary. Ukraine's homeownership exceeded 94 percent after rapid housing privatization following the Cold War, the highest in Europe by 2010. Mortgage holding was very low, meaning private equity was high. Fine for homeowners in normal times. However, the absence of mortgages means residents rather than banks suffer the financial consequences when they lose homes, see them damaged, or unfair eminent domain comes calling.[56] (Unfair can mean either failing to provide just compensation or taking too long to do so.) As in Manila, recovery programs focusing on government properties alone burden commercial and residential property owners. Programs addressing private property losses are fundamental to social and economic recovery.

Much of Ukraine's housing stock was in poor shape even before 2022. The implications for urban recovery are at least threefold. First, even as construction of new housing proceeds, that old will continue to crumble as was the case in Tokyo. Second, while past post-disaster contingencies have shown repairing rather than rebuilding is generally both cheaper and more helpful to homeowners who might be able to live in other parts of their homes as repairs proceed, the poor quality of Soviet-era construction might eliminate repairing as a viable option. Lastly, determining how much a property owner merits in the way of repair or rebuilding support should account for the structure's pre-damage condition. Assessment and coming to a satisfactory solution are sure to prove controversial, sometimes to the point of absurdity. Some Sarajevo residents refused to accept homes because of petty complaints even when residences were provided gratis. Another factor: By 2015 most Ukrainians could no longer afford to buy a home given increasing prices and an inability to secure mortgages given rampant price speculation.[57] Good plans will account for the housing market's evolution.

It is fortunate Ukraine's cities were—at least to some extent—moving away from Soviet-style urban planning prior to the war, a style in which regional or national authority plans dictated aspects of urban development for up to thirty years. Greater inclusiveness and flexibility are characteristics of post-Soviet approaches. A positive from the perspective of being more responsive to local requirements, downsides include uneven quality of urban development and possible failure to fully consider potential synergies via a city's relationship with surrounding rural and other urban areas.[58] Recovery planning provides an opportunity to address these potential ills by ridding urban planning of negative residual Soviet elements, overwriting previous poorly designed schemes, and establishing standards in keeping with more effective approaches. The 2020 New Leipzig Charter provides guidance for cities choosing to take advantage. A non-binding document, it aligns suggested policies with numerous European and world agreements that include the European Green Deal, Paris Agreement, and UN 2030 Agenda for Sustainable Development. The charter encourages greater influence for individual cities during national and EU decision-making. Ukraine joined the Leipzig Charter in 2016 "as a proclaimed intention to implement the European urban development values and principles in Ukrainian cities."[59] Additional organizations provide potentially complimentary post-disaster recovery insights.[60]

Without clearly articulated and enforced building standards and fraud-free inspection processes, Ukrainian urban recovery will be a hodge-podge of regulations and corresponding confusion. The July 2022 National Council for the Recovery of Ukraine from the Consequences of the War draft plan expressed several concerns in this regard. While all 397 of the country's settlements with the status of cities had development general plans, less than 60 percent met Ukrainian legislative standards.

National-level architectural and construction guidance falls short of what is needed to address the shortfall. Further, conservative if not reactionary regulations hamper introduction of innovative building materials, technologies, and procedures.[61] Coherent nationwide building standards and observant local plans are critical to convincing investors their money will not be wasted on substandard construction. Complementing standards with financing procedures allowing funders to provide loans or donations directly to beneficiaries speeds recovery by avoiding unnecessary layers of bureaucracy while reducing the opportunity for corruption.[62] Alternatively, Kyiv's designating a single node for routing all construction funding could go far toward ensuring funds only go to recipients whose plans meet national standards while another agency monitors related corruption at all echelons. These management bodies would also be the logical entities for ensuring contractors meet contractually mandated local hire and training requirements.

Orchestrating recovery activities as directed in plans will face challenges. Participating aid and other organizations will have competing agendas. Friction will arise as some refuse to work with others. (Select NGOs avoid working with military forces, for example.) Proper planning procedures include what the military calls "wargaming." This involves bringing relevant parties together and walking through a plan with each participant having the opportunity to ask for clarification or challenge elements thought in need of improvement. Designated "red teams" assume an adversarial role, their charter being to identify weaknesses planners can then address. The resultant process frequently employs an action->reaction->counteraction process with sufficient iterations to resolve shortcomings, the goal being to remove as many inefficiencies as possible. Proper wargaming requires participants to send sufficiently empowered representatives to agree on changes. The outcome should be deconfliction, a plan maximizing synergy, and freedom from undue delays.

The above-noted National Council for the Recovery of Ukraine from the Consequences of the War draft recovery plan broadly outlined objectives including recognition of cities' roles in national recovery. These are worth quoting at length:

> The key development goals for the next decade are to accelerate the economic growth of regions and territorial communities based on the effective use of domestic potential, job creation, improved employment, and accessibility of public service and services, which creates conditions for repatriation of migrants. The state will pay particular attention to supporting potential growth centres that can spread their positive impact on the development of neighbouring territories and affect the development of the region as a whole.... Reconstruction of Ukrainian cities and villages after the war is a complex process that must ensure modernisation and further development for decades ahead. New challenges related to the war—providing balanced resettlement of migrants, relocation of enterprises and businesses in all regions of the country, and creating a socially-oriented business environment as a prerequisite to economic development of communities—must be combined with the best modern world approaches and practices [in terms of] architecture and UN Sustainable

Development Goals. Human-centeredness, rational spatial planning, ensuring the balance of resettlement and jobs, sustainable urban mobility, inclusiveness, energy efficiency, environmental friendliness and many other current trends in human settlements should be the signs of our excellent recovery.[63]

The draft goes on to emphasize several key recovery and development principles, among them:

- Integrate green technologies and enhance sustainability,
- Maintain openness and transparency,
- Work toward integration into the European Union,
- Enhance civil protection,
- Incorporate inclusiveness of all the country's population, and
- Improve energy independence.[64]

Ukraine's steps to improve its development prior to the renewal of war in 2022 should abet these goals' attainment. The reduction in the number of separate governmental entities with the creation of 1,469 *hromadas* during the 2015-2022 period means fewer parties with which authorities have to deal. This should reduce the number of nodes fostering corruption while also easing monitoring. The accompanying decentralization means funds, decision-making authority, and planning responsibilities have left Kyiv for outlying authorities. Several urban areas have created their own development ties continentally and worldwide. These include links to the German and Swiss governments, USAID, UNDP in Ukraine, and the Canadian Partnership for Local Economic Development and

Democratic Governance (PLEDDG).⁶⁵ Though as of yet falling short of a comprehensive Ukrainian nationwide urban planning guidance system, a number of prewar laws and other forms of assistance likewise propel movement in the right direction.⁶⁶

The need for local control has grown given the destruction suffered by urban housing and a pre-war lack of building programs supporting those with lower incomes. Ukraine's urban rental markets remain underdeveloped. Resulting scarcity promises to fuel tensions as many whose homes have been destroyed move from elsewhere or return home on release from military service.⁶⁷ Another source of potential friction thus far receiving little attention is that between un-mobilized Ukrainian young men and the tens of thousands who are fighting. As of this writing, the country mobilizes only men between the ages of 25 and 60, meaning those 18-24 will tend to be better positioned geographically and economically to obtain available housing.⁶⁸ That currently serving soldiers will have some sense of entitlement when it comes to housing seems justified. Difficulties lying ahead in terms of too few rentals and too many prospective renters are evident when looking at western Ukrainian communities' handling of the population influx as individuals fled westward in 2022. National construction guidance, including priorities for the distribution of scarce materials, is essential for effective planning, oversight, and donor comfort.⁶⁹ Local input to this guidance and as-necessary exceptions should likewise be instituted. The time for a coherent and comprehensive national housing policy is now.

CHAPTER 6

The planners' road ahead is a rough one. Even Ukraine's desire to "build back better" receives frowns from donors who would prefer the country settle for a return to basic functionality. Others express concerns regarding the country's immature (by Western standards) federal-level contracting regulations and oversight.[70] Investors and donors alike will hesitate to provide funding until national leaders address so fundamental a deficiency. It is to these leaders we turn in the following section.

David McMahon, the demining expert quoted earlier, provided an example of the value in having plans and management promoting orchestration of and related resource sharing across the many organizations aiding the country's recovery:

> In other countries, the United Nations is the lead or has the lead in coordination and resource mobilization. And then the United Nations issues grants or contracts competitively. So donors give money to the United Nations and then competitive processes are put in place. I would say that due to the lack of coherence and the lack of coordination in the beginning [of Ukrainian recovery initiatives], NGOs have been able to secure their own bilateral funding from a lot of donors. There is thus almost a role reversal in Ukraine. NGOs in Ukraine are huge. They have substantial funding, more than the United Nations. I think it will be very difficult to put the genie back in the bottle when it comes to coordination…. It has taken the Ukrainian government two years to get their act together in terms of coordination, quality assurance, quality control, etc. So, I think it's going to be difficult to force these very large NGOs to do what the government says [and the lack of an orchestrating body introduces inefficiencies]. As an example, there are a lot of NGOs in the Mykolaiv

Oblast. The [demining] NGOs have decided to divide up the oblast geographically, which might not be the best use of their combined assets. For example, one NGO may have machines while another uses dogs. If each has its own geographic area, they may lack certain assets that could be used there more efficiently.[71]

■ Leadership and Management

Whilst the majority of Haligonians [residents of Halifax, Nova Scotia] saw the disaster as a chance to give unstintingly of their time, money, and possessions in order to alleviate the distress, others saw it as a golden opportunity for profit. Unscrupulous landlords raised rents astronomically.... [While] hundreds of men and women were working twelve and fifteen hours a day without thought of payment, organized labour held the city to ransom. Plumbers, quoting union rules, refused to work one minute beyond the regulation eight hours unless they received extra rates for overtime. The bricklayers, working on houses urgently needed for the homeless, would not allow plasterers to help in the repair of chimneys and, at the same time, demanded higher rates and bonuses from the Relief Commission.... Truckmen charged exorbitant prices for carrying salvaged furniture and belongings.[72]

— Michael J. Bird, *The Town that Died: The true story of the greatest man-made explosion before Hiroshima*

On November 10, the remainder of the Russian military was busy abandoning Kherson. Unlike the rout in Kharkiv and northern Donetsk, this was a prepared and well-organized retreat. This time around, the Russians didn't leave behind hundreds of brand-new tanks, howitzers, and BMPs. The Russian troops even had time to blow up Kherson's electrical installations.[73]

— Yaroslav Trofimov, *Our Enemies will Vanish*

CHAPTER 6

It is hard to overstate the magnitude of the challenges confronting Ukraine's urban leaders as they take steps to recover from the damage inflicted by an ongoing war while planning a continuation of those efforts once hostilities cease. Plenty are the unknowns despite history's lessons. To what extent, if at all, will cities such as Kharkiv reestablish former ties with occupied Donbas? How difficult will it be to educate Ukrainian children once taught with Ukrainian curricula, then Russia's, then once again their own? What will the long-term effects be on their trust in educators? Determining who are among the unidentified and unfound dead, IDPs, or refugees is important to families and friends. It is also fundamental to determining the disposition of unoccupied properties. Who and how will priorities for sure-to-be too scarce resources such as steel, power, and vehicles be determined to address demands for shelter, spurring national economic recovery, and supporting equitable aid distribution? How will city leaders find the elusive sweet spot balancing calls for memorializing those lost, yearnings for a familiar past, and innovation in light of future trends? What might Tokyo, Berlin, Manila, and Sarajevo reveal regarding adapting facilities to those physically or emotionally handicapped by war? To what extent should those same authorities prepare to constrain, tolerate, or regulate black markets…and for how long?

Addressing the above will require a partnership between Ukraine's national government and those serving at subordinate echelons. That the country had made significant, if at times too slow, progress in de-Sovietizing in the years between 1989 and 2022 suggests Ukrainians will be comfortable with continued adaptations. The army's interest in establishing something akin to the US Army Corps of Engineers is an example. Like America's army engineers, Ukraine's have skills readily adaptable to the country's recovery, demining and familiarity with military construction among them. Unlike the US corps, however, Ukraine's engineers have neither the responsibility nor the capability to manage civil construction, oversee environmental policy, administer waterways, and otherwise assist in nationwide rebuilding.[74] Creating such an entity would seem to offer numerous recovery benefits for Ukraine, especially given the desirability of dual-use protective features in both government and commercial construction. Ukrainians are gaining recovery experience with each passing day. Kherson's experiences with a months-long occupation offer insights regarding the difficulties reassuming governing responsibilities poses for returning authorities.

Government and commercial sectors have done yeoman's work in quickly restoring services to Ukraine's war-damaged cities. Quick restoration of power in particular has been well publicized. Other sectors have shown equally impressive rebounds. The World Health Organization reported over a thousand attacks on health facilities, transport, or supply chain links by May 2023. Losses were especially punishing given the diminished availability of civilian medical care due to demands for supporting the military. Spikes in local urban populations caused by influxes of those displaced from points east further strained the system. Even where available, increases in health-related products and services costs undercut individuals' ability to pay. All the more important, then that over two-thirds of the 896 facilities damaged countrywide had been fully or partially repaired by the end of the following month. Approximately 90 percent of medical facilities in the ten worst affected oblasts were functional. Other initiatives were put in place to address patients' ability to pay and the cost of medicines.[75]

Maintaining popular support can pose unexpected challenges. Ironically, liberating Ukrainian forces can be victims of their earlier restraint. The town of Kupyansk, with a population of about 30,000, had residents who

> weren't happy that the city had returned to Ukrainian rule…. The Russian takeover had been quick and painless, with uninterrupted electricity, heating, and water. And for seven months, there was no shelling. Now the power outlets had gone dead, the water taps were dry, shops and bakeries were closed, and one building after another was being destroyed by Russian artillery. "To tell you the truth, life was better under the Russians," said the woman, Marina…. Experience shapes perceptions. For the citizens of Kharkiv, which had resisted the Russians and suffered death and destruction from the first days of the war, the enemy was clear. But in Kupyansk, the worst for the people like Marina had begun only with the return of Ukrainian forces.[76]

Marina's logic may seem skewed. It is Russians threatening her life, but Ukraine's reticence to use more firepower before retaking the town meant she felt safer under Russian rule. Such perhaps unanticipated views are ones Kyiv and local officials cannot ignore. Gaining and maintaining public support becomes more difficult as suffering continues. Ukrainians' expectations regarding services will be higher under the Ukrainian government than Russian. Such was the case in immediate-post-WWII Hong Kong when residents freed of Japanese occupation anticipated the provision of water to their homes 24/7 after the British reassumed control.[77] That some Sarajevans refused to accept a postwar home rebuilt at no personal expense because of minor flaws was no less unrealistic.[78] There are times when locals expect more from an outsider than their own former government, however. US Army Corps of Engineers officer Carl Strock found Baghdad residents complaining because occupying Americans could not immediately provide consistent power in 2003.[79]

Well-managed expectations and visionary yet pragmatic plans are partners in successful recoveries. The pair provides for melding short and longer-term objectives just as it does employing today's technologies while incorporating the flexibility needed to introduce others to come. The extent to which the whole is greater than the sum of its parts depends on how well a recovery's elements work together. These pieces include not only those physical but others social, economic, and informational. Seizing the initiative in managing expectations should help leaders minimize disgruntlement. Establishing two-way communication channels for expectation management also provides a means for urban residents to become direct participants in day-to-day recovery activities. Encouraging reporting of damage speeds information gathering and responsiveness. Pairing this input with messages

CHAPTER 6

informing citizens of the sorts of information needed further speeds response as managers can immediately dispatch those with relevant expertise rather than needing to perform an initial reconnaissance.

Among the actions gaining a government both immediate and longer-term positive effects are reuniting families and identifying the dead. Collapsed buildings, hasty burials, and those who died in remote locations all present difficulties, first in finding remains, second in identifying them. Russia's relocating Ukrainians complicates the issue. The challenges in no way diminish expectations. Nor need those expectations be met by government officials alone. As with any crisis, leaders emerge from unexpected sources. Ralph Simmonds stepped forward despite the magnitude of the task in the aftermath of Halifax's explosion. He quickly

> recognized another need that wouldn't have occurred to him if he hadn't been on the scene. He sent a messenger back to his company to get all the three-by-five index cards they had to record where each article or corpse had been found and tie the label to the object or the body itself.[80]

Well-intentioned and helpful, Simmonds's accounting likely fell short of need given the magnitude of his city's losses. Paper-based methods proved both unwieldy and inaccurate in recovering the dead after the September 11, 2001 attacks on New York City's World Trade Center. Both Halifax and 9/11 demonstrate the density of casualties during urban catastrophes creates problems of its own. This is in considerable part due to a difference distinguishing urban disasters from those in most other environments: the basic unit of space is volume rather than area. The vertical dimension represented in tall buildings or below-ground facilities means casualties on a given plot of ground can be tens or hundreds of times greater than in open space. Officials in New York adopted an electronic barcoding system allowing firefighters to record the location, time, date, and nature of a finding during 9/11 recovery.[81] While little may remain of a body due to crushing, fire, or other devastation, clothing, a backpack, or another item can help determine status when body parts are limited or nonexistent. The association of an item with a missing individual can mean the difference between eternal anonymity and tentative identification. The association can also save time and expense; remains otherwise anonymous might be more readily identified as DNA testing need only focus on relatives familiar with an item.

New York City leaders drew on lessons from the Oklahoma City federal building bombing six years before when dealing with the aftermath of 9/11. They resultantly recognized their own victims' injuries would be physical, mental, and emotional. Many would require long-term—perhaps lifelong—rehabilitation or physical therapy in cases of lost limbs, eyesight, deafness, post-traumatic stress, or other ailments. Nagasaki also offers lessons...and a notable caution. The Japanese Wartime Casualties Care Law provided medical support for only sixty days to those injured. This effectively abandoned any needing care or medicines after suffering radiation exposure, for example.⁸² Appropriate programs will instead sustain care for decades, long after most would prefer to forget unpleasant events past. Effectively managing patient needs is a progressive process. IGOs and NGOs will depart. Their and other funding sources will end, some gradually, others precipitously. Some patients will recover. As in Oklahoma City, a number, recovered or otherwise, will require vocational training, modifications to dwellings, special transport capabilities, upgrades or replacement of artificial limbs or equipment, and additional needs ending only with the individual's passing. Select cases will require sustaining support for more than the victim alone, relatives or other long-term care providers also being in need. Challenges will include those pertaining to both civilian and former military personnel. The scope of time and type covers myriad possibilities. Leaders managing the response to and recovery from the World Trade Center attack quickly designated locations for the reception of families searching for information on loved ones. Representatives who were able to arrange for financial assistance and other support while also addressing emotional issues manned the sites. Officials from the Oklahoma City bombing shared that survivors were at greater risk of suicide, divorce, depression, and substance abuse.⁸³ As with the case of identifying the missing, addressing the needs of the emotionally or physically injured is not only an immediate and long-term undertaking. It is one sure to vary over time.

Ukrainians in currently occupied territory include military veterans and pensioners. Terminating payments because they suffer the misfortune of Russian occupation will trigger a sense of abandonment. Yet meeting these obligations will be expensive, support the occupier's economy, and potentially relieve Russia of having to assume payment responsibilities, ensuring that continuing this support would be unpopular with many in unoccupied Ukraine.

Coherently and effectively managing international support will be a gargantuan task. Although on a scale dwarfed by the challenges confronting war-torn Ukraine, the 2003 Regional Assistance Mission to Solomon Islands (RAMSI) led by Australia reinforces the value of designating a single node for coordinating aid activities. The three primary agencies representing Canberra were the Australian Federal Police (AFP), Australian military, and Department of Foreign Affairs and Trade (equivalent to the US Department of State). The trio of leaders heading these organizations benefited from creation of one conduit through which went all requests for support from Canberra. Having to deal with only a single entity meant those in the Solomon Islands knew exactly who to contact when a response lagged or a support request went astray. That the single node was responsible for receiving and tracking status of actions meant RAMSI representatives immersed in day-to-day activities could dedicate maximum effort to the challenges at hand while others in the capital took on a considerable administrative burden.[84] A similar node in Kyiv could serve both as a channel for external aid providers and point of contact for the country's city officials needing to coordinate for support.

An interviewee with extensive experience in Ukraine and conflict zones elsewhere felt the size of Ukraine makes it "virtually impossible to centralize supervision," though, as noted, making the effort is worthwhile even if the reality falls short.[85] The often short duration of providers' in-country rotations further complicates the situation. USAID largely operates on a contract basis for delivery of services. Those contractors sometimes require employees to stay in a theater for only three to four months, hardly enough time to acquire requisite understanding of their responsibilities much less provide insightful management. Overly frequent turnover largely negates effective management. The problem is sometimes compounded when organizations allow too frequent rest and rehabilitation periods or vacations. Other NGOs' representatives remain in disaster areas for months or years and take less frequent breaks. Norwegian Refugee Council (NRC) is one, making such a better choice if support infrastructure dictates limiting the number of aid providers. An obvious policy is for USAID and other major donors to require effective personnel policies in organizations they fund...as well as ensuring their own are likewise.

Semi-centralized management approaches in Ukraine include the UN's cluster structure in which functions are compartmentalized as a means of coordinating aid delivery. Cluster managers differ by focus. For example, the UN's World Food Program (WFP) oversees the food cluster.[86] Shelter (housing), food, demining, and health are among others employing the cluster approach. Clusters employ various modalities within themselves. Other modalities span multiple clusters, i.e., a given modality addresses how individuals receive assistance across multiple clusters. These include in-kind distributions (of food or seed, for example) and ways of providing services. Cash distribution is one such modality. It represents not a general aid function (and thus is not a cluster) but rather how aid reaches recipients. Cash distribution serves needs when purchasing housing, food, or paying medical expenses whether the cash comes in the form of actual money-in-hand, deposits to bank accounts, rechargeable debit cards, transfers to mobile phones, or another.[87]

An aid organization's participation in a cluster is voluntary but encouraged. Those choosing not to do so may find UN funding less forthcoming, meaning organizations with adequate alternative income sources might feel less motivated to partake. However, they may find benefits in participation go beyond funding. Cluster managers encourage participants to upload information regarding planned distributions. The accumulated data provides "building blocks" allowing other organizations to see who is receiving assistance, when, and for how long, thereby helping to preclude overlaps and potentially revealing additional groups or areas with as-of-yet unaddressed needs.

The cluster system is a step toward better orchestration. It is, however, imperfect. It does not guarantee effective addressing of need. Remaining with the example of food distribution, the WFP at times inadequately coordinated its distributions with other providers in one interviewee's experience. Nor did it accurately gauge local conditions. Too much of its food aid was still in-kind (actual foodstuffs) after evolved circumstances suggested alternative forms would be more effective. The distribution also failed to balance requirements and aid, some areas receiving more than was needed while others received less. Food aid in the form of cash (or its equivalent) would have been a better choice. It would also have been more agile, allowing quicker adaptations in where aid went while reducing overall logistical demands. Lack of adequate coordination with other organizations also meant some NGO food representatives found their efforts were redundant to those of the WFP or other groups. Some aid providers within a cluster have avoided such conflicts by maintaining formal or informal links with each other to deconflict their activities. Links included cross-cluster relationships, thereby helping to avoid stove-piping (the limiting of information to a select group and thus denying timely sharing with other providers). These cross-cluster communications are essential. Inefficiencies and waste arise in their absence. Without them, for example, money provided for food (which should theoretically meet 100 percent of a recipient's needs) might go to beneficiaries who are already receiving general purpose cash distributions intended to address food in addition to other necessities. Coordination between cluster leaders theoretically complements these in-the-field ties. At the highest UN echelons, a Humanitarian Coordination Team (HCT) made up of senior managers ideally maintains a collective vision covering all clusters and other forms of aid distribution.[88] The procedures are not foolproof. In one case, those delivering food boxes dumped them without coordinating for onward delivery, crediting themselves with having gotten the food to recipients nonetheless. As in organizations anywhere, performance quality is often personality driven. The more dedicated hold those under their purview to account. Less passionate managers' oversight has sometimes been little more than pro forma.[89]

Having one or more clever (and non-fawning) individuals responsible for evaluating and challenging leader decisions is no less important than the above-noted red-teaming during planning. Their responsibilities require advisers and leaders alike to "walk around the table" and view decisions' potential consequences from all relevant perspectives. Recovery, like war, can be a lucrative business. And, like war, the longer it goes, the greater the opportunity for profit. Aid organizations are too often a witting or unwitting accomplice of this profiteering-through-extended-misery. Politically-instigated famines during the 1980s and 1990s in Ethiopia and Somalia precipitated food aid that provided combatants resources for feeding their soldiers. The Khmer Rouge likewise drew on refugee camp foodstuffs to perpetuate the terror they inflicted on Cambodians the decade before. Manipulation of those who had limbs hacked off during Sierra Leone's late 20th-century fighting made recovery an aid windfall. Publicizing their misery generated NGO and faith-based organization money for perpetrators, doctors who provided treatment but no aftercare, and shady adoption programs involving amputee children.[90] Lise Grande, UN Humanitarian Coordinator in Yemen, made the difficult decision to terminate food delivery to those parts of the country under

CHAPTER 6

Houthi control in June 2019 after a year of the rebels ignoring demands to cease its misrouting.[91] Appointing advisers and capable managers enhances the chances senior authorities will foresee the potential consequences of their decisions while alerting them to what might be future signals to change course.

A Brief Further Look at Funding

> It was rare that returnees had a way to make a living. In the long run, lack of economic viability proved to be the ultimate obstruction to return.[92]
> — Peter Lippman, *Surviving the Peace: The Struggle for Postwar Recovery in Bosnia-Herzegovina*

> "This money should be spent on buying weapons," said Yevheniia Klyshal, a 29-year-old nutritionist who was waving a sign that read, "New roads won't win this war."... "I want the budget to be used for the defense of our country, not to repave sidewalks or put asphalt on roads that already look normal," said Tetiana Nagumuk, who was standing among protesters last week, a Ukrainian flag draped around her shoulders.[93]
> — Constant Méheut, "More Drones, Fewer Parks. Ukrainians Urge Spending Shift as War Drags On"

Funding will inevitably prove a continuing challenge for leaders at every echelon of the Ukrainian government. "That America would help out financially was never seriously in doubt" was not entirely true in the early months after WWII. It certainly can no longer be assumed given so many US politicians backing away from their country's world leadership role. Nor can Ukrainian city leaders trust changes in funding amounts won't be more like the UN's sudden termination of funding to the Philippines upon independence rather than the more gradual US one. Predictability, effective prioritization, and private investment will be crucial components in sustaining urban recovery.

That funding will evolve in terms of amounts, sources, and priorities (as donor and government agendas wax and wane) complicates leaders' ability to plan coherently. As the second quote above also hints, public expectations will do likewise, the same calls for holding off on what are perceived as uncritical expenditures later becoming complaints as aging infrastructure crumbles. Yet money is the ultimate persuader. There must be means to coerce when cooperation is not voluntarily forthcoming. As with the example of UN funding encouraging (semi-) voluntary participation within clusters, Kyiv can create a central recovery authority through which all funds flow (or at least all from sources willing to pool their assets). It is to this authority federal and lower echelon government organizations would turn for other than locally-raised funding. By working with the UN and other coordinating (and fund-controlling) bodies, the resulting collective would provide a powerful guidance body abetting recovery efficiency. There would be outliers. Some NGOs, IGOs, international governments, commercial interests, and others not in need of external funds will choose to operate independently. Ukrainian officials will then be left with the alternatives of foregoing their support or tolerating some level of lesser efficiency in what is in any case an undertaking in which efficiency is an ever-elusive goal. Akin to an orchestra of musical instruments, a conductor brings harmonious coherence. The alternative is cacophony.

A Closing Thought on Centralized Orchestration

> As early as 1941, while the bombs were still falling...the *Picture Post*...magazine recalled the sudden end of the war in 1918: "The plan was not there. We got no new Britain.... This time we can be better prepared. But we can only be prepared if we think now."[94]
> — David Adams and Peter Larkham, *The Everyday Experiences of Reconstruction and Regeneration*

> I saw no evidence of a clear strategic-level end-state for what we were about—the omens were not good.[95]
> — Tim Cross, commenting on a planned attack into 2003 Iraq in "Humanitarian Assistance and Reconstruction"

As the previous paragraph makes clear, creating one overarching recovery authority will not mean all participants partake of that ultimate managerial node. Should creating a centralized administrative entity prove impossible, as is likely, the lesser achievement of an overarching monitoring and advisory organization is an option. Either way, leaders will still need to balance the advantages of centralized guidance and capitalizing on insights only local managers possess. Both effectiveness and efficiency suggest recovery is best envisioned as a system, a network of networks. One or more orchestrating sub-establishments might work with NGOs (as does the UN currently with its cluster system), another with IGOs, and yet others with international state partners. How many management levels this would entail and what authority each would have are matters determined in conjunction with the organizations comprising each network. Networks and individual organizations would be encouraged to maintain relationships across network boundaries to minimize redundancy and waste. Such formal and informal contacts serve to avoid the stove-piping that so often plagues collective enterprises. Intelligence organizations are notorious in this regard, operating in self-imposed isolation in the sometimes legitimate, sometimes alleged service of protecting sources and avoiding leaks.[96] Whether aid and other organizations are allowed to opt in or out when it comes to orchestration is a matter for host governments to decide. The easier option is to let each organization make its own decision. The wiser one may be for the government to strongly encourage or require opting in. In the case of Ukraine, even a minimal level of voluntary participation would allow for better information sharing regarding lifesaving matters such as the locations of minefields, unexploded ordnance, and communities in critical need.

■ Housing, Building, and Employment

> Urban land with small lot divisions strongly resists change.[97]
> — Carola Hein, "Resilient Tokyo: Disaster and Transformation in the Japanese City"

Given the importance of destroyed architecture as a symbol of the identity of a certain ethnic group or nation as a whole, Sarajevo's Association of Architects during its city's siege in the 1990s coined the term "warchitecture" as a war against architecture.[98]

— Kostyantyn Mezentsev and Oleksii Mezentsev,
"War and the city: Lessons from urbicide in Ukraine"

"One of the immediate problems facing blitzed cities was the shortage of building materials, which remained rationed until the early 1950s…. Despite demobilization immediately after the end of the war, the nation's labour force was [also] severely hit."[99]

— David Adams and Peter Larkham,
The Everyday Experiences of Reconstruction and Regeneration

Thoughts of how to house those whose homes have been lost, how to rebuild city centers that meet both today's and coming decades' needs, and how to address these and other rebuilding challenges while respecting existing property rights will challenge the most talented of urbanists. Resulting solutions could be models for others during and following future wars. The scope of challenges alone—cities damaged but never occupied, others occupied but for a short span, those occupied long-term before recovery, and some perhaps never returning to their proper fold—are providing plentiful meat for case studies to come.

Housing and rebuilding generally will surely be the focus of several of those studies. Considerations will reach far beyond construction issues alone. Our quartet of Berlin, Tokyo, Manila, and Sarajevo leaves no doubt there will be difficulties in determining whether absent urban landowners are displaced and plan to return, elsewhere with no intention of coming back, or dead. Unknowns like these, those histories tell us, spawn related problems of determining how long a landowner should have to reclaim property and procedures regarding properties that go unclaimed. There will be plentiful additional issues. What of that challenge when property records have been destroyed? What rights, if any, do squatters on another's property have when alternative shelters are few? To what extent does property ownership constrain eminent domain legitimately wielded when the outcome better serves the greater whole? Is there a feasible compromise as in Tokyo when a percentage of properties could be involuntarily taken with (hopefully) equitable compensation paid? What is a fair basis for compensation when asserting eminent domain? Should existing construction codes guide rebuilding or is now the time to incorporate climate change adaptations, innovative building materials, and rezoning? Does rebuilding wait for clearance of destroyed structures or are incursions onto nearby agricultural, park, greenbelt, or other lands allowed in the interest of speed? Does housing get priority for limited materials and labor or does it await rejuvenation of factories and other enterprises providing more jobs? Or government, medical, office, or other structures? How should authorities deal with owners whose properties are undamaged but gouge fellow residents via extortionate rents? Does apportioning properties along ethnic or economic lines make sense (as in Singapore where the government established percentages for those of Chinese, Malay, Indians, and other groups when allocating apartments)?

Answers to the above will differ by location, extent of damage, materials and labor availability, demand, nature of local economies, and many other factors. Decisions regarding resolutions will ideally be made from a systems perspective, e.g., if City X can provide the bulk of the country's needs for some segment of an industry, the focus of City Y's recovery might be otherwise to avoid redundancy, speed recovery of another sector, or move some part of Ukraine's economy in a new direction. Alternatively, redundancy might be desirable for security reasons.

Seemingly mundane decisions will have unexpected consequences. Los Angeles and Tokyo offered differing perspectives on whether to repair or rebuild after each suffered an earthquake:

> Federal recovery funds went into the City of Los Angeles' multifamily housing loan program, which was focused on repairing rather than demolishing and rebuilding even in cases where repairs required stripping a structure down to its frame. Only 500 of more than 36,500 damaged units had to be demolished. Japanese officials looking back at their policy of rebuilding in lieu of repairing in Kobe believe better incentives for the latter should have been on the table after the January 1995 quake. They found that while rebuilding rather than repair improved the speed of rehousing and reduced recovery costs, landlords subsequently tended to charge higher rents once new buildings were in place. Many long-time residents were permanently shut out of their long-time pre-earthquake neighbourhoods as they could not afford the new rates. Both individuals and community cohesion suffered.[100]

An additional benefit of the Los Angeles approach was one we have already noted in a general context: occupants could sometimes continue to live in an unaffected part of their residence while repairs were ongoing. The result reduced personal turmoil, expense for the residents involved, and burden on local housing. Several other factors can influence the repair-or-rebuild decision. Los Angeles properties tend to be large enough to allow construction access with minimal disruption of occupants on surrounding properties. The same is not true in many Japanese or European urban locations where proximity and lot size mean the effects of construction are more constrained. It seems logical to assume Berlin's recovery was helped by its lower building density than sister cities Hamburg and Dresden in addition to the capital's related lesser susceptibility to firestorms. Economics will play a role. Landlords may favor rebuilding for reasons apparent after the 1995 Kobe tremors. What property owner would not choose to rebuild over making repairs when the former is faster, cheaper, and supports higher rents for resulting spiffier properties?[101] Urban government authorities may find it necessary to promote select practices in the service of community cohesion and fairness.

Approaches to Housing and Other Infrastructure Recovery in Ukraine's Cities

> The war has caused the biggest housing crisis in Ukraine's history.... The need for housing has not just increased but also diversified. A need for temporary crisis accommodation has emerged.... The data show that the share of people living in their own housing is decreasing in Ukraine while the share of renters is increasing.... Rent prices have increased, but the private rental sector remains poorly

protected and poorly regulated…. Tenants still risk facing illegal evictions and unjustified rent hikes…. About 39% of IDPs reported needing help with paying their rent [while] only 3% of those who had not moved required such help.[102]
— Anastasiia Bobrova, "Housing and war: housing policy in the first year of the full-scale war"

Appropriate housing cost policies balance renter and landlord requirements. Every aid hryvnia spent on housing could be one instead promoting job education, medical care, or another area of need. Ishikawa Hideaki, head of Tokyo's metropolitan government planning section, was one of those who had grand plans for the capital in the aftermath of its WWII destruction. They were not to be. Popular demand required quick provision of housing. Existing property rights hamstrung plans for innovative urban planning schemes and new greenbelts. Both funding limitations and Allied occupier restrictions on the nature of reconstruction constrained what reality allowed. Other obstacles blocked similarly grandiose plans for Berlin when planners' ambitions of demolishing areas beyond those ruined by war met funding shortages, existing property rights, and citizens' desire for rapid rebuilding proved insurmountable These are constraints Ukraine's mayors and staffs will find familiar as they contemplate their own recoveries from war.[103]

As was the case with their historical predecessors, Ukrainian urban residents have not waited for the war's end to address its damage. Private and public volunteer initiatives join crowdfunding efforts to assist residents. Repair Together, NEST, OKNO, and Brave to

Rebuild are among the organizations lending assistance. Kyiv's 2022 eOselia program included discounted mortgage loans of 3 percent interest for military personnel, educators, and medical workers with plans for a 7 percent interest rate for others. Despite initial missteps, local government roles in determining housing policies expanded that same year though their proficiency in managing this important sector remains to be seen.[104]

UN-Habitat representatives have been part of the United Nations Ukraine country team from the month after Russia's February 2022 renewed intrusions. Increased decentralization of housing initiatives means these and other outsiders can work with officials to better determine local needs, assist in allocating funding, and help meld external aid initiatives with increased tax income consequent of that decentralization. UN-Habitat and other organizations have also lent their expertise to local authorities as they hone their expertise given Ukraine's government decentralization being a fairly recent phenomenon.[105]

Organizations at home have likewise stepped up. Ukrainian urban planner Alexander Shevchenko's ReStart Ukraine, founded in the months after Russia's 2022 invasion, has drawn Ukrainian and international attention with its focus on green sustainability. Among its initiatives are several reminiscent of Berlin's disciplined rubble recycling. As the German capital saw rescued bricks cleansed of excess mortar, ReStart Ukraine promotes reuse of timber and plastic and pulverizing old concrete for use as aggregate. The organization joins others in resurrecting recollections of the Marshall Plan and soliciting assistance by foreign architects given their talents are shared with but 0.08 percent of Ukrainians, a far cry from the EU's 0.25 percent. Kharkiv, for example, turned to English architect Norman Foster, known for his designs of the glass dome atop the rebuilt German Reichstag and Apple's ring-shaped headquarters in Cupertino, California. As seems inevitable, local jealousies raised their heads. Foster's participation quickly drew criticism, a co-founder of Kharkiv's school of architecture decrying reliance on an outsider whose efforts could constitute "intellectual colonization."[106] Such resistance poses yet another challenge to urban leaders at a time when other matters seem worthier of attention.

World War II's recovered cities demonstrate our aforementioned truth that recovery is more than physical reconstruction alone just as going green means more than innovative technologies, clever designs, white rooftops, and greater reuse of resources. The City of Los Angeles is the core of the United States' second-largest urban area. Unlike many major urban conglomerations, it lacks a dominating central business district (CBD). Instead, a prominent City of Los Angeles CBD has company in many smaller but notable downtowns such as Burbank, Long Beach, and the South Coast Metro area. Though the existence of multiple regional CBDs has been unable to relieve the urban area of its horrendous traffic, it nonetheless does allow for dispersion of commercial enterprises and correspondingly shorter commutes for patrons and workers. Among the options available to Ukrainian urban recovery planners is that of supporting multiple urban cores versus one dominant.

Such macro considerations have micro partners. Twenty-first-century disasters in New York City (Hurricane Sandy, 2012), New Orleans (Hurricane Katrina, 2005), and Fukushima (2011) provide warnings regarding placement of key infrastructure nodes. New Orleans businesses ceased functioning when rising water destroyed computers located on lower building levels. Most of the two-thirds of Manhattan lying below Central Park lost power for three days when Hurricane Sandy's waters rendered an East 13th Street electrical substation inoperable, a substation built on the banks of the East River in a known flood zone. The ill-advised placement of the substation in NYC had company in the back-up generators for two major hospitals in the blacked-out area, components of which sat in flooded basements.[107] The threat to Tokyo resulting from reactors flooding at the Fukushima Daiichi nuclear facility reminds us of the systems nature of urban areas. Though 150 miles distant, Japan's prime minister at the time declared the capital escaped major disaster "by a wafer-thin margin" thanks to valiant efforts by power station employees and providential winds that took radiation out to sea.[108] Author Peter Frankopan cites estimates that between three and eleven trillion dollars-worth of assets are at flood risk in the United States, the spread of numbers depending on the extent and speed of sea level rise. That most damage would be urban is obvious when one considers how many cities lie on or near a coast. All nineteen nuclear reactors in the United Kingdom are in coastal locations. So too are the country's major fossil fuel power facilities in Scotland, Northern Ireland, and Wales.[109] The threat of future Russian aggression is not alone in having a claim on where Ukraine's key physical infrastructure nodes might be better located.

We can add Ukraine's recent past to the above housing and other physical infrastructure challenges. Berlin, Tokyo, and Manila: these immediate post-WWII cities experienced moderate demographic tensions. Sarajevo saw—and unfortunately continues to see—frictions more severe thanks to previously latent ethnic divides being rekindled by opportunistic politicians. Gray clouds of Russian interventionism dim recovery's potential in cities where sympathies expose hearts and too receptive minds to Russian propaganda. Yet overreaction in countering Russian influence has costs. Some in Kyiv favor policies reducing or outright banning access to Russian language material, the first language for 30 percent of their countrymen. Inhibiting use of Russian could enflame rather than mollify social differences. President Volodymyr Zelensky wisely refused to sign a parliamentary bill banning the import of literature from Belarus and Russia.[110] Further arguments against such knee-jerk policies include their being a violation of EU policies (cited by Zelensky as underlying his refusal) and the popular use of Russian in routine social intercourse and Ukrainian literature. Assuming once all-but-frictionless communities will remain unchanged in the wake of war flies in the face of history. Social structures need restoration no less than those physical.

A final note reminds us of the value of addressing resident expectations. Compare the unappreciative behavior of

Sarajevans who refused possession of properties repaired gratis with Hong Kong residents in the months after the colony was freed of Japanese occupation. Publicly sponsored housing was bare bones. So too were the rents. The walls of Hong Kong's sought-after apartments were bare concrete. Bathrooms were communal. The low rents and government landlords' enforcement of standards nonetheless meant demand was high.[111] Ukraine's urban housing policies should provide another case of finding balance. Whatever is erected will long endure. Building quickly and on the cheap will see "temporary" structures standing decades from now, ones costly in terms of maintenance, energy costs, and quality of life. Quality of construction and amenities should seek a sweet spot such that anyone refusing a property earns a new spot at the bottom of a waiting list. Building policies are music scores, government officials conductors. Successful orchestration is harmony when expectations match resources.

■ Health Care

> The Great Chicago Fire of 1871, the Johnstown Flood of 1889, the Galveston hurricane of 1900, and the Great San Francisco Earthquake of 1906.... How the cities emerged afterward depended almost entirely on the quality of their leadership, community spirit, and a little luck.[112]
>
> — John U. Bacon, *The Great Halifax Explosion*

> We know there are no full guarantees when working in an active conflict.[113]
>
> — *Médecins Sans Frontières* (MSF), "Kunduz Hospital Attack"

CHAPTER 6

Seventy-seven years after Manila suffered rats, destroyed medical facilities, and continued deaths from unexploded munitions, residents in retaken Kherson could be forgiven for believing history does indeed repeat itself. Still under sporadic Russian bombardment, residents continue to endure interrupted sleep, hazards from the sky, and fear of the invader's return. These act to weaken bodies, increasing vulnerability to disease no less than similar assaults on mind and physiques did for those who walked Philippine capital streets nearly four score years ago.[114]

The above *Médecins Sans Frontières* (MSF) quote cites another case of history seeming to repeat itself, this one reinforcing the dangers of providing aid in urban environments. The October 3, 2015 bombing by "friendly" forces of the MSF hospital in Kunduz, Afghanistan has company in another mistaken strike in Grenada 32 years before. There the pilot of an aircraft repeatedly asked for and received assurances that the building he planned to engage was occupied by enemy forces. It did have a similarly colored roof. It did otherwise fit the description relayed by the individual below calling for the bombing. The two men were sure the structures they described were the same. They were not. That bombed housed a US military headquarters, members of which were killed. A generation on, MSF reported that American military forces had been informed of their medical facility's location several days before the attack.[115] Mistakes happen in war. They are more likely when the environment is a densely packed urban one. Ensuring—and re-ensuring—military forces are aware of aid provider locations is therefore all the more important.

That is unfortunately no guarantee one or the other opponent will respect the sanctity of humanitarian operations. Russian forces target proscribed urban facilities in Ukraine; International Criminal Court arrest warrants for two Russian commanders accused of directing attacks on electricity facilities in late 2022 and early 2023 are a result.[116] Yet, as with the above-noted placement of artillery in proximity to residential housing, Ukrainian forces are not blame-free. An aid worker observed military personnel moving into a hotel elsewhere, one used by several NGO representatives, thereby making the structure a legitimate Russian target and putting the aid providers at increased risk.[117]

Urban warfare presents medical practitioners with casualty numbers and types less seen elsewhere. Previously noted difficulties associated with identifying urban dead stem not only from their larger numbers when artillery shell or air-delivered munition strikes. As in 9/11 New York City, collapsing buildings and fires can leave little evidence of bodies within. What evidence remains may be so badly damaged as to make identification impossible barring DNA with which to compare. The number of unidentified and unidentifiable deceased increases with the height of a building and severity of attack. Over 40 percent of the estimated 2,753 killed remained unidentified twenty-two years after the 9/11 attacks on the World Trade Center.[118] The nature of injuries differs also. Crush injuries are more common. Thoracic surgeons therefore find themselves in greater demand. The ubiquitous presence of glass means more eye injuries. The 1917 explosion that shook Halifax killed 1,963; another 199—over 10 percent of the number dead—were blinded. Others underwent surgery to remove glass particles from their eyes.[119] Similar injuries killed or wounded individuals when terrorists bombed the US embassy in Nairobi on August 7, 1998. Hearing gunfire as guards engaged the bomb-laden truck outside, curious in nearby buildings ill-advisedly rushed to windows to see. Two hundred twenty-four died with over 4,500 additional wounded. Over a quarter of the 290 treated at Nairobi's Kenyatta National Referral and Teaching Hospital had severe eye injuries.[120]

Kyiv estimates the country's veteran population will number 1.8 million by the war's end. The number increases to five million or 11 percent of Ukraine's pre-war population if we include immediate family members who might also need medical care. War-related trauma—including amputations, burns, spinal injuries, loss of hearing or sight, traumatic brain injuries, and PTSD—will exceed Ukraine's medical capacity even with outside assistance.[121] And that 11 percent fails to account for the many non-veterans or non-veteran family members who have experienced physical, mental, or emotional injury. A significant number of those enduring wounds will require long-term care no less than military veterans. Opportunities for NGOs and other providers to educate medical personnel specializing in amputee rehabilitation, PTSD treatment, and additional recovery-related fields are ripe for exploitation.

Ukraine's heavily mined terrain will continue to kill and wound long after other of this war's killers pause. Some mines are designed to kill. Others seek to maim. The latter ghoulishly capitalize on civilized militaries' commitments to their wounded. The dead can await recovery. All but walking wounded require additional soldiers to evacuate. Wounding also burdens logistical systems in ways the deceased do not, requiring additional transport, fuel, medical personnel, and other forms of support. Society assumes responsibility for continued care long after as rehabilitation continues. The number of limb injuries had already outstripped the number of Ukraine's specialists in the field less than two years after February 2022. Olha Rudneva, head of the Superhumans Center (an organization assisting Ukrainian military amputees), estimated that by September 2023, 20,000 Ukrainians had suffered at least one amputation since February 2022. Only five individuals had formal rehabilitation training for treating those with hand or arm amputations when the Russians attacked that month.[122]

Millions in Debris, Billions of Dollars: Disposing of Unexploded Ordnance in Ukraine

> The Russians had left behind a web of minefields and booby traps. The local police headquarters in Kherson had to be blown up because Ukrainian explosive ordnance teams determined that it couldn't be safely demined.[123]
>
> — Yaroslav Trofimov, *Our Enemies will Vanish*

CHAPTER 6

> Dealing with unexploded ordnance will be a very long-term undertaking for Ukraine.[124]
> — Pehr Lodhammar, Chief, Mine Action Programme Iraq, UN Mine Action Service

The miraculous progress in equipping and treating amputees notwithstanding, some will be unable to obtain work sufficient to support families or themselves. These are among the most tragic of war's legacies.

The Demining and Unexploded Ordnance Disposal Burden

> The job in Ukraine really feels like everything I've done up to this point has been a dress rehearsal. The presence of mines and explosive hazards are not only significantly affecting the Ukrainian economy but the global economy. The economic impact of what we are doing is huge…. Demining in urban areas is like fighting in urban areas. It's vastly more complicated. It's vastly more dangerous. It's very, very intensive and very, very expensive.[125]
> — Paul Heslop, Programme manager, Mine Action, United Nations Development Programme, Ukraine

> There's a rule of thumb in landmine removal: Every day of fighting means another month of demining.[126]
> — A.J. Caughey, "It will take decades to clear Ukraine's landmines"

Ukraine became the most heavily unexploded ordnance-contaminated country on the planet less than two years after the Russian's February 2022 invasion:[127]

Given the vast number of mines over an estimated 67,000 sq. mi. [174,000 square kilometers] of contaminated land, the main question confronting the Ukrainians was how to prioritize the work. Much of the area suspected of being mined by the Russians likely does not have any hazards, says [Paul] Heslop, the head of UN Mine Action in Ukraine. But "if only 1% of that land is actually contaminated, that's still 10 times as much land as is contaminated in Afghanistan," he adds. Deciding where to best deploy scant resources could mean the difference between resolving the problem in years or letting it drag on for decades.[128]

The Danish Refugee Council's estimate of 180,000 square kilometers of unexploded ordnance-contaminated land all but concurs with the number above. It represents an expanse roughly the size of Missouri.[129] Despite the near equality of the two estimates, both involve considerable speculation. Much of Ukraine remains occupied by the invaders. The extent of contamination there is open to supposition.[130] Mining has been a primary factor in fighting becoming a slog during which advances are akin to World War I combat. There is no reason to expect the situation will change appreciably as combat continues. However, focusing on the military effects of unexploded ordnance can cause one to overlook those munitions' dramatic effects on Ukraine's civilians and both the country's and world economy. Much of Europe's richest soil sits unfarmable. The consequences impact European food supplies and those of continents beyond. Cities also suffer contamination. The many tons of artillery shells, rockets, missiles, tank munitions, and more join mines as threats to some six million noncombatants, rural and urban alike.

unexploded ordnance had by November 2023 accounted for 264 innocent lives. Another 830 were maimed. Here again, these numbers do not account for Russian-controlled Ukrainian areas or terrain where heavy fighting continues.[131]

Much of the contamination never had a significant military purpose. Russians routinely emplace sophisticated booby traps when forced to withdraw from an area. Unmarked, they do not discriminate. Victims include soldiers, civilians, and those in Ukraine's national police units responsible for clearing retaken structures (primarily in urban areas). Most of the unexploded ordnance is not improvised explosive devices (IEDs) familiar from Syria, Afghanistan, Iraq, or other recent wars. Factory-made, their sophistication tends to exceed that of munitions encountered during these other conflicts.[132] Experts tasked with neutralization find systems never seen before their appearance in Ukraine.[133] A sense of the sophistication involved is apparent in the following POM-3 mine description by the Collective Awareness to UXO organization:

> The Russian POM-3 Medallion [is] a high-explosive fragmentation (HE-Frag), scatterable, anti-personnel (AP), bounding, self-destruct (SD) landmine designed to be dispersed/ejected from a variety of airborne and ground delivery systems. On dispersal from its container, the landmine is orientated by the use of a parachute. If it lands on soft ground, it is intended to position itself in the ground to a depth of its body height, if it lands on hard ground, six spring-loaded feet deploy and position the landmine in an upright position. Once in a suitable position, a seismic

rod sensor is forced into the ground. The POM-3 uses a proximity (PRX) seismic fuse with a self-destruct time of either 8 or 24 hours. On sensing a suitable seismic signature, the base unit ejects a fragmentation charge into the air that contains metal fragmentation rings that detonate, sending fragmentation out to a lethal radius of 16 meters.[134]

A Ukrainian source provides additional information:

> The mine's electronics unit registers soil vibrations and compares them with characteristics stored in its memory. If the vibrations match those of a person's step and have the amplitude that means the target is within effective range, a signal to detonate triggers the warhead.[135]

Image 5. Russian POM-3 Anti-Personnel Mine[136]

These mines; those artillery shells, bombs, missiles, rockets, rocket-propelled grenades, and tank rounds that never detonated; ammunition stockpiled and then abandoned:

CHAPTER 6

Their impact will be felt for decades across every facet of Ukrainian life. Lives yet to be claimed include those of children yet unborn. Removal, detonation in place, or disarming "will need up to $300 million per year over the next five years, causing the biggest drag on Ukraine's economy," concludes Paul Heslop, mine action program manager for the United Nations Development Programme in Ukraine. "What we're facing in Ukraine is very much what was faced in Europe at the end of World War II" where it took some fifteen years to reach satisfactory levels of deactivation.[137] The World Bank estimates dealing with unexploded ordnance will take one of every fourteen recovery dollars.[138] Heslop and his colleagues in the mine action community know addressing the unexploded ordnance challenge is but one part of the larger Ukrainian recovery system. To get the greatest bang for the buck (sorry), "the UN plans to target mine clearance in Ukraine that will have the biggest economic impact, helping the country to get back on its feet within a shorter timeframe, before dealing with the rest later."[139]

Unexploded Ordnance in Cities: War's Dangerous Lingering Legacy

> Hundreds of thousands of tons of ammunition had been stored in salt mines in the north of Germany.... Several mines blew up, sometimes with loss of life. In the summer of 1946, 9,000 tons of explosives blew up while being removed from a deep mine near Hanover, killing over eighty German and Polish workers.[140]
>
> — Douglas Botting, *From the Ruins of the Reich: Germany 1945-1949*

Another world war bomb found in Schmargendorf: defusing on Thursday[141]
— Berlin.de (The Official Website of Berlin), April 3, 2024

Heslop summarizes the increased challenges when an adversary deploys anti-personnel mines in built-up areas:

> So we are seeing some quite complex munitions being deployed in Ukraine. They are very difficult to clear in an open area…. You put those into an urban context, where you've got rubble and all sorts of distractions and metal contamination, and you're also operating at different levels…on the second or third floor, or on the roof of a building or even down in the cellar. It complicates clearance…. The easiest technique is just to leave them until the battery goes dead, which [for some munitions] can be nine months or so.[142]

Unexploded ordnance other than mines include fired munitions that failed to explode and individual items or stockpiles never fired. Russian munitions' poor detonation rates (as many "have been stored for decades") complicate neutralization according to Heslop. Regarding munitions Russians buy from North Korea, he observes, "I'm pretty sure the North Koreans aren't selling them their newest and latest munitions. The fail rate on [those] munitions is 30 percent-plus."[143] Dangers to children are exceptionally acute as many Russian anti-personnel mines do not look like bullets, artillery shells, or other common munitions. Most are made of plastic, increasing the chances a child might mistake them for toys.[144]

The variety of unexploded ordnance in conjunction with the heterogeneous nature of urban environments makes them especially challenging for deactivation. Detection needs to be capable of locating mines up to 25 centimeters (10 inches) underground in any terrain. Doing so in rubble exposes personnel to risks of shifting debris, collapse (especially when using removal equipment), difficulty of detection given the proliferation of concrete-reinforcing and other metals, and the possibility of unexploded ordnance on multiple levels above, below, and at ground level. Difficulty of detection increases the risk of damaging or destroying equipment in addition to endangering operators' lives. The low quality of Russian munitions aggravates these perils.[145]

Heslop described the magnitude of the problem assuming an average failure rate of 10 percent, not unusual for Russian ordnance:

> [Say you have an urban area] shelled by 1000 to 2000 shells per day. That's 100 to 200 shells per day that are unexploded in that town…. Some of the artillery and bombs fired on towns can go quite deep. [In other wartime locations, we've seen cases where] the bomb goes down right through the building, or the side of the building, and disappears. And the building falls in, not because the bomb exploded, but because of the kinetic energy…. And then you have to dig down into the hole and follow the hole down that snakes around in the ground until you find the bomb and extract the fuse, then destroy it… I think we're going to see a lot of that in Ukraine.[146]

The example goes far in explaining why deminers can find sustaining urban clearance funding difficult. Here the issue is one of metrics. Measuring demining progress in terms of the number of mines removed is all but useless.

Far more valuable than this measure of effort expended is the effect of munitions neutralization. Yet some donors—and deminers—continue to gauge demining effectiveness in terms of effort expended rather than benefits accrued from neutralization. An interviewee who requested anonymity explained the difficulties when donors accept the effort-expended approach as legitimate:

> Ukraine is [motivated by] outputs in terms of demining, so the metrics they use are the number of devices cleared, the number of square meters cleared, the cost per square meter. The Americans were in particular very guilty of cost per square meter in Afghanistan. The Americans would not pay for any clearance that would cost more than $.60/square meter. And I tried to explain to them that when you are dealing with IEDs in an urban area, it's very different from dealing with mines out in a field. You can probably get $.10/square meter in [a rural environment], but if it's in an urban environment it might be $100/square meter. What we use is the impact and the outcome of the clearing.... In the context of Ukraine, you've got a lot of damaged power infrastructure. So maybe you've got a rapid response team going around repairing transformers. You've got a lot of power transformers. If you had the option of clearing one transformer 100% or partially clearing ten transformers [allowing you] to provide electricity to 5,000 families while one transformer provides electricity to only 500 families, which do you do?.... You are leaving contamination behind, but are you not doing more by connecting the 5,000 families to the grid? And this is going to be even more relevant in an urban environment. You've got 100 buildings to clear. Which are going to be the first ones you do? It needs to be bridges. It needs to be power. It needs to be water. It needs to be basic health services.... It needs to be education. And if you want people to return from Western Europe, you

need to make it safe and restore the basic infrastructure or you won't be having people coming back. It's like any town planning activity. It has to be impact per outcome.... So what's the critical infrastructure in that town? How do you address that? How do you prioritize?.... And this is where I think some Ukrainian clearance entities have got it wrong at the moment. They will happily stand up and say, "We've cleared 500 devices today, or 5,000 devices today." But so what? So what? What does that mean? Where are you measuring the impact of clearing that 5,000 devices?[147]

While some Ukrainian unexploded ordnance disposal organizations might lag in recognizing appropriate demining metrics, the same is not true for others. These have wisely

> decided to focus on clearing land with a high economic output, cutting down the driving times to hospitals, restoring power, and rebuilding bridges and schools where real-time data showed it would impact the most people.... They worked together to develop a platform that combined data from government agencies, including the Ministries of Education, Defense, Agriculture, Energy, and Infrastructure, with information like cell phone data from Ukrainian mobile operators, which can reveal how many people are actually living in an area or using certain roads.[148]

It will take a concerted effort to overcome use of "number of mines removed" or "dollars per square meter" as metrics. The millions of unexploded ordnance items now in and yet to arrive in Ukraine make quoting impressive numbers attractive. Such metrics are also far easier to compile and understand, doing much to explain their continued popularity despite their limited utility or misleading character (the latter of which might also explain their attractiveness for groups prioritizing funding rather than quality performance). Claiming the collective quantity of rounds destroyed in an ammunition depot misleadingly inflates effort expended and effect accomplished. Pehr Lodhammar reminds us Ukraine contains "thousands of wrecks of personnel carriers and tanks, many of them carrying ammunition inside. Organizations will want to [claim] the extreme number of mines and unexploded ordnances they have removed because it's going to be thousands and thousands and thousands." He, like others, reminds us, "In Ukraine you need to focus on impact and outcomes."[149]

Paul Heslop introduces additional considerations demonstrating the complexity of demining decision-making. The challenge is in many ways comparable to medical triage. Is the patient (building or plot of land) worth putting on the operating table (decontaminating), or is another with a better chance of survival (greater safety or economic value) the wiser choice? Experts in New York City developed decision guidance regarding hard choices prior to COVID-19's arrival in 2020. It went unused while patients died as officials fearing political backlash dithered.[150] Along these triage-type lines, Heslop observed,

> In Ukraine there are going to be drivers. The first driver will be "Is there a direct human threat if that building is not cleared immediately?...If it's a warehouse on the edge of town...is it there a real need to clear that land quickly?" And then you've got the political dimension. In a city like Mariupol the issue is... "This makes no economic or humanitarian sense to clear it. It makes more sense to build

a new city five miles down the road." But politically can you make that decision?... If you don't rebuild, will you get elected in the next election?... But what will ultimately be the biggest driving factor is the consideration of whether the Ukrainian government thinks it is worth the economic cost of clearing it or accepting the possible cost in lives of not clearing it. That is a very complicated formula that I don't think has ever been properly established in terms of risk management and the risk of doing or not doing something.[151]

Heslop's comments make it clear that unexploded ordnance disposal is inherently speculative in ways beyond the obvious hazards to those doing the decontamination. Less evident: Demining is some of war's most ghoulish work, especially where population density dramatically increases the probability of coming across the deceased. Heslop understatedly recalled the devil's brew of danger and horror deminers confronted during operations in Iraq. Working in buildings confirmed the extent to which "clearing IEDs is dangerous and disagreeable at the best of times. When the munition is on the body of a child, or a woman, or an ISIS corpse, it may be primed, and you've got cats and dogs going eating bodies and dragging things around. It's very unpleasant."[152] This raises the question of procedures regarding how deminers should respond when they come across remains. Longtime deminer Lourie Venter explained that in Ukraine, discovering a body dictates "immediately reporting it to the National Police Unit (NPU) or the military. If none of them are present, it needs to be reported to any government authority. Mine action agencies are not allowed to handle human remains."[153]

Further Specifics Regarding Clearance of Unexploded Ordnance in Ukraine

> Urban clearance is a different ballgame as it has more "moving parts." [Its many challenges need] to be assessed before any person is allowed to clear in or around a structure. In Iraq and Syria, armoured plant equipment like front-end loaders and excavators assisted with the rubble clearance. This is something that I think will start [in Ukraine] after the war more seriously as it is difficult to commit too many resources [when equipment] can be destroyed in the blink of an eye.[154]
>
> — Lourie Venter, Global Clearance Solutions

> When you say it's going to be $40 billion dollars [to address Ukraine's demining in the long term], it attracts a lot of cowboys who think they are going to make a fortune. It also results in rivalries between ministries who want their slice of the pie. I think at the moment there are a lot of people jockeying for their slice of $40 billion. This is where the international community needs to get its shit together.[155]
>
> — Anonymous interview 4

Activities to neutralize mines and other unexploded ordnance constitute one of the several UN functional area clusters in Ukraine. What I will refer to as the mine action cluster is notable for its broad participation and mutual assistance characterizing the community. That said, unexploded ordnance operations are still stove-piped more than is desirable, the primary components being (1) military demining and (2) humanitarian demining. (For brevity, "demining" herein includes all unexploded ordnance operations.) The former encompasses activities supporting mobility operations such as clearing routes for offensive action and enhancing logistical movement. The latter, which is the responsibility of specialized national police units, the United Nations, and various NGO or other civilian organizations, broadly addresses demining for other than military purposes. Though labeled "humanitarian," this effort has a significant, even dramatic, economic impact as referenced earlier.

Ukraine has long experience with demining. Like the United Kingdom, Germany, Belgium, Japan, and any other country whose soil has seen combat since the introduction of explosive munitions, construction and other activities occasionally expose residual ordnance. Russian incursions in 2014 and the post-February 2022 deluge in particular, however, challenged, then overwhelmed, Ukraine's in-house capability to deal with this threat. Convoluted bureaucracy and corruption further limit effectiveness. David McMahon would like to see better orchestration of demining efforts at the highest levels to better avoid duplication and improve effectiveness. He sees promise in recent government initiatives that include willingness to accept input from the UN's experienced demining community. The Ministry of Economy of Ukraine organized a working group bringing together national, UN, and other relevant demining parties. The voluntary nature of its participation, however, means it lacks the teeth needed to impose greater efficiency and, importantly, to ensure communication and mutual understanding of standards by military and humanitarian deminers.[156]

Expediency understandably means military demining often falls short of international humanitarian unexploded ordnance clearance standards. Humanitarian organizations therefore often find it necessary to re-clear areas after military demining. The scope of the challenge and ongoing fighting have thus far prevented better coordination of military and humanitarian unexploded ordnance survey, clearance, and reporting activities despite Ukraine's creating a National Mine Action Authority (NMAA) tasked with that responsibility. The current demining structure exacerbates the challenge as neither the military nor State Emergency Services of Ukraine (SESU) report to the NMAA (though they do assist NMAA in setting priorities). It is a problem with which UN deminers are too familiar. They confronted the same issues during unexploded ordnance operations in Iraq and Syria (and will surely again should they go into in Gaza).[157] The sheer number of organizations supporting demining in Ukraine also complicates orchestration, leading as it does to fragmentation in planning, fundraising, and demining efforts. (The State Special Transport Service for example, focuses specifically on unexploded ordnance clearance of transportation infrastructure, buildings, industrial facilities, and agricultural land.)[158]

Ukraine's economy minister, Yulia Svyrydenko, outlined an ambitious plan to return 80 percent of the country's unexploded ordnance-contaminated land to economic viability in a decade. The government has contracted with the US data analytics organization Palantir to bring together dozens of what were previously separate data sources to identify demining efforts with the greatest economic impact.[159] The agreement provides for cooperation to:

- Digitize humanitarian demining operations and process automation as outlined in the National Mine Action Strategy for the period until 2033;
- Enhance digital capabilities for coordination of land release and assessment, region prioritization, and risk management in mine action;
- Enable assistance, leveraging Palantir's Artificial Intelligence Platform (AIP), for decision-making in mine action;
- Aid demining activity by helping the government analyse and prioritise where to focus its efforts to achieve the best humanitarian and economic outcomes.[160]

The demining community also conducts crowdsourcing by going into communities that have suffered contamination and collecting information on the location, extent, and type of contamination in the area; the number of casualties suffered; and whether there are witnesses to local munitions use, all of which goes into databases.[161] Various mine action organizations instruct members of local populations regarding unexploded ordnance identification, marking, recording, and reporting. Deminers use the results to improve resource allocation. Candidate areas first undergo a non-technical survey. A technical survey ensues, if the extent of contamination merits, to determine whether manual or mechanical clearance is advised.[162] Heslop provided examples of how valuable local input can be for those seeking to determine the nature of local contamination:

> Say there's a building that's collapsed. There's obviously been an explosion in the building…. So we asked, "Are there

any witnesses to what went on here?" And they said, "Yes, the next door neighbor was here when it happened." So we walked across and asked him. And he said, "On the hill over there, a T-72 [Russian tank] fired two rounds into the house, both exploded, and it collapsed." And I asked, "Is that all that happened?" And he said, "Yep." And so obviously the house is smoked, but I could say that there was no contamination because two rounds were fired and both exploded…. Now on another site, four rounds had been fired and three had gone off. So that gives us an indication that somewhere in that house there is an unexploded shell or it has gone through the building and is somewhere behind it. So there are ways to quickly evaluate buildings to determine whether they are contaminated.[163]

The value of this step-by-step approach is hard to overstate. Heslop further observes Ukraine is now a country with two types of terrain where its ground has been touched by the war: that which is possibly contaminated and that which is confirmed as contaminated. Much of the former is later found to be uncontaminated. The faster deminers can confirm status, the faster an area can regain its economic utility. A portion of contaminated areas will be "very, very heavily contaminated," some to the extent common sense dictates it being fenced, marked, and left untouched for the foreseeable future.[164] The combined inputs from residents, survey teams, and those responsible for demining go far in hastening determination of what land falls into which category.

Humanitarian deminer interactions with the Ukrainian public are not all take and no give. Mine action organizations began conducting explosive ordnance risk education (EORE; thank you, A.A. Milne) almost immediately after the February 2022 invasion. Urban and rural dwellers alike are anxious to have their communities demined; they are in many cases unable to work until clearance takes place.[165] Some do not wait. Deminers have found homeowners making repairs to properties in areas not yet made safe. Some pick up live munitions and bring them to those conducting unexploded ordnance disposal. Such actions demonstrate the importance of EORE. Additional means of instruction include stenciling messages on food sacks or other forms of aid, leaflets, and—thanks to the proliferation of cellphones—text and social media posts. School instruction from the age of six seeks to warn the youngest of unexploded ordnance dangers. Pehr Lodhammar believes "education is where we have saved the most lives." But EORE is not a "fire and forget" undertaking. He went on to commiserate that people's caution wanes over time. Others simply ignore cautions.[166] Nor are members of the general public alone in needing training and reminding. Whether an area has been declared completely decontaminated, cleared only sufficiently to allow access, or awaits deminers' attentions, utility workers restoring power lines, engineers repairing roads or bridges, and workers removing rubble all need to know how to operate at minimum risk to themselves, others, and their equipment.[167]

These well-conceived and relatively well-orchestrated initiatives can have significant payoffs. Heslop is optimistic collective demining efforts could result in eliminating 75-80 percent of the economic hardship imposed by unexploded ordnance in the next three to five years (barring, obviously, those communities suffering renewed introduction of munitions). His positivity recognizes pragmatism has to drive clearance operations. Echoing the need to focus on effects rather than raw effort, he reiterated the example of contaminated power stations. Clearing just the small amount of land necessary to make repairs while fencing and marking areas left for later clearance is the logical way ahead. Greater effectiveness can reduce but not negate the great costs involved. The assessed $300 million thought needed in the next five years only marks a first step toward an estimated ultimate price of over $37 billion.[168] Such numbers have to raise red flags in terms of potential corruption and bureaucratic management capacity. McMahon emphasizes the importance of competitive processes when awarding contracts. They are something his overarching organization (the United Nations Office for Public Services) emphasizes. Encouragingly, Kyiv has expressed interest.[169]

Closing Thoughts on Unexploded Ordnance Neutralization

> Full recovery from war is impossible. All wars leave indelible marks. They change the course of history. But something close to full recovery is possible. This can take decades for foundations like infrastructure, and generations for the people impacted by conflict.[170]
>
> — Team Zee Feed, "How Long Does It Take a City To Recover From War? Decades"

> From the mine action agencies I know are working in Ukraine, we all work together. We all trust each other.[171]
>
> — Lourie Venter, Global Clearance Solutions

CHAPTER 6

One would hope the challenges associated with demining's technical aspects were enough. That unexploded ordnance are proving sources of corruption and bureaucratic infighting as well as Ukrainian soldier and innocents' deaths frustrates and disgusts the more honest of their countrymen is understandable. Taras Kachka, the deputy minister for agriculture, estimates 40 percent of the grain harvested as of early 2024 is "black grain," that on which farmers avoid paying taxes to Kyiv. Dodges range from barter exchanges and unreported cash sales to sly international dealings and falsely claiming the land from which a harvest came is unfarmable due to mine contamination. Getting caught in the lie of false contamination is a low risk given the extent of agricultural land actually polluted. The damage done to Ukraine's coffers is in contrast real, and doubly so. In addition to profiting on black grain, farmers whose lands are unfarmable (or claimed as unfarmable) can partake of tax breaks. It is a policy requiring reevaluation and better policing. Dishonest farmers are in a sense doubling their harvest. They sell undeclared products while also using tax breaks to pay even less on what sales they do report. More sophisticated cheats falsify grain export documents to show taxes paid that never were before hiding profit in foreign accounts. Farming is not the only commercial sector shorting the country, but their actions are undeniably significant given agriculture accounted for 40 percent of Ukraine's export revenue pre-early 2022.[172]

Building on his earlier remarks, Heslop noted Ukraine's tribulations provide lessons for wars still to come:

> I've probably worked in nearly every mine-affected country in the last 30 years, and this is the combination of all previous countries' experience with the Ukrainian love of innovation and technology…. We're going to see a fundamental change in the way that humanitarian demining is done in the next three years in Ukraine that will affect mine action the whole world over.[173]

Whether Ukraine's technical demining advances also advise management and organization practices is a different issue, however. The country's still-too-Soviet-like bureaucracy is sand in the gears of government efficiency both nationally and locally. First, competing and stovepiped ministry operations such as those in defense and interior deny healthy synergies in demining and other sectors. It is a problem unlikely to find resolution as long as funding for unexploded ordnance operations remains dispersed. Independent monitoring to guard against misdirection of funds would be a prerequisite if centralized oversight falls to an organization like Ukraine's National Mine Action Authority (NMAA). Supervision could consist of a combined Ukrainian-international body, the latter including subject-matter experts and donors. For example, as of early 2024, the Swiss began requiring recipients of their demining systems to meet specified training standards. That most donors now appear to understand the importance of appropriate, effects-reflective metrics is reassuring. That others—and some Ukrainian governmental bodies—remain unconvinced is otherwise. Vetting of demining organizations to avoid inefficiency and waste is reportedly effective in the humanitarian arena where the UN applies procedures proven in other theaters.[174]

CHAPTER 6

That there appear to be less rigorous standards elsewhere is troubling. Such is the case when organizations hired by farmers understandably impatient to return their lands to operation avoid screening. These various shortcomings will continue to hamstring both warfighting and recovery efforts. One frustrated observer noted

> the mine problem, the unexploded ordnance problem all over Ukraine, is so cross-sectorial that it affects every aspect of recovery…. What Ukraine needs is a centralized database for all the land in Ukraine that tells how that land was used, how that land could be used, and what's the impact of that land being denied…. Though Ukraine has been an independent country for years, they still have a problem with the Soviet mindset [that hinders such effective responses]. I'll give you an example. We were approached a few months ago by the Ministry of Energy saying "We've got 10,000 sites that need to be assessed." And I said "Yes, we can probably help you with that. Give me the grids." And they said, "We can't give you the grids because that's classified. If the Russians get it, they will target it."… That's just absolutely classical Ukraine. Every time you find a solution to a problem, they find a problem to that solution.[175]

Two final points merit emphasis. Donors and Ukrainians alike would be wise to reconsider how they view demining. It is not solely a humanitarian undertaking. It is instead additionally, even primarily, an economic one. Giving economic concerns primacy well-served both donor (the United States) and recipients of post-World War II aid (in the form of the Marshall and other plans). Humanitarian deminers will not lessen their concerns for public safety should economic considerations be given greater weight. An expanded and more systems-aware approach would address not only immediate beneficiaries' welfare. It could also incorporate second and higher-order benefits beyond, economic considerations included. The previous logic of decontaminating a power station 100 percent and thereby aiding 500 or demining only sufficiently to permit the immediate return of ten stations to operation and thereby provide electricity to 5,000 applies here. Better to provide to-the-tap water to one thousand homes or delay that relative luxury while supplying ten factories with water needed to provide wages for ten thousand new employees whose taxes will bolster local economies?[176]

Second, Ukraine is ultimately responsible for solving its recovery problems, demining amongst them. Bureaucrats being what they are, it is likely beyond the pale to hope the Ministries of Defense, Interior, Economy, Digitization, and others will set aside jealousies and hunger for their slice of the budget pie barring reorganization of the federal government, firmly gripping corruption at the highest echelons, and finding leaders willing to objectively put country before fiefdom.[177] Unlike many aspects of recovery that should and are fast-tracking alongside wartime management, addressing major but necessary revisions to the government in Kyiv may have to await more peaceful times. Even then progress will be better measured in degrees than absolutes. After all, the world's leading national government bureaucracies have yet to conquer inefficiencies born of jealousy and infighting.

CHAPTER 6

The Mire of Collaboration

Manuel Roxas insisted that "errors of the mind rather than the heart must be forgotten and forgiven." Elpidio Quirino [President of the Philippines from 1948-1953] gave clemency to collaborators and enemy soldiers despite the massacre of his family in 1945.[178]

— Filipinas Heritage Library, "Manila Reborn: An Exhibit on the postwar reconstruction of a city"

Working in liberated communities was always interesting.... People were afraid to open their doors. That lack of trust lingered. People were rightfully afraid because you never know the bias of those knocking on the door.[179]

— Anonymous interview 1

Many people were very reluctant to give their names. A group of soldiers just down the road explained that while most pro-Russian locals are staying very quiet, Ukrainian patriots here may want to keep their head down to avoid being targeted.[180]

— Igor Kossov, "Pro-Russian sympathies make life harder for soldiers, cops in Kupiansk district"

Perhaps nothing presents as divisive and politically difficult a quagmire as the issue of collaboration with the enemy. Perhaps no topic involves so many contrasting interpretations of justice. Dealing with Philippine collaboration influenced the election for the country's first president. The bargains made, as often behind the political curtain as before, solidified domination by the Philippine elite that remains today. Part of the blame can be laid at the feet of a US government choosing to sidestep the issue before granting independence in 1946. Familiar from our example of

Kharkiv, tensions arose when contrasting the behaviors of those fleeing before the Japanese occupiers arrived, others refusing to participate in Manila's governing thereafter, and individuals taking positions under the occupying regime.

Jose P. Laurel chose the last, assuming the presidency when the Japanese granted Filipinos notional independence in autumn 1943. Laurel subsequently became embroiled in another of cities' wartime conundrums: how to deal with black marketeering. It was a challenge that put him squarely in the middle in terms of his countrymen's hunger and harshness of the occupier regime:

> The black market became the only market as food grew increasingly scarce. Most Filipinos, especially the urban dwellers, discovered that their daily business was the struggle for physical survival…. Eventually Laurel had to make bribery, black marketeering in food, and "racketeering" crimes punishable by death.[181]

Laurel asked Manuel Roxas to serve as food czar in the spring of 1944 as US forces advanced toward the island of Luzon from the south. Roxas accepted, stating

> "no Filipino can decline, under the circumstances now obtaining, to do what lies in his power to ameliorate the suffering of thousands of people due to the insufficiency or maldistribution of food supplies." Roxas reversed the existing restrictive policy in favor of one in which food could move freely and be sold at prices more competitive with the black market. Simultaneously, an effort was made to find hidden caches and prosecute speculators relentlessly.[182]

Laurel relieved Roxas of his position when food shortages and black market profiteering continued. The return of the Americans in 1944 muddied the waters in terms of dealing with senior officials who had served under the Japanese. Roxas was considered by many Filipinos as a leading collaborator. He was also a man the commander of US forces retaking the Philippines, General Douglas MacArthur, considered a particularly close friend according to MacArthur biographer D. Clayton James. Roxas had also served on the general's staff in 1941-42.[183] In his study on post-WWII collaboration in the Philippines, David Steinberg wrote that MacArthur believed "Roxas was innocent [of collaboration], that Roxas had helped the guerrilla movement, and that he personally was able to speak for Roxas' character." The general's support was key during the ensuing presidential campaign, one Roxas won while others similarly serving under the occupiers remained imprisoned awaiting charges of collaboration or treason.[184] Roxas himself later became an overt defender (and eventual pardoner) of persons who, like him, had served in the occupiers' government and could claim membership in the Philippines' long powerful and politically dominant elite. Steinburg summarized the lasting consequences:

> The elite survived. Incorporating into its membership the most articulate and powerful of its nonradical critics, it sapped the strength of its guerrilla opposition by assimilation.... To achieve this fusion, which has dominated postwar history in the Philippines, a quarantine of silence has been placed around the collaboration question. Guerrillas and collaborators have studiously ignored this tender spot as a prerequisite for permitting the collaboration wound to close naturally.... The new blood of a new generation was thought to be a healing agent. Now, as collaboration fades into the past, the scar is barely visible to the eye.[185]

Roxas declared blanket pardons for collaboration in 1948, explaining those cooperating with the Japanese "did everything within their power to prevent the perpetration by the enemy of acts of atrocity and savagery against their fellow-countrymen."[186]

France took a quite different approach when dealing with participants in the Vichy regime during Germany's WWII occupation. While the worst cases of collaboration were triable as treason, French law initially lacked an effective way to address lesser instances. Bringing no pride to the country's legal system, the solution was to create the retroactive crime of "national indignity." Further dubious were requirements that jurors in collaboration trials be individuals who had "never ceased to demonstrate their patriotic sentiments," resulting in a dominating influence by former resistance members. Trials were frequently conducted in an atmosphere of virulent anti-collaboration that compromised exercise of justice. Estimates vary, but 10,000 is a frequently quoted number for the number executed as collaborators, some after sentencing, the majority due to extrajudicial action. Raymond Aron, who later became one of the country's leading intellectuals, was originally vehemently anti-collaborationist. He assumed a more nuanced view just before the most famous collaboration trial, that of Marshal Philippe Pétain. For Aron, the difficulty in judging those who had served in the Vichy government was

> that the consequences of the acts had almost nothing in common with the intentions of the actors.... It is not impossible that the armistice and Vichy, for two and a half years, attenuated the rigours of the occupation. In

interposing the French administrative apparatus between the Gestapo and the French population, the policy...procured for the 40 million French who found themselves hostages multiple although mediocre advantages that are as difficult to quantify as to deny.[187]

In France as elsewhere, passions to punish lessened over time. The government granted general amnesty in 1953.[188]

That officials retain or re-assume government positions under an occupier should not surprise. Experienced leaders and staff are invaluable to an occupier as the US found after World War II in Japan, Germany, and (largely by exception) again in Iraq in the early years of the 21st century. Individuals gained these standings thanks to experience, talent, political connections, persevering in elections, or—very likely—some combination of the four. That they chose to collaborate suggested inherent moral depravity in some minds. We have seen the situation is not so straightforward. The mire becomes murkier yet when the challenge involves tackling the spiraling conundrum of what legitimately entails collaboration, how to deal with collaborators, and what can be done to placate the ill-will felt by others who refused to cooperate with an occupier. Ukraine's leaders will also have to address disruptions created by Russia's forced introduction of rubles; imposition of occupier passports; educational, psychological, and social influences of Russian propaganda; and other residuals associated with occupier policies.

Those conundrums regarding collaboration outside Kharkiv spotlighted the difficulty of distinguishing what we might call malicious collaborators versus maintenance collaborators, helpful but far from distinct categories. Oversimplifying, the first denotes persons supporting occupier agendas that deliberately undermine the absent legitimate authority. In contrast, maintenance collaborators provide services essential to their community regardless of who is in charge. Their political biases might favor one side or the other or be agnostic in terms of who is in control. Teachers who continue to teach, medical personnel who continue to treat, and city government authorities who continue to perform their duties are among those in this latter category. What they do relieves the occupier of otherwise having to commit manpower to accomplish the same tasks. Alternatively, the occupier might instead leave those tasks unmet or under-resourced. The consequences of not cooperating are readily imagined: children untaught, patients not treated, and vital services not provided.

Kupiansk was a Kharkiv Oblast town of some 27,000 in 2022. Its case is revealing. One observer claimed the Russians threatened the mayor with an ultimatum of "either you surrender the city or we destroy the city and kill everybody." There was no Ukrainian military force in the vicinity at the time. The major surrendered and informed residents it was permissible to accept Russian aid. The same observer blamed Western Ukrainian nationalists for imposing unrealistic standards once Kyiv reassumed control. One such demand directed that only Ukrainian be spoken in stores. "People continued to speak Russian," the same individual observed, not because they were pro-Russia, but because that was their language of upbringing and family life.[189]

CHAPTER 6

An August 2023 article in *The Kyiv Independent* presents an alternative view, one further reflecting the muddled environment of collaboration accusations, counter-accusations, rumor, innuendo, and difficulty of determining ground truth...if "truth" exists under such circumstances. The article cites interviews "with dozens of soldiers, police officers, and civilians around Kupiansk" who claimed "many of the local residents that remain are pro-Russian" though estimates of the actual number varied widely.[190] The mayor at the time of the occupiers' arrival reportedly "welcomed the Russians into his town, joining their occupation authority and aiding them with housing, transportation, and other needs, until Kupiansk was liberated in September 2022." The article went on to imply that distrust runs deep in the aftermath of Russia's departure. Divides include those between Ukrainian soldiers and local police, the former accusing the latter of interfering with military efforts to identify local casualties. Senior Kupiansk police investigator Andrii Subotin refuted the accusation. Whatever the elusive truth, difficulty in parsing rumor, wanton accusation, and fact sheds further light on the complexity of equitably dealing with collaboration.

The combined number of collaboration-related cases opened by the National Police of Ukraine and the State Bureau of Investigations totaled 4,593 as of early June 2023. Charges ranged from high treason to "aiding and abetting the aggressor state." Conviction's consequences include bans on holding public office, fifteen years imprisonment, and confiscation of property. Ukrainians who fled as Russians withdrew have been charged in absentia. Most departed with the occupiers. Some are thought to have gone elsewhere in Europe. Ukraine compiled an international extradition list to share with Interpol.[191]

■ The Other Mire: Corruption

> You are capable of many illegalities when your teeth are chattering with cold. Without heat you are only half a person.[192]
>
> — Ruth Andreas-Friedrich, *Battleground Berlin*

> I can also tell you that Ukraine looks like Europe but is like Europe at several different stages of its development, over a century or so. High tech meets the gilded age of Europe in a sense.[193]
>
> — Patrick Christian email to author

War imposes a new moral order. Some refuse to sacrifice ethical standards even under the most extreme circumstances as evident in Tokyo's judge Yamaguchi Yoshitada and teacher Kameo Hideshirô's choice to starve rather than partake of the black market. Author Peter Lippman suggests these men are the exception. He posits that war's social evils do not end when fighting stops:

> War starts with crimes and ends with crimes. These crimes are not limited to violence against people; just as rife is the practice of corruption, because law disappears during wartime…. A new set of rules takes over; in the course of a war, the culture of corruption becomes institutionalized, and it is difficult to extirpate the practice afterward.[194]

CHAPTER 6

Diaries describing Berlin life after WWII tell of people taking items from amidst the city's rubble. Ruth Andreas-Friedrich of Berlin was one. She observed,

> without a doubt, turning away from the law is easier than returning to it. We too, despite all efforts, keep catching ourselves interpreting the question of mine or yours rather carelessly. As long as there is nothing to buy, as long as all over Berlin goods worth millions are rotting in the streets, the struggle to remain an upright citizen remains unrewarding.[195]

Some London residents fell prey to the same loosening of morals, shocking others who expressed

> considerable surprise…over the amount of looting in bombing areas. It hasn't reached large-scale proportions, but the British are always surprised at any increase in lawlessness. The matter is further complicated by the fact that many of the articles picked up from the bombed houses are of little intrinsic value, a book or a piece of ribbon, or a bucketful of coal, that sort of thing.[196]

Such by and large minor corruption of morals, however, tends to be a transient phenomenon, Lippman's contrary remark notwithstanding. "Lesser" ill-behavior tends to give way to previous norms once authorities restore basic services and access to necessities. More troublesome is large-scale corruption that has greater and longer-lasting effects. Concerns regarding this scale of corruption dominate Congressional visits to Ukraine just as they do during virtually any major US overseas contingency involving aid dollars. Afghanistan and Iraq are recent examples.

Rampant corruption resulted in thefts of millions, depriving significant numbers of intended recipients (more on this later). But what of practices having a traditional social basis in another culture? Comments by two interviewees with extensive experience in aid environments cause one to ponder whether unconditionally imposing Western standards constitutes a best practice or whether some adaptation is called for:

> Much of what we consider corruption Ukrainians do not. Ukraine is a very high-contact culture. Personal relationships really matter. So things like the tender process are an anathema to some of them. If you know somebody, why would you not simply go with someone you know and trust?[197]

> The US has perceptions that always put the rule of law on top. That's often not the case on the ground. A lawyer in Ukraine explained how things work there. Something was okay as long as "it's not illegal." That was the standard. Many Western NGOs don't know how to operate in that environment.[198]

It can similarly be said that many Western governments don't know how to operate in these environments, the standard often being a contract is put out to bid with the lowest priced quality response receiving the work. It is a system that has millions of times proved itself effective. When operating properly, it is also a way of reducing opportunities for "sweetheart deals" that lead to higher project costs. There are inherent assumptions in these lowest-bidder award systems, including the belief that there are sufficient capable contractors to provide legitimate competition and that officials can prevent responders from striking deals behind the scenes. There are also inefficiencies. Drafting tenders and putting them out for bids takes time and money. Dealing with regulatory constraints such as providing veteran or minority preferences, requiring contracts be balanced between ethnic groups, and ensuring awardees are sufficiently "buying American" or not buying from proscribed sources increases costs and can lower deliverable quality. Alternatively, awarding contracts to familiar organizations having previously shown themselves able to produce at acceptable levels reduces time to award, issues with subcontractors, and supply chain challenges. Perhaps allowing use of familiar and proven contractors whose bids fall within a predesignated cost range merits consideration in some environments.

Non-competitive (or less competitive) processes undoubtedly can result in corrupt practices. The most obvious include kickbacks for officials making the awards and ensuring family or friends receive preferential treatment. But such awards are not inherently corrupt as seems to be the underlying assumption in US regulatory policies and official visitors' minds. Further, demanding adherence to US or other Western procedures can deny local contractors access to work. Even representatives from countries familiar with the US can find American regulations and procedures bamboozling. Such was the case when the United Kingdom's senior civilian representative in Basra, Iraq—Hilary Synnott—received guidance from the US Coalition Provisional Authority in early 2004. The US State Department's Sherri Kraham embarked on a PowerPoint presentation which purported to explain new rules that we should follow in tendering, contracting, and accounting for our project expenditure. It was an impressively professional performance and was followed by total silence.... So far as we were concerned [Sherri] might have descended from the planet Vulcan.... The message to us was incomprehensible.... I observed that we British unfortunately had no experience of America accounting procedures, and hence we were unfamiliar with the various regulations and acronyms to which Sherri had referred.... Therefore, it might prove difficult for us to confirm to the [US] Office of Management and Budget's wishes.[199]

A quote from an interviewee provides support for another extreme: Accepting some level of what might be thought the unacceptable...at least in the immediate term:

> Many contractors in Ukraine subcontract with multi-service vendors with which they have longstanding relationships. Most countries run on such informal systems.... Corruption is an everyday part of life in Ukraine as it is in much of Eastern Europe. Corruption makes things happen easier and quicker. It's something that's ingrained in the culture. It's not in anyone's interest to change that.... Corruption hasn't really been taken up by the government. People get removed, but they move on and still have their connections. You don't really hear of anyone being punished for it. If you start punishing, the country will grind to a halt.[200]

Both viewpoints merit comment in light of corruption challenges confronting Ukraine. The United Kingdom is hardly a developing nation unfamiliar with sophisticated financial guidance. As was the case in Basra, unilateral imposition of procedures convenient for the senior partner is unhelpful. It is also inefficient and could breed resentment. Though a couple of decades have passed since Synnott's experience, and therefore the US is hopefully now better attuned to coalition interactions, the misstep is interesting in light of a recognized parallel best practice. Outsiders wishing to assist another government's authorities have long understood matching adviser assignments to the existing structure of the bureaucracy receiving help is the way to go. Imposing the helpers' structure on the recipient is not. In instances like that confronted by Synnott, working out mutually compatible procedures ought to be standard practice. Similarly, being open to reasonable established local contracting approaches can enhance delivery effectiveness and speed without forgoing efforts to reduce corruption. Compiling information on local practices and monitoring average costs for given types of work is akin to compiling intelligence. Taking steps to prevent or punish egregious practices constrains abuses. No less obvious are the benefits of introducing acceptable standards of commercial intercourse.

Unquestioning imposition of Western standards might constitute faulty practice. Yet so is unqualified tolerance of malicious practices. Change is justified when a structure or existing procedures contain inherent flaws. Several individuals with experience in Ukraine are favorably impressed by the Zelensky government's apparent willingness to address what are unacceptable forms of corruption. Yet removal of perpetrators alone (in cases where the individual is in government) equates to tolerance. This is especially true for those in senior positions, individuals likely independently wealthy, possessing considerable commercial influence or ownership, or otherwise able to access comfortable fallback positions, ones perhaps offering compensation better than was available in their just-lost government role (though without the same opportunities for illicit gain). Simply removing such wrongdoers qualifies as no more than a slap on the wrist. The US is not free of de facto oligarchs, but they are not completely free of punishment threats. Linking continued aid to real punishment addresses both immediate and longer-term anti-corruption challenges. Penalties involving substantial financial confiscation, barring further commercial intercourse, and jail time would show Ukraine's government is serious and other than an oligarchic lapdog. There is admittedly the danger this stick could become a wrongly-wielded political implement. The possibility suggests that revised policies would require careful drafting, judicious checks, and—perhaps—outside monitors as long as international aid is forthcoming. The guidance seems clear: Outsiders should work within established structures and procedures to the extent feasible while encouraging (or demanding) tailoring when acceptance of the status quo would sustain unacceptable levels of corruption or other shortfalls. Concurrently, Ukrainian adoption of select Western practices could be a cure for some of the country's continued ailments. Outsider hesitation to invest in the growing Ukrainian green energy economy is perhaps hindered by that sector's potentially being unduly influenced by the earlier noted DTEK, the country's largest private energy company, one owned by its richest oligarch.[201] Stricter (and enforced) financial regulations and exposure to greater scrutiny available via entry into European or American stock markets could better align Ukrainian and Western standards to the former's benefit.

Determining what composes corruption can sometimes be difficult enough much less developing successful programs to mitigate its practice. An anonymous commentator related that a medical doctor in one of Ukraine's larger cities has a number of rich patients, this based on a favorable reputation as practitioner. As doctors tend to earn less than those in the US, the physician occasionally receives gifts from appreciative patients, an example being a fur coat.[202] The gift-giving is voluntary. Such situations in other contexts could present a problem for anti-corruption officials. As we will see below, one of four types of illicit exchanges associated with Berlin black marketeering was "underhand trade in which a party demands some additional good before providing a desired product or service for normal compensation." Acceptance of gifts in the government sector is generally proscribed in the West to avoid the appearance of corruption (and, likely, the virtual impossibility of determining whether the giving is completely devoid of coercion. Accepting token gifts, a meal not exceeding a given value or a plaque after presenting a speech, for example, is allowed. Worthy of note: Expectations in terms of corruption are not the same in the private sector, from which our example comes.) Not regulating gift-giving permits prospective contractors to shower officials awarding contracts with what would constitute bribes. Goods or services can be in short supply during and in the aftermath of a conflict. Food can be one such as was the case in Berlin, Tokyo, and Manila. Those examples demonstrate building materials are frequently another. In these cases, taking gifts in addition to standard payments has been, could be, and often would be a means of obtaining illicit priority for delivery. Parsing corruption, as with collaboration, tasks the wisdom of Solomon. Knowing that some activities have proven particularly attractive for corruption in the past, however, could somewhat ease the monitoring task. From Peter Lippman:

> In a "transitional" society recovering from the devastation of war and converting to a privatized economy, there are obvious venues for lucrative grand-scale transactions. These opportunities include road construction, corporate privatization, and privatization of state-owned land. In each of these areas a tightly knit group of public officials makes decisions that make all the difference to the profiteers…. It is generally the case that international officials are more comfortable ignoring high-end criminality—and conducting political negotiations with the kingpins—than confronting corruption. Periodic exhortations from international officials to combat corruption most often amount to mere rhetoric.[203]

Lippman's observations suggest certain sectors—and related government positions—merit special attention as habitual founts of corruption. As for his observation regarding international officials' negligence (dare we say laziness?), several solutions suggest themselves. These include more rigorous screening of potential officials, strengthening international and national laws in place allowing for recovery-plus of illicitly acquired funds from the corrupt, and better manning and financing anti-corruption organizations. We recall from our discussion of Sarajevo that crooked politicians, war profiteers, and militia leaders regularly supplemented their incomes via black marketeering. Failing to take on this challenge as war rages opens the door to proliferation of corruption once peace returns. It also allows criminals to solidify their positions during war's tumultuous times when limiting corruption is but one of many challenges in a chaotic environment. One senior Serbian criminal in Bosnia-Herzegovina created phantom companies, put legally-registered assets under the names of colleagues and family members, and arranged to have bad loans covered by the Republika Srpska government. His activities were among those involving "massive transfer of wealth from ordinary citizens to all manner of profiteers, war criminals, and political leaders commenced during the war and continued in the postwar period."[204] British officials reassuming London's responsibility for post-WWII Hong Kong managed prices and supply with an eye to interdicting corruption's worst, finding

> prices fell as supplies enabled entrepreneurs to restart and then to compete against each other.... Price control was applied to a narrow range of goods.... It was clear that the objective was to manage constrained supply and to set prices to encourage increased supply.... The government also imported key staples such as rice and distributed these at below cost in an attempt to hold inflation down.[205]

So-called petty corruption might seem of minor consequence. In countries where such low-level corruption is a pre-conflict norm, however (Ukraine being one of them), police expectations of a bribe in lieu of their issuing a traffic ticket and other practices by minor bureaucrats undermine government legitimacy, hinder genuine commercial enterprise, and risk leading to toleration of broader illicit acts such as avoiding or cheating on taxes. One could be sympathetic to the last. Having had to pay a bribe to get an appointment with an official, obtain a driver's license, or acquire another service, a resident might well assume he or she has already paid "taxes" a legitimate government would prevent.

In the later years of the 20th century, New York City made considerable strides in addressing its crime rate by introducing zero tolerance for illegal activity. Ukraine has taken similar initial steps to address petty corruption. Traffic tickets are now paid online at the point of violation; police officers carry a portable payment device tying payment to offenders' licenses. Similar online apps enable passport, car insurance, home title, and other transactions.[206] Imperfect, perhaps (that policeman can still offer not to write a ticket for a bribe less than the fine). But obvious efforts to redress what have been long-tolerated practices mean men and women on the street have become more likely to report corruption.[207] That Ukraine is already a digital society eases public anti-corruption support.[208]

Incompetent or corrupt bureaucrats are seeds from which broader corruption sprouts. Canadian Army General Rick Hillier recalled a Ukrainian officer he served with during a UN tour. Hillier's recollection makes it easy to understand why others less honest might turn to unethical practices in response to bureaucratic ineptitude or dishonest docking of wages, both too common during such contingencies:

> The Ukrainian officer was Major Andre Ponakarovski, a prince of a man and an excellent leader who had adapted from the Warsaw Pack system to the UN easily. He was completely dependable but, after eighteen months in theatre, needed a break, so we sent him home for three weeks' leave with his family over Christmas 1995. He departed, and four days later, when I went into the Operations Centre there he was. He could not afford financially to stay at home. Ukraine stopped his UN pay while he was there, and he had received no Ukrainian military pay for six months. As he said, if his three daughters wanted food and shoes, he had to stay and work.[209]

It is encouraging that initial Ukrainian government anti-corruption initiatives have made some, if insufficient, progress in addressing corruption at higher echelons. Some in these and private sector organizations are taking steps on their own. Ukrainian state-owned weapons and military hardware manufacturer Ukroboronprom revamped its senior manager selection process. Candidates now undergo screening by fifteen-person committees and are asked to take a polygraph test seeking to determine past corrupt behavior or an affinity for same. Questions can be blunt. They include "Have you ever been given money in an envelope? Did you ever take bribes? Do you have income other than your official one? Have you ever done anything that resulted in other people receiving bribes?" The initiatives come none too soon. Above-noted progress notwithstanding, an October 2023 *Christian Science Monitor* article reported many Ukrainians consider corruption a greater security threat than possible Russian use of nuclear weapons.[210] The US government has not hesitated to make public its view on the importance of Ukrainian anti-corruption efforts. An August 2023 US State Department memo bluntly announced, "Reforms in the energy sector, a bastion of corruption and oligarchic control, are essential to cementing Ukraine's European integration."[211]

Corruption at oblast, city, or lower government levels receives less attention than that at the federal. Interviewee Erik C. Kramer provides a Kyiv resident's perspective in this regard:

> I was here in 2016 for a year working out of the embassy…. Corruption back then was more in my face. I'll give you a couple of examples. I had to pay a bribe to get a gym membership. Twice when I went to see different museums, they were closed in the middle of the day. But the guy standing there said, "Hey, if you pay this much, you'll be able to come in." I have yet to have that happen this time around, and I'm even more integrated into society than I was before…. However, in business interactions I've seen it more frequently. There was a contract I was working on. My organization [sought to train elements of the] Ukrainian armed forces. There was a general officer in the Ministry of Defense who sent an intermediary asking for a facilitation fee of $10,000. I said "No way-no how."[212]

Kramer has found US military aid provides a "ray of hope" when it comes to corruption. Given all the "billions upon billions of dollars in equipment we've sent over here…it's seen as bad form to steal that equipment. There's almost a paranoia about it…. In my purview, they are being good stewards." Unfortunately, Kramer also found that awareness of the scrutiny associated with Western-donated equipment means it is at times used sparingly or not at all out of concern its damaging or loss in combat could be construed as misuse. He further observed the US Department of Defense sent a long-term inspector general corruption monitoring team to Ukraine in late 2023 or early 2024 and several contracts seeking to aid Ukraine in combating corruption were out for bid at the time. Kramer went on to identify potential tensions regarding Ukraine's relationship with China. Ukraine joined the Belt and Road Initiative in 2017 prior to Zelensky's 2019 assumption of the presidency. China took over Russia's status as Ukraine's number one trading partner even before the re-invasion of 2022 (though as a group, the EU remains larger).[213] Kyiv would obviously like to see less Chinese support for Russia, but they at the same time face challenges due to dependencies on the country's products, e.g., it is difficult to build drones without Chinese-made components.[214] China, not known for its above-board commercial dealings, could be a force working against anti-corruption initiatives.

■ The Specter of Ethnic Conflict

> Kharkiv is a Russian-speaking city, and people here used to be rather loyal to the Russian Federation. But now the situation has turned 180 degrees. The east of Ukraine has become more radically anti-Russian than the west of the country. There is a reason. It's one thing to see the horrors that they inflict on TV, and it's another to live them in real life.[215]
>
> — Mayor of Kharkiv Ihor Terekhov as quoted in
> *Our Enemies will Vanish*

> Nothing is more divisive for a government than having to make peace at the price of major concessions.... When the attainable peace terms fail to satisfy earlier war aims, powerful men and their supporters may—consciously or unconsciously—try to maintain their private advantages and political positions by objecting to the disappointing settlement.... Close behind charges of betrayal lurks the accusation of "treason."[216]
>
> — Fred Charles Ikle, *Every War Must End*

Ethnic conflict in the context of this book refers primarily to tensions between those sympathetic to or actively supportive of Russian agendas as contrasted to that portion of Ukraine's population with a stronger sense of their nation's legitimacy as a sovereign nation. The east and south have in recent decades housed a greater percentage well-disposed to Russia and correspondingly more likely to be receptive to Russian propaganda. These regions historically fell under Russian rule earlier than did the western part of the country. This goes far in explaining why more of the population there speaks Russian as its first language and is more Orthodox while Ukrainian and Catholicism become more common as one travels westward. (See Image 6).

Writer Even Conant explains the roots anchoring these biases:

> It's not just about geography or religion. "The biggest divide after all these factors is between those who view the Russian imperial and Soviet rule more sympathetically versus those who see them as a tragedy," says Adrian Karatnycky, a Ukraine expert at the Atlantic Council of the United States.... The Ukrainian language—spoken in

rural areas—was twice banned by decree of the tsar.... After the communist revolution of 1917, Ukraine was one of the many countries to suffer a brutal civil war before becoming a Soviet Republic in 1920. In the early 1930s, to force peasants into joining collective farms, Soviet leader Joseph Stalin orchestrated a famine that resulted in the starvation and death of millions of Ukrainians. Afterward, Stalin imported large numbers of Russians and other Soviet citizens—many with no ability to speak Ukrainian and with few ties to the region—to help repopulate the east. This, says former Ambassador to Ukraine Steven Pifer, is just one of the historic reasons that helps explain why "the sense of Ukrainian nationalism is not as deep in the east as it is in west."[217]

Despite Russian propaganda seeking to undermine unity, Ukrainian social divides are far less embedded than those continuing to fragment Bosnia-Herzegovina. There is in turn fortunately less chance of violence akin to BiH's internecine beatings, murders, rapes, kidnappings, community cleansings, and forced segregation. The habituality of Moscow's lies in addition to the blatancy of its repeated incursions onto Ukrainian territory further reduce the likelihood of internecine bloodshed. Undercutting reasons for optimism, however, is the belief by some in the east of the country that Kyiv has relegated the region to secondary status. Legitimate or not, perceptions of neglect paired with wealth differences can fuel beliefs that economic discrepancies are the result of deliberate policies. Residual sympathies for Soviet or Russian life will have two forms of reinforcement once the recent phase of hostilities ceases. First, Russian propaganda in the form of new housing as in Mariupol, higher salaries and pensions,

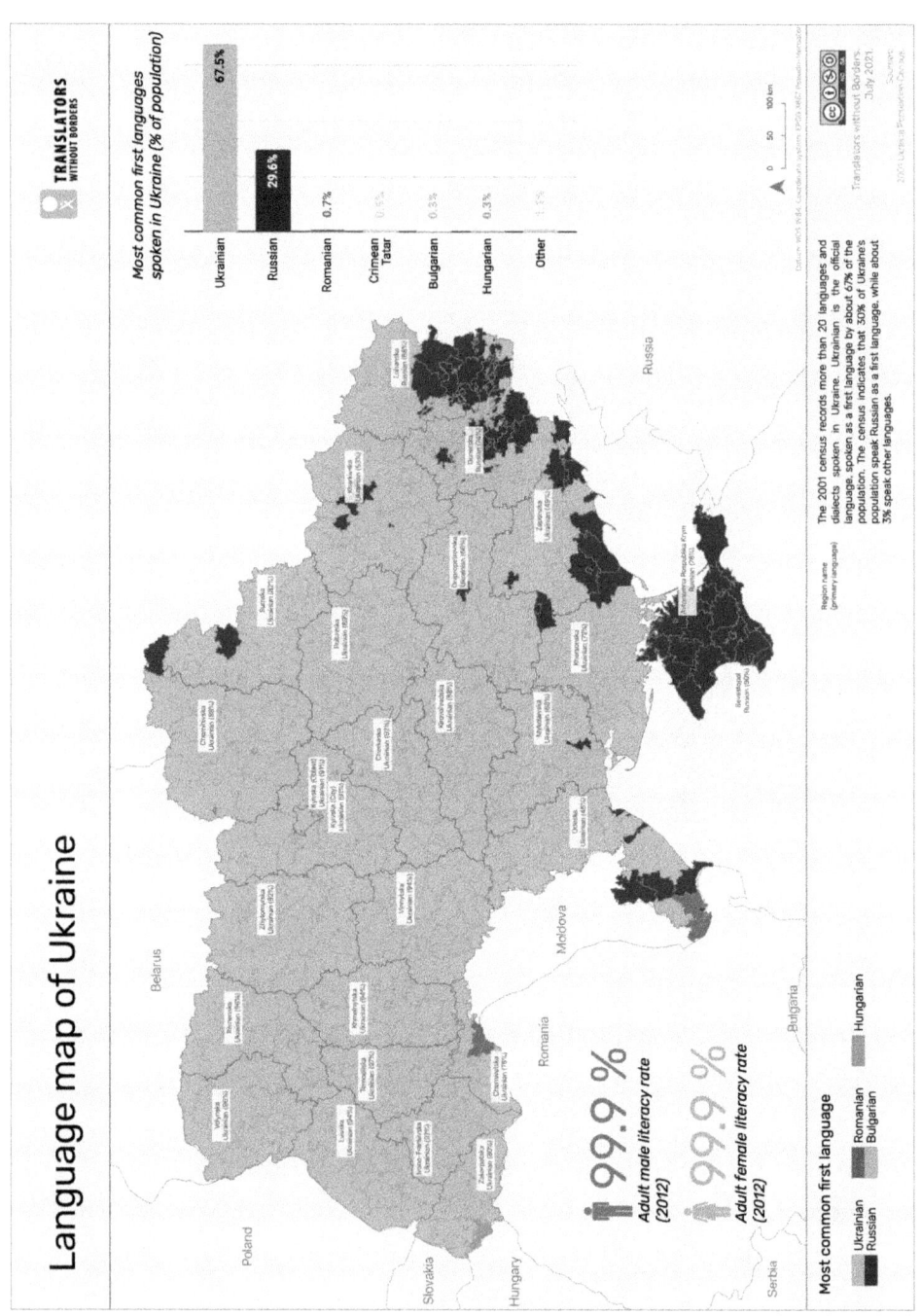

Image 6. Language Geography of Ukraine[218]

and other enticements accompanying Russian occupation will sway some. Second, the westward flight of factories, commercial enterprises, and accompanying jobs and wealth due to the most recent invasion complicates the economic situation in the east. Combined with severing economic relationships with Russia and Belarus, understandable hesitation by commercial interests to expose their investments to future Russian trepidations, and recovery costs nationwide, committing extensive funds to the East's depleted population and potential is a questionable policy from a harshly logical standpoint. On the other hand, Kyiv's recent counter-Russia policies can seem petty and potentially counterproductive. These include a program promoting use of lower case for the words "Russia," "Russian Federation," "Russian Empire," "Moscow," and select others, stating such usage does not constitute a violation of Ukrainian language standards in unofficial publications.[219] Russian television has been banned in Ukraine, a perhaps more understandable dictate given its utility as a propaganda vehicle. Russian pop music is likewise prohibited barring screening before presentation in Ukrainian media.[220]

All this is to say that while Ukraine's ethnic differences should not pose an existential threat, it would be naive to deem the issue unworthy of attention. This is especially true given Russia's efforts to undermine Ukrainians' sense of nation extending well beyond words. Theft of cultural treasures and deliberate targeting of libraries are among other actions crudely seeking to eliminate anything distinguishing Ukraine from its neighbor. We have noted efforts to purge the sense of Ukrainian separateness in occupied areas. Incentives to exchange Ukrainian passports for those Russian include not only making the latter mandatory to draw pensions. They are also necessary to open bank accounts, obtain business licenses, wed, obtain a death certificate, or register a vehicle. Russian language classes target students. Forced curricula promote a Russian view of the world. Textbooks portray Ukraine's government as Nazi-led (particularly ironic given Zelensky being Jewish).[221] The attacks on legitimate education could prove hard to reverse, especially when an occupation is lengthy. These challenges are complex, notably so given the young being primary targets. In addition to addressing years of educational disinformation, counter-approaches will have to deal with falsehoods without undermining the legitimacy of teachers and teaching. More discussion regarding education appears in the following section.

Though Ukraine's post-Cold War heads of state have had varying policies regarding relations with Russia, the country has done much to establish its sovereignty as a country and, increasingly, as a European country. We have seen most of the population favors closer bonding with the European Union and the West generally. Many likewise look at NATO membership as desirable. Nonetheless, social and emotional links with Russia can remain strong. Author Jonathan Masters addresses the dichotomy, one remaining despite

> more than fourteen thousand people [dying] in the fighting in the Donbas between 2014 and 2021, the bloodiest conflict in Europe since the Balkan Wars of the 1990s....

> Strong familial bonds...go back centuries. Kyiv, Ukraine's capital, is sometimes referred to as "the mother of Russian cities," on par in terms of cultural influence with Moscow and St. Petersburg. It was in Kyiv in the eighth and ninth centuries that Christianity was brought from Byzantium to the Slavic peoples. And it was Christianity that served as the anchor for Kievan Rus, the early Slavic state from which modern Russians, Ukrainians, and Belarussians draw their lineage.[222]

History's intermixing notwithstanding, Ukraine's post-Cold War leanings are increasingly apparent, and the lean is westward. Masters continues:

> In late 2013, President Yanukovych, acting under pressure from his supporters in Moscow, scrapped plans to formalize a closer economic relationship with the EU.... Many Ukrainians perceived Yanukovych's decision as a betrayal by a deeply corrupt and incompetent government, and it ignited countrywide protests known as Euromaidan..... Before the 2022 offensive, polls indicated that Ukrainians held mixed views on NATO and EU membership. More than half of those surveyed (not including residents of Crimea and the contested regions in the east) supported EU membership, while 40 to 50 percent were in favor of joining NATO.[223]

As we saw in our discussion of Mariupol's occupation, the percentages favoring stronger ties to NATO have since increased sharply.

In March 2023, Moscow's human rights ombudswoman, Tatyana Moskalkova, claimed over five million Ukrainians had fled to Russia after the 2022 invasion, a significantly higher number than more objective estimates.

The September before, Human Rights Watch described some such movements as "illegal forcible transfers," a war crime. Yet some speaking to HRW admitted leaving voluntarily. Reasons included finding work, being with relatives, and avoiding Ukrainian dictates that men under sixty are not to depart the country, a policy aimed at preventing those of draftable age from leaving.[224] Movement in the opposite direction is also taking place, this of Russians seeking better wages in occupied cities such as Mariupol as noted above.[225] Resolving the status of these occupation-sponsored immigrants awaits the retaking of Mariupol and other yet to be de-occupied cities.

Education and Information Campaigns in Previously Occupied Cities

> Before Ukrainian-Russian reconciliation occurs (if it never does), Ukrainians need to focus on Ukrainian-Ukrainian reconciliation to achieve a shared vision of the past and the future.[226]
>
> — Yaroslav Hrytsak, *Ukraine: The Forging of a Nation*

Sustaining education is difficult enough as bombs drop and artillery impacts a city. Ukraine has moved schools into subway stations and other underground facilities so as to not too greatly disrupt its children's educations (all the more important after their previously suffering what penalties COVID inflicted). Destruction of facilities and teacher departures deny students in other locations. Elsewhere, as we have seen, the issue for students, parents, teachers, and school administrators is one of how best to deal with Russian occupation: Continue schooling despite having to expose students to new curricula seeking to misinform or refuse participation when it is an option? The tradeoffs include forgoing all instruction despite STEM subjects (science, technology, engineering, and mathematics) reportedly being largely left unchanged while history, social studies, and other humanities curricula preach falsehoods.

There are, of course, ways to allay the worst of Russian mis- and disinformation even as areas remain under occupation. Social media, radio, television, and other means of reaching across the frontlines provide avenues for counter-propaganda and truth. But the focus here is less on these than how to confront the challenge of educating and informing once occupied areas are retaken. Again, post-WWII Japan and Germany provide insights of value. The examples are admittedly imperfect. It was the occupier seeking to undo years of indoctrination rather than a democratic government having to reverse the effects of an authoritarian occupier's skewed offerings.

Education and Re-Education in Post-WWII Japan

> Japan is at present swiftly expanding her education system in response to the clear call she has heard to play a leading role in world affairs. She regards education as the right arm of manifest destiny.[227]
> — Willard Price, *Where are you going, Japan?*, 1938

The rise of Japan after the defeat in World War II became the center of world admiration…. Human resources development through education has become the main key to the success.... We often feel amazed at the seriousness of the Japanese government in dealing with education problems.[228]

— Susy Ong, "Post-World War II Education Reform in Japan"

The 1868 restoration of the emperor jumpstarted Japan's creating one of the world's premier education systems. The road was a rocky one. It began with the emperor's admirable ambition that "education shall be so diffused that there may not be a village with an ignorant family nor a family with an ignorant member."[229] Subsequent decades saw experiments with French, American, German, and other approaches that to a greater or lesser extent informed the system that came to be by the later 1930s and the arrival of the Second World War. Notably, neither schools nor the young were the sole targets of state educational energies. Films touted Japan's inevitably successful military enterprises, the emperor as a deity, and duty of the Japanese to subordinate themselves to the welfare of the whole. Popular songs, some introduced by Christian missionaries, underwent tweaking of notes to make them friendlier to Japanese ears and altering of words in the service of revising history. These and other instruments of instruction, including textbooks, increasingly took on ultra-nationalistic and militaristic tones, a trend that accelerated post-1941.[230] Teachers and students were to swear support for the new educational aims. Elementary school students were a priority, the belief being their younger minds were more pliable. Courses supporting development of the Greater East Asia Co-Prosperity Sphere were thought to be most worthy of exploitation.²³¹ Mass education at home had complements as Japan made inroads into other countries. Occupiers sought to similarly sway populations in the Philippines, French Indonesia, Burma, Netherlands East Indies, and elsewhere as Japan's soldiers advanced. Youth were again particular targets for enlisting support. Many were willing subjects. Interest, however, was more in how Japanese instruction and any accompanying resources might support their own nationalist aims.²³²

Enter the Occupiers

> Redirecting an entire nation's thought processes in the short space of six and a half years was, of course, an unachievable task.... Nonetheless, in many areas, the occupation's programme of social and cultural reorientation laid the groundwork for a decisive rupture with the authoritarian past. Washington ascribed the popular acceptance of Japanese militarism to ideological manipulation in three areas: education, religion, and information.²³³
>
> — Takemae Eiji, *Inside GHQ: The Allied Occupation of Japan and its Legacy*

> In outlining the basic policy for education reform, SCAP [Supreme Commander for the Allied Powers] directed that dissemination of militaristic and ultra-nationalistic ideology and all military education and drill be discontinued. Inculcation of concepts and establishment of practices in harmony with representative government, international peace, dignity of the individual as well as such fundamental rights as freedom of assembly, speech, and religion were encouraged.²³⁴
>
> — General Staff, Supreme Commander, Allied Powers, *Reports of General MacArthur*

Led by General Douglas MacArthur, Japan's allied occupiers approached their objectives in a variety of ways. The allies banned "State Shintoism," Japan's de facto state-sponsored religion, given its history as a vehicle to promote militarism and expansionism. Similarly oriented textbooks were purged of offending passages or removed altogether and relegated to pulping. Educators of any type underwent investigation. Those thought unacceptable were removed. Others underwent reorientation and were later supervised to ensure instruction was aligned with occupier objectives.[235]

Japanese authorities' extraordinarily rapid post-surrender adaptation of education policies had in many ways already aced intentions by General MacArthur's staff to provide guidance.[236] The Ministry of Education published eleven "Education Policy Guidelines for the Development of New Japan" on September 15, 1945, only a month following Emperor Hirohito's surrender announcement. The guidelines directed abolition of military instruction and "an end to militaristic and ultra-nationalistic practices in schools."[237] Others among the eleven included:

- Instruction specially oriented toward students returning to school from factories or the military after premature removal from school
- Improve the capacity to think scientifically while fostering a spirit of peace
- Address the need to educate adults as well as Japan's youth, the former via educational programs in museums, libraries, art exhibitions, theater, and popular books
- Formation of local youth groups

▶ Reorganization of the Ministry of Education to incorporate directorates of scientific education and sports.

The result of the Japanese initiative to interdict even more stringent occupier policies meant the newly arrived occupiers spent more time screening Japanese reorientations than imposing original direction. It was nonetheless good fortune the Japanese had stolen a march on their occupiers. The Supreme Commander for the Allied Powers' (SCAP) initial team responsible for designing educational policy had only three members, this for an educational system with 18,000,000 students, half a million teachers, fifty thousand schools, and a budget which before the war was larger than that for the army and navy combined. The staff would later expand, ranging from a dozen to twenty-seven persons during the first two years of occupation. It was nevertheless by far the most understaffed component of the occupiers' machinery. SCAP issued its formal instructions regarding the revision of Japanese education on October 22, 1945.[238]

Themes underlying early Japanese revisions and this SCAP guidance included promoting the value of democratic ideals, those ideals extending beyond politics to encompass economics and day-to-day living. As conceived, equality was fundamental to democracy, the emphasis being less on social equality than offering all equal access to opportunity.[239] Students, teachers, and officials were encouraged to examine the legitimacy of texts and other educational materials and question authority. SCAP guidance additionally advocated discussion of topics such as social and religious freedom.[240]

The impact was quick and significant. The August 15, 1945 announcement of war's end had come during students' summer break. Classes resumed the following month. By October 3rd, teachers were directing their students to ink over or cut out entries in textbooks thought not in accordance with the Ministry of Education's guidance—those considered too militaristic, nationalistic, or undemocratic.[241] The Civil Information and Education Section approved the action as an interim fix until replacement texts became available. Students' shock was palpable. The psychological impact of despoiling:

> was considerable. Education specialist Nakamura Kikuji recalls: "The inked-over school books impressed indelibly on youthful minds the harsh finality of defeat. For many pupils, that moment of truth had a lasting influence on their lives." Before the surrender, children had been admonished to take scrupulous care of their texts. "Now we were suddenly told to smear the books with ink.... I felt as if I were defiling myself," wrote another Japanese. "That day for the first time, I felt besieged by a jumble of contending values, a feeling that has persisted ever since."[242]

Historian John Dower recorded a similarly stunned response by both students and teachers:

> This practice of "blackening over" (*suminuru*)...was a visceral undertaking—simultaneously a ritual exorcism of teachings that had only yesterday been deemed sacrosanct and a practical exercise in encouraging criticism of received wisdom. Yuri Hajime...was thirteen when hostilities ended. [His reaction] was typical in never forgetting this experience.... The Ministry of Education and a host of

publishers hastened to produce new textbooks appropriate to the times. In the meantime, he was required to deface his painstakingly copied language text. The mutilated text struck him as "abnormal and even grotesque," but the episode left him with a lasting awareness that received knowledge could be challenged and education in itself could be a relative thing.[243]

Herbert Wunderlich, who would become Chief of the Textbook and Curriculum Branch, found most textbooks contained so much material that inking-over or cutting was impractical. SCAP suspended the offending textbooks and all courses of instruction in three subjects thought most prevalently nationalistic: Japanese history, ethics, and geography, the last given its glorification of the wartime overseas empire.[244] Instruction would begin again only after introduction of replacement textbooks. It would not be until late May 1946 that the SCAP education division appointed authors. The writers were given approximately a month to complete their tasks. Work was to meet three primary dictates: (1) base content on historical fact, (2) incorporate social, economic, and cultural history, and (3) nurture critical thinking.[245] Censorship and guidelines extended to other influential mediums, radio and film among them. As with virtually all aspects of Japan's postwar recovery, education guidance was ever-adapting. To the original goal of eradicating militarism, ultra-nationalism, and expansionism was added barring any criticism of SCAP personnel or policies. It later further evolved to include censorship guarding against the influence of Communism.[246]

Education and Re-Education in Germany

> [Noble Prize winner in literature] Günter Grass, former Hitler Youth member of the 10th SS Panzer Division Frundsberg, once reflected on having been in the Hitler Youth generation of Germany, noting that he felt "too young to have been a Nazi, but old enough to have been formed by the Nazi regime."[247]
>
> — Elizabeth Fox, "Rebuilding Germany's Children"

> Another problem was the education and training of the younger generation, those who had grown up entirely or largely under the National Socialist regime. They were not the generation that had brought Hitler to power, but it was they who now had to bear the full measure of the physical and psychological consequences. Their ideals had been shattered overnight.... The care of these young people was, I thought, one of our most urgent duties. The age groups in question would soon influence political life in Germany. Their attitudes and ways of thinking would set the tone for the country. In the National Socialist years they had heard only official indoctrination. It was impossible to expect political judgment from people who were still children when Hitler came to power.... Punishment for the guilty was necessary, but so was instruction and enlightenment for the large groups of people who were not guilty but had been systematically misled.[248]
>
> — Konrad Adenauer, *Memoirs 1945-53*

> Like everything else in post-surrender Germany, reopening the schools was not easy.[249]
>
> — Earl F. Ziemke, *The US Army in the Occupation of Germany 1944-1946*

General Lucius Clay, as Military Governor of Germany after World War II, commiserated that at the start the

CHAPTER 6

task of addressing education responsibilities in the American zone

> seemed hopeless. Many German school buildings had been destroyed, others badly damaged, and still others were occupied either by troops or by displaced persons. Teaching staffs contained many ardent Nazis; in one city more than 60 percent of the staff had belonged to the party. Textbooks were so impregnated with Nazi ideology that even mathematics problems were expressed in military terms and logistics. German youth learned to add and subtract guns and bullets rather than apples and oranges. The hope of a new Germany rested in its youth, which was roaming the streets. It was essential that it be returned to school quickly before it formed lasting habits of indolence or violence.[250]

It is a situation Ukraine's leaders will find only too familiar as their soldiers reclaim occupied cities, towns, and villages.

Clay's remarks make it clear education was but one part of the recovery whole. Getting kids off the streets was fundamental to security. This quickly became a priority as the threat of postwar resistance faded and juvenile delinquency became a major concern. US officials closed all schools in May 1945. Others had not been open since September of the year before, this in cities such as Aachen that had fallen during the first weeks of the Allies' entry into Germany.[251] Saving the defeated from plagues of petty crime and worse was necessary to ensure stability and reinforce the occupiers' legitimacy as governors. Clay recognized it would be an uphill battle. Germany's youth, female and male, had for years been exposed to indoctrination. One author summed up the objectives driving leaders of the *Hitlerjugend* (Hitler Youth) as "mobilize and discipline an entire generation of German youth in the spirit of National Socialism; loosen their ties to the Church, the family, and the past; [and] inculcate the ideal that the State was everything and the individual nothing."[252]

How to approach education was still a matter of debate after Germany's surrender, a surprising situation given the length of time the Allies committed to civil affairs preparations. Clay himself resisted increasing education funding, believing "full bellies to be a first requisite to recapture minds."[253] Others feared reopening schools before replacing old with new textbooks and the removal of teachers with suspect leanings. The delays meant in-school education lagged that via press, film, and other mediums. It further meant there was a lack of orchestrating messaging used in various methods across the re-education effort. As in Japan, the goals pursued quickly evolved to include bolstering anti-Communism in addition to reorienting beliefs from those years of Nazi propaganda. Re-industrialization was also goal-worthy, one surely impeded if school openings were too-long delayed. Yet while Japanese authorities seized the initiative in redesigning their education system, occupiers in the US zone found themselves in a similar situation not only because German authorities seized the initiative but also due to American lethargy. This meant German legislation was in place prior to the occupier's introducing new policies. Those laws became drivers of change as they overtook any US efforts to establish guidance. It wasn't until November 1947 that US officials directed Germany's various *Land* governments to incorporate the above objectives even in the less demanding media arena. The same lack of attention meant coordination of education initiatives lacked orchestration in the US zone, across Allied partner sectors, and within German political parties.[254] Ultimately, it wasn't recognition of shortcomings in Germany itself that ignited progress. That began in 1947 when educators in the United States criticized lethargy in Europe.[255]

The Berlin mayor's office first published guidelines for school reopenings in May 1945, the month the war ended in Europe. Dictates barred use of any textbook or other resource published under the Third Reich. Teaching proceeded without texts, though reading lessons could employ German literary classics or postwar newspapers. Schools gradually again welcomed students, elementary grades and those for handicapped children receiving preference. London's guidance to the Commander-in-Chief of the British zone reflects a sense of the Western Allies' objectives in general. He was to (1) "reestablish in German education the former standard for objective facts, and...(2) foster...interest in the ideas of popular democracy." He was also to encourage school use of Allied films and educational broadcasts.[256]

As in Japan, speed in writing textbooks and providing the necessary paper (also in demand by newspapers, government offices, and other competitors) were much sought after.[257] Stopgap measures such as replacing Nazi texts with those from the Weimer Republic had limited success. A reader for fifth-year students contained nationalist and militarist passages such as Frederick the Great's speech to his soldiers before the battle of Leuthen during which he declared, "Let us beat the enemy or let us be buried by his batteries." Arithmetic texts presented problems based on territorial and economic losses resultant from the Treaty of Versailles. Considered better than the alternative, United States Forces European Theater caveated these offerings with "The fact of reprinting does not imply, seen from the educational and other points of view, that this book is absolutely without objection."[258] The Allied *Kommandatura* (Berlin's governing body during the early occupation) required unanimous approval of any textbooks used in the city. Nine prepared under American supervision and another seven overseen by the Soviets fortunately passed muster before Western-Soviet relations became so strained as to make unanimity overly difficult.[259] Were problems with providing textbooks not enough, many former teachers failed to pass even the first stage of clearance based on *Fragebogen*, the denazification questionnaires used to screen out unacceptable individuals. Partially as a result of this vetting, Munich's teachers' average age was fifty-seven while the city's student-teacher ratio was eighty-nine to one.[260]

Adult education recovered well in Germany's larger cities. The same was not true for the youngers' education given lack of sufficient facilities. Shortages persisted despite occupiers prioritizing educational buildings' repair and finding alternative housing for soldiers and displaced persons initially billeted in school facilities. Those visiting classrooms in colder weather found students bundled in heavy winter clothing, their schools without heat.[261] Authorities resisting liberalizing education systems presented other hurdles. Among them were church leaders who felt their authority threatened.[262]

Fears of youths roaming streets were not without basis. Lacking the firm oversight and authoritarian environment of their time in the Hitler Youth, those born before 1930 (and therefore the older among the ranks of that organization) openly protested against democratization, believing it would fail just as had the Weimar Republic.[263] This helped to drive the first official program for US Army contacts with civilians. German Youth Activities linked regional military government education sections with local youth groups beginning in April 1946. The US Army's athletic and other recreational facilities opened to young Germans. Local guests interfaced with American soldiers who had been directed to instill appreciation for democracy and fair play while demonstrating by example that soldiering did not equate with militarism. Films, games, dances, English lessons, and other activities joined sports with American soldiers being assigned full-time jobs as supervisors tasked with realigning youth attitudes. Unfortunately, these programs tended to disproportionately benefit the already better-off as most US facilities were in the occupier's more upscale neighborhoods.[264] Program similarities to the former *Hitlerjugend* training appear not to have been coincidental, though the focus on democratization, denazification, and demilitarization obviously marked a sharp departure.[265]

Clay ultimately acknowledged the importance of education not only for the young but German society in general. Perhaps his background as an engineer helps to explain his early reticence. Measuring progress in that field tends to rely on hard numbers little debatable, that in the education arena less so. Regardless, as in Japan, Allies' efforts bore fruit in turning a citizenry away from totalitarianism and toward democracy and respect for the individual's role in society. In Clay's own words,

> The results of an educational program are intangible and almost impossible to evaluate immediately, but they will record the success or failure of our occupation. It is difficult to produce evidence convincing to those who appropriate funds of the importance of exchange programs and the dissemination in Germany of examples of our own cultural life…. Our town meetings…made the citizen conscious of his right to question his public officials, and the latter realize that they too can learn from the citizen the failures and successes of their administration.[266]

Education Insights for Ukraine

> One of the peculiar characteristics of the Second World War was the deep note of pessimism which could be discerned in almost all public statements made in anticipation of the victory…. Thoughtful people realized that the military victory marked only a phase in a far more basic conflict, one involving economic, psychological, and diplomatic pressures, and one which would ultimately be determined on that most intangible yet fundamental of battlegrounds—the mind of the defeated peoples.[267]
>
> — Robert King Hall, "The Battle of the Mind: American Educational Policy in Germany and Japan"

CHAPTER 6

> The brainwashing of German adolescents was accomplished through the regime's schooling, physical training, and Fascist pageantry of the Hitler Youth organization.... In the wake of the indisputable failure and disillusionment of the Germans, Nazi principles simply could not withstand the impending wave of democracy that began to affect postwar Germany.[268]
>
> — Elizabeth Fox, "Rebuilding Germany's Children"

Human Rights Watch estimates that one million Ukrainian school-age children remained in Russian-occupied territories as of June 2024, just under half of those being in long-occupied Crimea. In addition to corrupting teaching by substituting propaganda falsehoods as facts (the previously mentioned claims that Ukraine is run by Nazis, for example), some receive military training as a component of their curriculum. HRW further reports Russian use of coercion that includes beatings and other physical abuse to pressure teachers to work or provide data on their students. Further complicating the issue in regions retaken by Ukrainian forces is Kyiv's September 20, 2022, Ministry of Education and Science directive that collaborating teachers should be removed. As with earlier noted policies regarding collaboration, specifics regarding what constitutes unacceptable collaboration remained unclear. There were educators resultantly subjected to criminal prosecution, administrative sanctions, delays in receiving salaries, and mandatory screening (disturbingly referred to as "filtration," the same term used to describe Russia's abusive vetting of select Ukrainians). As with earlier cases of too-hastily created collaboration guidance, legitimate

305

justifications for teaching while under occupation (such as providing instruction to children with disabilities who had been unable to evacuate) appear to have been granted inadequate if any consideration.[269]

We focus on education here, however, a topic on which the many-tentacled nature of postwar education programs in Japan and Germany fortunately offer insights. Where the two countries required significant revamping of their education programs, both eventually evolved to overcome years of dis- and misinformation. They also countered Communism's appeal, a nontrivial success aligning favorably with Ukraine's challenges ahead. Sympathy for Russia receives reinforcement where Ukrainians have access to Russian television, radio, or social media. What might be intermittent streams in Ukraine become a deluge in occupied territory. Countering willing and no-choice consumption will be difficult. More difficult yet: the above-mentioned refuting of mis-teachings and regaining the trust of Ukrainian youth in once-occupied areas. Here comparisons with Japan and Germany are more comparable, though Ukraine will benefit from the advantages of existing textbooks, proven teachers, experienced school administrators, and eighty-plus years of progress in refuting propaganda. Resemblances do not end there. Ukraine, as did Japan and Germany, faces multiple and ever-evolving tasks as it educates and re-educates its citizenry. Complicating those challenges is the continued existence of an antipathetic Russia. Educators in post-WWII Germany and Japan had to deal with residual militarism and ultra-nationalism. Shielding against the influences of Communist propaganda followed. Ukraine's will be an environment with an active and aggressive Russia continuing its efforts to bully, sway, intimidate, and convince those receptive and others less so to its messaging. One size will not fit all in counter-efforts. Urban centers' better access to the internet and other forms of media abet communication even as it now provides wider access to Russian messaging. Promulgating Kyiv's educational initiatives will require local adaptation of urban approaches while ensuring those messages are consistent throughout the country, in urban and rural environments alike.

The challenge of re-education encompasses not only addressing *what* students and others internalized from earlier instruction and propaganda. We have mentioned the legitimacy of the collective *who* doing the teaching. They too will undergo—should undergo—rigorous but legitimate questioning. Again as in Tokyo, Berlin, and elsewhere in those cities' countries, re-education will face the Gordian Knot of implanting a new norm of challenging authority even as another authority attempts to convince its truth is the right truth. Enlightenment will entail refuting years of in-person instruction, social media, television, radio, film, and more. Those occupying classroom chairs must believe once misplaced trust will not again prove a mistake if reoriented. An additional complication: sophisticated Russian brainwashing programs during occupation will incorporate the possibility of Ukraine's eventual return, making reorientation more difficult.

There accordingly may be value in studying other initiatives addressing youth indoctrination. Insights from elsewhere could draw on experiences in the United Kingdom where teachers found the misogynistic spoutings of social media influencer Andrew Tate had taken root amongst some male students. These "teachings" included blaming women in instances where they were raped and denigrating female judgment. Asking whether a student would feel the same were the victim a sister or mother caused a number to reconsider. In other cases, however, endeavors to reorient met resistance. The teacher was, after all, "just a woman."[270]

Ukrainian youth taken to Russia could suffer more intensive indoctrination. Some forced to undergo military training were exposed to particularly vehement anti-Ukrainian misinformation. One young man recalled, "When I saw myself in the uniform in photos and videos on the Internet, I thought for myself that I was a traitor and that I betrayed Ukraine. I swapped Ukraine for Russia… even though I knew I was forced to do it."[271]

History reassures. Re-education can prove successful even on a mass basis. The past also makes clear the pitfalls awaiting those not recognizing the importance of preparing early and putting resources in place to employ a broad spectrum of initiatives encompassing as many of the means and ways of instruction as are available. Much can be learned from the historical cases above, to include the need to persevere regardless of initial setbacks. Missteps and errors led Columbia Professor Robert Hall to write in 1948, "the battle for the German and Japanese minds seems disconcertingly close to defeat."[272] That Ukrainians will direct re-education programs rather than outsiders bodes well. That a feeling of neglect by portions of Ukraine's eastern-more population preceded the 2022 invasion means Russian endeavors will at times benefit from fertile soil. Much work lies ahead for Ukraine.

CHAPTER 7

CONCLUSION

> History's many lessons are available to any assisting Ukraine's recovery.... One particularly worthy of reiteration is a lesson powerfully reinforced given its virtual absence in 2003 Iraq: The importance of getting an early start.[1]
> — Russell W. Glenn, "Creating Light at Tunnel's End: Ukraine's Post-war Urban Recovery"

> Russia remains very much a "hard power," one not to be messed with, and quite capable of surprising the West again.[2]
> — Mungo Melvin, *Sevastopol's Wars: Crimea from Potemkin to Putin* (published in 2017)

The international community's restricted understanding and knowledge of the urban context are evident in...

- ▶ an inability to stay on top of rapidly moving situations in an urban context
- ▶ a registration system for affected populations which focuses on large self-settled camps rather than neighbourhoods: this tends to generate incomplete and inaccurate information which can hamper return to sites of origin by concentrating the distribution of support in the camps...

> over-reliance on satellite imagery to capture the complexity of the impact on the built environment

> uncoordinated action [leading to] limited recognition of socioeconomic factors...without meaningful communication with communities, owners, and previous occupants.[3]
>
> — Roger Zetter and George Deikun, "A new strategy for meeting humanitarian challenges in urban areas"

The value of our primary historical examples takes us only so far. Tokyo, Berlin, and Manila during WWII had one huge advantage Ukraine does not: The trio's governments (occupying government in the case of Manila) could largely focus on military operations to the neglect of what would follow. Post-war considerations were, unlike today, a future phase that little overlapped the ongoing war. Former US ambassador to Ukraine Marie Yovanovitch succinctly summarizes Kyiv's greater challenge: "Ukraine [is] fighting a two-front war: a war for territorial integrity and a war for what kind of a country it [will] become. The Ukrainians [have] to prevail in both fights to secure their future."[4]

In that light, we wrap up our consideration of what lies ahead as Ukraine's city folk move forward from the here and now to their there and then. Ukrainians as a whole are fortunate in having a government of their choosing to assist recovery, a government that has proven itself able to deal with the crisis of war while simultaneously maintaining a vision of what will follow. The country's collective next steps are no less threatened by hazards than is the case for those confronted with farmers' fields or urban denizens' paths concealing war's explosive remnants.

CHAPTER 7

Whether citizens and their leaders manage to successfully contain the beast of corruption remains to be seen. Several are the other perils touched on above that merit a final look. We therefore close with thoughts on the nature of progress and how to gauge success before returning briefly to the topics of black markets and social divides. And then there is the no longer unthinkable possibility of nuclear weapons use.

■ Adapting for Today, Readying for Tomorrow

> Victory is our first and only duty, but just as we prepare for war in a time of peace, so we should prepare for peace in a time of war. Through preparation we visualize a prosperity, sound and lasting.[5]
> — Bernard M. Baruch and John M. Hancock, "Report on War and Post-War Adjustment Policies" for James F. Byrnes, Director, Office of War Mobilization, February 15, 1944

> Few men have shown a more comprehensive foresight of its greatness, or greater boldness in the formation and execution of plans commensurate to the grandeur of an anticipated future. It is the more surprising, therefore, that in the matter of building city of incendiary wooden shells, Mr. Ogden should manifest a disposition to cling to the follies of the pasts instead of boldly grasping the necessities and realities of the future.[6]
> — Scott G. Berg, *The Burning of the World*, on a city business leader's promotion of wood buildings when rebuilding after Chicago's great 1871 fire

> In the aftermath of disaster, the very legitimacy of government is at stake.[7]
> — Lawrence J. Vale and Thomas J. Campanella, "Conclusion: Axioms of Resilience"

Ukrainians—those living in cities and otherwise—have experienced suffering on a scale heretofore unheard of in Europe this century.[8] Recalling our discussions from above (and momentarily stepping aside from the pseudo-promise to avoid statistical deluges), our considerations of post-WWII cities provide some small reason for thanks despite the punishment wrought on the country's urban areas. An estimated 2,316,000 houses in 115 bombed cities were destroyed and over 758,000 residents were killed or injured in Japan alone. The Office of the United Nations High Commissioner for Human Rights verified 30,457 noncombatant casualties in Ukraine in almost exactly two years of war from February 24, 2022 to February 15, 2024, 10,582 of whom were killed.[9] As of March 14, 2024, nearly 3.7 million had suffered displacement within their country while 6,486,000 had fled to other countries, 5,982,900 of those to elsewhere in Europe.[10]

Recovery in Tokyo was made further difficult by the postwar influx of new or returning residents, a 1945 population estimated at approximately three million increasing to seven million by 1952. Assessments estimated demand countrywide would require 4,200,000 additional living units in the years immediately following the arrival of peace. World War II cities generally suffered physical damage practically impossible to grasp: Berlin's postwar rubble constituted 55,000,000 cubic meters, Hamburg's 35,000,000, Cologne's 24,100,000. The pile would have been 12.3 kilometres (7.67 miles) high if there had been a way to stack Berlin's 1945 rubble on a US football field. A plane flying at 40,000 feet would have had to climb another 500 feet to avoid a collision. One could find rubble piles as late as 1990 in the German Democratic Republic (East Germany). Clearance of wartime debris was somewhat easier in Japan. Structures built of wood predominated; little but ash remained after attacks. Experience influenced cleanup efficiency within individual urban areas as some approaches proved better than others. Yet little in the way of lessons was passed from city to city. This was unfortunate given the considerable innovation showed in disposing of rubble and refuse by select urban areas.[11]

Though fortunately not of the same scale, the crude nature of Russia's attacks on Ukraine is reminiscent of World War II. That has less been the case for most recent conflicts involving more civilized governments. Coalition forces during Operation Desert Storm in 1991, for example, neutralized Iraqi power facilities not by destroying expensive, purpose-built, hard-to-replace generators. The choice was instead chaff, strips of metal foil causing system shorts but allowing rapid return to functionality.[12] Perhaps Russia lacks similar capabilities, leaving only more destructive means (or has the capability and chooses not to use it). Contrarily, the attackers may be opting to exercise the first application of their Strategic Operation for the Destruction of Critically Important Targets (or SODCIT) as suggested by intelligence officials. According to British Defence Ministry representatives, "Russia envisioned SODCIT as using long-range missiles to strike an enemy state's critical national infrastructure, rather than its military forces, to demoralize the population and, ultimately, force the states leaders to capitulate."[13] Whether not developing less damaging means or choosing not to employ them, the results lend credence to accusations that Russia's leaders violate international law. Researchers at the Yale School of Public Health join others in finding evidence to support that conclusion:

> Incidents are distributed across an overwhelming majority of Ukraine's oblasts, including areas well removed from the frontlines of fighting. This wide geospatial distribution is suggestive of an effort to cripple Ukraine's energy infrastructure in a manner potentially inconsistent with pursuit of direct and concrete military advantage in every instance. The wide geospatial distribution points to possible violations of the international humanitarian principles of distinction and proportionality, as well as the obligation to take all feasible precautions to minimize injury to civilians and damage to civilian objects.[14]

A Ukrainian woman monitoring political talk shows reported that Russian pundits explained these strikes as spurs to a hoped-for uprising to overthrow the Zelensky government. "It is insane," she concluded. "They do not understand us."[15]

The above pages tell us that what constitutes recovery success will be a matter of context, opinion, expectation, and emotion. Build back as before the war? Build back as was the city decades ago? Build back in a manner entirely new in terms of architecture, green awareness, and grasp of the future to come? Relevant lessons from the last century imply finding value in (1) soliciting and listening to the needs and wants of those who will live in their future city, and (2) recognizing temporary buildings rarely are. Building on the cheap or too casually adopting current architectural fads risks structures aging poorly as did many post-WW II.

Yes, Ukraine's tragic and—were Putin not what Putin is—unnecessary war offers a slim silver lining amidst its devastating blackness. Cities can be "built back better" given sufficient funding, patient willpower, constrained corruption, and willingness to meld residents' perspectives with those of officials, experts, and budgeteers. Ukraine's recovery could be the torch that cuts loose the dragging anchor of Soviet bureaucratic practices. A well-considered immigration policy could fire innovative thinking while also addressing the demographic specter of low birth rates made worse by the thousands who emigrated during the war and may not return. It is not a new phenomenon. Ukraine's deaths have outnumbered births since 2013. In January 2022, a month before Russia's renewed attacks, the country's population was 4.2 million fewer than nine years before.[16] A decrease in the number of births since February 2022 aggravates the problem. Unsurprising given young men fighting at the front, mass population displacements, and accompanying disruption of social life, the number of children born in Ukraine in 2022 was over 30 percent less than the year before.[17]

As do militaries during war, organizations supporting recovery need to evolve as conditions change. The cooperation marking demining operations, in which otherwise competing organizations readily exchange lessons drawn from ongoing activities, warrants emulation. The teamwork makes particular sense given the consequences of not keeping pace with changes in explosive munitions technology and evolutions in weapons employment. Cooperation and related adaptations can be slower in other sectors. A member of the NGO community commiserated that an international government agency providing food aid in Ukraine was slow to recognize the local economy in one region had rebounded nicely during their period of aid delivery. The agency's representatives continued to deliver food kits rather than transition to cash distribution. Food kits are appropriate when local conditions make maintenance of food supply chains and stocking shop shelves difficult. Once an economy returns to health, continued reliance on food kits becomes less efficient in terms of logistics and less likely to meet individual recipient needs. It can also impede further economic development by depriving shops of customers.[18] Lethargy in recognizing needed changes means providing aid recipients with what is on-hand whether needed or not and missing an opportunity to stimulate local markets.

The example helps expose another characteristic of effective recovery management: the existence of an organization with an overarching perspective and ability to compile and disseminate insights to relevant participants. Many military organizations long ago recognized the benefits of having internal lessons learned bodies. These compile lessons from ongoing operations and disseminate them to relevant participants. The better manned and funded of the organizations dispatch teams with the charter to observe, collect, analyze, and distribute lessons in real-time. Effectiveness dictates gathering and analyzing both negative and positive insights (or "areas to improve" and "areas to sustain" in the jargon). Assurance of anonymity for parties from whom lessons come helps reduce sharing inhibitions. Compilation of lessons also offers the less immediate benefit of informing future undertakings for which they can be adapted.

Ukraine's recovery can similarly benefit from insights provided by the past.[19] Berlin and Sarajevo tell us further rural-to-urban and urban-to-urban migration lies ahead. Berlin (again) and Tokyo inform that fighters returning from the front will be a significant part of this internal migration. Now, therefore, is the time to contemplate relevant options for gauging where these migrants will likely settle and prepare plans for housing and integrating new arrivals into local economies. Alternatively, officials might encourage settlement in select regions to stimulate economic recovery and bolster national defense. Although the purpose in the latter case would be to defend Ukrainian sovereignty rather than imperialism as was the case with Rome's encouraging settlement on the empire's periphery, promoting immigration into these regions and linking it to citizenship could conceivably bolster settlement in the east. Such an initiative could be linked to preliminary military training and border security operations. Additional implications for addressing the country's recent population losses are readily apparent.

Murphy's Law ensures the number of a location's available housing units and number of those seeking residence will be unequal. Wiesbaden, Germany's post-WWII mayor Georg Krücke faced such an imbalance as refugees fled west from the Soviets while others returned from their days in uniform. He directed the displaced be housed in abandoned apartments on a loan basis, a solution that could be available in parts of Ukraine. Other possible remedies include conversion of public or large commercial buildings for use as housing, offering tax or other incentives in the latter case. The country's good fortune in retaining a standing bureaucracy provides the means to begin these adaptations before hostilities cease, an advantage not seen in Iraq, Afghanistan, or other recent contingencies.

We know Ukraine's leaders realize the end of their shooting war will not be the end of Russian infringements on the country's sovereignty. Commendable as Ukraine's rapid repair of physical and cyber infrastructures has been, continuation of conflict in the information, economic, social, and cyber arenas is all but assured. Increased instances of sabotage in Europe's west suggest an additional threat.[20] Russia's ongoing attacks suggest physical infrastructure is a primary candidate for adaptation—if not significant redesign. Modifications could reduce both physical and cyber system vulnerabilities by decentralizing critical nodes, creating redundant routing options, and hardening select components. Ukraine is already instituting some of these initiatives, including moving components of its digital infrastructure to other countries. The World Bank reported the percentage of Ukraine's educational institutions with bomb shelters increased from 68 to 80 percent between January 2023 and February 2024.[21] Helpful, particularly given Russian attacks continue to reflect a bent toward wanton destruction rather than the behaviors of a

CHAPTER 7

country seeking territorial and population control. While attacks prior to spring 2024 favored (but were not limited to) power transmission infrastructure, others later targeted hydroelectric and thermal power generation plants and their more difficult to replace components, this as power generation capabilities generally were receiving particular attention during attacks early that year.[22]

Adaptations to the ongoing damage to larger, generally fossil fuel facilities include importing energy from elsewhere in Europe and scrounging replacement equipment from decommissioned Soviet-era plants. Other initiatives favor zero or low-emission alternatives. These can have security in addition to environmental benefits. DTEK is building wind and solar farms, infrastructure that is more robust in terms of survivability and often quicker to repair.[23]

■ Recovery Can't Wait

> There could be no more crushing demonstration of Germany's abject condition after VE-Day than this. It was, as the Germans themselves called it, *die Stunde Null*, hour zero: the moment of the hiatus when the people of a nation that had ceased to exist touched rock-bottom, when the hands of the stopwatch were reset to zero and began to tick toward an unthinkable future.[24]
>
> — Douglas Botting, *From the Ruins of the Reich: Germany 1945-1949*

> "We have to rebuild even if it's going to be destroyed again. We have no choice." It's building for the present, not for the future.[25]
>
> — Masha Gessen, "Democracy in Darkness: What Ukraine has already lost in its fight against Russia"

An estimated four to six million Ukrainians were living under Russian occupation as of February 2024. Multiple millions remain internally displaced or as international refugees. Another approximated million reside—voluntarily or otherwise—in Russia.[26] Addressing the above population returns and continued shifts means Ukrainian predispositions will sometimes have to give way to a postwar new normal. Prefabricated homes donated by Poland met potential residents' resistance. The buildings differ from the foundation and brick construction Ukrainians consider the norm.[27] This is far from the only case in which history and progress pull countrymen in different directions. Many Ukrainians and outsiders alike want the country to better align itself with the European sphere economically, politically, diplomatically, socially, and militarily as well. Others still feel the residual tug of Soviet legacy or Russian connections and would prefer to keep the West at arm's length. It is not year zero for Ukraine, but there is plentiful motivation to break with the past.

Corruption offers another opportunity for such a deliberate rupture. It proved a culprit in Tokyo, Berlin, Manila, and Sarajevo (and remains a troublesome commodity in the latter two's politics today). The less savory set up businesses specializing in the collection and resale of debris in Berlin, having others gather material to which neither they nor the business buyer had a right. Metal products—copper, brass (from door and other fittings), and steel used in construction—were markedly popular targets for looters given scrap dealers' hunger for the materials. Such thefts might stir unpleasant memories in coalition veterans of operations in Iraq earlier this century. Copper wire was among the many items routinely taken from buildings. The theft hindered re-establishment of local government services in addition to increasing recovery costs. Looting is a minor form of corruption when considering individual thieves' actions. Its consequences in sum are otherwise. Unfortunately, looting seems an inevitable partner of disaster. In addition to the semi-organized thefts in Germany's capital, our earlier discussions regarding Berlin noted how casually survivors viewed taking items not their own. Histories tend to give looting little more than passing comment despite its ubiquity and damage both to physical infrastructure and local government legitimacy (or that of an occupier, as was the case in Iraq). It has on occasion taken the shine off groups otherwise viewed as heroes. Few chose to delve too deeply into theft during recovery operations at the 9/11 World Trade Center site though it occurred with some regularity.[28] Veterans of operations in 2003 Iraq would vouch that intact property records were key to perceptions of their effectiveness. Deliberate destruction by insurgents served to undermine authorities who could no longer confirm ownership. Property records were equally important in Germany, Tokyo (recall the wise duplication of landownership files), and elsewhere in the months and years after World War II. On-hand documents were crucial to quickly resolving competing claims when millions of displaced returned home. Missing records exposed communities to further corruption when wealthier parties bribed officials or otherwise illicitly seized properties. Ideally, retaking cities such as Mariupol will include intact property records. Recovering them will not relieve officials of having to determine ownership when owners are deceased or cannot be found. Both require a search for wills and next of kin records. Challenges increase if either the play of chance or Russian malfeasance means property or other needed documents are no longer accessible. It is a situation further complicated when new occupants are those imported by the occupiers as in the case of Mariupol. Once again, developing policies is better done before occupied lands return to the rightful governing authority. (History offers options and cautions in this regard. Allied leaders meeting at Potsdam agreed to expel Germans from areas annexed by WWII Nazis to which they were imported. Thousands of them died during the ensuing movements.)[29] Property rights, fair determination of ownership, and rights of disposal have more than once proven fundamental to perceptions of government legitimacy. It is a point not lost on the authors of *The Resilient City: How Modern Cities Recover from Disaster*: "The power of property rights to stabilize the forms of cities—or stymie their evolution—cannot be overemphasized."[30]

Markedly unlike post-World War II Tokyo, Berlin, Manila, and even Sarajevo, Ukraine's cities are benefiting from officials' unwillingness to wait for the current round of Russia-induced violence to end. The State Agency for Restoration and Infrastructure Development of Ukraine had offered fifty contract tenders by the end of 2023. "De-occupied" regions received priority; lands in or around Kyiv, Odesa, and Kherson were among them. The Kyiv region had already seen over 12,500 structures restored by that point, over 11,000 of which were homes. The eclectic sources of aid further distinguishes Ukraine's recovery from that of cities following WWII. Again in the Kyiv region, these included Austrian charitable foundations (focusing on education-related facilities), Taiwan (a martial arts school), and Nordic Environment Finance Corporation (water, sewage, and heat infrastructure) among the many.[31] Much will doubtless remain to be done once artillery shells, missiles, bombs, and armed UAVs cease their visits, but Ukraine's urban areas should not experience an hour zero nor, hopefully, will the extent of suffering be as it was in those cities having to wait until war's end to begin renewal. The extent of suffering will be less yet if recovery planning accounts for more than physical infrastructure, putting effective capabilities in place to deal with returning displaced, preserving the social healing effects of maintaining urban communities, and readying for the diverse challenges inherent in addressing physiological and psychological injuries suffered by veteran and noncombatant alike. That much of the civilized world is providing Ukrainians previously unparalleled support means city residents, hospitals, and other victims have access to resources rarely available to urban Japan, Germany, and the Philippines eight decades ago, e.g., portable generators and batteries capable of powering utilities while local infrastructure awaits repair. These redundant layers are the more valuable given that Ukrainian cities' wartime recovery has to share scarce resources with the complementary creation of defensive infrastructure such as subterranean schools.[32]

Coherent recovery is impossible without some extent of overarching vision. Goods and services are of limited value if those needing them are unaware they exist or unable to access them. This implies running information programs broadcasting availability on the one hand and providing access to recipients on the other.[33] More insightful programs will foresee the inevitable tensions resulting when refugees and IDPs return to join others who never left, others who are recent first-time arrivals, and any among those whose favorable attitudes regarding things Russian find themselves among others less sympathetic.

Committing resources to address postwar challenges even as conflict rages is already paying significant dividends. We have more than once noted Russia's all-but-inevitable continued interference in Ukrainian affairs once military operations pause. Likely among them are interference in elections, gamesmanship along borders, cyberattacks on both state and commercial functions, theft from occupied cities, and de facto kidnapping, all with precedents. Receiving less attention is Russia's history of counterfeiting foreign currency. Preparing for attempts to disrupt Ukraine's economy in the aftermath of current fighting via this and other means is essential given Putin's reputation for vengeance and his country's previous counterfeiting of US and EU currency.[34] In addition, establishing supply chains for products either in short supply or previously obtained from Russia and Belarus merits priority. Ukraine is fortunate to have production capacity for many items that will be in demand. Notable exceptions include electrical panel components, glass (both categories being ones for which the country was 100 percent reliant on international suppliers before 2022), and cement (14 percent reliant).[35]

Ukraine will be able to draw on recent innovations in melding historical preservation and sustainable development. A third of world heritage sites are in urban areas. Four of Ukraine's eight are so; a fifth is the ancient city of Tauric Chersonese on the Black Sea in Crimea.[36] The 2011 United Nations Educational, Scientific, and Cultural Organization (UNESCO) Recommendation on the Historic Urban Landscape promotes "a holistic approach to managing historic urban areas." The voluntary program provides recommendations regarding civic engagement, planning, regulation, and financing in support of historical preservation, dealing with climate change, and sustainability.[37] Far from year zero, Ukrainians have firm foundations on which to build and many are willing to assist as they do so.

Monitoring, Measuring, and Managing Urban Recovery

> Targets create three common problems. They product perverse results when people focus excessively on them. They tempt managers to manipulate numbers. The obsession with measurement diverts people from useful activity to filling in forms.[38]
> — Bagehot, "Rule by algorithm"

Rather than deal with systems as a whole, contemporary decision-makers tend to concentrate their choices on discrete activities that are easier to identify and understand.

> The problem with that approach is that the more complex and disorganized the system, the more unpredictable the discrete, uninformed intuitive decisions of policy makers may have on driving specific outcomes. Failing to understand how discrete decisions have an impact on the system as a whole can produce unintended and counterproductive consequences. In the aftermath of Hurricane Katrina, for example, emergency officials barred all but authorized emergency responders from entering New Orleans. As a result, fuel handlers which had not been credentialed by officials could not make deliveries to emergency operations centers that were powered by generators. Without gas or fresh batteries, the centers lost power and became inoperable since officials failed to understand how the entire system worked. They fixed one problem—preventing unnecessary convergence at the disaster scene, but they also created another—disabling key command and control nodes.[39]
>
> — James Jay Calafano, "Thinking the Future"

Colonel (US Army) Gregory Fontenot commanded a brigade during its 1995-1996 deployment to Bosnia-Herzegovina. Coordinating mine removal was one of his unit's many responsibilities. A senior leader was impressed when he heard the brigade had facilitated the neutralization of 3,000 mines. As is the case with deminers in Ukraine today, Fontenot was aware the number meant little. The brigade's sector contained an estimated over one million mines. Three thousand mines was a drop in the proverbial bucket (less than 0.3 percent for those interested). The number removed was a measure of effort, a metric of little value other than recording work done. What was significant were the consequences of that labor: its measure of effect. Clearing those 3,000 mines opened forty-five otherwise unusable traffic routes.[40]

History's whispers tell us measuring progress is an arena as rife with pitfalls as helpful advice. Overlooking the importance of designing metrics that provide measures of effect rather than effort is one such shortcoming. A study focusing on strengthening Ukraine's regional and municipal governments provides a somewhat lengthy metrics matrix in its conclusion. Too many of its cells reflect only measures of effort.[41] The reasons for the shortfall are easy to grasp. For example, measuring effort—dollars allocated is a notoriously ineffective metric—is far easier than gauging the consequences of providing the funds. Confusing effort for effect (or settling for an easy-to-collect and simple to display measure in lieu of one effective) is so common as to have become a norm. Bagehot, in the first quotation above, recognizes some of the dangers when employing poorly designed measures: They can motivate wasteful or, even worse, harmful behaviors. Metrics often inherently establish targets. Targets are something motivated leaders seek to achieve. Measuring a unit's combat effectiveness in Vietnam by the number of enemy killed (body count) made killing more foes a target for ambitious leaders. Poorly conceived metrics can also incite outright bizarre behaviors. Hospital administrators directed patients be left in ambulances when a United Kingdom's health policy resulted in penalizing hospitals based on length of time taken to treat individuals after ambulance delivery. Universities are notorious for easy-to-measure but ineffective, even counterproductive measures. How many books and journal articles a faculty member writes is often key to promotions and tenure. Assessing how well one teaches or the impact of those writings—much tougher to determine—too often relies on dubious statistics...if any attempt is made to measure them at all.[42] A case involving the logistics company Maersk provides a nearly perfect example of a confusing effort for effectiveness. Maersk's "call-centre employees were judged on the time spent per complaint. [When] the firm changed the metric for judging success from time spent to other factors, such as issue resolution, customer satisfaction nearly doubled."[43]

Designing policies for Ukrainian recovery will demand means of gauging progress...or lack thereof. Relevant metrics will not only have to clear the above hurdle of reflecting effectiveness rather than effort expended. Measures must also inform relevant decision-makers at all relevant levels in all relevant organizations. Metrics design should additionally consider their possible second and higher-order effects. Ideally, metrics motivate positive behavior. But there is another edge to that blade. Two examples touched on above demonstrate the point. The first is body count as employed during the Vietnam War. Senior leaders considered the number of enemy dead as a measure of progress toward enemy defeat. It instead resulted in some less ethical leaders reporting any deceased Vietnamese as foe, an obvious inaccuracy as noncombatant casualties are, unfortunately, an inevitable part of war. Secondly, as the metric could influence performance reports, less honest leaders simply inflated their numbers. Lastly, the metric's designers were certainly remiss in failing to consider its worst potential consequence: the most unsavory could kill innocents and count them as foe.

The second example posed less of a threat to lives but was no more effective as a measure of success. Given the massive funding committed to recovery after the 2003 defeat of Saddam Hussein's forces in Iraq, leaders at the top considered how much an organization spent as reflecting progress. The metric was easy to tally, easy to understand, and universal: It applied to any organization regardless of type. However, ease of calculation, simplicity of understanding, and universality alone are insufficient justifications for metric design. In Iraq, negative consequences included dollars spent ineffectively or in ways for which determining effectiveness was impossible. The measure drove spending on larger projects rather than those of lesser dollar amounts that might have been more valuable. Putting a large sum toward a single project eases administration; it involves fewer contracts, fewer project managers, fewer reports, and less in the way of resources generally (transportation, security manpower, quality control experts...and the number of metrics one needs to design). Peter Lippman tells us the problem was not limited to Iraq, nor to government-funded undertakings. The same challenges plagued work in Bosnia-Herzegovina:

> Often international NGOs spent money in a hurry toward the end of their budgeting period in the fear that otherwise they could not justify new grants.... This led to wasteful spending and the creation of useless projects.... The international community's...reckless and wasteful expenditure

in the years immediately after the war encouraged local NGOs to sprout like mushrooms. It was crucial for international relief agencies and human rights workers to learn how to assess the sincerity of local NGO workers.... Phantom NGOs with a blank account, and perhaps a brochure, sometimes came into existence solely for the purpose of raking off the dollars and Deutschmarks that were flowing. In addition to these obviously criminal NGOs, there was a spectrum of NGO operations of varied usefulness from feel-good "trauma counseling" with short-lived or nonexistent results to the truly sincere, even heroic, multiethnic organizations.[44]

Demining expert Pehr Lodhammar put it succinctly in terms of his field. He and Greg Fontenot share an understanding of measuring effectiveness: "Success in mine action, unlike in the financial world and elsewhere, is not measured in the money we can raise. It's measured by what we can do with the money we are entrusted with by the member states."[45] Another interviewer provided a reinforcing example demonstrating why donors or others measuring effectiveness in terms of effort miss the point (e.g., number of mines removed per dollar donated):

> Consider the lesson learned from the Fallujah [Iraq] Iron Bridge experience. If the operation was measured in terms of contamination [number of mines removed] alone, the two IEDs destroyed during the week-long effort would seem costly in terms of effort expended yet more than commensurate when valued by the socioeconomic impact. Following clearance and repairs to the [bridge], travel time for some residents to the only maternity hospital in a 50 kilometer (31.1 mile) radius [was] reduced from two hours to five minutes.[46]

A third's remarks also reinforce Lodhammar's observations:

> We cleared one device [from a bridge in Fallujah, Iraq] and it was $100,000. That doesn't sound like good value for money, but that allowed the bridge to be repaired which now allows ten thousand vehicles a day to use the bridge and cuts the time for people trying to get to the hospital from four hours to fifteen minutes. So when you turn around and say what was the impact of that $100,000, it was probably ten thousand times what you'd have spent clearing a field of a thousand mines for $10,000. One is $10/per device and the other's $100,000 per device, but actually the impact was a thousand times more for the $100,000 spent.[47]

Should the above challenges not be daunting enough, creating measures helpful for informing every relevant authority level is often less straightforward than might be thought. Some organizations use a "stoplight" chart to reflect status. Green, for example, might mean 90 percent of an organization's vehicles are operational. Amber (in military-speak; yellow to most of the world) would be 70 to 89 percent are good to go while red reflects readiness of less than 70 percent of vehicles. Can the approach be effective in terms of reflecting a unit's vehicle readiness? Yes...but if a single measure encompasses all vehicle types rather than each type, it might well mislead. If a fuel delivery outlet for a large corporation has all its sales cars working but only half the trucks that make deliveries, higher headquarters might see an amber or even green rating when in fact the most important of the organization's services—getting product to customers—is significantly inhibited. Metric design counts.

A US Department of State representative recalled his time in Iraq and how a means of measuring status could deceive if misunderstood by those reporting or receiving the status. The issue at hand was the success of indigenous police training:

> My team said something in a report that [differed from the report by] the brigade. A call came from Camp Victory asking, "Why are you differing? You shouldn't be differing."... And I said, "If you ask a local leader, 'Are the police trained?' he could truthfully answer, 'Yes.'" So they have all green lights up on the chart, but I might have a red light because yes, they are trained, but they are going around intimidating the people. In our rush to brevity, we sacrifice accuracy, and then the poor general thinks he is informed, but he is not.[48]

The point reminds us of donors who mistakenly thought measures such as cost per square meter of mines removed reflected the benefits reaped by their funds. The number of hours spent training the police provided no measure of benefit. What those law enforcement personnel learned and how they applied their knowledge was the real metric of value. It was also one far harder to design and measure. So too with gauging the effects of unexploded ordnance neutralization.

The burden on metric designers tasked with tracking Ukrainian cities' recovery is a heavy one. Reports will have to inform (and thus be comprehensible to) managers at multiple Ukrainian government echelons and organizations, funding nations' representatives, NGOs, IGOs, and others. Resulting metrics will influence participant willingness to continue providing support. That implies considering these organizations' perspectives in the creative process. Interest in locations, types, and scope of Ukrainian corruption provides a prime example. The matter is not simply one of whether corruption is sufficiently constrained. Corruption of concern to one set of donors will be of little interest to others. Corruption metrics need to be dynamic as well, necessitating periodic revisiting by their designers. The corrupt are nothing if not adaptable. They quickly learn how to game existing countermeasures and metrics to their benefit. Agile measures make adaptation easier for those seeking to contain corruption. They also avoid the jolting consequences of having to create and present entirely new metrics as conditions evolve. The source reporting Maersk's initial metric misstep went on to observe, "often the problem stems from new regulations being introduced without thinking through the implications."[49] (Recall our comment about the need to consider a metric's second and higher-order effects.) This returns us to the value of wargaming. Remember its sequence of action->reaction->counteraction? The "enemy" (in our example corrupt parties) is smart, connected, and adaptive. That means wargaming the course ahead in terms of dealing with the corrupt needs to go beyond objectives as they are today to consider how goals will have to change in order to respond effectively or, preferably, stay a step ahead of corrupt individuals' maneuvers.

Corruption's penetration of Ukrainian society and ability to shapeshift in response to counters makes addressing the challenge something akin to whack-a-mole. Perhaps a necessary first step is to see corruption not as a single beast but rather as a phenomenon of many forms, all more or less adaptive in the ecosystem that is Ukrainian society. The organisms making up an ecosystem adapt to change, abandoning no longer lucrative niches and filling those newly revealed or abandoned by others. In terms of corruption in the ecosystem that is Ukraine, participants include individuals relying on ill-gotten gains for enrichment or survival, peripheral employees hired to facilitate day-to-day activities, and near-innocents caught up in such practices as paying for services that should be free. This dynamic, multi-faceted nature attracts piecemeal anti-corruption approaches. They are unlikely to do other than nibble at the outer crust of the challenge and—as in the case of policing black marketing or pursuing alleged collaborators—punish minnows while sharks escape unscathed. Significant results demand a systemic, long-term, continuous, similarly adaptive campaign plan melding efforts at all levels of government and across the public-private divide. Anti-corruption reforms put in place by Bolivia's National Tax Service earned the admiration of Norway's Anti-Corruption Resource Centre for its agility. Inherent in their success: recognizing the need for a comprehensive, vice piecemeal, approach:

> Steady changes over a number of years gradually closed the gaps by bringing reality in line with design expectations: different data was gathered on taxpayers; old and absent information technology was updated; the process for making tax payments was streamlined; more than 80%

of staff were replaced and their skill sets were expanded; and so on. This gap closure created a new system that worked.[50]

The center's analysis also noted the importance of initial anti-corruption program design, citing a frequent cause of failure as applying techniques used elsewhere to environments where they were less suitable. Problems arise when "design expectations do not draw directly, or even predominantly, from the world of the actors who deploy and use the anti-corruption initiative, but from the world of the designer."[51]

These findings and Ukrainian corruption's ubiquitous character suggest a multinational undertaking with international reach. Extending partnerships beyond design into a long-term relationship proved beneficial during a Sri Lankan government anti-corruption initiative:

> When the Sri Lankan State Accounts Department decided to introduce a more transparent approach to publication of financial statements...it required the long-term presence of design consultants working alongside departmental staff. This enabled the designers to move beyond the "discourse of rationality" to a closer contextual understanding. It also enabled greater staff participation in processes of design and implementation.[52]

Resulting anti-corruption policies should recognize local practices without unquestionably accepting their legitimacy. Metrics and objectives need to pursue reasonable ends. Users need to recognize progress will be gradual and some extent of corruption percolates within even the most ethical of world societies. International reach will be necessary if Ukraine is to seize oligarch, crooked farmer, and other of the corrupts' illicit gains. Assistance provided Kyiv in recovering these monies would be another example of other parties providing soft aid.

Effective aid delivery is inevitably multi-faceted. Measuring effectiveness is a function of many variables, among them: what is delivered (Does it meet recipient needs?), what form delivery takes (Are recipients put at risk? Does the aid undermine economic recovery?), who receives it (Does it go to individuals or groups in need?), and when and where delivery comes (Does it arrive in a timely fashion where need exists?). Dropping aid in a convenient location without arranging for follow-on transport might tick the "delivered" block for the lazy or scared when recipients are in a dangerous location. Favoring recipients with marginal if any need because they reside in a safe location is not unheard of.[53] Such forms of aid corruption allow providers to report favorable statistics and thereby continue to receive funding. The ability to provide guidance for delivery to those most in need and monitor whether appropriate whats, whos, whens, and wheres are on the receiving end remains a mark on the wall not always reached.

The example of police training makes it clear that careful definition and monitoring of how users employ a metric is crucial to its value. The example below demonstrates how shortcomings in metric design, misleading reporting (deliberate or otherwise), and inattention to conditions on the ground can combine to misinform and lead to waste:

One food kit can support three people. Regardless of how many it was actually helping, it was being recorded as going to three people. Taking reporting shortcuts like that is pretty common in NGO work. Some INGOs [international nongovernmental organizations] were going to big cities and distributing aid to those who didn't really need it [because it was easy. One mega-donor] adapted and demanded rural distribution as well, but not until mid-2023. Until then it was a wild west environment and they only cared about how much money was spent.[54]

To be fair, distributing large amounts of support in any form under dangerous conditions or when needs are urgent is a task demanding exceptional management skills and dedication by employees and volunteers. Waiting to establish a firm understanding of the crisis environment delays provision of aid, perhaps at the cost of lives. Early days and weeks are periods of simultaneously providing support and learning on-the-job. Yet too often the same mistakes made initially are allowed to remain in place. Having one or more macro-perspective organizations to provide guidance via identifying where residents are wanting, what type of support they need, and how urgent that need is would be a mega-step toward improved early (and continuing) delivery effectiveness. Larger organizations can shorten their individual learning curves by similarly putting boots on the ground in the form of troubleshooting quality control teams. Ideally these organizational teams would be part of a collective in which teams inform both their own representatives and those of other groups.

To summarize, quality metrics focus on effects, avoid motivating negative behaviors, encourage positive behaviors, and provide sufficiently granulated results to support decision-making at all relevant echelons. Creation of ready-to-use metrics waiting "on the shelf" for immediate use once support operations begin would be another leap forward. These standing metrics will need adaptation to fit local or evolving conditions. More effective aid organizations already employ solid practices in this regard. Rather than providers making assumptions, representatives gauge needs by requiring recipients to complete preliminary questionnaires with questions such as "Are your family members skipping meals?" Following up with the same question after aid delivery provides a basis for refining support. Managers can adapt base levels when assisting elderly, special needs, or other exceptional recipients. Familiarity with an environment can spawn further efficiencies. Delivery of some aid via Ukraine's Ukrposhta (National Postal System) may be feasible, for example, as Ukrposhta is well regarded in the country and a proven quantity. The organization has long distributed pension payments and has control mechanisms in place to reduce fraud, e.g., representatives require identification verification before making disbursements. Alternatively, cash cards or payments to mobile phones via apps allowing remote replenishment can be even quicker and cheaper when local conditions permit.[55]

Metrics are managers' GPS. Leaders establish goals and plot a course to their accomplishment. Chances of success are slim if they don't know whether they are on or off track. Successful recovery requires not just understanding how the uncountable (and everchanging) pieces of the whole fit together. It demands managers seek out and take advantage of available synergies. Synergy during recovery means more than merely the whole being greater than the sum of its parts. It comes to encompass timeliness, accurate scoping, minimizing waste, and resilience in the face of changing conditions. One might not be able to predict the future—to determine exactly what will happen and where and when an occurrence will take place. But effective metrics can aid in forecasting the likelihood of possible outcomes: They can point to possible results and provide reasonable probability estimates that each will come to be. This in turn provides a basis for calculating risk. Lucius Clay put education on the back burner early in his post-WWII tenure in Germany, assigning priority to food provision. The choice seemed the logical one...at first. But rarely are recovery decisions of an either-or nature. They are instead judgments regarding proportion. What percentage of resource A is best allocated to need 1 vice needs 2, 3, or otherwise? Perfect understanding of how a recovery system's parts create a whole and influence each other is management nirvana. It isn't going to happen. Having a reasonable grasp is essential. Successful recovery, like war waged well, demands a systems approach to orchestration.[56] Consciously capitalizing on synergistic relationships constitutes systems management at rarely attained levels, levels artificial intelligence might in future years more often make achievable. In the meantime, pursuit improves outcomes even when it falls short of perfection.

One among many examples demonstrates the complexity inherent in recovery while hinting at the benefits of capitalizing on potential synergies. Housing is the most damaged sector of Ukraine's infrastructure. Resulting problems in addressing housing infrastructure's physical component—not only apartment buildings, dormitories, and stand-alone houses, but also other sub-infrastructures overlapping it: streets, power and water supply, schools, and much more—have economic and social counterparts. Issues include how to rebuild while maintaining or restoring communities; how to address ethical, economic, and other divides (existent or latent); how best to manage the turmoil of returning IDPs and refugees (another potential source of tension); and how to address the too many factors yet to completely show themselves: climate change, further Russian aggression, new or improved means of generating and transmitting power, new technologies such as self-driving vehicles, and resident desires for safer pedestrian walkways and bikeways. (Vehicle-related accident numbers in Ukraine are well above those for the EU with pedestrians disproportionately being victims.) Advances in disaster response merit a look. The above call for wiser placement of and better protection for power generation equipment, mainframe computers, and other infrastructure elements should address both further Russian aggression and natural disasters such as flooding. Tokyo's commendable disaster planning system includes maps for residents that specify safe emergency evacuation locations. These locations include clever initiatives such as pop-up toilets and park benches convertible to cooking grills.[57] Then there is the already budding recurrence of debates familiar from Tokyo, Berlin, Manila, Sarajevo: Determining the most effective, popularly desired, culturally appreciative, security conscious, and resource conservative way of rebuilding...each of these in tension with the others but also a source of potential synergies. And speaking (well, writing actually) of tension, there is the friction between centralized orchestration and decentralized decision-making during recovery. Though on a micro-scale in comparison with what confronts Ukraine's cities, the following observations regarding the response to the 9/11 attacks on the World Trade Center suggest an approach to dealing with this particular tension:

> Orders were being given on the spot by junior officers without the big picture. Clearly the vacuum had to be filled and a centralized command structure had to be reestablished…. "We had to get a citywide command center up because we had a citywide problem…. We decided to leave [local decisions] on the scene to [the] officers already on the scene"…but the big picture would be managed from Police Plaza.[58]

In other words, guidance from the top allowed those below to make informed decisions in light of conditions on the ground.

Ten percent of Ukraine's housing stock has been damaged or destroyed as I ready to send this manuscript to its press. Russian attacks assure more harm to come even as the country repairs, restores, or replaces. Elsewhere, unexploded ordnance renders intact structures uninhabitable. Return of IDPs and refugees, imported Russians, and

Ukrainians moving to new jobs, university, or otherwise mean both permanent and temporary housing will be in demand. There will also be individuals moving from rural environs seeking employment in cities, their farmland no longer viable thanks to Russian mines too numerous to remove in the near term (and, potentially in some cases, ever). The pain is real, but there is reason to trust solutions will not be too distant once fighting ceases. Such was not the case in Germany after World War II when the last of displaced person camps closed only in 1966. Yet we must at the same time guard against over-optimism. Those dislodged from New Orleans by Hurricane Katrina in some cases remained in temporary housing ten years later, this in the advanced society of the United States.[59] Ukraine is poor in comparison to the European Union norm. It has historically been considerably more corrupt than most Western peers. Its population is aging and diminished in numbers. The road ahead is rife with such potholes as well as mines. Recent recovery undertakings in Iraq, Afghanistan, Sierra Leone, Haiti, and elsewhere are often more sobering than sources of insights to guide the way ahead.

Amidst the organizations bringing together recovery donors, planners, architects, and other partners, one stands out with its efforts to provide coherent oversight. Created in January 2023 at the initiative of the G7 countries, European Commission, and Ukraine,

> the Multi-agency Donor Coordination Platform for Ukraine coordinates the support for...immediate financing needs of Ukraine and future economic recovery and reconstruction needs across different sources and

established instruments for financing. Its goal is also to direct resources in a coherent, transparent, and inclusive manner, enabling efficient planning and delivery of assistance to Ukraine and avoiding duplication.[60]

Announcing membership expansion at the Platform's first meeting in 2024, the European Commission explained,

> As of February 2024, it includes four additional temporary members, namely the Republic of Korea, The Netherlands, Norway, and Sweden as well as observers from six EU Member States - Denmark, Estonia, Latvia, Lithuania, Poland and Spain. To join the Platform as temporary members, states have contributed since February 2022, or have committed to contribute, at least 0.1% of the country's 2022 GDP and at least USD 1 billion. To join as observers, states have contributed since February 2022, or have committed to contribute, at least 0.05% of the country's 2022 GDP or at least USD 300 million (USD 200 million for EU Member States). Membership and observer status are contingent on continued support to Ukraine and will be reassessed on a regular basis. International financial institutions, such as the European Investment Bank, the European Bank for Reconstruction and Development, the International Monetary Fund and the World Bank, also participate in the platform to coordinate efforts to address Ukraine's financing needs, both in the short to medium-term.... In this regard, it will coordinate international efforts to support a sustainable, resilient, inclusive, and green economic recovery which enhances strong democratic institutions, rule of law, and anti-corruption measures.[61]

Included in their self-imposed tasks, platform members are to coordinate economic aid in conjunction with Ukrainian objectives and major donor conditions with an eye toward the country's eventual membership in the EU. If the cooperative venture can succeed in meeting its objectives, benefits would include a consistent flow of aid money to Ukraine in at least the immediate term. The charter, however, appears to take a very much macro perspective on coordination, meaning the requirement to apportion aid between competing sectors in a manner capitalizing on opportunities for synergy could remain unmet. Undoubtedly a step in the right direction, a more robust charter or creation of a subordinate organization to take on these highly complex additional tasks will be necessary to minimize waste and provide effective oversight at the execution level. That desire to maintain a consistent funding flow is at once highly desirable and a bear to achieve, the more so given the number of participating donors and nature of politics in some of the largest donor countries. Confidence in sustained levels of funding allows planning long-term, the benefits of which include efficiencies otherwise impossible. The internal debates hindering US aid commitments to Ukraine in early 2024 have precedence. That the United States eventually did much to assist allies, former enemies, and others after World War II is well known. Less touted are the Congressional squabbles and other factors delaying that assistance. Reasons behind the delays included inexperience in creating an alliance of the complexity needed to deter the Soviet Union, discomfort in dealing with future unknowns, and fears that once started, curtailing aid would prove impossible.[62] Ironically both the funding challenges and subject of deterrence are all too familiar in today's Ukraine.

CHAPTER 7

■ Black Markets and Ukraine's Urban Recovery

This town is in a hell of a mess. There's gang warfare going on and we're fishing bodies out of the Passig River all the time. Everybody is trying to control the black market, prostitution, and various rackets including stealing and fencing. There are political factions vying for control of the system.[63]

— Major Dalton O'Brien (US Army), commenting on just retaken Manila

The postwar challenge in Sarajevo and throughout Bosnia was far more complex than simply recovering from the physical scars of the conflict. The black market dealing and smuggling channels that proved so essential to the Bosnian war effort at the same time contributed to the criminalization of the state, economy, and society—with serious repercussions for reconstruction.... While Bosnia's formal, aboveground economy struggled to recover, the informal, underground economy flourished—generating substantial revenue and employment and becoming part of the basic survival strategy for many in the face of bleak economic prospects. In 2002, the World Bank estimated that the underground economy represented between 50 and 60 percent of Bosnia's GDP.... While the physical scars of war are the most visible, the social repercussions may be more consequential.[64]

— Peter Andreas, *Blue Helmets and Black Markets*

Inter arma enim silent leges (In time of war, the law is silent.)[65]

— Cicero

Tokyo, Berlin, Manila, and Sarajevo: Black markets were among the wartime and postwar phenomenon common to all. Above discussions present only too clearly the mixed bag black markets present to authorities and residents. Downsides include loss of tax revenue, promotion of crime (often of the violent sort), breeding of corruption, and their preying on the hungry, destitute, and otherwise vulnerable. Among benefits: provision of necessities—food arguably foremost—and jobs. Without them the calories needed to survive can be too few. With them, foodstuffs and more find themselves misdirected from legitimate sources to the underground economy.

Ignoring black markets risks criminal violence, populations under the thumb of organized crime and the corrupt, and city governments' legitimacy and funding put at risk. Ukraine's cities will hopefully avoid the worst of black markets' underlying causes: starvation, an inability to keep killing cold at bay, and lack of medicines and other life essentials. That there will be some extent of black marketing seems inevitable. If not food, war's destruction suggests there will be competition for construction materials, household goods, other hard-to-get items, and—regrettably—weapons.

The below is a brief return to our four exemplar cities and what they might offer in the way of managing black market challenges in Ukrainian cities, to include Mariupol and others that might in the future return to their rightful country's fold. To the original quartet of examples we add a fifth: Bosnia-Herzegovina's Arizona Market, recent history's arguably most prominent and rigorously studied example of an informal market's birth and development.

CHAPTER 7

Once Again: Tokyo, Berlin, Manila, and Sarajevo

> The poorest searched smouldering refuse heaps for cast-off items that might somehow be bartered for a scrap to eat or something to wear. Black markets (*yami'ichi*, literally "dark market") run by Japanese, Koreans and Formosans mushroomed to replace collapsed distribution channels and cash in on inflated prices.... Black market yami goods fetched prices more than 30 times higher than those for officially controlled commodities. Such markets also were awash with food stores, clothing and industrial equipment pilfered from military stockpiles by corrupt industrialists, bureaucrats and former military officers whose illegal activities made black marketeering a low-risk, high-growth industry.[66]
>
> — Takemae Eiji, *Inside GHQ: The Allied Occupation of Japan and Its Legacy*

> It was surely some kind of record for speed. Three days after the end of the war—and a full ten before the first American soldier set foot in Japan—[a] newspaper advertisement appeared for what would be the nation's first postwar black market.... By August 20, only five days after Japan had officially conceded defeat, the Ozu open-air market was ready to roll.[67]
>
> — Robert Whiting, *Tokyo Underworld: The Fast Times and Hard Life of an American Gangster in Japan*

For all the problems Tokyo's black markets caused Japanese and American officials, it is undeniable they provided a means to supplement official ration's starvation calorie levels while also providing employment for those socially marginalized—war widows, orphans, and war wounded among them. Though Douglas MacArthur's headquarters would succeed in closing down many before 1950, Japanese authorities in Tokyo sometimes resisted. The markets provided goods not elsewise available, goods essential to economic recovery.[68] Initially stocked by corrupt officials with stores stockpiled in readiness for an Allied land invasion that never came, black markets became battlegrounds of another sort as Japanese, Korean, and Chinese gangs fought for control. Authorities—occupying and local—never succeeded in completely taming Tokyo's markets. Several of their original locations continue to host small, albeit much evolved, markets today.

Berlin's seventy million cubic meters of rubble constituted nearly a fifth of that within the boundaries of what was Germany in 1938.[69] Consequently short of housing sufficient to protect its population from the elements, capital residents suffered further from a food distribution infrastructure that at times fell well short of amounts authorized for ration card holders. Such was the case in November 1946 when but 342 of a promised 1,500 tons of vegetables reached the American Berlin sector. Nor was quality assured even when quantities hit their targets. It was not unusual for logisticians to substitute lower-grade products when better ones were not at hand.[70] Growling stomachs drew the hungry to black markets. There they became part of one or more of what Dr. Paul Steege concludes were four types of market exchanges:

- *Underhand trade* in which a party demands some additional good before providing a desired product or service for normal compensation. For example, a plumber requires he be given several pounds of potatoes in addition to money before he agrees to repair broken fixtures.

- *Barter/Trade-in-kind/gray marketing* wherein there is an exchange of controlled goods outside of the monetary economy, e.g., a veterinarian performs pet surgery in exchange for jewelry.

- *Black market trade*: Unlawful trading in rationed goods or the means to obtain those goods (such as coupons or ration cards) in exchange for money. A person selling ham at an inflated price without demanding the required meat coupon would constitute black market trade.

- *Racketeering* in which the goal was personal enrichment. Large-scale black market trading or actions that significantly undermine an economy's functions. Also called "professional black marketing."[71]

Usurious profits made participation in black market sales too lucrative to ignore for some. Police in Berlin estimated between 5 and 7 percent of rationed food products ended up there. The losses were between 10 and 12 percent for rationed textiles. Frequent Berlin grocery store break-ins fed illicit sales. Store owners waylaid their stock. Murders and other serious crimes had direct links to black marketing. Prosecution alone failed to staunch the flow.[72] Black market sellers and buyers' fluid adaptations to officials' efforts to close them down further challenged any seeking to mitigate the illegal activities.

The August 1946 US creation of barter centers to reduce suffering of the desperate and control runaway black marketeering little slowed the juggernaut. Berlin's youth crime spiked three months later as 14 to 18 year-olds turned to theft to feed themselves, help family members, or supply racketeers.[73] Similar official markets in the Soviet sector spawned black markets in locations nearby as items exchanged in the legitimate forums made their way to those otherwise.[74] Manipulation became political art. The aforementioned CARE packages with their some 40,000 calories and luxuries such as candies, coffee, and canned meats scored a public relations coup for American officials.[75] Berliners quickly recognized the obviousness of Russian attempts to buy votes by boosting distribution in the runup to city elections. The effort only reinforced resident distrust of the Soviets whose reputation would never recover from their barbarous acts on capturing the city. Their reputation suffered further when it became known that the Communist Party of Germany's kitchen tailored meals depending on rank. "Normal" party workers got but a bowl of stew while party secretaries dined on multiple course meals accompanied by wine, a stark contrast between proclamations of communist equality and reality at the table.[76] This as Berliners died both directly due to starvation and other disorders magnified by poor diets.[77]

Black markets in wartime and postwar Manila further demonstrated variety. The University of Santo Tomas prisoner of war camp housed many American and other civilians captured following the January 1942 fall of Manila. The camp had its own black market system through which internees could purchase a wide variety of items. The just under 3,700 imprisoned ate cats, pigeons, dogs, and rats. The importance of such trade is evident in the camp's death rate. Three to four died of starvation daily in the period just before the camp's February 1945 liberation.[78]

As in Tokyo and Berlin, Manila's black markets contained items pilfered from legitimate sources after the city was retaken. Corrupt officials capitalized on their access to such goods. Many gained considerable wealth built on their fellow residents' misery. The Philippine government suffered from its own apathy in addressing this corruption as members of the insurgent Hukbalahap movement turned to the markets for weapons, ammunition, and other items essential to their struggle.[79] An American military investigation revealed sales of surplus US jeeps by a group that included the sons of Manila's mayor, Secretary of Labor, and police chief. Atrocities committed by these men to protect their business included ordering the murder of an American investigator's infant daughter.[80]

With criminal elements so firmly embedded in its military and government organizations, it would have courted unbelievability had Sarajevo not been home to rampant black marketeering during and after the city's siege. Similarly unsurprising: inter-ethnic cooperation even as leaders condemned other groups in public pronouncements. Food, cigarettes, fuel, and other product sales "thrived along Serb Sarajevo's boundary with Croat-controlled areas" during the fighting.[81] The tentacles of illicit operations extended beyond Sarajevo proper. In the words of Serb Sarajevo's mayor:

> We have at least 150 mafia guys who drive unregistered Volkswagens. They wear uniforms, carry pistols and the most contemporary weapons, (sun)glasses, walk around,

and no one dares engage them. They steal, walk, kill, engage in black market operations...from Ilidza, Rajlovac, Vogosca, to Ilijas, and we all fear them.[82]

Those unregistered Volkswagens were available for purchase. Hundreds were stolen from the VW plant in Vogosca (a town less than ten kilometers northwest of Sarajevo) in a scandal implicating both local and Republika Srpska authorities. The vehicles were never recovered.[83]

These markets continued to thrive before police action eventually imposed some measure of government control after the war, but not before members of Sarajevo's underground numbered themselves "among the wealthiest and best protected of Sarajevo's new elite," this while most Sarajevans were earning "only a small fraction of what they did in 1970 and are correspondingly impoverished."[84] The city's inflation surged in the decade after the war thanks to the number of international organizations there, a surge diminishing only as donor fatigue set in. Construction was an exception in an otherwise stagnated economy due in considerable part to international donations. Cultural structures received particular attention. Unfortunately, some served to emphasize ethnic differences rather than healing. A massive mosque and cultural center were among the prominent buildings thought by some to be out of place amongst Sarajevo's traditional architecture and more secular Muslims. Lawlessness permeated capital life. Competing claims regarding property ownership proved a bureaucratic quagmire given the combination of forcibly ousted tenants, resistance to minority representatives in majority-dominated ethnic communities, previous owners gaming return procedures to their advantage, and long duration occupation of publicly-owned properties under socialist Yugoslavia residents thought constituted ownership. Continued voting along ethnic party lines joined corruption and bureaucratic interference to reinforce economic inertia, although the majority claimed to reject ethnic exclusivity.[85] Author Peter Andreas summarized this unfortunate vestige of Sarajevo's black marketeering:

> A legacy of the war was the criminalization of the city, as power and influence shifted during wartime to those most connected in the shadowy world of clandestine transactions. While physical destruction was the most visible legacy of the siege, the city's political and social transformation was the most consequential and long lasting.[86]

Corruption fueled by Sarajevo's wartime black marketing became the muscle propelling postwar misdirection of aid money. Bosnia's recovery reportedly saw up to $1 billion of some $5 billion in international aid funds disappear into corrupt pockets.[87] Few suffered for their greed. Local politicians supported international requests for an amnesty law pardoning deserters and draft dodgers, cleverly expanding it to include crimes involving misuse of aid or black marketing. What cases did go to court focused on the higher profile of war crimes, relegating organized criminality to a distant second. Novelist Loren Estleman once wrote of a city government "too busy counting violent crimes to estimate the number of rats in residence."[88] Estleman was writing of actual rats in Detroit, but his words well fit post-war Sarajevo, a case of fiction describing reality. Lack of public confidence in Sarajevo and Bosnia's legal systems generally gave witnesses pause when considering coming forward to testify. Given the frequent use of brutality during and after the war, that hesitation was surely also motivated by fear of violent retribution.[89]

With some exceptions, Sarajevo's black markets were considerably less vital to residents as a means of avoiding starvation or freezing to death in winter than was the case in Berlin. Their legacy remains far more potent, however. It permeates city politics and ethnic divisions more than two decades later. Actual elements of those markets linger as well, with sales of tobacco products primary among them. Elimination of black markets during the war and in its immediate aftermath may be undesirable if the illicit exchanges are life-sustaining. Even if otherwise, complete elimination in the immediate aftermath of fighting is well-nigh impossible. Former UNHCR Chief of Operations in Sarajevo during the siege helped put the situation in perspective. An organization's arms or aid should not appear in a black market, but it is wrong to assume the blame lies with the agency whose logo is stamped on the bag of flour:

> Some aid does go adrift. Even in the best of supermarkets, in the most sophisticated of countries, "shrinkage" occurs. A percentage goes missing. The trick is to keep it as low as possible. We normally pride ourselves on very little shrinkage within our own ranks. The troubles normally begin once we have delivered it, once we have handed it over. As often as not, this is to local authorities.[90]

CHAPTER 7

The Arizona Market

> At the Arizona Market, stall owners and patrons come from all of Bosnia's ethnic groups and even across borders from neighboring Croatia and Serbia to sell goods and find deals. Coffee shops at the Arizona Market serve people of all religious faiths and ethnicity. On a daily basis, Bosniaks, Serbs, and Croats interact, socialize, exchange information and sometimes discover how similar they really are.[91]
>
> — Benjamin Feit and Michael Morfit, "A Neutral Space: The Arizona Market as an Engine for Peace and a New Economy in Bosnia and Herzegovina"

> By 2005, the Arizona Market bore little resemblance to the rustic trading area it had been less than five years earlier. None of the wooded stalls remained. Retailers, including two bank branches, had moved into permanent buildings with full utilities, and Italproject was paying about $17 million in taxes to the District…but the venture counted on the presence of a Supervisor to keep the district from returning to low-level warfare or worse.[92]
>
> — Bruce R. Scott and Edward N. Murphy, "Brcko and the Arizona Market"

The likelihood of black marketing in post-war Ukraine begs the question of the extent to which the country's mayors should attempt to influence their operation. Mayors cannot tackle the challenge alone. As in Sarajevo, black markets depend on a system of supply, demand, and connections no less than does legitimate commercial intercourse. Policies regulating their operations will have to have both urban area-wide and broader influence.

Prominent if not preeminent in any discussion of recent informal markets is that which arose fifteen kilometers southwest of Brcko, Bosnia-Herzegovina after cessation of fighting in the northern portion of the country. The city of Brcko was in a unique situation. It was the node where two portions of Republika Srpska came together at a very narrow junction, making it appear as the link between two lungs. (See Image 3 on page 97.) The non-Serb residents of the town had suffered terribly as a result of this geographical fluke given Serb efforts to control the vital terrain. Over half of those living within its boundaries were Bosniak when Brcko fell to Serb forces in 1992. Those forces conducted a brutal cleansing. Forced ousters and killings combined with an influx of Serbs fleeing from elsewhere left the town with an estimated population of 45,000 by 1996, 97.5 percent of whom were Serb as compared to 20 percent before the city's fall.[93]

Those negotiating the General Framework for Peace in Bosnia and Herzegovina (commonly known as the Dayton Accords based on where the negotiations took place) recognized Brcko's critical status and need to deny its unhindered control by either Republika Srpska or those in Sarajevo. To do otherwise would divide Republika Srpska or block local movement between the Federation of Bosnia-Herzegovina and Croatia. The Accords therefore dictated Brcko would have a multi-ethnic governing body. US military forces were to ensure opposing parties respected this special status as they patrolled a local Zone of Separation extending

> for a distance of approximately two (2) kilometers on either side of the Agreed Cease-Fire Line. No weapons other than those of the IFOR [Implementation Force] are

permitted in this Agreed Cease-Fire Zone of Separation except as provided herein. No individual may retain or possess any military weapons or explosives within this four kilometer Zone without specific approval of the IFOR. Violators of this provision shall be subject to military action by the IFOR, including the use of necessary force to ensure compliance.[94]

This Zone of Separation (ZOS) in the vicinity of Brcko was the responsibility of not the UN or NATO but the US Department of Defense (DoD) which in turn assigned it to the US Army. The de facto possession by a neutral party was why the Arizona Market rose from what was nothing more than empty space beside a major road. Protected and administered by the Americans, local political bosses could not levy their habitual extortionate taxes, could not favor cronies with business advantages, and (ideally) could not conduct criminal activity within the ZOS.[95] As such, the ZOS became a haven free from the worst of ethnic prejudice and corresponding violence that had fueled the war. Critically, the ambiguity of the Dayton Agreement provided the DoD great flexibility in how they conducted security operations. That included lack of a specific date when American sovereign control would end.[96] Unlike so many past contingencies in which outsiders unwisely set a departure date for their forces, any party wanting to benefit from activities within the ZOS had to obey the Americans' rules or risk missing out.

The initial unit responsible for security of the ZOS southwest of Brcko was 1st Brigade, 1st Armored Division commanded by Colonel Gregory Fontenot. A platoon of soldiers, to include its four M1 Abrams tanks, manned a location along Bosnian Highway 18-1, designated Route Arizona by the Americans.[97] Unannounced and unexpected, in March 1996 a man driving a battered Trabant drove toward the checkpoint and stopped a short distance from the Americans. He unloaded some bags of sugar, cassette tapes, and bottles of liquor, setting them along the roadside. Other cars soon pulled off the road on seeing the goods available for sale. Such was the start of the Arizona Market. Asked by the soldiers what he was doing, the man responded he "felt safer" in the presence of the Americans within the ZOS where opposing ethnic groups were prohibited from carrying arms. He returned the next day. Others soon joined him. Within two months 250-300 persons were on-site either buying or selling, their parked cars stretching over a mile along the roadside. (Mijo Anić, the mayor of Ravne-Brcko, a Croat area, said other markets had previously existed in the area, but no Croat was going to risk establishing an enterprise in an area controlled by Serbs or Bosniaks, a situation applying to all three ethnic groups and their relations with the other two.)[98] Foreseeing the seemingly inevitable, Fontenot arranged for locals to clear mines from nearby fields.[99] (Doing so was a responsibility of the former opposing forces as dictated in the Dayton Accord.)[100] A wide range of foodstuffs, liquor, automobile parts, clothing, and more was exchanging hands between over a thousand daily participants less than three months after arrival of that lone Trabant.[101] Fontenot would recall the earliest days when people began to turn up at the checkpoint. It was a safe place to gather to meet people from the other side, or even neighbors. And it was not long before people were selling cigarettes and gasoline and peppers. Then a fellow came one day with a van, and he set up a small stand to sell coffee, and that helped attract more people. The next thing we knew, we had cars parking along the road and people congregating, at least during the daytime. Soon the crowds became an obstruction for those using the highway.... There were thousands of mines [in the vicinity].... NATO forces were forbidden to clear them by the Dayton Treaty. That was up to the Bosniaks, Croats, and Serbs. So I persuaded them to help, and I coordinated the mine clearing.... Next thing you know stands were beginning to appear and there was again a shortage of space and the need to clear more mines and add gravel.[102]

The Arizona Market's evolutions would continue. "Feeling safer" was the critical component. Customers could buy products, eat, drink, or socialize at more than one thousand stalls by mid-1999. One hundred and fifty trucks sold wares directly from their chassis. Estimates of the number employed reached 2,500 with an additional 7,500's welfare linked to the market. Stabilization Force civil affairs personnel estimated weekend visitors during summer months at fifteen to twenty-five thousand. [Stabilization Force (SFOR) was NATO's new designation for what was previously Implementation Force]. Estimates pegged annual trade at US$50 million. Stalls paid a fee and vehicles paid to park, the funds going to Mijo Anić's Ravne-Brcko government as the market land was Croat-owned.[103] Sellers came to include Bosnia-Herzegovina's Bosniaks, Croats, and Serbs. Hungarians, Poles, and Turks were among other merchants. There were no taxes collected, a sore point with local political leaders.[104] The Arizona Market remained completely within the ZOS and was therefore not subject to local oversight.[105]

As in Sarajevo, leaders from Croat, Serb, and Bosniak factions were said to have been among those meeting at market locations. US Army representatives became Arizona Market proponents given its facilitating social exchange, commercial cooperation, employment, and economic sustainment. Prior to his turning the area over to his successor, Fontenot championed the Posavina Working Group bringing local community, civilian organization, and military representatives together to consider economic and political issues.[106] The market also benefited from the early influence of Anić. A political moderate, the mayor resisted pressures from local power brokers who resented his increased influence and income resultant of the market.[107] It was he, working with Fontenot and other American military officers, who assisted in planning mine removal, installation of sewerage, provision of gravel, and providing funds to local authorities for infrastructure improvements.[108]

The market's growth came to include less savory commercial enterprises, prostitution and sale of pirated materials and stolen goods among them. Merchants, for example, were purportedly selling copper piping stolen from neighboring communities by various military groups.[109] More serious accusations included human trafficking. Calls for its closure came from the United Nations mission in Bosnia-Herzegovina; local political leaders unhappy with the loss of influence and inability to access related fees; and other influential sources local, regional, and international. American military forces maintained control in the face of both verbal and physical assaults, the latter including multiple attempts by local police to seize control of the market and close it down, this at the direction of Tuzla canton authorities (Tuzla canton being directly to the Arizona Market's south and resultantly an area its leaders believed was losing potential tax revenue).[110] Fontenot and his successors recognized there were problems with sanitation infrastructure as the market grew, conflicts between shop operators and original owners of the land on which the market sat, and some extent of criminal enterprise and other unsavory activity.[111] However, the possibility these complaints might be inflated by one or more of the many parties opposing the Arizona Market's existence suggested considered judgment rather than kneejerk reaction. Inspections by high ranking military personnel and checks on accusations resulted in conclusions that claims were exaggerated.[112] The market's evolution continued. By early 2000 it contained an estimated 2,000 stalls, drew thousands of daily shoppers, and supported some 10,000 persons.

On November 16th of that year, Office of High Representative Supervisor Gary Matthews released his "Supervisory Order on Arizona Market" that would better regulate and considerably change the nature of the market. All in-place business licenses were subject to revalidation. Any unlicensed enterprise had to apply for one within thirty days or be closed down. The market would operate on fixed hours with penalties for any violators. A police substation would be located within the market. The supervisory order also required the Brcko District mayor to create a task force from members of his police force. His government was to develop a comprehensive market regulation plan.[113] Henry Clarke took over the supervisor position in April 2001. Also pressured to close the market, he concluded the primary challenge was not criminality but rather the continued lack of sufficient infrastructure.[114] He refined his predecessors' guidance, to include voiding all gambling licenses for enterprises in the market.[115] Regarding the considerable infrastructure issues, Clarke also initiated a search for a private investor to manage the enterprise. The cooperative Italian-Bosnian commercial venture, Italproject, signed a 250 million convertible mark (KM) contract with the Brcko District the following year (an approximate equivalent of US$140 million, KM being the currency of Bosnia-Herzegovina).[116]

The Arizona Market today occupies a purpose-built facility much like those housing shopping centers around the world. Estimated annual tax revenues provide the equivalent of ten million euros to government authorities from what one source states is "the largest market in the former Yugoslavia."[117] While formalizing the physical configuration of the market and bringing it within Bosnia-Herzegovina's tax structure addressed some of the Arizona Market's more obvious ills, sanctifying its operations could not eliminate all problems, some of which are arguably worse today than in its initial years. Located in a country still rife with corruption, the market reportedly continues to support smuggling, human trafficking, and drug sales. Nor, as we look back at conditions in post-WWII Tokyo and Berlin, should accusations of robbery and violent crime related to the market come as a shock. The Global Initiative Against Transnational Organized Crime reports criminal organizations have recruited police who actively participate in these illicit operations. The assistant chief of the Brcko District criminal police was arrested in 2018 with 130,000 euros worth of pure cocaine in his vehicle. His is but one of several law enforcement agencies from which officers have been arrested or suspended for corruption or criminality. Training, equipment, and funding have proved insufficient to keep corruption and police crime at bay, the Global Initiative Against Transnational Organized Crime finding,

> it is striking that there are so many cases of corruption in such a small area despite the fact that police are paid better than in other parts of Bosnia and Herzegovina, have good equipment, receive training and support from the international community, and work in a new building that cost more than €5 million.[118]

Fortunately, law enforcement officials have also scored several successes in interdicting drugs, weapons, and other illicit goods.[119]

As with initiatives to contain corruption, a pragmatic approach to black marketing seeks not to eliminate the scourge but rather minimize its worst features. Local and international authorities kept the Arizona Market from closing, thereby maintaining a location feted for inter-ethnic cooperation, local employment, additional indirect sustainment for thousands, and providing buyers with a source for goods either not readily available elsewhere or only at higher prices. Yet corruption directly related to market activities and inherent across the Brcko region and Bosnia-Herzegovina generally continues to limit the facility's potential. As of December 2021, Brcko and surrounds was one of the country's poorest regions with an average monthly salary equivalent to 502 euros, the lowest in the country.[120]

The Arizona Market has evolved in ways other than physical. Local hypermarkets in the Brcko region originally bridled at its competition. They adapted by providing retail brands known for quality, standardizing their pricing, providing superior retail service, increasing the assortment of goods offered, and providing customers with a clean environment in which to shop. Arizona Market's produce sector countered by becoming 90 percent wholesale. Many sellers in other arenas are likewise adapting to changing conditions. As with Tokyo's black markets, the Arizona Market has become a more formal and legitimate entity. Whether it can similarly become one less corrupt and criminal has yet to be seen.

Looking back on that single individual's initiative on pulling up by the roadside, Fontenot explained,

> The way I try to explain the Arizona Market is that it had become an entrepôt in the classic sense. That is, markets grow up. Cities develop and things happen because of the conditions that prevail at the time. You've got a sheltered bay, so a harbor happens. You have a ford on a river, so a city happens. Frankfurt am Main is a good example. In this instance, the Arizona Market formed around that

checkpoint because it was a place of reasonable safety that you could meet at.[121]

He went on to observe that much of what the US military took on as the market matured and conditions in the vicinity of Brcko attained some sense of stability would generally have fallen under civilian responsibility, in this case the High Commissioner in Sarajevo. Understandably, however, it took the various civilian organizations supporting the High Commissioner longer to deploy their assets. The military is designed and trained to respond quickly. Civilian organizations, often ad hoc in situations such as those confronted in Bosnia-Herzegovina, are not. The military becomes the default solution. It is the military on whom nations and the international community will rely until the UN, some other IGO, or a purpose-built NGO exists that is capable of mobilizing personnel and equipment needed to manage immediate crisis situations. As many militaries practice a form of guided decentralized management called "mission command," they are also well suited to balancing the demands of overarching political objectives with local conditions on the ground. Ukraine, with its standing government, is less likely to default to this alternative, though temporary stints of military government might be necessary in cases of retaking urban areas currently enemy-occupied.

Further Thoughts on Controlling Black Markets

> The ICRC reckons that every major disaster now attracts…about a thousand national and international aid organizations…. The United Nations Development

Program (UNDP) estimates that the total number of INGOs exceeds thirty-seven thousand.[122]

— Linda Polman, *The Crisis Caravan: What's Wrong with Humanitarian Aid?*

Local [Sarajevo] residents both despised and depended on the [black] market.[123]

— Peter Andreas, *Blue Helmets and Black Markets*

[Interviewer: How likely is Ukraine to have black markets after the ongoing fighting?] Why should we expect Ukraine's going to be any different? It's a mechanism by which goods can be more efficiently distributed.

— Anonymous interview 6

The list of attempts seeking to constrain, contain, regulate, or eliminate black markets in Tokyo, Berlin, Manila, Sarajevo, and southwest of Brcko offers several courses of action...all of which suffered setbacks or failed altogether. Sarajevo, Sierra Leone, and too many other humanitarian assistance missions demonstrate war is good business for those involved in black marketing and other enterprises such as renting properties to aid providers, supplying food, or sustaining combatants or relief representatives. Ignoring black markets' existence during war in hopes of addressing the challenge later is an ill-advised approach threatening to extend the conflict as well as put the corrupt in post-conflict positions of power that undermine local economies for years if not decades after war's end. Time, rebounding economic activity, and policing eventually circumscribed those in Tokyo, Berlin, and Manila, constraining their operations to within tolerable limits. Sarajevo and Brcko District continue to host more robust illicit exchanges a quarter-century after conflict's end.[124] Bosnia-Herzegovina ranks eighth worldwide in tobacco consumption, a habit fed by prices among Europe and Central Asia's lowest. Black market purchases account for up to 49 percent of tobacco products, making them the country's largest component of illicit market sales.[125] Occupation authorities in Tokyo and Berlin—in conjunction with local city leaders—outlawed black markets, apparently unaware or uncaring of their vital importance to those suffering hunger and facing the possibility of starvation. Children and youths in Manila, like those in other post-WWII cities, turned to deception and crime in order to secure food and other items for themselves and, if not orphans, family members. As with anti-drug campaigns in 20th-century US cities, it was more often the purchaser of small amounts of black market goods suffering arrest while bigger fish remained unscathed. Those fish included buyers fed by scavengers tasked with scrounging metal products from Berlin's wrecked buildings and copper stolen and then sold in the Arizona Market. Intimidation and racketeering undermined both occupier and government legitimacy as well as ration systems. Ever able to adapt, early efforts to close them down were no more than a hand thrust into a bucket of water, a disturbance that when removed left conditions unchanged.

Wrecked commercial infrastructure, shortages of essential products, supply chain disruption, and criminal or corrupt domination of market sectors are war's legacy. Ukrainian urban areas liberated from Russian occupation will be particularly vulnerable. Cities already retaken suffered occupier theft of production means, deliberate damage to infrastructure, crippled local and regional economic systems, and wartime damage to surrounding agricultural resources (e.g., mined farms and interruption of seed, fertilizer, and other commodity availability). The propensity for corruption suggests criminals will capitalize on black market opportunities by hoarding needed materials, favoring specific groups, and misdirecting goods to more profitable uses as was the case in occupied Tokyo. Neither ceasefires nor treaties will stop Russian endeavors to undermine Ukrainian sovereignty. Denying or limiting select imports; restricting Black Sea routes; manipulating regional export markets; spreading false rumors regarding products; fabricating scandals; hindering the country's transitions to the European Union: these comprise only a token list of ways the bear to the east will seek to undermine Ukraine's stability that simultaneously encourage black marketeering.

Ukraine should be able to address black markets' worst ills, *carpe diem*-like, by seizing the moment before such enterprises become entrenched, at least in cities unoccupied by Russia. Success will require addressing black marketing in a comprehensive and orchestrated manner. Initiatives could include supporting competing well-regulated and supervised markets, to include making select goods more competitive by subsidizing prices and thereby spurring legitimate private sector growth. Other initiatives might involve licensing commercial functions and continuing to address low-level corruption, all such programs being employed coherently and in a mutually-supporting fashion rather than fragmentally. Prescient planning holds potential for avoiding trial-and-error stabs at solutions. Multinational cooperation with Kyiv and its cities will be key to countering international gangs and other forms of super-national crime seeking to capitalize on informal markets. Doubters need only to look at the 1990s number of criminals fleeing Western European law enforcement who smoothly immersed themselves in Sarajevo's illicit economy.

Ukraine's military will be a key component of the country's recovery strategy. Just how it will fit in this healing merits contemplation even as war continues. Here Sarajevo tells us toleration of armed forces corruption during war ingrains continued pollution in its aftermath. Kyiv appears fortunate in that a Sarajevo-level of military corruption is not the Ukrainian norm…though past actions of some Ukrainian military personnel in the BiH capital ensure complacency would be misplaced.

Do Ukrainian cities have black markets in the 21st century's third decade? Replies one Kyiv resident:

> The black markets are here, whether it's drugs, guns, humans, you name it. Pretty much everything is for sale. The mafia is really big. It is huge. What's interesting about the mafia is before the war they worked pretty closely with the Russian mafia…. Unless you are connected with the mob or have a relationship with the government, you are not going to get into the arms market. The mob is heavily involved in running bars here. Prostitution is everywhere. There's a black market for everything.[126]

Poverty spiked in 2022 Ukraine, rising from 5.5 percent to 24.2 percent, though the World Bank reported this was disproportionately felt not in urban but rather rural villages. Unofficial estimates of unemployment pegged it at 36 percent. Inflation had risen to 26.6 percent by the end of that year. The initial response by those no longer able to rely on a sufficient salary was to take appliances, cell phones, and other items to pawn shops, thus keeping exchanges within the licit economy.[127]

Perfection in addressing Ukraine's ills will be no more possible than elsewhere. As with any recovery effort, however, trying and falling short of the desired mark is preferable to letting the status quo and play of chance have their way. In terms of corruption, the threat of simple removal from office, a slight fine, or even a short stint in prison has not proved sufficient to dissuade many from participation. Late 11th-century author Nizam al-Mulk's suggestion regarding how to deal with the corrupt retains considerable merit. From his *Siyasat Nameh* or *Book of Politics*:

> If an official assesses a farmer more than is due to the authorities, the sum he unjustly raised should be demanded of him and returned to the farmer, and if the official has any property, it should be confiscated as an example to other agents, so they refrain from tyrannical acts.[128]

There is no reason such a policy need apply to government officials alone.

If it is a donor's funds that have been misused, confiscation would reimburse the donor. That policy component would be in keeping with some nations such as Norway, which attaches conditions to their foreign aid that include repayment in cases where aid conditions go unmet.[129]

For misappropriated funds sent overseas for safekeeping, penalties for both the appropriator and shielding entity (country or commercial) would seem fair and doable in this age of global finance.

Black marketing shares with prostitution some level of support from a portion of virtually any population. Closing down operations in one location sees them reemerge elsewhere. Demand will be unending as long as needs exist. Vigorous prosecution might reduce activity for a while without eliminating root causes and, therefore, continued provision. Our examples from the past recommend some mix of legitimizing, redressing demand, and punishment of the most influential among providers and partakers to transition black to gray and, eventually, white markets. Graduating penalties depending on the nature of service provided would permit continuation of essential availability while reducing less needed or more harmful practices. Selling foodstuffs semi-legitimately acquired might be de-criminalized or considered only a misdemeanor while stealing from stocks meant to serve fulfillment of rations would merit prosecution as a felony, for example, as would any violence associated with the marketing. Licensing, training, provision of market locations or priority for access to buildings and other resources in short supply, and reduced taxes could be granted in exchange for assistance in bringing the worst perpetrators and those in illicit supply chains to justice. The worst of those preying on Ukrainians' essential needs would pay the greatest prices in terms of financial penalties and imprisonment. Policy development should keep the goal of transition to a capitalist market economy in mind with eventual full integration in the legitimate economy the goal as occurred in Tokyo.

Closing the Ethnicity Gap in Ukraine's Information Operations Armor

> Ukraine was trying to swim west in an eastern tide.... Eastern Ukraine will think they should have first claim on recovery funds because of the devastation [but] the relative depopulation, devastation, and Eastern Ukraine being smaller [if parts remain under Russian occupation] is only going to strengthen Ukraine's Western orientation.... I wonder about how difficult it's going to be to restimulate the economy in eastern Ukraine. How likely are private investors going to be to invest their money east of Kyiv?
>
> — Anonymous interview 6

East-west. Rural-urban. Russia-sympathetic versus West-leaning. Veteran-younger male. The next pause in (and, hopefully, end of) Ukraine's combat operations with Russia will see a re-festering of previous social differences and, possibly, introduction of others new.

- East-west: The pre-2022 sense among some in eastern Ukraine that benefits apportioned by Kyiv failed to provide them their fair share is almost sure to reassert itself. Perceptions of disproportionate allocations of wealth may be reinforced by reduced employment opportunities caused by the loss of commercial enterprises that fled to the less exposed west of the country. Kyiv's sensitivity to conditions in once-occupied areas will be called for. Akin to WWII Manila, occupied Ukrainians are being forced to convert their savings and other investments to rubles. Ill-will is assured barring equitable resolution of how to reconvert these funds fairly.

- Rural-urban: That monies spent and unexploded ordnance decontamination operations conducted in Ukraine's more densely populated (urban) areas will reach more of the country's population and have more immediate political impact will work against efforts to equitably balance recovery benefits between city dwellers and those in rural areas.

- Russia-sympathetic versus West-leaning: This, the most prominent among Ukraine's social divides and most vulnerable to Russian exploitation, will be the specter blocking the light of prospective resolution to east-west, rural-urban, and other perceived inequities. Given long-standing and remaining ties with Russia, information operations would be well advised to emphasize anti-Putin or anti-Moscow themes rather than ones generally anti-Russian.

- Veteran-younger male: Veterans returning home to find their jobs occupied by 18 to 24-year-olds never sent to fight will be a potential source of demonstrations and latent antipathy, a tension ripe for exploitation by both the unfortunate neighbor to the east and less savory politicians at home.

All of these greater or lesser divides will be available for exploitation at the national level and locally. The latter highlights risks that Kyiv runs with its decentralization of political decision-making and public expenditure. As in the post-war Philippines, where President Manuel Roxas's decentralization policies helped Hukbalahap insurgents cultivate support against Manila, Kyiv's progressive decentralization policies carry with them opportunities for those wanting to capitalize on Ukraine's social antagonisms. Kyiv would be well advised to retain those policies while taking steps to counter abuse.

Effectively addressing these extent and potential social fissures once again suggests a carefully conceived, prudently designed, socially aware information and counter-Russian propaganda campaign (understanding "information" and "propaganda" in this sense have broader meanings that include economic, social, and other actions beyond media activities). Such campaigns do not constitute a Western strength. Ukraine's effectiveness in offsetting Russia's cyber and information campaigns since the February 2022 attacks bode well for succeeding where other populations and governments' naivety and lack of diligence expose them to Russian, Chinese, and additional malign influences. As with anti-corruption efforts, mending rifts and defeating Russian efforts to exploit (or create) seams in Ukraine's social fabric call for a comprehensive, constant, and agile campaign.

Preparing for the No Longer Unthinkable: The Nuclear Threat to Ukraine's Cities

> Due to Halifax's lack of preparation, civic institutions were immediately overwhelmed by the tasks in front of them.[130]
> — John U. Bacon, *The Great Halifax Explosion*

> Some 400 persons were in the tunnel shelters in Nagasaki at the time of the explosion. The shelters consisted of

CHAPTER 7

> rough tunnels dug horizontally into the sides of hills with crude, earth-filled blast walls protecting the entrances. The blast walls were blown in but all the occupants back from the entrances survived, even in those tunnels almost directly under the explosion. Those not in a direct line with the entrance were uninjured. The tunnels had a capacity of roughly 100,000 persons. Had the proper alarm been sounded, and these tunnel shelters been filled to capacity, the loss of life in Nagasaki would have been substantially lower.[131]
>
> — *The United States Strategic Bombing Survey Summary Report (European War)*

The hold of the *Mont-Blanc* held 250 tons of closely-packed TNT, 62 tons of gun cotton, and 2,366 tons of highly unstable picric acid as it entered Halifax, Nova Scotia's harbor. A last-minute addition to the manifest had packed an additional 246 tons of benzol, a fuel considered the latest "super gasoline."[132] The departing *Imo* approached from the opposite direction. Violating the Canadian city of Halifax's shipping channel procedures, *Imo* crossed the channel centerline and struck the explosives-laden vessel. A fire broke out, the *Mont-Blanc*'s crew and harbor pilot abandoning the ship, leaving it to drift toward the docks. As the men rowed to their escape, people throughout Halifax, ignorant of the ship's contents, went to their windows or paused along shore to watch the blazing ship. It was 9:04 on the morning of December 6, 1917 when the explosion

> tore through the ship's steel hull like wet tissue paper, converting the vessel into a monstrous hand grenade. The heat vaporized the water surrounding the ship and the people trying to tie her up and put out the fire. The remains of these victims were never found because there

were no remains to be found.... *Mont-Blanc* disintegrated, leaving only two recognizable parts: the anchor shank, which weighed half a ton and was found 4 miles away...and an iron deck cannon, intended to protect the ship from U-boats, which landed 3 miles away.... The explosion also produced something we recognize all to readily today: a mushroom cloud.[133]

The explosion broke virtually every window in Halifax, shards of glass killing, blinding, or otherwise maiming the hundreds entertained by the fire and smoke on the now no longer existent ship. Buildings collapsed, torn apart by the tremors traveling through the ground or the slower blast of air, though any form of "slow" seems a misnomer when the speed of the concussion leaving the blast area was 2,100 miles per hour. The resulting tsunami, 35 feet high, rushed inland, destroying over 1,600 structures and grounding the *Imo*.[134] Structural wood, now turned to tinder, ignited as furnaces and stoves spewed their fuels over the damaged landscape. Six thousand buildings were destroyed in total. Nearly 1,800 from Halifax's population of just over 60,000 died instantly or later succumbed to their injuries.[135] Another 9,000 suffered wounding. Twenty-five thousand were rendered homeless. The people's agonies were not over. The following day and that next brought a severe storm with gales so powerful that ships in the harbor dragged their anchors. Sixteen inches of snow meant rescue parties could not reach many areas. Temperatures rose sharply on December 9th, three days after the explosion. Melted snow became rivers streaming down roads and flooding basements. Another snowstorm followed the next day.[136]

CHAPTER 7

Author Michael J. Bird summarized the situation:

> There was no gas or electricity. Little water flowed through the mains; the public transportation system had ceased to exist; the railway artery was severed; telephones were not working and the telegraph lines, the only other means of communication with the outside world, were down. For some time after the *Mont Blanc* blew up the city was unnaturally quiet. Then it was bedlam. Everything that was ordered, familiar, and tranquil was gone and horror, fear, and chaos reigned in their place. The elements of civilized society were broken down and for many all that remained was the jungle law of self-preservation. For others lay ahead the tasks of rescue and salvage, of counting the dead and estimating the damage, or rehabilitation and reconstruction.[137]

The Halifax explosion was the largest man-caused blast in history at the time. The equivalent of 2.7 kilotons of TNT (one kiloton being 1,000 tons), it was just under one-fifth the power of the bomb dropped on Hiroshima thirty-eight years later and a blast at the lower-end range of Russia's tactical nuclear weapons today, providing some context for Ukrainian planners.[138] That is from detonation alone. Radiation would add to the dangers. Should Putin make so appalling a decision as to use a nuclear weapon, an eastern-more Ukrainian city seems the likely target. Chances of interception would be less.

The physical damage wrought by a tactical nuclear weapon need not exceed the scope already suffered by Ukraine's cities during conventional weapons attacks. There would be a difference in suddenness of the consequences, shock value, concentration of the damage, and immediate demands on medical, rescue, and other service providers. Utility interruptions akin to those in Halifax are a given. The electromagnetic pulse would render both traditional and more modern communications inoperable. The spectrum of injuries would be similar to that of 1917 other than those radiation related. There would be no trace of some. Physical injuries would run the gamut. Many would suffer strains on their emotional and mental health. Criminality and social disorder would follow, as might an enemy attack to exploit the resulting confusion. Caregivers could be driven to emphasize urgency over organization as in Halifax where

> with thousands in desperate need of immediate help just to make it through the day, doctors, nurses, and others frequently failed to record where their patients were when they had been injured, what wounds they had suffered, where they lived, or even their names.… Where, exactly, would the soldier leave the note?.… But this essential expedience would help explain why hundreds of victims went unidentified, making it much more difficult for family members to find their loved ones in the days that followed.[139]

And thus the case of Edith O'Connor's father who never again saw the daughter he thought had perished with the rest of his family.

Yet while Halifax was like most cities at the time in being unprepared for a major catastrophe, some cities elsewhere in the Americas were otherwise. Boston had formed the United States' first Committee on Public Safety in February 1917, two months before the US entered

World War I.[140] Whether its preparations accounted for compound disasters such as suffered by Halifax (explosion followed by severe storm, flooding, and a second storm) is unknown to this author, but the wise would not discount the possibility of a nuclear attack in Ukraine having the company of frigid temperatures, floods, conventional attack, or accompanying use of chemical, biological, or radiological weapons. Compound disasters are not as unusual as one might think as Japan's 2011 combination of earthquake, tsunami, and Daiichi nuclear reactor failures in Fukushima reminds us.

Halifax benefited from its hosting a number of military personnel, this the result of the city being a wartime depot. Those men and women rushed to assist overwhelmed local authorities. Soldier and sailor patrols were given the authority to arrest or shoot looters.[141] A partnership of sorts formed between Halifax and Boston, the latter dispatching trucks and gasoline. The fuel was necessary not only to make up for losses in Canada but ensure arriving vehicles did not further burden on-hand supplies.[142]

Looters, treating the injured, and supporting the homeless were not the only concerns. Just as Koreans living in Tokyo were blamed for the fires resultant of the 1923 earthquake, Haligonians attacked the homes of Germans and arrested sixteen of German birth (though they had been reporting monthly to the police as required).[143] We have observed that Ukraine has its own social divides and know Russia will seek to exploit those rifts. Disasters can create others. While many Halifax property owners freely offered unoccupied dwellings to the homeless, others demanded extortionate rents. Merchant integrity was likewise uneven as some took the opportunity to dramatically increase prices. Remember the above recollection of workers demanding overtime and bricklayers refusing to allow others help make repairs. While most tales of looters being shot proved rumor, newspaper reports of soldiers being granted permission kept numbers down.[144]

Despite the destruction, some residents of a targeted city will prefer to remain in or near their communities if feasible, preferably in proximity to neighbors and others they trust. As was the case in post-earthquake Los Angeles, repairing rather than rebuilding will speed recovery and in some instances allow families to remain in less damaged parts of dwellings as work progresses. Construction in Halifax took advantage of the city's tragic opportunity when repairing or replacing buildings, turning to more robust materials and updated techniques. Builders replaced wood structures with Hydrostone, for example, a form of concrete manufactured across the narrows from the devastated city. One result was a 23-acre Hydrostone "English style garden" neighborhood designated a Canadian national historic landmark in 1994.[145]

As in Halifax, recovery will be harder for the widowed or orphaned. Ukraine's urban leaders should keep up-to-date family member rosters to the extent possible, not an easy task when so many have been displaced. But even a reasonable effort is better than none. More advanced efforts in this regard could include collection of DNA data, a boon in cases where pre-speech children or cognitively challenged suffer separations. DNA would also aid identification of both the living and deceased should disfiguration be severe. Reliance on paper documentation alone is a non-starter given the fragility of such records. Tokyo reminds us of the need to have redundant copies of public records as a guard against destruction. As in the case of orphans, in Halifax the often overlooked circumstances of pets similarly overtaxed officials. Though residents took in many suddenly ownerless, putting down the injured or unclaimed involved numbers forcing SPCA workers to work overtime.[146]

These many observations are drawn from a wartime Halifax not at war. If Russian use of a nuclear weapon in an urban area is in conjunction with a military operation, street fighting and bombardment with conventional weapons could follow the initial attack's damage, social disruption, and chaos. Demands on Ukrainian forces would include simultaneous calls for civil assistance and fighting the enemy, the latter taking priority. Otherwise the former could quickly become mute. In such a case, urban residents would have to rely on those surviving among their emergency response personnel, medical providers, and—ultimately—each other. (The last save many lives in the immediate aftermath of a disaster. I have in other writings attached the label "first-first responders" to neighborhood good Samaritans in consequence.) The near-astounding 2022 response of men and women in defense of their cities' demonstrates the capabilities of Ukraine's citizenry. Introduction of a tactical nuclear weapon would impose a quantum leap in challenges. Readiness means preparing all whose courage could again be called upon.

■ Closing Thoughts

Ukraine's resilience in the face of Russian attacks has been accomplished via a remarkably adaptable assemblage of local, national, and transnational infrastructure.... A common threat brings people together. Longstanding research shows that shared threats drive social cohesion. Ukraine saw an unprecedented surge in solidarity after the Russian invasion. Polling data a few months into the war showed a record high of 85% of Ukrainians self-identifying foremost as Ukrainian citizens (instead of as members of a minority group or residents of their regions)—up from 64% the previous year.[147]

— Daniel Armanios, et.al, "What Ukraine Can Teach the World About Resilience and Civil Engineering"

Irpin was retaken on March 28, one month and a day after the invasion. [The Russians] retreated north toward Belarus, leaving a trail of devastation in their wake. Their tank tracks still mark the asphalt on the highways.... Gleaming modern apartment buildings were incinerated; residential homes reduced to rubble; schools shelled, burned and flooded.[148]

— Linda Kinstler, "Architects Plan a City for the Future in Ukraine, While Bombs Still Fall"

Russia is going to regard any successful reconstruction as a strategic defeat. I can see them trying to defeat any successful reconstruction with sabotage, propaganda...any way they can.

— Anonymous interview 6

The first quotation above brings a sense of hope when envisioning the long years of recovery lying ahead for the people of Ukraine. History whispers caution. An "unprecedented surge in solidarity" can prove fragile. The ties that bind tend to weaken once members of a group—country, alliance, coalition, or another—sense threat's waning. Suppressed antagonisms reemerge. Thoughts of personal welfare surface. Those for the collective whole slip into a subordinate place.

War has brought other changes aiding individual cities' recoveries and will continue to so serve in the aftermath of current hostilities. Confidence and trust in local institutions has in some cases surpassed that for others more centralized, confidence and trust granted when local institutions meet the demands of war. Local officials throughout the country established "points of invincibility" where residents could access the internet, recharge equipment, and find warmth to defeat the outside chill.[149]

To imply the only balance of importance is that between levels of government would be to mislead. The number of parties involved in Ukraine's urban recovery is myriad and varies from city to city. Yet those parties inevitably share characteristics such as the desire to be heard, assist others in greater need, and redress social tensions. The badly damaged city of Irpin, a suburb of 65,000 just sixteen miles northwest of Kyiv, provides an example. Partially occupied in the opening days of the invasion, some half of its buildings suffered damage or destruction [10,596 of 22,149 according to Rebuild Ukraine (RebuildUA), including 9,690 of 20,256 residential or nearby "outbuildings," 48 percent of Irpin's housing stock].[150] In Irpin alone, United Nations Development Programme representatives estimated 410,000 tonnes of rubble would need removing in the fighting's aftermath.[151]

(Should it interest, that's 451,820 US tons, nearly seven per resident.) Cutting-edge approaches to estimating the extent of damage include drone and satellite imagery. It is unclear whether photo collection includes crowdsourcing requests for pre-war photographs usable should returning to previous architecture be desirable.[152]

Irpin resident Iryna Yarmolenko was among those who put together a call for architects worldwide to submit proposals for rebuilding. An article described how some submissions "reimagined Irpin's architectural landmarks as gleaming modernist complexes, with monumental glass additions supporting whatever facades could still be saved. They were expensive, ambitious designs, experiments in conceiving of a future still to come, a future radically unlike the past."[153]

Iryna Matsevko, historian and deputy vice chancellor at the Kharkiv School of Architecture, commiserated that Bosnia-Herzegovina's war a generation before provides a lens on what possibly lies ahead for Ukraine. "Already," she observed, "we are seeing how international institutions are coming to Ukraine and pursuing the same strategies that will lead to failure."[154] The likelihood of Irpin's more ambitious rebuilding proposals seeing realization are no greater than was the case with Tokyo's following World War II. Like Tokyo, Berlin, and elsewhere, residents waited for no one's plans or approval, taking repairs into their own hands–replacing glass or covering voids where windows once offered protection from the cold; hauling rubble away from their properties; and rebuilding to the extent personal funds, materials availability, and time allowed.

CHAPTER 7

Interpretations of what tomorrow's Irpin should look like vary dramatically. Inevitably impacting rebuilding plans and their execution: the hundreds if not thousands of unexploded artillery shells, bombs, rockets, tank rounds, and other ordnance littering public and private properties.

While some dream, others' feet remain firmly planted in reality. Domestic and international organizations participating in recovery brainstorming included the earthbound as well as ephemeral. Essential services, windows, heating systems: these received top priority, the nice-to-haves forced to wait. More ambitious master plan proposals still linger in the wings. If adopted, they will need to be adapted after necessity has its say. Another reminder of past recoveries from war: Irpin's cultural structures are among the damaged. These include the city library, museum, and House of Culture.

Thus far the spirits of the Ukrainian people have not lagged, sacrifices to win the war being willingly taken. One Irpin couple expressed commonly-held views: "First, we need to win, and then we need more money," the wife proposed. Her husband confirmed the priority: "Give us five HIMARS. We will rebuild the House of Culture ourselves."[155] Guns before butter. Thanks to early planning, funding, and voluntary support from much of Europe and beyond, Ukraine's cities have to some extent benefited from both simultaneously. (HIMARS is the US High Mobility Artillery Rocket System, a weapon capable of launching multiple rockets ground-to-ground.)

Urban recovery cannot help but be somewhat Janus-faced. The question becomes one of how much the look back in time is one of remembrance rather than commiseration. Restoring the grandeur of a city's center and rebuilding its treasured historical icons: these are salutes to past glory serving as stones on the path for others to come. Some reminders of a more difficult past have their place, preserving damage to iconic buildings, perhaps. Yet one might ask whether it is not better to link history's brilliance with future promise. Urban leaders would be wise to ensure reminders of past suffering inspire pride rather than loathing, innovation in lieu of reactionism. *New York Times* journalist Linda Kinstler writes,

> Ukrainian defense forces blew up the Irpin bridge in the first week of the full-scale invasion in an effort to cut off one of the main entry points into Kyiv and prevent the Russian Army from advancing toward the capital…. The destroyed bridge is slated to become a memorial to the Ukrainian Army's victory in the Kyiv region.[156]

Whether the destroyed span remains as a memorial remains to be seen. Passion for memorials in the immediate aftermath of disaster runs hot, the heat dissipating over time. Irpin's memorial bridge would lose relevancy as rust stains its concrete fragments and new generations replace old. What are meant to commemorate can come to instead be reminders of divisive antipathies (particularly ironic were the memorial a bridge).

By remaining largely intact, Ukraine's local and national bureaucracies share a trait with Japan's dramatic recovery. Capitalizing on recent construction innovations will help overcome many future challenges. Ukraine benefits from a further advantage. Whereas Japan was largely bereft of natural resources, Ukraine is historically Europe's breadbasket, this in addition to possessing coal, iron ore, and other natural gifts. Fundamental to national recovery, they are also temptations that will prove irresistible to those with bent ethics. Many remain unconvinced of the Zelensky government's commitment to purging corruption while individuals with questionable pasts remain in key positions and removal constitutes little punishment for perpetrators. Nizam al-Mulk's aforementioned wisdom suggests more effective deterrents.

Authors have compared successful preventive medicine approaches to stacking slices of Swiss cheese. Steps to reduce the spread of COVID included masks, vaccinations, physical distancing, and effective testing. Each approach was itself insufficient, having holes through which the virus could pass. Overlapping slices (coordinating different approaches) closes many holes. Overcoming corruption shares this approach. Corruption's many forms, its practitioners' ability to evolve in the face of countermeasures, their skills in recognizing emerging niches and capitalizing on opportunities, the amounts of money involved: Containment must orchestrate multiple approaches to seal loopholes. Anti-corruption policies and practices must likewise be dynamic if they are to keep up with—or ideally forestall—illicit adaptations. Artificial intelligence (AI) will in future years help in forecasting evolutions and interdicting them. Crowd sourcing, social media, insights from savvy NGOs, and assistance from willing technology companies will be among the keys to a more corruption-free recovery in the interim.

As the world increasingly urbanizes, so too have its wars. More so than with other forms of disaster, mankind has much to say regarding the extent of popular suffering and type and degree of war-wrought damage. Target choices and methods of attack impact both immediate and longer-term recovery. Are the targets exclusively military, dual-use in character, or undeniably civilian? Urban complexity can stupefy military leaders faced with such considerations. US forces bombing targets in 1991 Baghdad consciously avoided destruction of medical facilities while disabling power plants, transportation nodes, and fuel supplies that might benefit the adversary. Medical care suffered regardless. Hospitals lacked power once back-up generators ran out of fuel. Doctors, nurses, and critical support personnel could not travel to work. Reality reminded that medical care systems are more than physical facilities alone. The earlier note regarding use of chaff to temporarily render Iraqi power stations inoperable rather than destroying generators taking years to replace reminds us that how an adversary conducts its attacks can be as significant as what it targets.[157]

If one accepts that it takes a village to raise a child, then it takes the best of our closely interconnected world to help a country recover from war. Ukraine will experience complications post-WWII cities did not. Kyiv must account for the continued threat of Russian aggression even as it addresses recovery. Significant higher-order effects will exist as well, e.g., attending to private investor reticence to invest. Continued defense means continuing costs of conscription, mobilization, training, equipping, and sustaining a professional armed forces. Luring back able young who became international refugees is highly desirable, their skills important in rebuilding. Doing so will be another claim on recovery funding, and it comes with risks.[158] Returning soldiers will justly expect governmental support. To see it spent on others who did not commit to defending Ukraine—whether while still in the country or otherwise—will be a sore point. Perhaps the answer lies in a modified version of the US GI Bill. While funding for veterans would come with few strings attached, educational offerings seeking to attract potential international returnees would incur an obligation to serve Ukraine in an approved role for a designated period (doctor, nurse, teacher, or law enforcement officer for example). Alternatively, funding for returnee education might incur an obligation of military service given the need to maintain a robust and professional defense force.

Many have stepped forward to assist Ukraine even as Russia's invaders continue to pursue illicit goals. The essentiality of support from the most prominent players rightfully dominates attention, the European Union, G7 nations, other individual countries, and major NGOs and IGOs among them. Additional organizations' actions will go unnoticed other than in the small sphere within which they operate, but their sometimes limited undertakings can have disproportionate effects. Unsurprisingly, people turn to their cultural and community touchstones in times of need. Libraries, museums, schools, universities, and other social hubs play an outsized role in this regard. They can be sources of reassurance for the physically and emotionally injured as well as for residents seeking nothing more than moments of calm. Such was the case when California's Porter Ranch community evacuated after a 2016 methane gas leak, residents suffering breathing problems, headaches, nosebleeds, and other ailments. Local library staff stepped forward. Industrial-strength air purifiers meant the displaced had a haven while their homes were off limits. The library was also a conduit for information and place for submitting claims against the responsible utility. Alert to the pulse of their community, librarians coordinated meditation and yoga classes for the stressed.[159] All this was provided in addition to services routinely part of a library's charter. For the thousands of veterans returning from fighting, libraries and other community centers can be not only a place to learn how others have dealt with challenges like theirs. They can also serve as a location for education foregone because of wartime service.[160] Historically targets for those wanting to destroy social and cultural landmarks, libraries and their kin become catalysts of a different sort as cities recover from war as do community members as a whole.

NOTES

ACKNOWLEDGEMENTS

1   Russell W. Glenn, "Creating Light at Tunnel's End: Ukraine's Post-war Urban Recovery," *Journal of Strategic Security* 16, no. 4 (2023): 1-14, https://digitalcommons.usf.edu/jss/vol16/iss4/1/.

CHAPTER 1

1   Fred Charles Ikle, *Every War Must End* (NY: Colombia University Press 1971), 2 and 18.

2   Bernard M. Baruch and John M. Hancock, "Report on War and Post-War Adjustment Policies," report for James F. Byrnes, Director, Office of War Mobilization, February 15, 1944, 3, https://fraser.stlouisfed.org/files/docs/historical/eccles/032_14_0003.pdf.

3   Jennifer Popowycz, "The Allied Responses to the Warsaw Uprising of 1944," (January 18, 2022), https://www.nationalww2museum.org/war/articles/allied-responses-warsaw-uprising-1944.

4   Lawrence J. Vale and Thomas J. Campanella, "Warsaw: Reconstruction as Propaganda," in *The Resilient City: How Modern Cities Recover from Disaster*, ed. Lawrence J. Vale and Thomas J. Campanella (NY: Oxford, 2005), 135-36.

5   Kenneth Hewitt, "Proving Grounds of Urbicide: Civil and Urban Perspectives on the Bombing of Capital Cities," *ACME: An International E-Journal for Critical Geographies* 8, no. 2 (2009): 341-42 and 340.

6   *Rebuilding Ukraine by Reinforcing Regional and Municipal Governance*, OECD Multi-level Governance Studies (Paris: OECD Publishing, 2022), 8, DOI: https://doi.org/10.1787/63a6b479-en. The decrease in those living below subsistence level was 52 to 23 percent. Internet usage increased from 23 to 63 percent.

7   "Lessons in Asian resilience," *The Economist* 447, no. 9350 (June 10, 2023): 34.

8   "French cities: Revival-upon-Med," *The Economist* 448, no. 9365 (September 30, 2023): 44.

9   "Ukraine's energy: The battle against General Winter," *The Economist* 449, no. 9366 (October 7, 2023): 45.

10 David L. Stern, "Russia destroyed Ukraine's power sector: so it's being rebuilt eco-friendly," *The Washington Post*, July 7, 2024, A16.

11 Evidence of deliberate targeting of civilian infrastructure is sufficient that the International Criminal Court has issued arrest warrants for two Russian commanders accused of ordering attacks on electricity facilities during the period October 2022 to March 2023. "The world this week: Politics," *The Economist* 450, no. 9387 (March 9, 2024): 9.

12 David L. Stern, "Heavy destruction of energy network leaves Ukraine fearing winter," *The Washington Post*, May 19, 2024, A16.

13 Michael Beschloss, *The Conquerors: Roosevelt, Truman and the Destruction of Hitler's Germany, 1941-1945* (NY: Simon & Schuster, 2002), 159.

14 Constant Méheut, "More Drones, Fewer Parks. Ukrainians Urge Spending Shift as War Drags On," *The New York Times*, December 22, 2023, https://www.nytimes.com/2023/12/22/world/europe/ukraine-spending-war-russia.html.

15 Yaroslav Hrytsak, *Ukraine: The Forging of a Nation*, trans. Dominique Hoffman (London: Sphere, 2023), 415.

16 Russell W. Glenn, *Come Hell or High Fever: Readying the World's Megacities for Disaster* (Canberra: Australian National University Press, 2023), 60, https://press.anu.edu.au/publications/come-hell-or-high-fever. I have slightly altered the wording in the quotation to make it more relevant to this book. Population values for Tokyo, Manila, and Kyiv are from *Demographia World Urban Areas*, 19th ed. (Belleville, IL: Wendell Cox Consultancy, August 2023), 21 and 24, http://www.demographia.com/db-worldua.pdf.

17 Kristin Ljungkvist, "A New Horizon in Urban Warfare in Ukraine?" *Scandinavian Journal of Military Studies* 5, no. 1 (2022): 91–98, https://doi.org/10.31374/sjms.165.

18 Louis Dimarco, "Urban Operations in Ukraine: Size, Ratios, and the Principles of War" (Modern War Institute at West Point, June 20, 2022), https://mwi.westpoint.edu/urban-operations-in-ukraine-size-ratios-and-the-principles-of-war/.

19 Demographia, *Demographia World Urban Areas*, 18th ed. (Belleville, IL: Wendell Cox Consultancy, July 2022), 24 and 27.

20 Glenn, *Come Hell or High Fever*, 47.

21 State of Berlin, "Berlin in Brief: Berlin after 1945," (online article, undated), https://www.berlin.de/berlin-im-ueberblick/en/history/berlin-after-1945.

22 Demographia, *Demographia World Urban Areas*, 15th ed. (Belleville, IL: Wendell Cox Consultancy, April 2019), 5.

23 Peter Andreas, *Blue Helmets and Black Markets: The Business of Survival in the Siege of Sarajevo* (Ithaca, NY: Cornell University Press, 2008), 5.

24 Thomas Helling, *The Great War and the Birth of Modern Medicine: A History* (NY: Pegasus Books, 2022), 113-14.

25 Lucius D. Clay, *Decision in Germany*, (Garden City, NY: Doubleday & Company, 1950), 32.

CHAPTER 2

1 Edward R. Murrow, *This is London* (NY: Schocken, 1989), 161.

2 Douglas Botting, *From the Ruins of the Reich: Germany 1945-1949* (NY: Crown, 1985), 122.

3 Seth E. Jones, "Russia's Ill-Fated Invasion of Ukraine: Lessons in Modern Warfare" (Center for Strategic and International Studies briefing, June 1, 2022), https://www.csis.org/analysis/russias-ill-fated-invasion-ukraine-lessons-modern-warfare.

4 "The World Factbook: Ukraine – Details," US Central Intelligence Agency, undated, https://www.cia.gov/the-world-factbook/static/maps/UP-map.jpg.

5 Marcus Butler, "Russia's Response to the Challenges of Urban Warfare in the Russo-Ukrainian War," *Towson University Journal of International Affairs* (Jan 13, 2023), https://wp.towson.edu/iajournal/2023/01/13/russias-response-to-the-challenges-of-urban-warfare-in-the-russo-ukrainian-war/.

6 Jones, "Russia's Ill-Fated Invasion of Ukraine."

7 Hewitt, "Proving Grounds of Urbicide," 365-66.

8   Human Rights Watch, "Ukraine: Russian Missile Strike on Lviv a Possible War Crime," July 19, 2023, https://www.hrw.org/news/2023/07/19/ukraine-russian-missile-strike-lviv-possible-war-crime.

9   "Lviv mayor calls for every Ukrainian region and city to have an EU partner," European Committee of the Regions, October 17, 2023, https://cor.europa.eu/en/news/Pages/WGU-Lviv.aspx.

10 "Lviv: A city embraces innovation, even amidst war," *United Nations Development Programme*, January 18, 2023, https://stories.undp.org/lviv-a-city-embraces-innovation-even-amidst-war; and Office of the United Nations High Commissioner for Refugees (UNHCR), "Ukraine Emergency," 2023, https://www.unrefugees.org/emergencies/ukraine/.

11 Kostyantyn Mezentsev and Oleksii Mezentsev, "War and the city: Lessons from urbicide in Ukraine," *Czasopismo Geograficzne* 93, no. 3 (2022): 504, https://doi.org/10.12657/czageo-93-20.

12 The National Council for the Recovery of Ukraine from the Consequences of the War, Draft Ukraine Recovery Plan: Materials of the "Construction, urban planning, modernization of cities and regions" working group (July 2022), 2 https://uploads-ssl.webflow.com.

13 World Bank, "Updated Ukraine Recovery and Reconstruction Needs Assessment Released," February 15, 2024, https://www.worldbank.org/en/news/press-release/2024/02/15/updated-ukraine-recovery-and-reconstruction-needs-assessment-released. Transportation was second at 15 percent with commerce and industry (14%), agriculture (12%), and energy (10%) following respectively.

14 Iryna Kosse, "Rebuilding Ukraine's Infrastructure after the War," Vienna Institute for International Economic Studies Policy Notes and Reports 72, July 2023, 12.

15 National Council for the Recovery of Ukraine from the Consequences of the War, 2 and Kosse, "Rebuilding Ukraine's Infrastructure after the War," 12.

16 "The Prague Charter: Recommendations for Post-war Urban Renewal of Ukraine," Conference on Architecture and Building Culture Policies 2022 summary, March 2023, 12 and 26.

17 National Recovery Council, "Ukraine's National Recovery Plan" (July 2022), 2, https://www.urc-international.com/urc2022-recovery-plan.

18 National Recovery Council, "Ukraine's National Recovery Plan," 3.
19 National Recovery Council, "Ukraine's National Recovery Plan," 25, 27, 29, and 35.
20 Canadian Urban Institute, "CityTalk: How Are Ukrainian Cities and Municipalities Planning Their Recovery?" CityTalk Canada (December 15, 20220, https://canurb.org/fr/citytalk-news/citytalk-how-are-ukrainian-cities-and-municipalities-planning-their-recovery/. ReStart Ukraine's presentation given during the CityTalk event is at https://www.youtube.com/watch?v=V3gU1Bt-XgY.
21 A small sample of these recovery initiatives includes Torbjörn Becker, et al., *A Blueprint for the Reconstruction of Ukraine: Rapid Response Economics 1*, Centre for Economic Policy Research Press, 2022; "The Prague Charter: Recommendations for Postwar Urban Renewal of Ukraine;" Claire Mills, Philip Brien, and Patrick Butchard, "Post-conflict reconstruction assistance to Ukraine," House of Commons Library research briefing no. 9728, June 15, 2023; *Rebuilding Ukraine: Principles and policies*; World Bank Group staff, "Relief, Recovery, and Resilient Reconstruction: Supporting Ukraine's Immediate and Medium-Term Economic Needs," Informal approach paper, April 21, 2022; Kyiv International Institute of Sociology, *A Study of Recovery Initiatives in Ukraine*, June 2023; and "Supporting Ukraine: A Study on Potential Recovery Strategies for Ukraine," Boston Consulting Group, January 2023.
22 Canadian Urban Institute, "CityTalk."
23 Vasyl Filipchuk and Yehor Kiyan, "Rebuilding Ukraine: Initiatives, Approaches, Recommendations," International Center for Policy Studies, 2023, 12.
24 Henri-Paul Normandin, "Ukraine Recovery and Reconstruction: Cities Must Be Part of It," German Marshall Fund (November 14, 2022), https://www.gmfus.org/news/ukraine-recovery-and-reconstruction-cities-must-be-part-it.
25 OECD, "The architecture of infrastructure in Ukraine," OECD Policy Responses on the Impacts of the War in Ukraine (July 1, 2022), https://www.oecd.org/en/publications/the-architecture-of-infrastructure-recovery-in-ukraine_d768a2e4-en.html.
26 OECD, "The architecture of infrastructure in Ukraine."

27 OECD, "The architecture of infrastructure in Ukraine;" European Union, "Ukraine Relief and reconstruction" (July 2022), https://www.google.com/Ukraine_Relief_and_Reconstruction.pdf; and European Committee of the Regions, "European Alliance of Cities and Regions for the Reconstruction of Ukraine," European Union (undated), https://cor.europa.eu/en/our-work/cooperations-and-networks/european-alliance-cities-and-regions-reconstruction-ukraine.

28 Botting, *From the Ruins of the Reich*, x.

29 Junichi Hasegawa, *Replanning the blitzed city centre: A comparative study of Bristol, Coventry and Southampton 1941-1950* (Philadelphia: Open University Press, 1992), 2.

30 Oksana Udovyk, Ievgen Kylymnyk, Daniel Cuesta-Delgado, and Guillermo Palau Salvador, "Making Sense of Multi-Level and Multi-actor Governance of Recovery in Ukraine," United National University world Institute for Development Economics Research, (June 2023), https://www.wider.unu.edu/sites/default/files/Publications/Working-paper/PDF/wp2023-82-making-sense-multi-level-multi-actor-governance-recovery-Ukraine.pdf.

31 "A fragile grid: Taiwan's energy," *The Economist* 451, no. 9397 (May 18, 2024): 33.

32 National Council for the Recovery of Ukraine from the Consequences of the War, 7 (first page numbered 7; pagination in document is inconsistent); and Jadwiga Rogoza, "Ukraine in the face of a demographic catastrophe," Centre for Eastern Studies, July 11, 2023, https://www.osw.waw.pl/en/publikacje/osw-commentary/2023-07-11/ukraine-face-a-demographic-catastrophe.

33 Office of the United Nations High Commissioner for Refugees (UNHCR), "Ukraine Emergency," 2023, https://www.unrefugees.org/emergencies/ukraine/.

34 National Council for the Recovery of Ukraine from the Consequences of the War, 3.

35 Marta Pastukh, Mathias Merforth, Viktor Zabreba, and Armin Wagner, "Anchoring green recovery of urban mobility in Ukraine: Eight building blocks," Transformative Urban Mobility Initiative (TUMI) (October 20, 2022), https://transformative-mobility.org/anchoring-green-recovery-of-urban-mobility-in-ukraine-eight-building-blocks/.

36 Momar D. Seck and David D. Evans, "Major US Cities Using National Standard Fire Hydrants, One Century After the Great Baltimore Fire," Fire Research Division, Building and Fire Research Laboratory, United States Department of Commerce National Institute of Standards and Technology (Gaithersburg, Maryland, August 2004), https://www.govinfo.gov/app/details/GOVPUB-C13-c33f9384233e5a13eca491ede462acdf; and "#112 – A Guide to Fire Department Connection (FDC) Sizes and Threading," Quick Response Fire Supply, June 12, 2018, https://blog.qrfs.com/112-a-guide-to-fire-department-connection-fdc-sizes-and-threading/.

37 Marta Pastukh, et al., "Anchoring green recovery of urban mobility in Ukraine: Eight building blocks;" and Janette Sadik-Khan, *Street Fight: Handbook for an Urban Revolution* (NY: Viking, 2013).

38 Kosse, "Rebuilding Ukraine's Infrastructure after the War," 14-15.

39 Kosse, "Rebuilding Ukraine's Infrastructure after the War," 18.

CHAPTER 3

1 Vale and Campanella, "Warsaw: Reconstruction as Propaganda," 135-36 and 137.

2 Yaroslav Trofimov, *Our Enemies will Vanish: The Russian Invasion and Ukraine's War of Independence* (NY: Penguin, 2024), 73.

3 John Green, *The Anthropocene Reviewed* (NY: Penguin Random House, 2023), 208.

4 Ukrainian urban populations from *Demographia World Urban Areas*, 17th annual edition (Belleville, IL: Wendell Cox Consultancy, May 2021), 23 and 27.

5 UkraineTrek, "Kherson city, Ukraine," November 8, 2023, https://ukrainetrek.com/kherson-city; and Statistics Times, "Population of Cities in Ukraine," September 9, 2021, https://statisticstimes.com/demographics/country/ukraine-cities-population.php.

6 World Population Review, "Sarajevo Population," 2023, https://worldpopulationreview.com/world-cities/sarajevo-population.

7 Alex Wellerstein, "Counting the Dead at Hiroshima and Nagasaki," *Bulletin of the Atomic* Scientists (August 4, 2020),

https://thebulletin.org/2020/08/counting-the-dead-at-hiroshima-and-nagasaki/; and The Committee For the Compilation of Materials on Damage Caused by the Atomic Bombs in Hiroshima and Nagasaki, *Hiroshima and Nagasaki: The Physical, Medical, and Social Effects of the Atomic Bombings.* trans. Eisei Ishikawa and David L Swain (NY: Basic Books, 1981): 353-54 and 420-21. Estimates for both the pre-bombing population of Nagasaki and the number killed during and in the immediate aftermath of the attack differ considerably. John Dower, for example, concludes, "probably around...75,000 [died] in Nagasaki – with the great majority of these deaths occurring during or shortly after the bombings." He continues, "Some estimates are considerably higher." John W. Dower, *Ways of Forgetting, Ways of Remembering: Japan in the Modern World* (NY: The New Press, 2012), 146.

8   Trofimov, *Our Enemies will Vanish*, 77.

9   There are many article-length considerations regarding Ukraine's recovery from different perspectives. For example, Nataly Martynovych, Elina Boichenko, and Maryna Dielini, "Rebuilding of Ukraine After War: Special Restoration Regimes and Stimulation of Sustainable Development of Territories," *International review for spatial planning a sustainable development A: Planning Strategies and Design Concepts*, 11, no. 4 (2023): 54-70, DOI: https://www.jstage.jst.go.jp/article/irspsd/11/4/11_4/_article.

10 Robert Guillain, *I Saw Tokyo Burning: An Eyewitness Narrative From Pearl Harbor to Hiroshima*, trans. William Byron (Garden City, NY: Doubleday & Company, 1981), 176.

11 H. Bruce Franklin, *War Stars: The Superweapon and the American Imagination* (NY: Oxford University Press, 1988), 98.

12 Dayna L. Barnes, *Architects of Occupation: American Experts and the Planning for Postwar Japan* (Ithaca, NY: Cornell University Press, 2017), 169.

13 Urban Areas Division, "Effects of Air Attack on Urban Complex Tokyo-Kawasaki-Yokohama," United States Strategic Bombing Survey, June 1947, 1, https://www.ibiblio.org/hyperwar/NHC/NewPDFs/USAAF.

14 Glenn, *Come Hell or High Fever*, 22.

15 Hewitt, "Proving Grounds of Urbicide," 356 and 358. Hewitt mistakenly identifies the aircraft as B-27s but correctly notes the bombing was done by Superfortress aircraft. The correct

designation for the Superfortress is B-29. The US Strategic Bombing Survey cites seven raids as the number causing "practically all of the physical damage and most of the casualties" in Tokyo and the industrial and port areas of Kawasaki and Yokohama to its immediate south, all coming between the months of March and May 1945. Urban Areas Division, "Effects of Air Attack on Urban Complex Tokyo-Kawasaki-Yokohama," 1.

16 *The United States Strategic Bombing Survey Summary Report (European War)*, September 30, 1945, 87; and Thomas M. Coffey, *Iron Eagle: The Turbulent Life of General Curtis LeMay* (NY: Crown, 1986), 165.

17 Hewitt, "Proving Grounds of Urbicide," 356 and 358.

18 Cary Lee Karacas, "Tokyo From the Fire: War, Occupation, and the Remaking of a Metropolis," (PhD diss., University of California, Berkeley, 2006), 96. The original source is Wesley Frank Craven and James Lea Cate, eds., *The Army Air Forces in World War II, Volume Five, The Pacific: Matterhorn to Nagasaki, June 1944 to August 1945* (Chicago: University of Chicago Press, 1953), 617.

19 Karacas, "Tokyo From the Fire," 97.

20 Karacas, "Tokyo From the Fire," 100.

21 Hewitt, "Proving Grounds of Urbicide," 358.

22 Hewitt, "Proving Grounds of Urbicide," 358.

23 Hewitt, "Proving Grounds of Urbicide," 359.

24 Harry Emerson Wildes, *Typhoon in Tokyo: The Occupation and its Aftermath* (London: George Allen & Unwin, 1954), 2 and 260; and John W. Dower, *Embracing Defeat: Japan in the Wake of World War II* (NY: W. W. Norton, 2000), 45.

25 William J. Sebald and Russell Brines, *With MacArthur in Japan: A Personal History of the Occupation* (NY: W.W. Norton, 1965), 39.

26 Urban Areas Division, "Effects of Air Attack on Urban Complex Tokyo-Kawasaki-Yokohama," 1.

27 Karacas, "Tokyo From the Fire," 104. In contrast with the above estimate of 80 percent of Tokyo's industry destroyed, Karacas states, "45 percent of the city's factories" suffered destruction during the war.

28 Dower, *Embracing Defeat*, 47.

29 *United States Strategic Bombing Survey Summary Report (European War)*, 87.

30 Ohno, *The History of Japanese Economic Development*, 118-19.

31 Urban Areas Division, "Effects of Air Attack on Urban Complex Tokyo-Kawasaki-Yokohama," 9.

32 Urban Areas Division, "Effects of Air Attack on Urban Complex Tokyo-Kawasaki-Yokohama," 16-17.

33 Owen Griffiths, "Need, Greed, and Protest in Japan's Black Market, 1938-1949," *Journal of Social History* 35, no. 4 (Summer 2002): 826 and 854n50, http://www.jstor.org/stable/3790613.

34 Griffiths, "Need, Greed, and Protest in Japan's Black Market, 1938-1949," 828.

35 Griffiths, "Need, Greed, and Protest in Japan's Black Market, 1938-1949," 829.

36 Griffiths, "Need, Greed, and Protest in Japan's Black Market, 1938-1949," 831.

37 Griffiths, "Need, Greed, and Protest in Japan's Black Market, 1938-1949," 834.

38 Karacas, "Tokyo From the Fire," 220 and 226-27.

39 Griffiths, "Need, Greed, and Protest in Japan's Black Market, 1938-1949," 835.

40 Wildes, *Typhoon in Tokyo*, 262.

41 Sebald and Brines, *With MacArthur in Japan*, 44 and 53.

42 Karacas, "Tokyo From the Fire," 231.

43 Griffiths, "Need, Greed, and Protest in Japan's Black Market, 1938-1949," 836-37.

44 Karacas, "Tokyo From the Fire," 213.

45 Karacas, "Tokyo From the Fire," 214-15.

46 Karacas, "Tokyo From the Fire," 212.

47 Karacas, "Tokyo From the Fire," 38-39.

48 Karacas, "Tokyo From the Fire," 111 and 216.

49 Dower, *Embracing Defeat*, 99-100.

50 Griffiths, "Need, Greed, and Protest in Japan's Black Market, 1938-1949," 858. Griffiths reports Yamaguchi's death as taking place in November. Dower cites the month as October. Other sources likewise vary as to the month of death but cite either September or October.

51 Yoshikawa Hiroshi, *Ashes to Awesome: Japan's 6,000-Day Economic Miracle*, trans. Fred Uleman (Tokyo: Japan Publishing Industry Foundation for Culture, 2021), 15.

52 Yoshikawa, *Ashes to Awesome*, 15-17; and Griffiths, "Need, Greed, and Protest in Japan's Black Market, 1938-1949," 837.

53 Griffiths, "Need, Greed, and Protest in Japan's Black Market, 1938-1949," 838-39.

54 Griffiths, "Need, Greed, and Protest in Japan's Black Market, 1938-1949," 839.

55 Ohno, *The History of Japanese Economic Development*, 120-21.

56 Ohno, *The History of Japanese Economic Development*, 122.

57 Dower, *Embracing Defeat*, 115. To put this in some context, Patrick Christy, addressing aid given between 1946 and 1952, wrote, "After World War II, the United States also understood the strategic importance of using foreign assistance and other tools to aid and rebuild post-war Japan. Between 1946 and 1952, Washington invested $2.2 billion — or $18 billion in real 21st-century dollars adjusted for inflation — in Japan's reconstruction effort." Patrick Christy, "America's Proud History of Post-War Aid," *U.S News and World Report* (June 6, 2014), https://www.usnews.com/opinion/blogs/world-report/2014/06/06/the-lessons-from-us-aid-after-world-war-ii.

58 Karacas, "Tokyo From the Fire," 148.

59 Karacas, "Tokyo From the Fire," 134.

60 Karacas, "Tokyo From the Fire," 156.

61 Karacas, "Tokyo From the Fire," 174.

62 Karacas, "Tokyo From the Fire," and 201.

63 Karacas, "Tokyo From the Fire," 166.

64 Karacas, "Tokyo From the Fire," 156-57.

65 For more on Japan's industrial expansion after World War II, see Simon Parker, *Assembled in Japan: Electrical Goods and the Making of the Japanese Consumer* (Berkeley: University of California Press, 1999).

66 Karacas, "Tokyo From the Fire," 199.

67 Karacas, "Tokyo From the Fire," 191.

68 Yoshikawa, *Ashes to Awesome*, 25.

69　Wildes, *Typhoon in* Tokyo, 267.

70　Dower, *Embracing Defeat*, 93; and Karacas, "Tokyo From the Fire," 207 and 210.

71　Karacas, "Tokyo From the Fire," 188.

72　Wildes, *Typhoon in* Tokyo, 268.

73　Dower, *Ways of Forgetting, Ways of Remembering*, 260.

74　Sebald and Brines, *With MacArthur in Japan*, 57, 295, 296, and 297.

75　Karacas, "Tokyo From the Fire," and 176.

76　Wellerstein, "Counting the Dead at Hiroshima and Nagasaki."

77　Susan Southard, *Nagasaki: Life After Nuclear War* (NY: Viking, 2015), 138, 160, 166-67, and 178; and Douglas MacArthur, *Reminiscences* (NY: Crest, 1965), 357-58.

78　Dower, *Embracing Defeat*, 61.

79　Dower, *Embracing Defeat*, 89.

80　Southard, *Nagasaki*, 168-69.

81　Barry Turner, *The Berlin Airlift: The Relief Operation that Defined the Cold War* (London: Icon, 2017), 20 and 58-59.

82　Inge E. Stanneck Gross, *Memories of World War II and Its Aftermath, 1940-1954* (Eastsound, WA: Island in the Sky Publishing, 2005), 122.

83　Roger Moorhouse, *Berlin at War* (NY: Basic Books, 2012), 307.

84　Moorhouse, *Berlin at War*, 321 and 325.

85　Hewitt, "Proving Grounds of Urbicide," 350.

86　Hewitt, "Proving Grounds of Urbicide," 350-52.

87　Moorhouse, *Berlin at War*, 331.

88　William Stivers and Donald A. Carter, *The City Becomes a Symbol: The US Army in the Occupation of Berlin 1945-1948* (Washington, D.C.: Center for Military History, 2017), 65.

89　Moorhouse, *Berlin at War*, 332.

90　Moorhouse, *Berlin at War*, 297.

91　Clay, *Decision in Germany*, 32.

92　Moorhouse, *Berlin at War*, 367.

93　Frank Howley, *Berlin Command* (NY: G. P. Putnam's Sons, 1950), 83; Turner, *Berlin Airlift*, 27; and F.S.V. Donnison, *Civil Affairs and Military Government North-West Europe, 1944-1946* (London: Her Majesty's Stationary Office, 1961), 272.

94 Lucius D. Clay to Vasily D. Sokolovsky, 20 April 1946, *The Letters of General Lucius D. Clay*, ed. Jean Edward Smith (Bloomington, IN: Indiana University Press, 1974), 1: 201; and Troy Sacquety, "Gen. Lucius D. Clay, a 'brilliant administrator,'" United States Army Special Operations Command, January 11, 2019, https://www.army.mil/article/216006/gen_lucius_d_clay_a_brilliant_administrator.

95 Stivers and Carter, *The City Becomes a Symbol*, 67-71.

96 Lucius D. Clay (signed Omar N. Bradley) to US War Department, 9 July 1945, *The Letters of General Lucius D. Clay*, ed. Jean Edward Smith (Bloomington, IN: Indiana University Press, 1974), 1: 49-50; Lucius D. Clay (signed Dwight D. Eisenhower) to George C. Marshall, 11 July 1945, *The Letters of General Lucius D. Clay*, ed. Jean Edward Smith (Bloomington, IN: Indiana University Press, 1974), 1: 51-52; and Earl F. Ziemke, *The US Army in the Occupation of Germany, 1944-1946* (Washington, D.C.: Center of Military History, 1975), 305.

97 Ziemke, *The US Army in the Occupation of Germany*, 305.

98 Office of the Chief Historian, *The First Year of the Occupation: Part One – The Transition from Combat to Military Occupation (8 May – 17 July 1945)*, Occupation Forces in Europe Series, 1945-46 (Frankfurt-am-Main: Headquarters European Command, United States Army, 1947), 93.

99 Office of the Chief Historian, *The First Year of the Occupation: Part One*, 171.

100 Author made minor text additions to original map from William Stivers and Donald A. Carter, *The City Becomes a Symbol: The US Army in the Occupation of Berlin 1945-1948* (Washington, D.C.: Center for Military History, 2017), 25.

101 Filip Slaveski, *The Soviet Occupation of Germany: Hunger, Mass Violence, and the Struggle for Peace, 1945-1947* (Cambridge, UK: Cambridge University Press, 2013), 104.

102 Slaveski, *The Soviet Occupation of Germany*, 90-91.

103 Richard Bessel, *Germany 1945: From War to Peace* (NY: Harper, 2009), 254.

104 Stivers and Carter, *The City Becomes a Symbol*, 141-42.

105 Howley, *Berlin Command*, 96; Donnison, *Civil Affairs and Military Government*, 283; and Botting, *From the Ruins of the Reich*, 139 and 141.

106 Howley, *Berlin Command*, 118, 122, and 123.

107 Stivers and Carter, *The City Becomes a Symbol*, 168-172.

108 Sinclair McKay, *Berlin: Life and Loss in the City That Shaped the Century* (London: Viking, 2022), 339-42.

109 Howley, *Berlin Command*, 141.

110 Howley, *Berlin Command*, 135.

111 Gross, *Memories of World War II*, 121.

112 Ruth Andreas-Friedrich, *Battleground Berlin: Diaries 1945-1948*, trans. Anna Boerresen (NY: Paragon, 1990), 140.

113 Paul Steege, *Black Market, Cold War: Everyday Life in Berlin, 1945-1949* (Cambridge: Cambridge University Press, 2007), 108-9. Frank Howley, US commandant for the American sector at the time wrote that two thousand froze to death that winter. Howley, *Berlin Command*, 219.

114 Giles Milton, *Checkmate in Berlin: The Cold War Showdown that Shaped the Modern World* (NY: Henry Holt, 2021), 206.

115 Oliver J. Fredericksen, *American Military Occupation of Germany, 1945-1953*, The Historical Division, Headquarters, US Army Europe (Darmstadt, Germany, 1953), 115. A later US Army study states the money dispatched to the United States by soldiers was far greater: "By the third week of July dollar remittances had reached seven times the total earning of US personnel in Berlin." Stivers and Carter, *The City Becomes a Symbol*, 118.

116 Stivers and Carter, *The City Becomes a Symbol*, 119.

117 Kevin Conley Ruffner, "The Black Market in Postwar Berlin: Colonel Miller and an Army Scandal," *Prologue Magazine* 34, no. 3 (Fall 2002), https://www.archives.gov/publications/prologue/2002/fall/berlin-black-market-1.html.

118 Giles MacDonough, *After the Reich: From the Liberation of Vienna to the Berlin Airlift* (London: John Murray, 2007), 374 and 378.

119 Bessel, *Germany 1945*, 352.

120 Stivers and Carter, *The City Becomes a Symbol*, 82-83.

121 Bessel, *Germany 1945*, 352-53.

122 MacDonough, *After the Reich*, 521; Howley, *Berlin Command*, 89-90. The quotation is from Lucius D. Clay to BG Edward H. White, Office of the Comptroller, United States Forces European Theater, November 2, 1946, *The Letters of General Lucius D. Clay*, ed. Jean Edward Smith (Bloomington, IN: Indiana University Press, 1974), 1: 276. Some of the problems associated with the market are evident in Delbert Clark, "U.S. Barter Center in Berlin Failing," 25, *The New York Times* (December 15, 1946), https://timesmachine.nytimes.com/timesmachine/1946/12/15/issue.html

123 Office of the Chief Historian, *The Second Year of Occupation: Volume III*, Occupation Forces in Europe Series, 1946-47 (Frankfurt-am-Main: Headquarters European Command, 1947): 122.

124 Malte Zierenberg, *Berlin's Black Market: 1939-1950* (NY: Palgrave Macmillan, 2015), 167.

125 Stivers and Carter, *The City Becomes a Symbol*, 120.

126 Clay to BG Edward H. White, 1: 276-79.

127 Zierenberg, *Berlin's Black Market*, 169. The excerpt is from page 8 of the January 5, 1947 issue of *Telegraf*.

128 Zierenberg, *Berlin's Black Market*, 197.

129 Margaret L. Geis and George J. Gray, Jr., *Relations of Occupation Personnel with the Civil Population,1946 -1948*, Occupation Forces in Europe Series, 1946-1948 (Historical Division, Headquarters, European Command, 1951), 44.

130 Geis and Gray, *Relations of Occupation Personnel with the Civil Population, 1946 -1948*, 11.

131 Slaveski, *The Soviet Occupation of Germany*, 104.

132 Slaveski, *The Soviet Occupation of Germany*, 105.

133 *Annual Narrative Report, 1 January-31 December 1950: Occupation Forces in Europe Series, 1950*. Karlsruhe, Germany: Historical Division, European Command, undated, 130-31 and 174.

134 Lawrence J. Vale and Thomas J. Campanella, "Warsaw: Reconstruction as Propaganda," 142.

135 Marta Pastukh, et al., "Anchoring green recovery of urban mobility in Ukraine: Eight building blocks."

136 Brian Ladd, "Double Restoration: Rebuilding Berlin after 1945," in *The Resilient City: How Modern Cities Recover from Disaster*, ed.

Lawrence J. Vale and Thomas J. Campanella (Oxford: Oxford University Press, 2005), 117.

137 Ladd, "Double Restoration," 120-22; and Glenn, *Come Hell or High Fever*, 312.

138 Ziemke, *The US Army in the Occupation of Germany*, 303.

139 Ladd, "Double Restoration," 125-26.

140 Ladd, "Double Restoration," 126.

141 Ladd, "Double Restoration," 126 and 128. For more on reconstruction in Berlin and its role in the East-West competition, see Kateryna Kozlova, "Please, Don't Stop: How Berlin Started the Reconstruction and Has Never Finished," *Bird in Flight* (December 26, 2022), https://birdinflight.com/en/architectura-2/20221226-postwar-berlin.html.

142 Philip McCouat, "Bernardo Bellotto and the Reconstruction of Warsaw," *Journal of Art in Society* (2015), https://www.artinsociety.com/bernardo-bellotto-and-the-reconstruction-of-warsaw.html; and Ladd, "Double Restoration," 130.

143 Glenn, "Creating Light at Tunnel's End."

144 Ladd, "Double Restoration," 131.

145 Turner, *Berlin Airlift*, 62.

146 George Sharpe, *Brothers in Blood: A Battalion Surgeon in the South Pacific* (Austin, Texas: Diamond Books, 1989), 199 and 200.

147 Lawrence J. Vale and Thomas J. Campanella, "Conclusion: Axioms of Resilience," in *The Resilient City: How Modern Cities Recover from Disaster*, ed. Lawrence J. Vale and Thomas J. Campanella (NY: Oxford, 2005): 342.

148 Unless otherwise cited, this description of damage inflicted on Manila during its recapture draws heavily on Russell W. Glenn, "Urban Disaster Wrought by Man: The Battle for Manila, 1945," *Journal of Strategic Security* 16, no. 3 (2023), https://digitalcommons.usf.edu/jss/vol16/iss3/3/.

149 Glenn, "Urban Disaster Wrought by Man."

150 United States Philippine War Damage Commission, *First Semi-annual Report For Period Ending December 31, 1946* (Washington, D.C.: United States Government Printing Office, 1947), 3.

151 Hartendorp, "Short History of Industry and Trade in the Philippines," 96.

152 James M. Scott, *Rampage: MacArthur, Yamashita, and the Battle of Manila* (NY: W.W. Norton, 2018), 424, 426, and 202.

153 Juan Labrador, *A Diary of the Japanese Occupation* (Manila: Santo Tomas University Press, 1989), 283.

154 Scott, *Rampage*, 424 and 426.

155 Scott, *Rampage*, 433.

156 Scott, *Rampage*, 431-32.

157 For more on the War Damage Corporation's relevance to WWII recovery, see C. Arnold Fraleigh, "Compensation for War Damage to American Property in Allied Country," *The American Journal of International Law* 41, no. 4 (October 1947): 748-69; and Ernest Schein, "War Damage Compensation Through Rehabilitation: The Philippine War Damage Commission," *Law and Contemporary Problems* 16 (1951): 519-542.

158 Bureau of the Census and Statistics, *Bulletin of Philippine Statistics* 1, no. 1 (Manila: Bureau of Printing, September 1945), 1 and 16.

159 US Secretary of State, "The Philippine Rehabilitation Program Report to the President," Far Eastern Series volume 67, August 31, 1954, 5-11, Available at https://books.google.com/books/about/The_Philippine_Rehabilitation_Program.html; and Filipinas Heritage Library, "Manila Reborn: An Exhibit on the postwar reconstruction of a city" Google Arts and Culture (undated), https://artsandculture.google.com/story/manila-reborn-filipinas-heritage-library/.

160 Salvador Araneta, "Basic Problems of Philippine Economic Development," *Pacific Affairs* 21, no. 3 (September 1948): 285, and Ricardo Trota Jose, "July 4, 1946: The Philippines gained Independence from the United States," The National WWII Museum, July 2, 2021, https://www.nationalww2museum.org/war/articles/july-4-1946-philippines-independence.

161 Shirley Jenkins, "Philippine White Paper," *Far Eastern Survey* 20, no. 1 (January 10, 1951): 2.

162 United States Philippine War Damage Commission, *First Semi-annual Report* 9.

163 Harold M Vinacke, "Post-War Government and Politics of the Philippines," *The Journal of Politics* 9, no. 4 (November 1947): 723.

164 Bureau of the Census and Statistics, *Bulletin of Philippine Statistics*, 2, no. 1 (Manila: Bureau of Printing, March 1946), 203-04 and

258. The actual numbers were imports P57,867,195; exports P1,344,169 (P: Philippine peso).

165 US Secretary of State, "The Philippine Rehabilitation Program Report to the President," Far Eastern Series volume 67, August 31, 1954, 1, 3-4, and 13.

166 Bureau of the Census and Statistics, *Bulletin of Philippine Statistics* 1, no. 2 (Manila: Bureau of Printing, December 1945), 171.

167 Bureau of the Census and Statistics, *Bulletin of Philippine Statistics* 1, no. 2, 113.

168 Bureau of the Census and Statistics, *Bulletin of Philippine Statistics* 1, no. 2, 115.

169 Bureau of the Census and Statistics, *Bulletin of Philippine Statistics* 1, no. 1, 16, 128, and 133.

170 Bureau of the Census and Statistics, *Bulletin of Philippine Statistics* 1, no. 2, 116.

171 Bureau of the Census and Statistics, *Bulletin of Philippine Statistics* 1, no. 2, (Manila: Bureau of Printing, December 1945), 133. David Joel Steinberg instead cites estimates "that between 6,623,000,000 and 11,148,000,000 pesos were issued by the Japanese during the occupation. The actual amounts printed will never be known, however, since field commanders had their own presses." David Joel Steinberg, *Philippine Collaboration in World War II* (Ann Arbor, MI: University of Michigan Press, 1967), 88.

172 Bureau of the Census and Statistics, *Bulletin of Philippine Statistics* 1, no. 1, 5.

173 Bureau of the Census and Statistics, *Bulletin of Philippine Statistics* 1, no. 1, 172 and 176.

174 Bureau of the Census and Statistics, *Bulletin of Philippine Statistics* 1, no. 1, 41.

175 Bureau of the Census and Statistics, *Bulletin of Philippine Statistics* 1, no. 1, 24.

176 Bureau of the Census and Statistics, *Bulletin of Philippine Statistics* 1, no. 2, 145.

177 United States Philippine War Damage Commission, *Seventh Semiannual Report of the United States Philippine War Damage Commission For Period Ending December 31, 1949* (Washington, D.C.: United States Government Printing Office, 1950), 1.

178 Bureau of the Census and Statistics, *Bulletin of Philippine Statistics* 1, no. 2, 117-19.

179 Lawrence M. Greenberg, "Between Liberation and Independence," in *The Hukbalahap Insurrection: A Case Study of a Successful Anti-Insurgency Operation in the Philippines – 1946-1955* (Washington, D.C.: Center for Military History, 1987), 31-32, https://apps.dtic.mil/sti/pdfs/AD1112093.pdf.

180 Tristan Miguel Santos Osteria, "Building from Within: Indigenous Nation-building and State-making During the Filipino Third Republic, 1946-1957," (PhD diss, Texas A&M University, December 2016), 219.

181 Osteria, "Building from Within," 4 and 52-53.

182 Osteria, "Building from Within," 61.

183 Osteria, "Building from Within," 67.

184 Osteria, "Building from Within," 120-21.

185 Osteria, "Building from Within," 213.

CHAPTER 4

1 For those interested in a detailed analysis of conflict-induced casualties in Sarajevo, see Ewa Tabeau, Marcin Żółtkowski, and Jakub Bijak, "Population Losses in the 'Siege' of Sarajevo, 10 September 1992 to 10 August 1994," Demographic Unit - LRT research report, May 10, 2002, https://www.icty.org/x/file/About/OTP/War_Demographics/en/galic_sarajevo_020510.pdf.

2 Kateryna Kozlova, "A Facelift Worth Billions: Urbanist on Why Post-war Restoration of Sarajevo Only Made It Worse," *Bird in Flight*, June, 17 2022, https://birdinflight.com/en/architectura-2/20220617-sarajevo-after-war.html.

3 Gruia Bădescu, "Dwelling in the Post-War City Urban Reconstruction and Home-Making in Sarajevo," *Revue D'etudes Comparatives Est-Ouest* 4, no. 46 (2015), 37

4 "Your land is my land: Imperialism then and now," *The Economist* 451, no. 9400 (June 8, 2024): 74.

5 Carola Hein, "Resilient Tokyo: Disaster and Transformation in the Japanese City," in *The Resilient City: How Modern Cities Recover from Disaster*, ed. Lawrence J. Vale and Thomas J. Campanella (NY: Oxford, 2005): 223.

6   Michael J. Bird, *The Town that Died: The true story of the greatest man-made explosion before Hiroshima*, (Toronto: McGraw-Hill, 1962), 160.

7   Green, *The Anthropocene Reviewed*, 211.

8   This background description draws on Office of the Historian, "The Breakup of Yugoslavia, 1990-1992," Foreign Service Institute, US Department of State, undated, https://history.state.gov/milestones/1989-1992/breakup-yugoslavia.

9   Robert J. Donia, *Sarajevo: A Biography* (Ann Arbor: University of Michigan Press, 2006), 293 and 297.

10 Karacas, "Tokyo From the Fire," 211.

11 "Bosnia and Herzegovina-Details," The World Factbook, US Central Intelligence Agency, undated, https://www.cia.gov/the-world-factbook/countries/bosnia-and-herzegovina/map.

12 Alice Autumn Weinreb, "Matters of Taste: The Politics of Food and Hunger in Divided Germany 1945-1971," (PhD diss., University of Michigan, 2009), 128 and 135, https://www.academia.edu/85272407/Matters_of_Taste_The_Politics_of_Food_in_Divided_Germany_1945_1971.

13 Mezentsev and Mezentsev, "War and the city," 500 and 502.

14 Peter Lippman, *Surviving the Peace: The Struggle for Postwar Recovery in Bosnia-Herzegovina* (Nashville, TN: Vanderbilt University Press, 2019), 43.

15 Haris Piplas, *Non-Aligned City: Urban laboratory of the new Sarajevo*, PhD diss., University of Sarajevo, undated, 226. SDS is the *Srpska Demokratska Stranka* (Serbian Democratic Party).

16 Piplas, *Non-Aligned City*, 227-28.

17 Donia, *Sarajevo*, 303.

18 Donia, *Sarajevo*, 304-05; and Andreas, *Blue Helmets and Black Markets*, 101-03.

19 Piplas, *Non-Aligned City*, 230.

20 Lippman, *Surviving the Peace*, 24-25.

21 Richard Holbrooke, *To End a War* (NY: Random House, 1998), 196 and 207.

22 Lippman, *Surviving the Peace*, 25.

23 Lippman, *Surviving the Peace*, 46.

24 Holbrooke, *To End a War*, 226.
25 Holbrooke, *To End a War*, 199.
26 Donia, *Sarajevo*, 288.
27 Holbrooke, *To End a War*, 249 and 291-93; and David Owen, *Balkan Odyssey* (NY: Harcourt Brace & Company, 1995), 199.
28 Donia, *Sarajevo*,), 339.
29 Holbrooke, *To End a War*, 335-37; and Donia, *Sarajevo*, 322-23.
30 Susan Orlean, *The Library Book* (NY: Simon & Schuster, 2018), 202.
31 Orlean, *The Library Book*, 101.
32 Kozlova, "A Facelift Worth Billions."
33 Orlean, *The Library Book*, 289.
34 Donia, *Sarajevo*, 314.
35 Bădescu, "Dwelling in the Post-War City," 41.
36 Ewa Tabeau, Jakub Bijak, and Neda Loncaric, "Death Toll in the Siege of Sarajevo, April 1992 to December 1995: A Study of Mortality Based on Eight Large Data Sources," Demographic Unit, Office of the Prosecution, International Criminal Tribunal for the Former Yugoslavia, August 18, 2003, 2. Numbers of killed and wounded due to the siege vary widely, in part due to different time periods used in the estimates. Much higher numbers appear to not discriminate between total deaths for a given timespan and those directly attributable to the siege. This study appears to be among the most rigorous analyses of losses.
37 Donia, *Sarajevo*, 334.
38 Donia, *Sarajevo*, 340 and 343.
39 "Russia's war on Ukraine's libraries," *Labour Hub* (December 21, 2023), https://labourhub.org.uk/2023/12/21/russias-war-on-ukraines-libraries/.
40 Gruia Bădescu, "Post-War Reconstruction in Contested Cities: Comparing Urban Outcomes in Sarajevo and Beirut," in *Urban Geopolitics: Rethinking Planning in Contested Cities*, ed. Jonathan Rokem and Camillo Boano (August 21, 2017), 17-31, http://dx.doi.org/10.4324/9781315659275-3.
41 Lippman, *Surviving the Peace*, 3.
42 Lippman, *Surviving the Peace*, 74-75.

43 Lewis MacKenzie, *Peacekeeper: The Road to Sarajevo* (Toronto: HarperCollins, 1994), 217.
44 Bădescu, "Dwelling in the Post-War City," 41.
45 Lippman, Surviving the Peace, 65.
46 Lippman, Surviving the Peace, 65.
47 Bădescu, "Dwelling in the Post-War City," 49.
48 Bădescu, "Dwelling in the Post-War City," 54-55.
49 Bureau of Democracy, Human Rights, and Labor, "2016 Report on International Religious Freedom: Bosnia and Herzegovina," US Department of State, 2016, https://www.state.gov/reports/2016-report-on-international-religious-freedom/bosnia-and-herzegovina/.
50 Bădescu, "Dwelling in the Post-War City," 39.
51 Bădescu, "Post-War Reconstruction in Contested Cities."
52 Lippman, *Surviving the Peace* 4 and 33.
53 Bădescu, "Dwelling in the Post-War City," 39-40.
54 Lippman, *Surviving the Peace* 31.
55 T. Hasic, "Sustainable Reconstruction of Post-War Cities: The Case of Sarajevo," *Open House International Journal* 27, no. 4 (2002): 73. Hasic's dissertation provides expanded coverage of reconstruction in BiH. See Tigran Hasic, "Reconstruction Planning in Post-Conflict Zones: Bosnia and Herzegovina and the International Community," (PhD diss. Stockholm: The Royal Institute of Technology, 2004).
56 Linda Kinstler, "Architects Plan a City for the Future in Ukraine, While Bombs Still Fall: Irpin was one of the first Ukrainian cities to be destroyed and liberated. Now it's become a laboratory for rebuilding," *The New York Times,* November 7, 2022, updated November 11, 2022), https://www.nytimes.com/2022/11/07/magazine/ukraine-rebuild-irpin.html.
57 Andreas, *Blue Helmets and Black Markets*, 58.
58 Andreas, *Blue Helmets and Black Markets*, 97.
59 Andreas, *Blue Helmets and Black Markets*, 39.
60 Andreas, *Blue Helmets and Black Markets*, 8- 9 and 47.
61 Andreas, *Blue Helmets and Black Markets*, 50.

62 Glenn, *Come Hell or High Fever*, 250-51 and 270-71, http://doi.org/10.22459/CHHF.2023.

63 Andreas, *Blue Helmets and Black Markets*, 15.

64 Andreas, *Blue Helmets and Black Markets*, 36-37.

65 Mark Cutts, "The humanitarian operation in Bosnia, 1992-95: the dilemmas of negotiating humanitarian access," Policy Research Unit UNHCR Working Paper no. 8, May 1999, 22, https://www.unhcr.org/media/humanitarian-operation-bosnia-1992-95-dilemmas-negotiating-humanitarian-access-mark-cutts, as quoted in Andreas, *Blue Helmets and Black Markets*, 38.

66 Andreas, *Blue Helmets and Black Markets*, 18 and 28-29.

67 Andreas, *Blue Helmets and Black Markets*, 24.

68 Donia, *Sarajevo*, 287.

69 Lippman, *Surviving the Peace*, 25.

70 Dr. Haris Piplas as quoted in Kozlova, "A Facelift Worth Billions."

71 Bădescu, "Post-War Reconstruction in Contested Cities."

72 Dr. Haris Piplas as quoted in Kozlova, "A Facelift Worth Billions."

73 Bădescu, "Post-War Reconstruction in Contested Cities."

74 Lippman, *Surviving the Peace*, 57.

75 Kozlova, "A Facelift Worth Billions."

76 Piplas, *Non-Aligned City*, 296-97.

77 Hasic, "Sustainable Reconstruction of Post-War Cities," 76.

78 Bureau of Democracy, Human Rights, and Labor, "2016 Report on International Religious Freedom: Bosnia and Herzegovina."

79 Sabina Niksic, "Top European court says that Bosnian minorities are treated like 'second-class citizens,'" Associated Press, August 29, 2023, https://apnews.com/article/bosnia-court-ethnic-elections-serbs-croats-dayton-f98eb45e5230a40fe0e4524311ff8e99.

80 Niksic, "Top European court says that Bosnian minorities are treated like 'second-class citizens.'"

81 "Prospecting for hope: Bosnia," *The Economist* 449, no. 9375 (December 9, 2023): 47. The article appears online as "A mining project revives a dying Bosnian town," https://www.economist.com/europe/2023/12/07/a-mining-project-revives-a-dying-bosnian-town.

CHAPTER 5

1. John Gittings, "The Conflict Between War and Peace in Early Chinese Thought," *The Asia-Pacific Journal* 10, Issue 12, no. 5 (March 12, 2012), https://apjjf.org/2012/10/12/johngittings/3725/article.
2. Trofimov, *Our Enemies will Vanish*, 80.
3. As quoted in Volodymyr Kravchenko, "Borderland City: Kharkiv," *East/West Journal of Ukrainian Studies* 8, no. 1 (2020), DOI: https://doi.org/10.21226/ewjus572, 184.
4. "Within range," *The Economist* 450, no. 9386 (March 2, 2024): 46.
5. Luke Harding, *Invasion: The Inside Story of Russia's Bloody War and Ukraine's Fight for Survival* (NY: Vintage, 2022), 88-89.
6. Kravchenko, "Borderland City: Kharkiv," 188.
7. Kravchenko, "Borderland City: Kharkiv," 191.
8. Luke Harding, Peter Beaumont, Jon Henley, and Martine Farrer, "Ukraine facing humanitarian crisis amid relentless Russian missile attacks," *The Guardian* (March 2, 2022), https://www.theguardian.com/world/2022/mar/02/ukraine-cities-bombardment-russia-attack-kyiv-kharkiv-russian-war-invasion.
9. Masha Gessen, "The Devastation of Kharkiv, Ukraine: Russian attacks have terrorized the civilian population in the Ukrainian city," *The New Yorker* (March 22, 2022), https://www.newyorker.com/culture/photo-booth/the-devastation-of-kharkiv.
10. Volodymyr Kravchenko, *Kharkov/Kharkiv: a borderland capital*. (NY: Berghahn Books, 2023), 265.
11. Kravchenko, *Kharkov/Kharkiv*, 268; and "Russian site recruits 'volunteers' for Ukraine," *BBC News* (March 5, 2014), https://www.bbc.com/news/blogs-trending-26435333.
12. Kravchenko, *Kharkov/Kharkiv*, 269-70.
13. Andrew Higgins, "Kharkiv, Ukraine's second-largest city, is a major target of Russia. Here's why," *The New York Times*, February 24, 2022), https://www.nytimes.com/2022/02/24/world/europe/kharkiv-russia.html.
14. Kravchenko, *Kharkov/Kharkiv*, 272.
15. Kravchenko, *Kharkov/Kharkiv*, 273 and 276-80, and Brian Mefford, "Death of Kharkiv Major Kernes marks end of era," Atlantic Council, December 22, 2020, https://www.atlantic-

council.org/blogs/ukrainealert/death-of-kharkiv-mayor-kernes-marks-end-of-era/.

16 Viktoriia Onyshchenko, "Ready, Set, Go: Decolonization! How New Law Changes Public Spaces of Ukraine," Transparency International-Ukraine (July 27, 2023), https://ti-ukraine.org/en/blogs/ready-set-go-decolonization-how-new-law-changes-public-spaces-of-ukraine/.

17 Onyshchenko, "Ready, Set, Go: Decolonization!"

18 Mason Clark, George Barros, and Kateryna Stepanenko, "Russia-Ukraine Warning Update: Initial Russian Offensive Campaign Assessment," Institute for the Study of War, February 24, 2022, https://www.understandingwar.org/backgrounder/russia-ukraine-warning-update-initial-russian-offensive-campaign-assessment.

19 Isabelle Khurshudyan and Miriam Berger, "Why Kharkiv, a city known for its poets, has become a key battleground in Ukraine," *The Washington* Post, February 28, 2022, https://www.washingtonpost.com/world/2022/02/28/kharkiv-ukraine-russia-war-east/.

20 "Ukraine: Cluster Munitions Launched Into Kharkiv Neighborhoods: Russian Forces' Indiscriminate Attacks May Amount to War Crimes," Human Rights Watch (March 4, 2022), https://www.hrw.org/news/2022/03/04/ukraine-cluster-munitions-launched-kharkiv-neighborhoods.

21 Sebastien Roblin, "Ukraine says it captured documents revealing that an elite Russian unit lost over 130 tanks in failed attacks on Kharkiv," *Business Insider* (May 20, 2022), https://www.businessinsider.com/captured-documents-say-elite-russian-unit-lost-tanks-kharkiv-ukraine-2022-5; Gessen, "The Devastation of Kharkiv, Ukraine;" and Kateryna Stepanenko and Frederick W. Kagan, "Russian Offensive Campaign Assessment, May 13," Institute for the Study of War (May 13, 2022), https://www.understandingwar.org/backgrounder/russian-offensive-campaign-assessment-may-13.

22 "Amnesty says Russia guilty of war crimes in Kharkiv shelling," Reuters (June 13, 2022), https://www.reuters.com/business/aerospace-defense/amnesty-says-russia-guilty-war-crimes-kharkiv-shelling-2022-06-13/.

23 "A Tale of Five Cities," *The Economist* 449, no. 9377 (December 23, 2023): 13 (of the "Holiday specials" section).

24 "The race to save Kharkiv," *The Economist* 451, no. 9392 (April 13, 2024): 40.

25 Isabelle Khurshudyan, "Russia unleashes attacks on Kharkiv border area," *The Washington Post*, May 12, 2024, A10.

26 "The race to save Kharkiv;" and Alec Russell, "The second battle for Kharkiv: Ukrainian city goes underground to defy Russian missiles," *Financial Times* (October 19, 2023), https://www.ft.com/content/c1719b5c-c30f-4415-a2dd-dc0b4025886b; and Brandon J. Weichert, "Russia Launching Massive 6,600-Pound Glide Bombs at Ukraine," June 23, 2024, https://nationalinterest.org/blog/buzz/russia-launching-massive-6600-pound-glide-bombs-ukraine-211570.

27 Russell, "The second battle for Kharkiv."

28 "The race to save Kharkiv," 40.

29 Adam Taylor, Anastacia Galouchka, and Kostiantyn Khudov, "Ukraine dreams of rebuilding but Russian destruction continues," *The Washington Post*, June 21, 2023, https://www.washingtonpost.com/world/2023/06/21/ukraine-recovery-reconstruction-economy-kharkiv/.

30 Kravchenko, *Kharkov/Kharkiv*, 282.

31 The foundation self-describes as follows: "The Norman Foster Foundation promotes interdisciplinary thinking and research to help new generations of architects, designers and urbanists to anticipate the future." Norman Foster Foundation, undated, https://normanfosterfoundation.org/. The quotation is from Taylor, Galouchka, and Khudov, "Ukraine dreams of rebuilding."

32 "UN4Kharkiv: Integrated Rehabilitation of Settlements (Territories) in Ukraine with a pilot project in the city of Kharkiv," United Nations Economic Committee for Europe Housing and Land Management, undated, https://unece.org/housing/un4kharkiv-rehabilitation.

33 Taylor, Galouchka, and Khudov, "Ukraine dreams of rebuilding."

34 Taylor, Galouchka, and Khudov, "Ukraine dreams of rebuilding."

35 Taylor, Galouchka, and Khudov, "Ukraine dreams of rebuilding."

36 Reliefweb, "The path to recovery: rebuilding hope in Kharkiv," United Nations Office for Project Services press release, December 19, 2023, https://reliefweb.int/report/ukraine/path-recovery-rebuilding-hope-kharkiv.

37 Tony Judt, *Postwar: A History of Europe Since 1945* (NY: Penguin, 1945), 35 and 49.

38 Joshua Yaffa, "The Hunt for Russian Collaborators in Ukraine," *The New Yorker* (January 30, 2023), https://www.newyorker.com/magazine/2023/02/06/the-hunt-for-russian-collaborators-in-ukraine.

39 Sinclair McKay, *Berlin: Life and Loss in the City That Shaped the Century* (London: Viking, 2022), 4.

40 Russell Falcon, "Explained: Why Kharkiv is one of Ukraine's most vulnerable cities," *NewsNation* (February 24, 2022), https://www.newsnationnow.com/us-news/explained-why-kharkiv-is-one-of-ukraines-most-vulnerable-cities/.

41 Olena Konoplia, "What Life is Like in the De-Occupied Territories of Ukraine," *Ukraine World* (blog) December 26, 2022, https://ukraineworld.org/en/articles/analysis/de-occupied.

42 Konoplia, "What Life is Like in the De-Occupied Territories of Ukraine."

43 Konoplia, "What Life is Like in the De-Occupied Territories of Ukraine."

44 Yaffa, "The Hunt for Russian Collaborators in Ukraine."

45 "Ukraine: New Laws Criminalize Collaboration with an Aggressor State," Library of Congress, April 4, 2022, https://www.loc.gov/item/global-legal-monitor/2022-04-04/ukraine-new-laws-criminalize-collaboration-with-an-aggressor-state/. The source identifies the two laws as "Law No. 2108-IX on Amendments to Certain Legislative Acts regarding the Establishment of Criminal Liability for Collaboration Activities (Criminal Liability for Collaboration Law), and Law No. 2107-IX on Amendments to Certain Legislative Acts on Ensuring the Responsibility of Individuals Who Carry Out Collaboration Activities (Individual Responsibility for Collaboration Law)."

46 "Holodomor," Holocaust and Genocide Studies, College of Liberal Arts, University of Minnesota, 2024, https://cla.umn.edu/chgs/holocaust-genocide-education/resource-guides/holodomor.

47 Yaffa, "The Hunt for Russian Collaborators in Ukraine."

48 Yaffa, "The Hunt for Russian Collaborators in Ukraine," and Judt, *Postwar*, 39.

49 Yaffa, "The Hunt for Russian Collaborators in Ukraine."

50 Trofimov, *Our Enemies will Vanish*, 286-87.

51 Judt, *Postwar*, 42-43.

52 Julian Jackson, *France on Trial: The Case of Marshal Petain* (Cambridge, MA: Belknap, 2023), xxix.

53 Judt, *Postwar*, 45 and 50.

54 Jackson, *France on Trial*, 31-32 and 35-36; and Dov Jacobs, "A Narrative of Justice and the (Re)Writing of History: Lessons Learned from World War II French Trials," in *The Hidden Histories of War Crimes Trials*, ed. Kevin Jon Heller and Gerry Simpson (Oxford: Oxford University Press, 2013), 124-26 and 132, https://academic.oup.com/book/26719/chapter/195545738.

55 Yaffa, "The Hunt for Russian Collaborators in Ukraine."

56 For several descriptions of such abuse, see Yaffa, "The Hunt for Russian Collaborators in Ukraine."

57 Yaffa, "The Hunt for Russian Collaborators in Ukraine."

58 Sam Harshbarger, "Challenges after Russian Withdrawals in Ukraine," New Lines Institute, (August 10, 2023), https://newlinesinstitute.org/state-resilience-fragility/challenges-after-russian-withdrawals-in-ukraine/.

59 Judt, *Postwar*, 33.

60 Valentyna Romanova, "Ukraine's resilience to Russia's military invasion in the context of the decentralization reform," Research Gate (May 2022), https://www.researchgate.net/publication/360447277_Ukraine's_resilience_to_Russia's_military_invasion_in_the_context_of_the_decentralisation_reform.

61 Hanna Arhirova, "'We survived': Kherson comes alive after Russian withdrawal," Associated Press (November 19, 2022), https://apnews.com/article/russia-ukraine-europe-business-46c1061fc44458c903cf12fa442c57e1.

62 Liam James, "Russia claims it has seized Kherson as mayor agrees to conditions to keep city running," *Independent* (March 3, 2022), https://www.independent.co.uk/news/world/europe/russia-ukraine-kherson-take-fall-b2027325.html; and Ivan Krasikov, "Crimean Canal Key to its Liberation," Institute for War & Peace Reporting, December 1, 2022, https://iwpr.net/global-voices/crimean-canal-key-its-liberation.

63 James, "Russia claims it has seized Kherson."

64 Harding, *Invasion*, 183.

65 "Timeline: Key developments in Ukraine's Kherson since invasion," Aljazeera (November 9, 2022), https://www.aljazeera.com/news/2022/11/9/timeline-key-developments-in-ukraines-kherson-since-invasion; and "Ukraine says 300,000 people are running out of food in occupied Kherson," Reuters (March 22, 2022), https://www.reuters.com/world/europe/ukraine-says-300000-people-are-running-out-food-occupied-kherson-2022-03-22/.

66 Jakob Hedenskog, "The Russian Occupation of Ukraine's Southern Regions," Stockholm Centre for Eastern European Studies report no. 5, June 2, 2022, https://sceeus.se/en/publications/the-russian-occupation-of-ukraines-southern-regions/.

67 Trofimov, *Our Enemies will Vanish*, 295.

68 "Kherson: How is Russia imposing its rule in occupied Ukraine?" BBC (May 11, 2022), https://www.bbc.com/news/world-61338617; and Anonymous interview 1.

69 "Russia hands out passports in occupied Ukraine cities," BBC (June 11, 2022), https://www.bbc.com/news/world-europe-61770997.

70 Marc Santora, "Moscow says babies born in occupied Kherson will automatically get Russian citizenship," *The New York* Times, July 11, 2022, https://www.nytimes.com/2022/06/16/world/europe/ukraine-kherson-babies-russian-citizenship.html.

71 "Timeline: Key developments in Ukraine's Kherson since invasion."

72 "Timeline: Key developments in Ukraine's Kherson since invasion."

73 James FitzGerald, "Ukraine war: Putin endorses evacuations from occupied Kherson," BBC (November 5, 2022), https://www.bbc.co.uk/news/world-europe-63523043; and Kateryna Stepanenko, Riley Bailey, Grace Mappes, Yekaterina Klepanchuk, and Frederick W. Kagan, "Russian Offensive Campaign Assessment, November 3," Institute for the Study of War, November 3, 2022, https://www.understandingwar.org/backgrounder/russian-offensive-campaign-assessment-november-3.

74 Paul Adams and James FitzGerald, "Ukraine war: Celebrations as Kyiv takes back key city Kherson," BBC (November 11, 2022), https://www.bbc.com/news/world-europe-63601312.

75 Liz Cookman, "Kherson is Liberated but Not Yet Freed," *Foreign Policy* (November 18, 2022), https://foreignpolicy.com/2022/11/18/kherson-ukraine-liberation-russia-occupation/.

76 Arhirova, "We survived."

77 "Ukraine: Russians Pillage Kherson Cultural Institutions: Art and Artifacts Stolen," Human rights Watch, December 20, 2022, https://www.hrw.org/news/2022/12/20/ukraine-russians-pillage-kherson-cultural-institutions.

78 Igor Burdyga, "Russia promised Kherson it would stay forever. It left chaos behind," openDemocracy (December 5, 2022), https://www.opendemocracy.net/en/odr/kherson-russian-occupation-retreat-looting/.

79 Holly Williams, "Russian attacks after occupation ends," *CBS News* (February 26, 2023), https://www.cbsnews.com/news/kherson-ukraine-60-minutes-2023-02-26/.

80 Elizabeth Piper, "Insight: Traitor next door? Fear stalks Kherson after Russian occupation ends," Reuters (May 18, 2023), https://www.reuters.com/world/europe/traitor-next-door-fear-stalks-kherson-after-russian-occupation-ends-2023-05-18/.

81 Harshbarger, "Challenges after Russian Withdrawals in Ukraine."

82 Radio Free Europe/Radio Liberty Ukrainian Service, "Red Cross: Mayor Of Ukrainian City Of Kherson Is In Russian Custody," September 18, 2023, https://www.rferl.org/a/ukraine-kherson-mayor-red-cross-russia-custody/32597782.html.

83 "Ukraine: Russians Pillage Kherson Cultural Institutions."

84 Michelle Bachelet, "High Commissioner updates the Human Rights Council on Mariupol, Ukraine," Office of the High Commissioner for Human Rights, June 22, 2022, https://www.ohchr.org/en/statements/2022/06/high-commissioner-updates-human-rights-council-mariupol-ukraine.

85 Paul Niland, "Putin's Mariupol Massacre is one of the 21st century's worst war crimes," Atlantic Council Ukraine Alert (May 24, 2022), https://www.atlanticcouncil.org/blogs/ukrainealert/putins-mariupol-massacre-is-one-the-worst-war-crimes-of-the-21st-century/.

86 Trofimov, *Our Enemies will Vanish*, 184.

87 "The Path to Recovery: How Regions Surviving Russian Occupation are Rebuilding," *Forbes* (December 21, 2023), https://forbes.ua/ru/brandvoice/krok-za-krokom-yak-uzhe-zaraz-trivae-vidnovlennya-regioniv-shcho-perezhili-rosiysku-okupatsiyu-21122023-17873. Amos Fox, writing a year previously,

estimated 350,000 from a population of 430,00 had fled. Amos C. Fox, "The Russo-Ukrainian War and the Principles of Urban Operations," *Small Wars Journal* (November 10, 2022), https://smallwarsjournal.com/jrnl/art/russo-ukrainian-war-and-principles-urban-operations.

88 Human Rights Watch, "'Our City Was Gone,' Russia's Devastation of Mariupol, Ukraine," February 2024, 2, https://www.hrw.org/feature/russia-ukraine-war-mariupol/report; and Rob Picheta, "Putin should face war crimes probe over 'devastating' assault on Mariupol, HRW report finds," CNN, February 8, 2024, https://www.cnn.com/2024/02/08/europe/mariupol-hrw-report-putin-russia-ukraine-intl/index.html.

89 Jen Kirby, "What Mariupol's fall means for Russia – and Ukraine," Vox, May 17, 2022, https://www.vox.com/2022/5/17/23037687/mariupol-evacuation-ukraine-russia.

90 Joel Gunter, "Ukrainian city of Mariupol 'near to humanitarian catastrophe' after bombardment," *BBC News* (March 2, 2022), https://www.bbc.com/news/world-europe-60585603; and Fox, "The Russo-Ukrainian War;" and Harding, *Invasion*, 120.

91 Human Rights Watch, "Our City Was Gone," 45, 54, 55, and 56; and "'The Hope Left Us:' Russia's Siege, Starvation, and Capture of Mariupol City," Global Rights Compliance, June 2024, 64, https://globalrightscompliance.com/wp-content/uploads/2024/06/20240612-Mariupol-ReportENG.pdf. The Global Rights Compliance document provides a detailed timeline of early 2022 Mariupol events in its Annex I.

92 Human Rights Watch, "Our City Was Gone."

93 Mason Clark, George Barros, and Kateryna Stepaneko, "Russian Offensive Campaign Assessment, March 24," Institute for the Study of War (March 24, 2022), https://www.understandingwar.org/backgrounder/russian-offensive-campaign-assessment-march-24; Max Hunder, "Timeline: Russia's siege of the Ukrainian city of Mariupol," Reuters (March 30, 2022), https://www.reuters.com/world/europe/russias-siege-ukrainian-city-mariupol-2022-03-30/; Bachelet, "High Commissioner updates;" Mstyslav Chernov, "20 Days in Mariupol: The Team that documented the city's agony," Associated Press, March 21, 2022, https://apnews.com/article/russia-ukraine-europe-edf7-240a9d990e7e3e32f82ca351dede; and Human Rights Watch, "Our City Was Gone," 18 and 79-80.

94 Mason Clark, Kateryna Stepanenko, and Karolina Hird, "Russian Offensive Campaign Assessment, April 10," Institute for the Study of War (April 7, 2022), https://www.understandingwar.org/backgrounder/russian-offensive-campaign-assessment-april-10; Bachelet, "High Commissioner updates;" and Trofimov, *Our Enemies will Vanish*, 166.

95 David Kortava, "In the Filtration Camps," *The New Yorker* (October 3, 2022), https://www.newyorker.com/magazine/2022/10/10/inside-russias-filtration-camps-in-eastern-ukraine.

96 "Russia's Filtration Operations and Forced Relocations," US Department of State, undated, https://www.state.gov/russias-filtration-operations-and-forced-relocations/.

97 Frederick Kagan, Kateryna Stepanenko, and Karolina Hird, "Russian Offensive Campaign Assessment, April 16," Institute for the Study of War (April 16, 2022), https://www.understandingwar.org/backgrounder/russian-offensive-campaign-assessment-april-16; and Kateryna Stepanenko, Karolina Hird, and Frederick W. Kagan, "Russian Offensive Campaign Assessment, May 12," Institute for the Study of War (May 12, 2022), https://www.understandingwar.org/backgrounder/russian-offensive-campaign-assessment-may-12.

98 Kateryna Stepanenko and Karolina Hird, "Russian Offensive Campaign Assessment, May 18," Institute for the Study of Warfare (May 18, 2022), https://www.understandingwar.org/backgrounder/russian-offensive-campaign-assessment-may-18.

99 Kateryna Stepanenko, Karolina Hird, Mason Clark, and George Barros, "Russian Offensive Campaign Assessment, May 23," Institute for the Study of Warfare (May 23, 2022), https://www.understandingwar.org/backgrounder/russian-offensive-campaign-assessment-may-23.

100 Pamela Falk, "No doubt we are failing the people of Mariupol,' U.N. relief official says," *CBS News*, April 18, 2022, https://www.cbsnews.com/news/mariupol-ukraine-united-nations-humanitarian-crisis/.

101 Niland, "Putin's Mariupol Massacre."

102 "The Path to Recovery: How Regions Surviving Russian Occupation are Rebuilding."

103 Human Rights Watch, "Our City Was Gone."

104 Lori Hinnant, Vasilisa Stepanenko, Sarah El Deeb, and Elizaveta Tilna, "Russia scrubs Mariupol's Ukraine identity, builds on death," Associated Press (December 22, 2022).

105 "To endure a long war, Ukraine is remaking its army, economy and society," *The Economist* 448, no. 9364 (September 23, 2023): 20, https://www.economist.com/briefing/2023/09/21/to-endure-a-long-war-ukraine-is-remaking-its-army-economy-and-society.

106 "To endure a long war, Ukraine is remaking its army, economy and society."

107 "The Path to Recovery: How Regions Surviving Russian Occupation are Rebuilding."

108 "The Path to Recovery: How Regions Surviving Russian Occupation are Rebuilding."

109 Elina Beketova, "Behind the Lines: Russia's Ethnic Cleansing," Center for European Policy Analysis (CEPA), July 27, 2023, https://cepa.org/article/behind-the-lines-russias-ethnic-cleansing/; Elina Beketova, "Behind the Lines: The Sugar-Coated Myths of Mariupol," Center for European Policy Analysis (CEPA), August 24, 2023, https://cepa.org/article/behind-the-lines-the-sugar-coated-myths-of-mariupol/; Vitaly Shevchenko, "Ukraine war: Life in Mariupol under Russian occupation," BBC, March 12, 2023, https://www.bbc.com/news/world-europe-64887890; and "The Spoils of War," *The Economist* (June 22, 2024): 38.

110 Shevchenko, "Ukraine war: Life in Mariupol under Russian occupation;" Kaela Malig, "'20 Days in Mariupol' Filmmaker on What is Left of the City After the Russian Invasion," Frontline on PBS, November 21, 2023, https://www.pbs.org/wgbh/frontline/article/20-days-in-mariupol-filmmaker-q-and-a/; Adam Robinson, Erwan Rivault, and Olga Robinson, "The Russians hunting for cheap flats in occupied Mariupol," BBC, August 5, 2023, https://www.bbc.com/news/world-66393949; Luke Harding, "'It's like the USSR': residents on life in Mariupol a year since Russian occupation," *The Guardian*, May 18, 2023, https://www.theguardian.com/world/2023/may/18/its-like-the-ussr-residents-on-life-in-mariupol-a-year-since-russian-occupation; Picheta, "Putin should face war crimes probe over 'devastating' assault on Mariupol;" and Human Rights Watch, "Our City Was Gone." Harding states lack of a Russian passport already disqualifies potential pension recipients from payments.

111 Patrick Lane, "A grim day in Russian-occupied Ukraine," The World in Brief, *The Economist* (July 1, 2024), https://view.e.economist.com.

112 Shevchenko, "Ukraine war: Life in Mariupol under Russian occupation."

113 "'The Hope Left Us,'" 61.

114 "Russia's FSB Raids Jehovah's Witness Office in Occupied Mariupol," *The Moscow Times* (Jan. 15, 2024), https://www.themoscowtimes.com/2024/01/15/russias-fsb-raids-jehovahs-witness-office-in-occupied-mariupol-a83726.

115 "Russia's FSB Raids Jehovah's Witness Office in Occupied Mariupol."

116 Human Rights Watch, "Our City Was Gone."

CHAPTER 6

1 Donnison, *Civil Affairs and Military Government*, 272.

2 "Winning the electricity war: How Ukraine tamed Russian missile barrages and kept the lights on," *The Economist* (March 12, 2023), https://www.economist.com/europe/2023/03/12/how-ukraine-tamed-russian-missile-barrages-and-kept-the-lights-on.

3 "The battle within," *The Economist* 448, no. 9364 (September 23, 2023): 18.

4 Some among these questions receive attention in Sofia Dyak, "From War into the Future: Historical Legacies and Questions for Postwar Reconstruction in Ukraine," *Architectural Histories*, 11, no. 1 (2003): 1-11, https://journal.eahn.org/article/id/9805/.

5 János Brenner, "Some ideas for a post-war recovery of Ukrainian cities," *Urban Research & Practice*, 16, no. 2 (2023, published online July 5, 2022): 297-98 (294-300), https://doi.org/10.1080/17535069.2022.2097646. For more discussion on this governmental reorganization, see I. Savchuk I. Savchuk, "New Administrative and Territorial Division of Ukraine – New Challenge for National Interest," *National Interest Academic Journal* 1, no.1 (2020): 37-45.

6 Trofimov, *Our Enemies will Vanish*, 327.

7 Photographs by the author.

8   Penny Pritzker, US Special Representative for Ukraine's Economic Recovery, Remarks to the Chicago Council on Global Affairs, Chicago, Illinois, February 14, 2024, https://www.state.gov/special-representative-pritzkers-remarks-on-ukraines-economic-recovery/.
9   "'The battle within,'" 19.
10 Patrick Christian email to Dr. Russell W. Glenn, Subject: RE: Ukraine article/Corruption in Ukraine, January 3, 2024.
11 Murrow, *This is London*, 182-183.
12 Kyiv School of Economics, "The total amount of damage caused to the infrastructure of Ukraine due to the war reaches $152.2 billion – estimate as of September 1, 2023," October 3, 2023, https://kse.ua/about-the-school/news/the-total-amount-of-damage-caused-to-the-infrastructure-of-ukraine-due-to-the-war-reaches-151-2-billion-estimate-as-of-september-1-2023/.
13 David W. Ellwood, *Rebuilding Europe: Western Europe, America and Postwar Reconstruction* (London: Longman, 1992), 61; and Beschloss, *The Conquerors*, 159.
14 Christian email.
15 Christian email.
16 Lippman, Surviving the Peace, 64.
17 Kinstler, "Architects Plan a City for the Future in Ukraine."
18 Glenn Kessler, "Eighty percent of Ukraine-Israel bill will be spent in U.S. or by U.S. military," *The Washington Post*, April 28, 2024, A4.
19 David McMahon (Head of Mine Action Project Unit, Peace and Security Cluster, UNOPS Ukraine) interview with Dr. Russell W. Glenn, May 6, 2024.
20 McMahon interview.
21 Anonymous interview 2.
22 Jamison Medby email to Dr. Russell W. Glenn, Subject: Working weekends, December 25, 2023.
23 Mark Landler, "Allies Pledge Billions for Ukraine's Recovery as Zelensky Stresses Urgency," *The New York Times*, June 21, 2023, https://www.nytimes.com/2023/06/21/world/europe/ukraine-war-recovery.html; "Lawrence Summers, Philip Zelikow and Robert Zoellick on why Russian reserves should be used to help

Ukraine," *The Economist* (July 27, 2023), https://www.economist.com/by-invitation/2023/07/27/lawrence-summers-philip-zelikow-and-robert-zoellick-on-why-russian-reserves-should-be-used-to-help-ukraine; and Jeff Stein, "U.S., allies move to tap interest on frozen Russian assets to aid Ukraine," *The Washington Post*, May 26, 2024, A21. A number of potentially less controversial means of indirectly using seized Russian assets to finance Ukraine receive attention in "Don't seize: capitalize," *The Economist* 450, no. 9386 (March 2, 2024): 12.

24   Faculty of Architecture & the Built Environment, "Tools for Post Conflict Urban Recovery), Delft University of Technology (undated)," https://postconflictrecovery.org/unun/. The $282 billion estimate for the value of seized Russian assets is from "Don't seize: capitalize": 12.

25   Cities 4 Cities United 4 Ukraine, "Municipal Partnerships with Ukraine (undated)," https://cities4cities.eu.

26   Council of Europe Office in Ukraine, "Cities4Cities: new matchmaking platform launched to support Ukrainian local and regional authorities," (March 29, 2022), https://www.coe.int/en/web/kyiv/-/cities4cities-new-matchmaking-platform-launched-to-support-ukrainian-local-and-regional-authorities.

27   Jones, "Russia's Ill-Fated Invasion of Ukraine."

28   Jeff Crisp, Tim Morris, and Hilde Refstie, "Displacement in urban areas: new challenges, new partnerships," *Disasters* 36, Issue s1 (June 11, 2012), 535-536, https://onlinelibrary.wiley.com/doi/10.1111/j.1467-7717.2012.01284.x.

29   Crisp, Morris, and Refstie, "Displacement in urban areas: new challenges, new partnerships."

30   Crisp, Morris, and Refstie, "Displacement in urban areas: new challenges, new partnerships."

31   "A new Marshall Plan?: Donors already wondering how to help Ukraine rebuild," *The Economist* 445 (November 12, 2022), 54-56, https://www.economist.com/international/2022/11/08/donors-are-already-mulling-a-marshall-plan-for-ukraine.

32   Jaroslav Lukiv, "Germany plans to halve military aid for Ukraine," BBC (July 18, 2024), https://www.bbc.com/news/articles/c0kr91zqp0lo.

33   "A new Marshall Plan?"

34 Crisp, Morris, and Refstie, "Displacement in urban areas: new challenges, new partnerships."

35 Linda Polman, *The Crisis Caravan: What's Wrong with Humanitarian Aid?* (NY: Metropolitan Books, 2010), 11.

36 Marie Yovanovitch, *Lessons from the Edge*, 142.

37 Polman, *The Crisis Caravan*, 187.

38 Lippman, *Surviving the Peace*, 99.

39 Steven Erlanger, "NATO Will Offer Ukraine a 'Bridge' to Membership, Hoping That's Enough," *The New York Times*, June 26, 2024, https://www.nytimes.com/2024/06/26/world/europe/nato-ukraine-washington-membership-summit.html?smid=nytcore-ios-share&referringSource=articleShare.

40 Glenn, *Come Hell or High Fever*, 298.

41 World Health Organization, "Early success in health system recovery in Ukraine, new WHO report highlights," news release (June 21, 2023), https://www.who.int/europe/news/item/21-06-2023-early-success-in-health-system-recovery-in-ukraine—new-who-report-highlights; and Landler, "Allies Pledge Billions for Ukraine's Recovery."

42 Anonymous interview 1.

43 Peter Frankopan, *The Earth Transformed: An Untold History* (NY: Alfred A. Knopf, 2023, 113 and 314.

44 Karl Jensen and Anthony Funkhouser Microsoft Teams interview with Dr. Russell W. Glenn, February 19, 2024.

45 Glenn, *Come Hell or High Fever*, 251.

46 Trofimov, *Our Enemies will Vanish*, 165.

47 "Activating and Strengthening Ukraine's Reconstruction Capacity," Ukrainian Industry Expertise SE, NGO International Economic Research Institute, and US Agency for International Development white paper, undated, 5.

48 "Largest earthquakes in Ukraine on record since 1900 – list, stats and map," Volcano Discovery, April 25, 2024, https://www.volcanodiscovery.com/earthquakes/ukraine/largest.html.

49 "Extreme weather is making parts of Australia uninhabitable," *The Economist* (December 20, 2022), https://www.economist.com/asia/2022/12/20/extreme-weather-is-making-parts-of-australia-uninhabitable.

50 Robert Jay Lifton, *Surviving Our Catastrophes: Resilience and Renewal from Hiroshima to the Covid-19 Pandemic* (NY: The New Press, 2023), 31.

51 Bird, *The Town that Died*, 137.

52 John U. Bacon, *The Great Halifax Explosion: A World War I Story of Treachery, Tragedy, and Extraordinary Heroism*, (NY: William Morrow, 2017), 325.

53 Bacon, *The Great Halifax Explosion*, 328.

54 Bacon, *The Great Halifax Explosion*, 329.

55 Lippman, *Surviving the Peace*, 19.

56 Ievgeniia Dulko, "Rebuilding Narratives: The Role of Urban Planning in Post-war Ukraine," PhD diss., University of Illinois at Chicago (2023), 25-26.

57 Dulko, "Rebuilding Narratives," 25-26.

58 Dulko, "Rebuilding Narratives,"19-20.

59 Dulko, "Rebuilding Narratives," 23-24.

60 These include the Stronger Cities Consortium, "Urban area-based approaches in post-disaster contexts: Guidance Note for Humanitarian Practitioners" (undated), 8, https://www.iied.org/sites/default/files/pdfs/migrate/10825IIED.pdf; and Urban Settlements Working Group, "Area-Based Approaches in Urban Settings: Compendium of Case Studies," May 2019, 4, https://sheltercluster.s3.eu-central-1.amazonaws.com/public/docs/201905013_urban_compendium.pdf that "considers the whole population affected by a crisis living in a specific geographic area [that is] in need of multi-sectoral support [from] multiple stakeholders."

61 National Council for the Recovery of Ukraine from the Consequences of the War, 5 (first page numbered 5; pagination in document is inconsistent).

62 Boston Consulting Group, "Supporting Ukraine: A Study on Potential Recovery Strategies for Ukraine" (January 2023), https://media-publications.bcg.com/Supporting-Ukraine-Potential-Recovery-Strategies-Feb-2023.pdf.

63 National Council for the Recovery of Ukraine from the Consequences of the War, 1 (second page numbered 1; pagination in document is inconsistent).

64 National Council for the Recovery of Ukraine from the Consequences of the War, 1 (third page numbered 1; pagination in document is inconsistent).
65 Dulko, "Rebuilding Narratives," 22-23.
66 Dulko, "Rebuilding Narratives," 24.
67 Dulko, "Rebuilding Narratives," 29.
68 Erik C. Kramer telephonic interview with Dr. Russell W. Glenn, February 16, 2024; and Nathan Rott, Claire Harbage, and Hanna Palamarenko, "As Ukraine seeks to replenish its depleted army, a divide grows among its civilians," NPR (January 31, 2024), https://www.npr.org/2024/01/31/1226251649/ukraine-russia-war-conscription-military. The primary reason for sparing younger males from forced military service appears to be preservation of this group in the service of Ukrainian recovery, to include future economic growth. Interestingly, Rott, et. al, note Ukraine started requiring female medical personnel between the ages of 18 and 60 to register for service with the military. Mid-April marked President Volodymyr Zelensky's signing of a law requiring all men between 18 and 60 to register with the military though the age at which Ukrainian men could be mobilized remained at 25. Olga Voitovych, Radina Gigova, Svitlana Vlasova and Christian Edwards, "Zelensky signs law overhauling Ukraine's mobilization rules," CNN (April 16, 2024), https://www.cnn.com/2024/04/16/europe/zelensky-signs-mobilization-law-intl-latam/index.html.
69 Jensen and Funkhouser interview.
70 Jensen and Funkhouser interview.
71 McMahon interview.
72 Bird, *The Town that Died*, 152.
73 Trofimov, *Our Enemies will Vanish*, 324.
74 Jensen and Funkhouser interview.
75 World Health Organization European Region, "Case studies of health system recovery in Ukraine: focus on the role of the private sector" (2023), 1, https://www.who.int/europe/publications/i/item/WHO-EURO-2023-7706-47473-69781.
76 Trofimov, *Our Enemies will Vanish*, 285-86.
77 Neil Monnery, *Architect of Prosperity: Sir John Cowperthwaite and the Making of Hong Kong* (London: London Publishing Partnership, 2017), 190.

78 Helena Holm-Pedersen, staff member of the Return and Reconstruction Task Force (RRTF) in 1999 Sarajevo, as quoted in Lippman, *Surviving the Peace*, 70.
79 Glenn, *Come Hell or High Fever*, 322.
80 Bacon, *The Great Halifax Explosion*, 234.
81 Joseph Pfeifer, *Ordinary Heroes: A Memoir of 9/11* (NY: Portfolio, 2021), 114-15.
82 Southard, *Nagasaki*, 121.
83 Pfeifer, *Ordinary Heroes*, 120-21.
84 For more on RAMSI, see Russell W. Glenn, *Counterinsurgency in a Test Tube: Analyzing the Success of the Regional Assistance Mission, Solomon Islands (RAMSI)* (Santa Monica, CA: RAND, 2007).
85 Anonymous interview 1.
86 Anonymous interview 2.
87 Anonymous interview 2.
88 Anonymous interview 2.
89 Anonymous interview 1.
90 Philip Gourevitch, "Alms Dealers," *The New Yorker* (October 4, 2010), https://www.newyorker.com/magazine/2010/10/11/alms-dealers.
91 Russell W. Glenn, *"Achieving Convergence during Humanitarian Assistance and Disaster Relief Operations in the World's Largest Urban Areas; Proceedings of the 'Current and Future Operations in Megacities' Conference, Tokyo, Japan, July 16-18, 2019"* (Fort Eustis, VA: US Army Training and Doctrine Command, October 1, 2019), 94, https://community.apan.org/wg/tradoc-g2/mad-scientist/m/tokyo-megacities-conference-2019/294569.
92 Lippman, *Surviving the Peace*, 69.
93 Méheut, "More Drones, Fewer Parks."
94 David Adams and Peter Larkham, *The Everyday Experiences of Reconstruction and Regeneration: From Vision to Reality in Birmingham and Coventry* (Milton Park, UK: Routledge, 2019), 22-23.
95 Tim Cross, "Humanitarian Assistance and Reconstruction," in *British Generals in Blair's Wars*, ed. Jonathan Bailey, Richard Iron, and Hew Strachan (Farnham, UK: Ashgate, 2013), 69.

96 For but one of many sources decrying the inefficiencies of stove-piping, see Steven K. O'Hern, *The Intelligence Wars: Lessons from Baghdad* (Amherst, NY: Prometheus Books, 2008), 213-218.
97 Hein, "Resilient Tokyo," 230-31.
98 Mezentsev and Mezentsev, "War and the city," 499.
99 Adams and Larkham, *The Everyday Experiences of Reconstruction and Regeneration*, 27.
100 Glenn, *Come Hell or High Fever*, 277.
101 Glenn, *Come Hell or High Fever*, 308-09.
102 Anastasiia Bobrova, "Housing and war: housing policy in the first year of the full-scale war," Cedos (March 22, 2023), https://cedos.org.ua/en/researches/housing-and-war-annual-review/.
103 Hein, "Resilient Tokyo," 226.
104 Bobrova, "Housing and war."
105 United Nations Habitat, "Scoping Mission to Ukraine" (October 2-14, 2022), https://unhabitat.org/sites/default/files/2022/11/ukraine_mission_report_oct22_public.pdf.
106 Sabastien Malo, "The Green Dream to Rebuild a Sustainable Ukraine from the Rubble of War," *Politico* (September 11, 2022), https://www.politico.com/news/magazine/2022/09/11/ukraine-russia-sustainability-00054910.
107 Glenn, *Come Hell or High Fever*, 299.
108 Glenn, *Come Hell or High Fever*, 5.
109 Frankopan, *The Earth Transformed*, 16.
110 Dulko, "Rebuilding Narratives," 61; and Francesca Ebel and Kostiantyn Khudov, "Ukrainians are breaking their ties with the Russian language," *The Washington Post*, July 28, 2023, https://www.washingtonpost.com/world/2023/07/28/ukrainians-are-breaking-their-ties-with-russian-language.
111 Monnery, *Architect of Prosperity*, 106-07.
112 Bacon, *The Great Halifax Explosion*, 226.
113 *Médecins* Sans Frontières, "Kunduz Hospital Attack: On 3 October 2015, US airstrikes destroyed our trauma hospital in Kunduz, Afghanistan, killing 42," undated, https://www.msf.org/kunduz-hospital-attack-depth.
114 Moorhouse, *Berlin at War*, 297.

115   *Médecins* Sans Frontières, "Kunduz Hospital Attack."
116   "The world this week: Politics," (March 9, 2024).
117   Anonymous interview 1.
118   Jacob Knutson, "About 40% of New York 9/11 victims' remains have yet to be identified," Axios, September 11, 2023, https://www.axios.com/2023/09/11/9-11-victims-remains-identification.
119   Bird, *The Town that Died*, 186 and 114.
120   W.A. Odhiambo, S.W. Guthua, F.G. Macigo, and M.K. Akama, "Maxillofacial injuries caused by terrorist bomb attack in Nairobi, Kenya," *International Journal of Oral and Maxillofacial Surgery* 31, no. 4 (August 2002): 374-377, available at https://www.sciencedirect.com/science/article/abs/pii/S0901502701901997.
121   Evgeniy Maloletka, "Upward of 20,000 Ukrainian amputees face trauma on a scale unseen since WWI," Independent (September 4, 2023), https://www.independent.co.uk/news/ap-lviv-europe-rehabilitation-united-states-b2404307.html.
122   Maloletka, "Upward of 20,000 Ukrainian amputees face trauma on a scale unseen since WWI."
123   Trofimov, *Our Enemies will Vanish*, 327.
124   Pehr Lodhammar (former Chief Mine Action Programme Iraq, UN Mine Action Service) interview with Dr. Russell W. Glenn, February 16, 2024.
125   Paul Heslop (Programme manager - Mine Action, UN Development Programme Ukraine) interview with Russell W. Glenn, March 21, 2024.
126   A.J. Caughey, "It will take decades to clear Ukraine's landmines. Without more women, it will be even slower — and more dangerous," Bluemarble (August 24, 203, updated January 30, 2024), https://globalaffairs.org/bluemarble/ukraine-full-of-landmines-without-women-cleanup-will-take-longer.
127   Vera Bergengruen, "Ukraine Is Using AI to Help Clear Millions of Russian Landmines," *Time* (November 2, 2023), https://time.com/6330445/demining-ukraine/.
128   Bergengruen, "Ukraine Is Using AI."
129   Danish Refugee Council, "Ukraine: Strengthening national mine action capabilities," February 9, 2024, https://pro.drc.ngo/resources/news/ukraine-strengthening-national-mine-action-capabilities/.

130 Heslop interview.

131 Bergengruen, "Ukraine Is Using AI."

132 McMahon interview.

133 Heslop interview; and "Background Briefing on Landmine Use in Ukraine," Human Rights Watch, June 15, 2022, https://www.hrw.org/news/2022/06/15/background-briefing-landmine-use-ukraine.

134 "POM-3 Landmine," Collective Awareness to UXO, 2024, https://cat-uxo.com/explosive-hazards/landmines/pom-3-landmine.

135 "Russians are mining the territory of Ukraine with POM-3 'Medallion' landmines," Militarnyi, March 30, 2022, https://mil.in.ua/en/news/russians-are-mining-the-territory-of-ukraine-with-pom-3-medallion-landmines/#google_vignette. I have edited the online translation from Ukrainian for clarity.

136 Operational Environment Data Integration Network, "POM-3 (Medallion) Russian Anti-Personnel Mine," US Army Training and Doctrine Command G-2 Worldwide Equipment Guide, undated, https://odin.tradoc.army.mil/WEG/Asset/POM-3_(Medallion)_Russian_Anti-Personnel_Mine.

137 AFP, "Ukraine De-Mining Like Europe After WWII: UN," *Kyiv Post* (June 22, 2023), https://www.kyivpost.com/post/18531.

138 World Bank, "Updated Ukraine Recovery and Reconstruction Needs Assessment Released," February 15, 2024, https://www.worldbank.org/en/news/press-release/2024/02/15/updated-ukraine-recovery-and-reconstruction-needs-assessment-released. World Bank estimates are as follows: "The highest estimated recovery and reconstruction needs are in housing (17% of the total), followed by transport (15%), commerce and industry (14%), agriculture (12%), energy (10%), social protection and livelihoods (9%), and *explosive hazard management (7%)*." (emphasis added)

139 AFP, "Ukraine De-Mining."

140 Douglas Botting, *From the Ruins of the Reich: Germany 1945-1949*, (NY: Crown, 1985), 259.

141 "Another world war bomb found in Schmargendorf: defusing on Thursday," Berlin.de (The Official Website of Berlin), April 3, 2024, https://www.berlin.de/en/news/8799736-5559700-another-world-war-bomb-found-in-schmarge.en.html.

142 Heslop interview. There are no verified reports of use of antipersonnel mines by the Ukrainian military. Both sides use anti-vehicle mines.
143 Heslop interview.
144 Heslop interview.
145 Lodhammar interview.
146 Heslop interview.
147 Anonymous 4 interview.
148 Bergengruen, "Ukraine Is Using AI."
149 Lodhammar interview.
150 Glenn, *Come Hell or High Fever*, 189.
151 Heslop interview.
152 Heslop interview.
153 Lourie Venter (United Nations Mine Action Service, Iraq, November 2016-February 2022) interview with Dr. Russell W. Glenn, March 19, 2024.
154 Venter interview.
155 Anonymous 4 interview.
156 McMahon interview.
157 Venter interview.
158 Danish Refugee Council, "Ukraine." DRC lists the following as among members of Ukraine's humanitarian mine action network:
 • "The National Mine Action Authority (NMAA) serves as the primary body responsible for developing and approving mid-term and long-term National Plans for Mine Action, alongside operative plans.
 • The Mine Action Centre (MAC) plays a pivotal role in ensuring effective planning, organisation, and coordination of mine action activities. During the war, MAC is the main body to coordinate mine action activities in Ukraine.
 • The Centre of Humanitarian Demining (CHD) acts as a think tank in collaboration with NMAA and MAC, collating and summarising information on demining needs from various sources. CHD also leads fundraising and cooperation with the donors.
 • The State Emergency Service of Ukraine (SES) is one of the bodies which assumes the critical task of detecting and disposing

of explosive devices throughout Ukraine. Under the SES umbrella, there is the Interregional Centre for Humanitarian Demining and Rapid Response responsible for the practical implementation of HMA processes, data collection, etc. [I use the acronym SESU in lieu of SES elsewhere in this section.]
• The State Special Transport Service (SSTS), with one of their main focuses being mine clearance of transport infrastructure, industrial facilities, buildings, and agricultural land."

159 Bergengruen, "Ukraine Is Using AI."
160 Ben Mascall, "Palantir and Ministry of Economy of Ukraine Sign Demining Partnership," April 3, 2024, Palantir [Investor Relations], https://investors.palantir.com/news-details/2024/Palantir-and-Ministry-of-Economy-of-Ukraine-Sign-Demining-Partnership/; and Venter interview.
161 Lodhammar interview.
162 Venter interview.
163 Heslop interview.
164 Heslop interview.
165 Venter interview.
166 Lodhammar interview.
167 Heslop interview.
168 AFP, "Ukraine De-Mining;" and Bergengruen, "Ukraine Is Using AI."
169 McMahon interview.
170 Team Zee Feed, "How Long Does It Take a City To Recover From War? Decades," *Zee Feed* (July 25, 2023), https://zeefeed.com.au/cities-recover-war/.
171 Venter interview.
172 "Against the grain: Funding fighting," *The Economist* 451, no. 9396 (May 11, 2024): 59; and Anonymous interview 4 interview.
173 Bergengruen, "Ukraine Is Using AI."
174 Lodhammar interview and Venter interview.
175 Anonymous interview 4.
176 Heslop interview.
177 Anonymous interview 4.
178 Filipinas Heritage Library, "Manila Reborn."

179 Anonymous interview 1.
180 Igor Kossov, "Pro-Russian sympathies make life harder for soldiers, cops in Kupiansk district," *The Kyiv Independent*, August 15, 2023, https://kyivindependent.com/pro-russian-sympathies-make-life-harder-for-soldiers-cops-in-kupiansk-district/.
181 Steinberg, *Philippine Collaboration in World War II*, 90.
182 Steinberg, *Philippine Collaboration in World War II*, 107.
183 D. Clayton James, *The Years of MacArthur: Volume One, 1880-1941*. (Boston: Houghton Mifflin, 1970), 563.
184 Steinberg, *Philippine Collaboration in World War II*, 115.
185 Steinberg, *Philippine Collaboration in World War II*, 164.
186 Manuel Roxas, "Message of His Excellency Manuel Roxas President of the Philippines Asking the Concurrence of Congress to the Amnesty Proclamation," Government of the Philippines, January 29, 1948, https://www.officialgazette.gov.ph/1948/01/29/message-of-president-roxas-asking-the-concurrence-of-congress-to-the-amnesty-proclamation/.
187 Jackson, *France on Trial*, xxx.
188 Jacobs, "A Narrative of Justice," 136.
189 Anonymous interview 1.
190 Kossov, "Pro-Russian sympathies."
191 Kossov, "Pro-Russian sympathies."
192 Andreas-Friedrich, *Battleground Berlin*, 195.
193 Christian email.
194 Lippman, *Surviving the Peace*, 302.
195 Andreas-Friedrich, *Battleground Berlin*, 43.
196 Murrow, *This is London*, 214.
197 Anonymous interview 2.
198 Anonymous interview 1.
199 Hilary Synnott, *Bad Days in Basra: My Turbulent Time as Britain's Man in Southern Iraq* (NY: I.B. Tauris, 2008), 221.
200 Anonymous interview 1.
201 Stern, "Russia destroyed Ukraine's power sector."

202 Anonymous interview 7.

203 Lippman, *Surviving the Peace*, 298.

204 Lippman, *Surviving the Peace*, 14.

205 Monnery, *Architect of Prosperity*, 50-51.

206 Christian email.

207 Christian email.

208 Jensen and Funkhouser interview.

209 Rick Hillier, *A Soldier First: Bullets, Bureaucrats and the Politics of War* (Toronto: HarperCollins, 2009), 150.

210 Dominique Soguel, "As corruption costs lives on the battlefield, Ukrainians demand change," *The Christian Science Monitor* (October 25, 2023), https://www.csmonitor.com/World/Europe/2023/1025/As-corruption-costs-lives-on-battlefield-Ukrainians-demand-change.

211 Natasha Bertrand and Alex Marquardt, "US increases pressure on Ukraine to do more to counter corruption," CNN (October 3, 2023), https://www.cnn.com/2023/10/03/politics/us-ukraine-pressure-counter-corruption/index.html.

212 Kramer interview.

213 "Eyeing Russia's backyard: China and Ukraine," *The Economist* 449, no. 9375 (December 9, 2023): 37-38.

214 Kramer interview.

215 Trofimov, *Our Enemies will Vanish*, 207.

216 Ikle, *Every War Must End*, 60.

217 Conant, "How History, Geography Help Explain Ukraine's Political Crisis."

218 "Language Data for Ukraine," Translators without Borders/CLEAR Global Source, map created March 2022 with Data wrapper using 2001 Ukraine census data, https://clearglobal.org/language-data-for-ukraine/.

219 RFE/Rl's Crimea Realities, "Ukraine Allows Russia-Related Words to be Written in All Lowercase," Radio Free Europe, September 22, 2023, https://www.rferl.org/a/ukraine-lower-case-russia-related-words-language/32604577.html.

220 Trofimov, *Our Enemies will Vanish*, 20.

221 David Lewis, "Life in occupied Ukraine," interview by Scott Detrow, NPR (January 21, 2024), https://www.npr.org/transcripts/1225969992.; and Robyn Dixon, et. al, "In Russia's presidential election, Ukrainians cast ballots at gunpoint," *The Washington Post*, March 17, 2024, A16.

222 Jonathan Masters, "Ukraine: Conflict at the Crossroads of Europe and Russia," Council on Foreign Relations backgrounder, February 14, 2023, https://www.cfr.org/backgrounder/ukraine-conflict-crossroads-europe-and-russia.

223 Masters, "Ukraine: Conflict at the Crossroads of Europe and Russia."

224 Masha Gessen, "Ukrainians Forced to Flee to Russia," *The New Yorker* (August 14, 2023), https://www.newyorker.com/magazine/2023/08/21/the-ukrainians-forced-to-flee-to-russia? (Also published as "Another Country" in the August 21, 2023 issue of *The New Yorker*).

225 Beketova, "Behind the Lines: Russia's Ethnic Cleansing."

226 Hrytsak, *Ukraine: The Forging of a Nation*, 373.

227 Willard Price, *Where are you going, Japan?* (London: Willian Heinemann, 1938), 18.

228 Susy Ong, "Post-World War II Education Reform in Japan," *Journal of Strategic and Global Studies* 2, no.2 (July 2019): 85.

229 Price, *Where are you going, Japan?*, 20.

230 Price, *Where are you going, Japan?*, 21 and 23; and Yoko H. Thakur, "History Textbook Reform in Allied Occupied Japan, 1945-52," *History of Education Quarterly* 35, no. 3 (Autumn 1995): 263.

231 Teodoro A. Agoncillo, *History of the Filipino People*, 8th edition (Quezon City: Garotech, 1990), 396-97.

232 "Japanese Attempts at Indoctrination of Youth in Occupied Areas," Research and Analysis Branch, Office of Strategic Services, Current Intelligence Study no. 3, March 23, 1945, 1.

233 Takemae Eiji, *Inside GHQ: The Allied Occupation of Japan and its Legacy* (NY: Continuum, 2002), 347 and 348.

234 General Staff, Supreme Commander, Allied Powers; *Reports of General MacArthur: MacArthur in Japan: The Occupation: Military Phase, Volume I Supplement* (Washington, D.C.: US Government Printing Office, 1966), 205.

235 General Staff, *Reports of General MacArthur, Volume I Supplement*, 205.

236 Harry Wray wrote in a 1996 article that prior to 1975 and the release of previously classified documents, most scholarship credited Washington for Japan's re-education policy. Unclassified materials supported the alternative that it was SCAP in Tokyo which was responsible for development. More recent scholarship supports yet a third possibility: while SCAP was certainly responsible, much of what became policy was virtually rubberstamping changes put in place by the Japanese, some even before the arrival of SCAP in the Japanese capital. For more on the first two of these alternatives, see Harry Wray, "Education Policy Formation for the Allied Occupation of Japan," *Nanzan Review of American Studies* 18 (1996): 1-25.

237 Eiji, *Inside GHQ*, 350.

238 Ong, "Post-World War II Education Reform in Japan," 86-87; and Robert King Hall, "The Battle of the Mind: American Educational Policy in Germany and Japan," *Columbia Journal of International Affairs* 2, no. 1 (Winter 1948): 61.

239 Dower, *Embracing Defeat*, 249.

240 Ong, "Post-World War II Education Reform in Japan," 88-89.

241 Dower, *Embracing Defeat*, 247; and Thakur, "History Textbook Reform," 264 and 265.

242 Eiji, *Inside GHQ*, 361-62.

243 Dower, *Embracing Defeat*, 247.

244 Dower, *Embracing Defeat*, 247.

245 Thakur, "History Textbook Reform," 269.

246 Thakur, "History Textbook Reform," 266.

247 Elizabeth Fox, "Rebuilding Germany's Children: Nazi Indoctrination and Postwar Reeducation of the Hitler Youth," *Furman Humanities Review* 27, Article 4 (2016): 31, https://scholarexchange.furman.edu/fhr/vol27/iss1/4/. Originally quoted in Jan-Werner Müller, *Another Country: German Intellectuals, Unification and National Identity* (New Haven: Yale University Press, 2000), 10.

248 Konrad Adenauer, *Memoirs 1945-53* (Chicago: Henry Regnery, 1966), 64.

249 Ziemke, *The US Army in the Occupation of Germany*, 277.

250 Lucius D. Clay, *Decision in Germany* (Garden City, NY: Doubleday & Company, 1950), 299.

251 Ziemke, *The US Army in the Occupation of Germany*, 276-77.

252 Fox, "Rebuilding Germany's Children," 36-37.

253 Harold Hurwitz, "Comparing American Reform Efforts in Germany: Mass Media and the School System" in *Americans as Proconsuls: United States Military Government in Germany and Japan, 1944-1952*, ed. Robert Wolfe (Carbondale: Southern Illinois University Press 1984), 333.

254 Hurwitz, "Comparing American Reform Efforts in Germany," 337 and 333.

255 Hurwitz, "Comparing American Reform Efforts in Germany," 329.

256 F.S.V. Donnison, *History of the Second World War: Civil Affairs and Military Government North-West Europe 1944-1946* (London: Her Majesty's Stationary Office, 1961), 373-74.

257 Clay, *Decision in Germany*, 300.

258 Ziemke, *The US Army in the Occupation of Germany*, 359-60.

259 Stivers and Donald A. Carter, *The City Becomes a Symbol*, 110.

260 Ziemke, *The US Army in the Occupation of Germany*, 277 and 359

261 Clay, *Decision in Germany*, 299-300.

262 Fox, "Rebuilding Germany's Children," 44.

263 Fox, "Rebuilding Germany's Children," 45 and 46-47.

264 Stivers and Donald A. Carter, *The City Becomes a Symbol*, 145-47.

265 Fox, "Rebuilding Germany's Children," 56.

266 Clay, *Decision in Germany*, 303.

267 Hall, "The Battle of the Mind," 59, 59-70.

268 Fox, "Rebuilding Germany's Children," 32.

269 Human Rights Watch, "Education under Occupation Forced Russification of the School System in Occupied Ukrainian Territories," June 2024, https://www.hrw.org/report/2024/06/20/education-under-occupation/forced-russification-school-system-occupied-ukrainian.

270 *Firstpost* staff, "UK Schools developing lessons to re-educate teens brainwashed by Andrew Tate's misogynistic content," *Firstpost* (January 8, 2023), https://www.firstpost.com/world/uk-

schools-developing-lessons-to-re-educate-teens-brainwashed-by-andrew-tates-misogynistic-content-11949582.html.

271 Ivana Kottasová, Olga Voitovych, and Svitlana Vlasova, "Russia's war machine is trying to turn Ukrainian teenagers into soldiers," *CNN World* (March 15, 2024), https://www.cnn.com/2024/03/14/europe/ukrainian-teenagers-russian-soldiers-cmd-intl/index.html.

272 Hall, "The Battle of the Mind," 68.

CHAPTER 7

1 Glenn, "Creating Light at Tunnel's End."

2 Mungo Melvin, *Sevastopol's Wars: Crimea from Potemkin to Putin* (London: Osprey, 2017), 632-33.

3 Roger Zetter and George Deikun, "A new strategy for meeting humanitarian challenges in urban areas," *Forced Migration Review* 38 (October 2011): 48 (48-50), https://www.fmreview.org/technology/zetter-deikun.

4 Yovanovitch, *Lessons from the Edge*, 201. Though Yovanovitch is writing in 2015 of Russia's incursions into Crimea and Donbas the year before, her insight applies no less post-February 2022.

5 Baruch and Hancock, "Report on War and Post-War Adjustment Policies," 1.

6 Scott G. Berg, *The Burning of the World* (NY: Pantheon Books, 2023), 251.

7 Vale and Campanella, "Conclusion," 340.

8 The next several paragraphs are adapted from Glenn, "Creating Light at Tunnel's End."

9 "Number of civilian casualties in Ukraine during Russia's invasion verified by OHCHR from February 24, 2022 to February 15, 2024," Statista Research Department, February 23, 2024, https://www.statista.com/statistics/1293492/ukraine-war-casualties/

10 "Ukraine Situation Flash Update #67," United Nations Humanitarian Commission for Refugees Regional Bureau of Europe, March 25, 2024, 1, https://reliefweb.int/report/ukraine/ukraine-situation-flash-update-67-25-march-2024.

11 Ishida Yorifusa, "Japanese Cities and Planning in the Reconstruction Period: 1945-55," in *Rebuilding Urban Japan After 1945*, ed. Carola Hein, Jeffry M. Diefendorf, and Ishida Yorifusa (NY: Palgrave MacMillan, 2003), 18 and 23; Jeffry M. Diefendorf, "War and Reconstruction in Germany and Japan," in *Rebuilding Urban Japan After 1945*, 227; and Jeffry M. Diefendorf, *In the Wake of War: The Reconstruction of German Cities after World War II* (NY: Oxford University Press, 1993), 27.

12 Glenn, *Come Hell or High Fever*, 89.

13 Marc Santora, Matthew Mpoke Bigg, and Ivan Nechpurenko, "Brace for Bombs, Fix and Repeat: Ukraine's Grim Efforts to Restore Power," *The New York* Times, December 1, 2022, https://www.nytimes.com/2022/12/01/world/europe/russia-ukraine-war-infrastructure.html.

14 "Bombardment of Ukraine's Power Generation and Transmission Infrastructure, 1 October 2022 to 30 April 2023: A Remote Assessment," Fletcher Ukraine Digital Verification Lab, February 29, 2024, https://sites.tufts.edu/fletcherrussia/bombardment-of-ukraines-power-generation-and-transmission-infrastructure-1-october-2022-to-30-april-2023-a-remote-assessment/.

15 David Eggers, "The Profound Defiance of Daily Life in Kyiv," *The New Yorker* (January 5, 2023), https://www.newyorker.com/news/dispatch/the-profound-defiance-of-daily-life-in-kyiv.

16 The National Council for the Recovery of Ukraine from the Consequences of the War, 7 (the first page 7 in the document).

17 Rogoza, "Ukraine in the face of a demographic catastrophe." This resource also provides statistics showing Ukraine's deaths have outnumbered births since at least 1991 rather than 2013 as reported by the National Council for the Recovery of Ukraine from the Consequences of the War.

18 Anonymous interview 2.

19 The following two paragraphs draw on Glenn, "Creating Light at Tunnel's End."

20 For example, see Mared Gwyn Jones, "NATO has upped 'vigilance' amid suspected Russian sabotage operations – Stoltenberg," euronews, May 28, 2024, https://www.euronews.com/my-europe/2024/05/28/nato-has-upped-vigilance-amid-suspected-russian-sabotage-operations-stoltenberg; and Bojan Pancevski, "Russian Saboteurs Behind Arson Attack at

German Factory," *The Wall Street Journal*, June 23, 2024, https://www.wsj.com/world/europe/russian-saboteurs-behind-arson-attackat-german-factory-c13b4ece.

21 World Bank, "Updated Ukraine Recovery and Reconstruction Needs Assessment Released."

22 David L. Stern, "Heavy destruction of energy network leaves Ukraine fearing winter," The Washington Post, May 19, 2024, A16; and "The winter ahead Russia has destroyed half of Ukraine's energy infrastructure. What does that mean for the upcoming heating season," Meduza.io, June 19, 2024, https://meduza.io/en/feature/2024/06/19/the-winter-ahead.

23 "Racing against time: Ukraine's electricity supply," *The Economist* 452, No. 9406 (July 20, 2024): 39.

24 Botting, *From the Ruins of the Reich*, 139.

25 Masha Gessen, "Democracy in Darkness: What Ukraine has already lost in its fight against Russia," *The New Yorker* (February 5, 2024): 34-43, https://www.newyorker.com/magazine/2024/02/05/ukraines-democracy-in-darkness. Gessen is quoting Mustafa Nayyem, head of Ukraine's federal agency for reconstruction.

26 Gessen, "Democracy in Darkness," 34-43.

27 Gessen, "Democracy in Darkness," 34-43.

28 William Langewiesche, *American Ground: Unbuilding the World Trade Center* (NY: North Point Press, 2002), 16 and 159-61.

29 Sinclair McKay, *Berlin: Life and Loss in the City That Shaped the Century* (London: Viking, 2022), 292.

30 Vale and Campanella, "Conclusion," 346.

31 "The Path to Recovery: How Regions Surviving Russian Occupation are Rebuilding."

32 Victoria Butenko, "'We are totally ready': Ukraine prepares for fresh attacks on energy as winter nears," CNN (November 10, 2023), https://www.cnn.com/2023/11/10/europe/ukraine-energy-grid-russian-strikes-intl-cmd/index.html.

33 Zetter and Deikun, "A new strategy," 49.

34 US Customs and Border Protection, "Philadelphia CBP Officers Seize More than $6.5 Million in Fake Currency from Russia," September 29, 2022, https://www.cbp.gov/newsroom/local-

media-release/philadelphia-cbp-officers-seize-more-65-million-fake-currency-russia; and Heather Schlitz, "Customs officials in Philadelphia seize $6.5 million in fake money from Russia," *Business Insider* (October 1, 2021), https://www.businessinsider.com/65-million-fake-counterfeit-money-russia-philadelphia-chicago-2021-10.

35 "Activating and Strengthening Ukraine's Reconstruction Capacity," 8.

36 UNESCO World Heritage Convention, 2024, https://whc.unesco.org/en/statesparties/ua.

37 "UNESCO Recommendation on the Historic Urban Landscape," United Nations Educational, Scientific, and Cultural Organization, 2024, https://whc.unesco.org/en/hul; and "Recommendation on the Historic Urban Landscape," United Nations Educational, Scientific, and Cultural Organization, November 10, 2011 available via the above website.

38 Bagehot, "How the British government rules by algorithm," *The Economist* 436 (August 22, 2020): 48, https://www.economist.com/britain/2020/08/20/how-the-british-government-rules-by-algorithm.

39 James Jay Calafano, "Thinking the Future," *The Whitehead Journal of Diplomacy and International Relations* 10, no. 2 (Summer/Fall 2009), https://ciaotest.cc.columbia.edu/journals/shjdir/v10i2/f_0018623_15949.pdf.

40 Gregory Fontenot, "Measures of Effectiveness in Stability Operations 1995–1996, Operation Joint Endeavor, Bosnia-Herzegovina," briefing given at the Israel Defense Forces–US Joint Forces Command Joint Urban Operations Office 2006 Urban Operations Conference, Tel Aviv, Israel, June 6, 2006; and Gregory Fontenot email message to author, Subject: Mine question, 12:57 PM, December 5, 2023.

41 Rebuilding Ukraine, 391-93.

42 Bagehot, "How the British government rules by algorithm."

43 Bartleby, "The secret to cutting corporate red tape," *The Economist* 438 (March 13, 2021): 63, https://www.economist.com/business/2021/03/13/the-secret-to-cutting-corporate-red-tape.

44 Lippman, *Surviving the Peace*, 68-69.

45 Lodhammar interview with Dr. Russell W. Glenn.
46 Pehr Lodhammar, "How Iraq is Changing What We Do: Measuring Clearance in Urban Environments," *The Journal of Conventional Weapons Destruction* 22, no. 2 (August 2018): 34 and 35.
47 Anonymous interview 4. Pehr Lodhammar similarly uses the Fallujah bridge to demonstrate the importance of measuring effects rather than effort. His description of the event differs in minor details from that quoted here in terms of the time saved to reach the hospital and the number of devices removed from the bridge (recalling the number was two rather than one). The differences do not diminish the example's value in getting the point across. See Pehr Lodhammar, "How Iraq is Changing What We Do: Measuring Clearance in Urban Environments," *The Journal of Conventional Weapons Destruction* 22, no. 2 (August 2018): 34 and 35.
48 Anonymous interview 5.
49 Bartleby, "The secret to cutting corporate red tape," 63.
50 Richard Heeks, "Understanding success and failure of anti-corruption initiatives," Anti-Corruption Resource Centre U4 Brief, March 2011, 3.
51 Heeks, "Understanding success and failure of anti-corruption initiatives," 1.
52 Heeks, "Understanding success and failure of anti-corruption initiatives," 4.
53 Anonymous interview 1.
54 Anonymous interview 1.
55 Anonymous interview 2.
56 Glenn, "Creating Light at Tunnel's End."
57 Glenn, *Come Hell or High Fever*, 190.
58 L. Douglas Keeney, *The Lives They Saved: The Untold Story of Medics, Mariners, and the Incredible Boat Lift that Evacuated Nearly 300,000 People From New York City on 9/11* (Guilford, Connecticut: Lyons Press), 155-56.
59 Glenn, "Creating Light at Tunnel's End."
60 "Multi-agency Donor Coordination Platform for Ukraine," 2024, https://coordinationplatformukraine.com/.
61 Directorate-General for Neighbourhood and Enlargement Negotiations, "Multi-agency Donor Coordination Platform for

Ukraine meets in expanded format, to advance Ukraine's recovery and reconstruction," European Commission news article, February 14, 2024, https://neighbourhood-enlargement.ec.europa.eu/news/multi-agency-donor-coordination-platform-ukraine-meets-expanded-format-advance-ukraines-recovery-and-2024-02-14_en.

62 Chester J. Pach, *Arming the Free World: The Origins of the United States Military Assistance Program, 1945-1950* (Chapel Hill, NC: University of North Carolina Press, 1991), 209-10, 228-32.

63 Sharpe, *Brothers in Blood*, 197.

64 Andreas, *Blue Helmets and Black Markets*, and 163.

65 As quoted in Michael Walzer, *Just and Unjust Wars: A Moral Argument with Historical Illustrations* (London: Allen Lane, 1978), 3; and Rebecca Lewis, *Does the Law Really Matter?: The Role of the Law of Armed Conflict in Contemporary Air Operations* (Canberra: Air Power Development Centre, 2005), 15, https://airpower.airforce.gov.au/publications/does-law-really-matter-role-law-armed-conflict-contemporary-air-operations.

66 As quoted in "Tokyo 'Black Markets, 1945," Old Japan website (undated), https://www.oldtokyo.com/tokyo-black-market-1945/.

67 As quoted in "Tokyo 'Black Markets, 1945."

68 Kosei Hatsuda and Akito Sakasai, "The Black Market as City: New Research on Alternative Urban Space in Occupied Japan (1945-1952)," summary of presentation, Princeton Mellon Initiative in Architecture, Urbanism & the Humanities (March 7, 2016), https://arc-hum.princeton.edu/black-market.

69 Steege, *Black Market, Cold War*, 20.

70 Steege, *Black Market, Cold War*, 42-43.

71 Steege, *Black Market, Cold War*, 50.

72 Steege, *Black Market, Cold War*, 55-56.

73 Steege, *Black Market, Cold War*, 122.

74 Steege, *Black Market, Cold War*, 124-25.

75 Steege, *Black Market, Cold War*, 38.

76 Steege, *Black Market, Cold War*, 85-86.

77 Steege, *Black Market, Cold War*, 62.

78 Jeremy Collins, "Interview with James M. Scott, Author of *Rampage: MacArthur, Yamashita, and the Battle of Manila*," The National World War II Museum (February 3, 2020), https://

www.nationalww2museum.org/war/articles/interview-james-m-scott-author-rampage-macarthur-yamashita-and-battle-manila.

79 Lawrence M. Greenberg, *The Hukbalahap Insurrection: A Case Study of a Successful; Anti-Insurgency Operation in the Philippines – 1946-1955* (Washington, D.C.: US Army Center of Military History, 1987), 31, 33, and 50, https://apps.dtic.mil/sti/pdfs/AD-1112093.pdf.

80 Greenberg, *The Hukbalahap Insurrection*, 54.

81 Donia, *Sarajevo*, 325.

82 Donia, *Sarajevo*, 325.

83 Donia, *Sarajevo*, 325.

84 Donia, *Sarajevo*, 345-46.

85 Donia, *Sarajevo*, 337 and 344-51.

86 Andreas, *Blue Helmets and Black Markets*, 123.

87 Andreas, *Blue Helmets and Black Markets*, 123. For more on the Community Stabilization Program, see Russell W. Glenn, et. al, *Evaluation of USAID's Community Stabilization Program (CSP) in Iraq: Effectiveness of the CSP Model as a Non-lethal Tool for Counterinsurgency* (Washington, D.C.: United States Agency for International Development, 2009), https://pdf.usaid.gov/pdf_docs/PDACN461.pdf.

88 Loren D. Estleman, *The Lioness is the Hunter* (NY: Tom Doherty Associates, 2017), 171.

89 Andreas, *Blue Helmets and Black Markets*, 124-26.

90 Larry Hollingworth, *Aid Memoir* (NY: Refuge Press, 2021), 458.

91 As quoted in Bruce R. Scott and Edward N. Murphy, "Brcko and the Arizona Market," Harvard Business School paper 9-905-411 (August 14, 2006): 16. The original document from which the quotation is taken is Benjamin Feit and Michael Morfit, "A Neutral Space: The Arizona Market as an Engine for Peace and a New Economy in Bosnia and Herzegovina," briefing prepared for the United States Agency for International Development DG Partners Conference, December 2002.

92 Scott and Murphy, "Brcko and the Arizona Market," 20.

93 Scott and Murphy, "Brcko and the Arizona Market," 9.
94 Article IV (Redeployment of Forces), Paragraph 2(b), "General Framework Agreement for Peace in Bosnia and Herzegovina," United Nations Peacemaker, November 21, 1995, available at https://peacemaker.un.org/node/9388. This dictate applied to the Zone of Separation throughout Bosnia-Herzegovina, not just in the vicinity of Brcko.
95 Bruce R. Scott, *Capitalism: Its Origins and Evolution as a System of Governance* (NY: Springer, 2011), 279-80.
96 Scott, *Capitalism*, 281.
97 Dean E. Murphy, "Bosnian Swap Meet May Be a Peace Model," *Los Angeles Times*, September 22, 1996; and Gregory Fontenot telephone interview with Russell W. Glenn, February 12, 2024.
98 Fontenot interview.
99 Adam Moore, "Localizing Peacebuilding: The Arizona Market and the Evolution of US Military Peacebuilding Priorities in Bosnia," *Journal of Intervention and Statebuilding* (July 2019), 2-3, https://doi.org/10.1080/17502977.2019.1610991; and Article IV (Redeployment of Forces).
100 Gregory Fontenot telephone conversation with the author, December 14, 2023.
101 Moore, "Localizing Peacebuilding," 2-3.
102 Scott and Murphy, "Brcko and the Arizona Market," 14.
103 Fontenot interview, February 12, 2024. Mijo Anić was a relative moderate. Fontenot recalled, "Anić said the land was Croatian owned, and I believed him."
104 Robert William Farrand, *Reconstruction and Peace Building in the Balkans: The Brcko Experience* (Lanham, MD: Rowman and Littlefield, 2011), 229; and Moore, "Localizing Peacebuilding, 3-4. Another source states there were "about 2,000 sellers" by the end of 1996. Katherine C. Sredl; Clifford J. Shultz, II; and Ružica Brečić, "The Arizona Market: a Marketing Systems Perspective on Pre- and Post-War Developments in Bosnia, with Implications for Sustainable Peace and Prosperity," *Journal of Macromarketing* 37, no. 3 (2017): 306-07, DOI: 10.1177/0276146717712359. It seems likely the number of those offering wares and services, which the same source says included night clubs and casinos by that year, differed depending on weather, day of the week, season, and other factors.

105 Scott and Murphy, "Brcko and the Arizona Market," 14; and Sredl, Shultz, and Brečić, "The Arizona Market," 305.
106 Moore, "Localizing Peacebuilding," 7.
107 Scott and Murphy, "Brcko and the Arizona Market," 16-17.
108 Moore, "Localizing Peacebuilding," 6.
109 Sredl, Shultz, and Brečić, "The Arizona Market," 307.
110 Moore, "Localizing Peacebuilding," 8.
111 Farrand, Reconstruction and Peace Building in the Balkans, 223.
112 Moore, "Localizing Peacebuilding, 5 and 8; Scott and Murphy, "Brcko and the Arizona Market," 16; and Farrand, *Reconstruction and Peace Building in the Balkans*, 230.
113 Office of the High Representative, "Supervisory Order on Arizona Market," November 16, 2000, https://www.ohr.int/ohr_archive/supervisory-order-on-arizona-market/; and Scott and Murphy, "Brcko and the Arizona Market," 18. Also see Gary Matthews (Deputy High Representative, Supervisor for Brcko), "Supervisory Order on the Use of Land in Arizona Market, Office of the High Representative," February 17, 2001, https://www.ohr.int/ohr_archive/supervisory-order-on-the-use-of-land-in-arizona-market/. An extensive list of related documents from the Brcko Final Award Office with links to each is at Office of the High Representative, Brcko Final Award Office, 2015, https://www.ohr.int/ohr_archive_taxonomy/brcko-final-award-office/page/11/.
114 Scott and Murphy, "Brcko and the Arizona Market," 18.
115 Henry Clarke (Deputy High Representative and Supervisor of Brcko), "Amendment to the Supervisory Order on Arizona Market of November 16, 2000," April 3, 2002, https://www.ohr.int/ohr_archive/amendment-to-the-supervisory-order-on-arizona-market-of-november-16-2000/.
116 Moore, "Localizing Peacebuilding," 8.
117 "Brcko: A market for organized crime," Global Initiative Against Transnational Organized Crime, undated, https://riskbulletins.globalinitiative.net/see-obs-012/03-brcko-market-for-organized-crime.html.
118 "Brcko: A market for organized crime."
119 The appearance and very brief description of the evolved Arizona Market can be found at "Arizona Market," Faculty of

Economics Brcko, University of East Sarajevo, 2020, https://tobd.ba/objekti/313/trznica-arizona.

120 "Brcko: A market for organized crime."
121 Fontenot interview.
122 Polman, *The Crisis Caravan*, 10.
123 Andreas, *Blue Helmets and Black Markets*, 83.
124 "Brcko: A market for organized crime."
125 "Smoking: An Endemic Problem in Bosnia and Herzegovina," World Bank Group, November 20, 2012, https://www.worldbank.org/en/news/feature/2012/11/20/smoking-an-endemic-problem-in-bosnia-and-herzegovina; and "Half of the Smokers in BiH buy Cigarettes and Tobacco on the black Market," *Sarajevo Times* (December 10, 2022), https://sarajevotimes.com/half-of-the-smokers-in-bih-buy-cigarettes-and-tobacco-on-the-black-market/.
126 Anonymous 3 interview.
127 Harry Taylor and Emily Dugan, "Heavy shelling reported in Kharkiv region after overnight attacks in Kherson – as it happened," (April 30, 2023), https://www.theguardian.com/world/live/2023/apr/30/russia-ukraine-war-live-russian-soldiers-likely-placed-in-holes-in-the-ground-for-misdemeanours-says-uk.
128 Quoted in Sarah Chayes, *Thieves of State: Why Corruption Threatens Global Security* (NY: W.W. Norton, 2015), 10-11.
129 Chayes, *Thieves of State*, 187.
130 Bacon, *The Great Halifax Explosion*, 235.
131 *United States Strategic Bombing Survey Summary Report (European War)*, 102.
132 The description of events regarding the explosion of the ship are adapted from Bacon, *The Great Halifax Explosion*; and Bird, *The Town that Died*.
133 Bacon, *The Great Halifax Explosion*, 168. Bird disagrees with Bacon in terms of how far the two parts of the ship traveled, but in both cases the distances were well over a mile.
134 "Halifax explosion," *Encyclopedia Britannica*, March 7, 2024, https://www.britannica.com/event/Halifax-explosion.

135 "Halifax explosion." Readers can find a list of the dead at "Halifax Explosion: A List of those that Died," Nova Scotia Archives, April 2024, https://archives.novascotia.ca/remembrance/.

136 Bacon, *The Great Halifax Explosion*, 255-258, 281, and 288.

137 The description of events regarding the explosion of the ship are adapted from Bacon, *The Great Halifax Explosion*; and Bird, *The Town that Died*.

138 Estimates of the kiloton equivalent of the Hiroshima atomic bomb vary with most values being in the 13-16 kiloton range. Though they also vary, the values for the bomb later dropped on Nagasaki are generally 50 percent greater than those for the first-dropped bomb. See, for example, "What are Tactical Nuclear Weapons?", Union of Concerned Scientists, June 1, 2022, https://www.ucsusa.org/resources/tactical-nuclear-weapons; "The Atomic Bombs Dropped on Hiroshima and Nagasaki," Hiroshima Peace Museum, undated, https://hpmmuseum.jp/modules/exhibition; and "Atomic bomb," European Nuclear Society, undated, https://www.euronuclear.org/glossary/atomic-bomb/.

139 Bacon, *The Great Halifax Explosion*, 228.

140 Bacon, *The Great Halifax Explosion*, 228-29.

141 Bacon, *The Great Halifax Explosion*, 234.

142 Bacon, *The Great Halifax Explosion*, 284.

143 Bacon, *The Great Halifax Explosion*, 286-87.

144 Bacon, *The Great Halifax Explosion*, 293.

145 Bacon, *The Great Halifax Explosion*, 347; "Not Your Grandfather's Mining Industry," Mining Association of Nova Scotia, undated, https://notyourgrandfathersmining.ca/the-hydrostones, and "Hydrostone District National Historic Site of Canada," Parks Canada Agency, undated, https://www.pc.gc.ca/apps/dfhd/page_nhs_eng.aspx?id=788.

146 Bacon, *The Great Halifax Explosion*, 295-96.

147 Daniel Armanios, Jonas Skovrup Christensen, and Andriy Tymoshenko.

148 Kinstler, "Architects Plan a City for the Future in Ukraine."

149 Armanios, Christensen, and Tymoshenko, "What Ukraine Can Teach the World," 101.

150 Rebuild Ukraine, "Irpin: Digitization of Destroyed Infrastructure (Kyiv region)," undated, 6-7, https://eng.rebuildua.net/irpin.

151 Reliefweb, "In Ukraine, recovery can't wait: Clearing landmines and rubble makes it safer for displaced families to come home," July 1, 2022, https://reliefweb.int/report/ukraine/ukraine-recovery-cant-wait-clearing-landmines-and-rubble-makes-it-safer-displaced-families-come-home.

152 Rebuild Ukraine, "Irpin: Digitization of Destroyed Infrastructure (Kyiv region)," 2.

153 Linda Kinstler, "Architects Plan a City for the Future in Ukraine, While Bombs Still Fall."

154 Kinstler, "Architects Plan a City for the Future in Ukraine." Descriptive material in the following paragraphs draws on this source.

155 Kinstler, "Architects Plan a City for the Future in Ukraine."

156 Kinstler, "Architects Plan a City for the Future in Ukraine."

157 Glenn, "Urban Disaster Wrought by Man."

158 Anonymous interview 6.

159 Orlean, *The Library Book*, 77.

160 One example in this regard is the Los Angeles library system's Career Online High School (COHS), offering some nine hundred courses via which adults can obtain a diploma rather than a high school equivalency certificate. Orlean, *The Library Book*, 77.

ABOUT THE AUTHOR

Dr. Russell W. Glenn spent sixteen years in the think tank community before joining the faculty of the Strategic and Defence Studies Centre at the Australian National University in Canberra, this after over twenty-five years service with the US Army. He and his wife, Dee, now live in Williamsburg, Virginia.

BIBLIOGRAPHY

- "Activating and Strengthening Ukraine's Reconstruction Capacity," Ukrainian Industry Expertise SE, NGO International Economic Research Institute, and US Agency for International Development white paper, undated.
- Adams, David, and Peter Larkham, *The Everyday Experiences of Reconstruction and Regeneration: From Vision to Reality in Birmingham and Coventry*. Milton Park, UK: Routledge, 2019.
- Adams, Paul, and James FitzGerald, "Ukraine war: Celebrations as Kyiv takes back key city Kherson," BBC (November 11, 2022), https://www.bbc.com/news/world-europe-63601312.
- Adenauer, Konrad, *Memoirs 1945-53*. Chicago: Henry Regnery, 1966.
- AFP, "Ukraine De-Mining Like Europe After WWII: UN," *Kyiv Post* (June 22, 2023), https://www.kyivpost.com/post/18531.
- "After the Retreat: Ukraine," *The Economist* 448, no. 9358 (August 12, 2023): 40-41.
- "Against the Grain: Funding Fighting," *The Economist* 451, no. 9396 (May 11, 2024): 59.
- Agoncillo, Teodoro A., *History of the Filipino People*, 8th edition. Quezon City: Garotech, 1990.
- "Amnesty Says Russia Guilty of War Crimes in Kharkiv shelling," Reuters (June 13, 2022). https://www.reuters.com/business/aerospace-defense/amnesty-says-russia-guilty-war-crimes-kharkiv-shelling-2022-06-13/.
- Andreas, Peter, *Blue Helmets and Black Markets: The Business of Survival in the Siege of Sarajevo*. Ithaca, NY: Cornell University Press, 2008.
- Andreas-Friedrich, Ruth, *Battleground Berlin: Diaries 1945-1948*. Translated by Anna Boerresen. NY: Paragon, 1990.
- *Annual Narrative Report, 1 January-31 December 1950: Occupation Forces in Europe Series, 1950*. Karlsruhe, Germany: Historical Division, European Command, undated.

▷ "Another World War Bomb Found in Schmargendorf: Defusing on Thursday," Berlin.de (The Official Website of Berlin), April 3, 2024, https://www.berlin.de/en/news/8799736-5559700-another-world-war-bomb-found-in-schmarge.en.html.

▷ Araneta, Salvador, "Basic Problems of Philippine Economic Development," *Pacific Affairs* 21, no. 3 (September 1948): 280-285.

▷ Arhirova, Hanna, "'We Survived': Kherson Comes Alive after Russian Withdrawal," Associated Press (November 19, 2022), https://apnews.com/article/russia-ukraine-europe-business-46c1061f-c44458c903cf12fa442c57e1.

▷ Arhirova, Hanna, and Yuras Karmanau, "Ukraine's Defense Minister Resigns Following Zelenskyy's Announcement of His Replacement," *PBS News Hour* (September 4, 2023), https://www.pbs.org/newshour/world/ukraines-defense-minister-resigns-following-zelenskyys-announcement-of-his-replacement.

▷ "Arizona Market," Faculty of Economics Brcko, University of East Sarajevo, 2020, https://tobd.ba/objekti/313/trznica-arizona.

▷ Armanios, Daniel, Jonas Skovrup Christensen, and Andriy Tymoshenko, "What Ukraine Can Teach the World About Resilience and Civil Engineering," *Issues in Science and Technology* 40, no. 1 (Fall) 2023: 98-103, https://issues.org/wp-content/uploads/2023/10/98-103-Armanios-et-al.-What-Ukraine-Can-Teach-the-World-Fall-2023.pdf.

▷ Article IV (Redeployment of Forces), Paragraph 2(b), "General Framework Agreement for Peace in Bosnia and Herzegovina," United Nations Peacemaker, November 21, 1995, available at https://www.osce.org/files/f/documents/e/0/126173.pdf.

▷ "Atomic bomb" European Nuclear Society, undated, https://www.euronuclear.org/glossary/atomic-bomb/.

▷ "The Atomic Bombs Dropped on Hiroshima and Nagasaki," Hiroshima Peace Museum, undated, https://hpmmuseum.jp/?lang=eng.

▷ Axe, David, "One of Ukraine's Best Brigades Defends One of Its Most Vulnerable Cities," *Forbes* (February 1, 2022), https://issues.org/wp-content/uploads/2023/10/98-103-Armanios-et-al.-What-Ukraine-Can-Teach-the-World-Fall-2023.pdf.

▷ Axe, David "The Ukrainian Army Is on the Attack. This Is How the War with Russia Could End," *Forbes* (May 5, 2022), https://

www.forbes.com/sites/davidaxe/2022/05/05/an-advancing-ukrainian-army-just-showed-us-how-the-war-with-russia-could-end.

▷ Bachelet, Michelle, "High Commissioner Updates the Human Rights Council on Mariupol, Ukraine," briefing, United Nations Human Rights Office of the High Commissioner (June 16, 2022), https://www.ohchr.org/en/statements/2022/06/high-commissioner-updates-human-rights-council-mariupol-ukraine.

▷ "Background Briefing on Landmine Use in Ukraine," Human Rights Watch, June 15, 2022, https://www.hrw.org/news/2022/06/15/background-briefing-landmine-use-ukraine.

▷ Bacon, John U., *The Great Halifax Explosion: A World War I Story of Treachery, Tragedy, and Extraordinary Heroism*. NY: William Morrow, 2017.

▷ Bădescu, Gruia, "Dwelling in the Post-War City Urban Reconstruction and Home-Making in Sarajevo," *Revue D'etudes Comparatives Est-Ouest*, 4, no. 46 (2015), 35-60.

▷ Bădescu, Gruia, "Post-War Reconstruction in Contested Cities: Comparing Urban Outcomes in Sarajevo and Beirut," *Urban Geopolitics: Rethinking Planning in Contested Cities*, Edited by Jonathan Rokem and Camillo Boano (August 21, 2017): 17-31, http://dx.doi.org/10.4324/9781315659275-3.

▷ Bagehot, "How the British Government Rules by Algorithm," *The Economist* 436 (August 22, 2020): 48, https://www.economist.com/britain/2020/08/20/how-the-british-government-rules-by-algorithm.

▷ Barnes, Dayna L., *Architects of Occupation: American Experts and the Planning for Postwar Japan*. Ithaca, NY: Cornell University Press, 2017.

▷ Bartleby, "The Secret to Cutting Corporate Red Tape," *The Economist* 438 (March 13, 2021): 63, https://www.economist.com/business/2021/03/13/the-secret-to-cutting-corporate-red-tape.

▷ Baruch, Bernard M., and John M. Hancock, "Report on War and Post-War Adjustment Policies," report for James F. Byrnes, Director, Office of War Mobilization, February 15, 1944, https://fraser.stlouisfed.org/files/docs/historical/eccles/032_14_0003.pdf.

▷ Becker, Torbjörn, et al., *A Blueprint for the Reconstruction of Ukraine: Rapid Response Economics 1*, Centre for Economic Policy Research Press, 2022.

- Beketova, Elina, "Behind the Lines: Russia's Ethnic Cleansing." Center for European Policy Analysis (CEPA), July 27, 2023, https://cepa.org/article/behind-the-lines-russias-ethnic-cleansing/.
- Beketova, Elina, "Behind the Lines: The Sugar-Coated Myths of Mariupol," Center for European Policy Analysis (CEPA), August 24, 2023, https://cepa.org/article/behind-the-lines-the-sugar-coated-myths-of-mariupol/.
- Berg, Scott G., *The Burning of the World*. NY: Pantheon Books, 2023.
- Bergengruen, Vera, "Ukraine Is Using AI to Help Clear Millions of Russian Landmines," *Time* (November 2, 2023), https://time.com/6330445/demining-ukraine/.
- Bertrand, Natasha, and Alex Marquardt, "US Increases Pressure on Ukraine to Do More to Counter Corruption," CNN (October 3, 2023), https://www.cnn.com/2023/10/03/politics/us-ukraine-pressure-counter-corruption/index.html.
- Beschloss, Michael, *The Conquerors: Roosevelt, Truman and the Destruction of Hitler's Germany, 1941-1945*. NY: Simon & Schuster, 2002.
- Bessel, Richard, *Germany 1945: From War to Peace*. NY: Harper, 2009.
- Bird, Michael J., *The Town that Died: The True Story of the Greatest Man-made Explosion before Hiroshima*. Toronto: McGraw-Hill, 1962.
- Bobrova, Anastasiia, "Housing and War: Housing Policy in the First Year of the Full-Scale War," Cedos (March 22, 2023), https://cedos.org.ua/en/researches/housing-and-war-annual-review/.
- "Bombardment of Ukraine's Power Generation and Transmission Infrastructure, 1 October 2022 to 30 April 2023: A Remote Assessment," The Yale School of Public Health's (YSPH) Humanitarian Research Lab (HRL), February 29, 2024, https://hub.conflictobservatory.org/portal/apps/sites/#/home/pages/power-1.
- "Bosnia and Herzegovina—Details," The World Factbook, US Central Intelligence Agency, undated, https://www.cia.gov/the-world-factbook/countries/bosnia-and-herzegovina/map.
- Boston Consulting Group, "Supporting Ukraine: A Study on Potential Recovery Strategies for Ukraine" (January 2023), https://media-publications.bcg.com/Supporting-Ukraine-Potential-Recovery-Strategies-Feb-2023.pdf.
- Botting, Douglas, *From the Ruins of the Reich: Germany 1945-1949*. NY: Crown, 1985.

BIBLIOGRAPHY

▷ "Brcko: A market for organized crime," Global Initiative Against Transnational Organized Crime, undated, https://riskbulletins.globalinitiative.net/see-obs-012/03-brcko-market-for-organized-crime.html.

▷ Brenner, János, "Some ideas for a post-war recovery of Ukrainian cities," *Urban Research & Practice*, 16, no. 2 (2023, published online July 5, 2022): 294-300, https://doi.org/10.1080/17535069.2022.2097646.

▷ Burdyga, Igor, "Russia promised Kherson it would stay forever. It left chaos behind," openDemocracy (December 5, 2022), https://www.opendemocracy.net/en/odr/kherson-russian-occupation-retreat-looting/.

▷ Bureau of the Census and Statistics, *Bulletin of Philippine Statistics*, Vol. 1, no. 1, (Manila: Bureau of Printing, September 1945).

▷ Bureau of the Census and Statistics, *Bulletin of Philippine Statistics*, Vol. 1, no. 2, (Manila: Bureau of Printing, December 1945).

▷ Bureau of Democracy, Human Rights, and Labor, "2016 Report on International Religious Freedom: Bosnia and Herzegovina," US State Department, 2016, https://www.state.gov/reports/2016-report-on-international-religious-freedom/bosnia-and-herzegovina/.

▷ Butenko, Victoria, "'We are totally ready': Ukraine prepares for fresh attacks on energy as winter nears," CNN (November 10, 2023), https://wp.towson.edu/iajournal/2023/01/13/russias-response-to-the-challenges-of-urban-warfare-in-the-russo-ukrainian-war/.

▷ Butler, Marcus, "Russia's Response to the Challenges of Urban Warfare in the Russo-Ukrainian War," *Towson University Journal of International Affairs* (Jan 13, 2023), https://wp.towson.edu/iajournal/2023/01/13/russias-response-to-the-challenges-of-urban-warfare-in-the-russo-ukrainian-war/.

▷ Calafano, James Jay, "Thinking the Future," *The Whitehead Journal of Diplomacy and International Relations* 10, no. 2 (Summer/Fall 2009), https://ciaotest.cc.columbia.edu/journals/shjdir/v10i2/f_0018623_15949.pdf.

▷ Canadian Urban Institute, "CityTalk: How Are Ukrainian Cities and Municipalities Planning Their Recovery?" CityTalk Canada (December 15, 20220, https://canurb.org/fr/citytalk-news/citytalk-how-are-ukrainian-cities-and-municipalities-planning-their-recovery/.

▷ Carter, Donald, *The City Becomes a Symbol: The US Army in the Occupation of Berlin, 1945-1948*. Washington, DC: Center of Military History, 2017.

▷ Caughey, A.J., "It will take decades to clear Ukraine's landmines. Without more women, it will be even slower—and more dangerous," Bluemarble (August 24, 203, updated January 30, 2024), https://globalaffairs.org/bluemarble/ukraine-full-of-landmines-without-women-cleanup-will-take-longer.

▷ Chayes, Sarah, *Thieves of State: Why Corruption Threatens Global Security*. NY: W.W. Norton, 2015.

▷ Chernov, Mstyslav, "20 Days in Mariupol: The Team that documented the city's agony," Associated Press, March 21, 2022, https://apnews.com/article/russia-ukraine-europe-ed-f7240a9d990e7e3e32f82ca351dede.

▷ Christian, Patrick, email to Dr. Russell W. Glenn, Subject: RE: Ukraine article/Corruption in Ukraine, January 3, 2024.

▷ Christy, Patrick, "America's Proud History of Post-War Aid," *U.S News and World Report* (June 6, 2014), https://www.usnews.com/opinion/blogs/world-report/2014/06/06/the-lessons-from-us-aid-after-world-war-ii.

▷ Cities 4 Cities United 4 Ukraine, "Municipal Partnerships with Ukraine" (undated), https://cities4cities.eu.

▷ Clark, Delbert, "US Barter Center in Berlin Failing," 25, *The New York Times* (December 15, 1946), https://timesmachine.nytimes.com/timesmachine/1946/12/15/305855372.html?pageNumber=25.

▷ Clark, Mason, George Barros, and Kateryna Stepanenko, "Russia-Ukraine Warning Update: Initial Russian Offensive Campaign Assessment," Institute for the Study of War (February 24, 2022), https://www.understandingwar.org/backgrounder/russia-ukraine-warning-update-initial-russian-offensive-campaign-assessment.

▷ Clark, Mason, Kateryna Stepanenko, and Karolina Hird, "Russian Offensive Campaign Assessment, April 10," Institute for the Study of War (April 7, 2022), https://www.understandingwar.org/backgrounder/russian-offensive-campaign-assessment-april-10.

▷ Clark, Mason, George Barros, and Kateryna Stepanenko, "Russian Offensive Campaign Assessment, March 24," Institute for the Study of War (March 24, 2022), https://www.understandingwar.

org/backgrounder/russian-offensive-campaign-assessment-march-24-2024.

▷ Clarke, Henry (Deputy High Representative and Supervisor of Brcko), "Amendment to the Supervisory Order on Arizona Market of November 16, 2000," April 3, 2002, https://www.ohr.int/ohr_archive/amendment-to-the-supervisory-order-on-arizona-market-of-november-16-2000/.

▷ Clay, Lucius D., *Decision in Germany*. Garden City, NY: Doubleday & Company, 1950.

▷ Clay, Lucius D., (signed Omar N. Bradley) to US War Department, 9 July 1945, *The Letters of General Lucius D. Clay*. Edited by Jean Edward Smith. Bloomington. IN: Indiana University Press, 1974, 1: 49-50.

▷ Clay, Lucius D., (signed Dwight D. Eisenhower) to George C. Marshall, 11 July 1945, *The Letters of General Lucius D. Clay*. Edited by Jean Edward Smith. Bloomington, IN: Indiana University Press, 1974, 1: 51-52.

▷ Clay, Lucius D., to Vasily D. Sokolovsky, 20 April 1946, *The Letters of General Lucius D. Clay*. Edited by Jean Edward Smith. Bloomington, IN: Indiana University Press, 1974, 1: 201.

▷ Clay, Lucius D., to BG Edward H. White, Office of the Comptroller, United States Forces European Theater, 2 November 1946, *The Letters of General Lucius D. Clay*. Edited by Jean Edward Smith. Bloomington, IN: Indiana University Press, 1974, 1: 276-79.

▷ Coffey, Thomas M., *Iron Eagle: The Turbulent Life of General Curtis LeMay*. NY: Crown, 1986.

▷ Collins, Jeremy, "Interview with James M. Scott, Author of *Rampage: MacArthur, Yamashita, and the Battle of Manila*," The National World War II Museum (February 3, 2020), https://www.nationalww2museum.org/war/articles/interview-james-m-scott-author-rampage-macarthur-yamashita-and-battle-manila.

▷ Committee For the Compilation of Materials on Damage Caused by the Atomic Bombs in Hiroshima and Nagasaki, *Hiroshima and Nagasaki: The Physical, Medical, and Social Effects of the Atomic Bombings*. Translated by Eisei Ishikawa and David L Swain. NY: Basic Books, 1981.

▷ Conant, Eve, "How History, Geography Help Explain Ukraine's Political Crisis," *National Geographic* (January 31, 2014), https://www.nationalgeographic.com/science/article/140129-protests-ukraine-russia-geography-history.

- Cookman, Liz, "Kherson is Liberated but Not Yet Freed," *Foreign Policy* (November 18, 2022), https://foreignpolicy.com/2022/11/18/kherson-ukraine-liberation-russia-occupation/.
- Council of Europe Office in Ukraine, "Cities4Cities: new matchmaking platform launched to support Ukrainian local and regional authorities," (March 29, 2022), https://www.coe.int/en/web/kyiv/-/cities4cities-new-matchmaking-platform-launched-to-support-ukrainian-local-and-regional-authorities.
- Crisp, Jeff, Tim Morris, and Hilde Refstie, "Displacement in urban areas: new challenges, new partnerships," *Disasters* 36, Issue s1 (June 11, 2012), 535-536, https://doi.org/10.1111/j.1467-7717.2012.01284.x.
- Cross, Tim, "Humanitarian Assistance and Reconstruction," in *British Generals in Blair's Wars*. Edited by Jonathan Bailey, Richard Iron, and Hew Strachan. Farnham, UK: Ashgate, 2013.
- Cutts, Mark, "The humanitarian operation in Bosnia, 1992-95: the dilemmas of negotiating humanitarian access," Policy Research Unit UNHCR Working Paper no. 8, May 1999, 22, https://www.unhcr.org/media/humanitarian-operation-bosnia-1992-95-dilemmas-negotiating-humanitarian-access-mark-cutts.
- Danish Refugee Council, "Ukraine: Strengthening national mine action capabilities," February 9, 2024, https://pro.drc.ngo/resources/news/ukraine-strengthening-national-mine-action-capabilities/.
- Demographia, *Demographia World Urban Areas*, 15th Edited by Belleville, IL: Wendell Cox Consultancy, April 2019.
- Demographia, *Demographia World Urban Areas*, 17th Edited by Belleville, IL: Wendell Cox Consultancy, May 2021.
- Demographia, *Demographia World Urban Areas*, 18th Edited by Belleville, IL: Wendell Cox Consultancy, July 2022.
- Demographia, *Demographia World Urban Areas*, 19th Edited by Belleville, IL: Wendell Cox Consultancy, August 2023, http://www.demographia.com/db-worldua.pdf.
- Diefendorf, Jeffry M., *In the Wake of War: The Reconstruction of German Cities after World War II*. NY: Oxford University Press, 1993.
- Diefendorf, Jeffry M., "War and Reconstruction in Germany and Japan," in *Rebuilding Urban Japan After 1945*, Edited by Carola Hein, Jeffry M. Diefendorf, and Ishida Yorifusa (NY: Palgrave MacMillan, 2003), 227.

▷ Dimarco, Louis, "Urban Operations in Ukraine: Size, Ratios, and the Principles of War," Modern War Institute at West Point (June 20, 2022), https://mwi.westpoint.edu/urban-operations-in-ukraine-size-ratios-and-the-principles-of-war/.

▷ Directorate-General for Neighbourhood and Enlargement Negotiations, "Multi-agency Donor Coordination Platform for Ukraine meets in expanded format, to advance Ukraine's recovery and reconstruction," European Commission news article, February 14, 2024, https://neighbourhood-enlargement.ec.europa.eu/news/multi-agency-donor-coordination-platform-ukraine-meets-expanded-format-advance-ukraines-recovery-and-2024-02-14_en.

▷ Dixon, Robyn, et. al, "In Russia's presidential election, Ukrainians cast ballots at gunpoint," *The Washington Post*, March 17, 2024, A16.

▷ Donia, Robert J., *Sarajevo: A Biography*. Ann Arbor: University of Michigan Press, 2006.

▷ Donnison, F.S.V., *History of the Second World War: Civil Affairs and Military Government North-West Europe 1944-1946*. London: Her Majesty's Stationary Office, 1961.

▷ "Don't seize: capitalize," *The Economist* 450, no. 9386 (March 2, 2024): 12.

▷ Dower, John W., *Embracing Defeat: Japan in the Wake of World War II*. NY: W. W. Norton, 2000.

▷ Dower, John W., *Ways of Forgetting, Ways of Remembering: Japan in the Modern World*. NY: The New Press, 2012.

▷ Dulko, Ievgeniia, "Rebuilding Narratives: The Role of Urban Planning in Post-war Ukraine," PhD diss., University of Illinois at Chicago (2023).

▷ Dyak, Sofia, "From War into the Future: Historical Legacies and Questions for Postwar Reconstruction in Ukraine," *Architectural Histories*, 11, no. 1 (2003): 1-11, DOI: https://doi.org/10.16995/ah.9805.

▷ Ebel, Francesca, and Kostiantyn Khudov, "Ukrainians are breaking their ties with the Russian language," *The Washington Post*, July 28, 2023, https://www.washingtonpost.com/world/2023/07/28/ukrainians-are-breaking-their-ties-with-russian-language/.

▷ Eggers, David, "The Profound Defiance of Daily Life in Kyiv," *The New Yorker* (January 5, 2023), https://www.newyorker.com/news/dispatch/the-profound-defiance-of-daily-life-in-kyiv.

- Eiji, Takemae, *Inside GHQ: The Allied Occupation of Japan and Legacy*. NY: Continuum, 2002.
- Ellwood, David W., *Rebuilding Europe: Western Europe, America and Postwar Reconstruction*. London: Longman, 1992.
- Erlanger, Steven, "NATO Will Offer Ukraine a 'Bridge' to Membership, Hoping That's Enough," *The New York Times*, June 26, 2024, https://www.nytimes.com/2024/06/26/world/europe/nato-ukraine-washington-membership-summit.html.
- Estleman, Loren D., *The Lioness is the Hunter*. NY: Tom Doherty Associates, 2017.
- European Committee of the Regions, "European Alliance of Cities and Regions for the Reconstruction of Ukraine," European Union (undated), https://eur-lex.europa.eu/legal-content/EN/TXT/PDF/?uri=CELEX:52022XR5222.
- European Union, "Ukraine Relief and reconstruction" (July 2022), https://www.eeas.europa.eu/sites/default/files/documents/Factsheet_Ukraine_Relief_and_Reconstruction.pdf.pdf.
- "Extreme weather is making parts of Australia uninhabitable," *The Economist* (December 20, 2022), https://www.economist.com/asia/2022/12/20/extreme-weather-is-making-parts-of-australia-uninhabitable.
- "Eyeing Russia's backyard: China and Ukraine," *The Economist* 449, no. 9375 (December 9, 2023): 37-38.
- Faculty of Architecture & the Built Environment, "Tools for Post Conflict Urban Recovery," Delft University of Technology (undated), https://postconflictrecovery.org/unun/.
- Falcon, Russell, "Explained: Why Kharkiv is one of Ukraine's most vulnerable cities," *NewsNation* (February 24, 2022), https://www.newsnationnow.com/us-news/explained-why-kharkiv-is-one-of-ukraines-most-vulnerable-cities/.
- Falk, Pamela, "No doubt we are failing the people of Mariupol, UN relief official says," *CBS News*, April 18, 2022, https://www.cbsnews.com/news/mariupol-ukraine-united-nations-humanitarian-crisis/.
- Farmer, Paul, *Haiti after the earthquake*. NY: PublicAffairs, 2011.
- Farrand, Robert William, *Reconstruction and Peace Building in the Balkans: The Brcko Experience*. Lanham, MD: Rowman and Littlefield, 2011.

- Feit, Benjamin, and Michael Morfit, "A Neutral Space: The Arizona Market as an Engine for Peace and a New Economy in Bosnia and Herzegovina," briefing prepared for the United States Agency for International Development DG Partners Conference, December 2002.
- Filipchuk, Vasyl, and Yehor Kiyan, "Rebuilding Ukraine: Initiatives, Approaches, Recommendations," International Center for Policy Studies, 2023.
- Filipinas Heritage Library, "Manila Reborn: An Exhibit on the postwar reconstruction of a city" Google Arts and Culture (undated), https://artsandculture.google.com/story/manila-reborn-filipinas-heritage-library/gQVxQknmPODGJA?hl=en.
- *Firstpost* staff, "UK Schools developing lessons to re-educate teens brainwashed by Andrew Tate's misogynistic content," *Firstpost* (January 8, 2023), https://www.firstpost.com/world/uk-schools-developing-lessons-to-re-educate-teens-brainwashed-by-andrew-tates-misogynistic-content-11949582.html.
- FitzGerald, James "Ukraine war: Putin endorses evacuations from occupied Kherson," BBC (November 5, 2022), https://www.bbc.co.uk/news/world-europe-63523043.
- Fontenot, Gregory, email message to author, Subject: Mine question, December 5, 2023.
- Fontenot, Gregory, "Measures of Effectiveness in Stability Operations 1995—1996, Operation Joint Endeavor, Bosnia-Herzegovina," briefing given at the Israel Defense Forces—US Joint Forces Command Joint Urban Operations Office 2006 Urban Operations Conference, Tel Aviv, Israel, June 6, 2006.
- Fontenot, Gregory, telephone conversation with author, December 14, 2023.
- Fontenot, Gregory, telephone interview with Russell W. Glenn, February 12, 2024.
- Fox, Amos C., "The Russo-Ukrainian War and the Principles of Urban Operations," *Small Wars Journal* (November 10, 2022), https://smallwarsjournal.com/index.php/jrnl/art/russo-ukrainian-war-and-principles-urban-operations.
- Fox, Elizabeth, "Rebuilding Germany's Children: Nazi Indoctrination and Postwar Re-education of the Hitler Youth," *Furman Humanities Review* 27, Article 4 (2016): 31-59, https://scholarexchange.furman.edu/fhr/vol27/iss1/4/.

▷ "A fragile grid: Taiwan's energy," *The Economist* 451, no. 9397 (May 18, 2024): 32-33.

▷ Fraleigh, C. Arnold, "Compensation for War Damage to American Property in Allied Country," *The American Journal of International Law* 41, no. 4 (October 1947): 748-69.

▷ Franklin, H. Bruce, *War Stars: The Superweapon and the American Imagination*. NY: Oxford University Press, 1988.

▷ Frankopan, Peter, *The Earth Transformed: An Untold History*. NY: Alfred A. Knopf, 2023.

▷ Fredericksen, Oliver J., *American Military Occupation of Germany, 1945-1953*. Darmstadt, Germany: The Historical Division, Headquarters, US Army Europe, 1953.

▷ "Free but under fire: Ukraine," *The Economist* 449, no. 9371 (November 11, 2023): 48-49.

▷ "French cities: Revival-upon-Med," *The Economist* 448, no. 9365 (September 30, 2023): 44.

▷ Geis, Margaret L., and George J, Gray, Jr., *Relations of Occupation Personnel with the Civil Population, 1946 -1948*. Occupation Forces in Europe Series, 1946-1948, Historical Division, Headquarters, European Command, 1951.

▷ "General Framework Agreement for Peace in Bosnia and Herzegovina," United Nations Peacemaker, November 21, 1995, available at https://peacemaker.un.org/bosniadaytonagreement95.

▷ General Staff, Supreme Allied Headquarters Pacific, *Reports of General MacArthur, MacArthur in Japan: The Occupation: Military Phase, Volume I Supplement*. Washington, DC: Government Printing Office, 1966.

▷ Gessen, Masha, "Democracy in Darkness: What Ukraine has already lost in its fight against Russia," *The New Yorker* (February 5, 2024): 34-43 https://www.newyorker.com/magazine/2024/02/05/ukraines-democracy-in-darkness.

▷ Gessen, Masha, "The Devastation of Kharkiv, Ukraine: Russian attacks have terrorized the civilian population in the Ukrainian city," *The New Yorker* (March 22, 2022), https://www.newyorker.com/culture/photo-booth/the-devastation-of-kharkiv.

▷ Gessen, Masha, "Ukrainians Forced to Flee to Russia," *The New Yorker* (August 14, 2023), https://www.newyorker.com/magazine/2023/08/21/the-ukrainians-forced-to-flee-to-russia (Also published as "Another Country" in the August 21, 2023 issue of *The New Yorker*).

▷ Gittings, John, "The Conflict Between War and Peace in Early Chinese Thought," *The Asia-Pacific Journal* 10, Issue 12, no. 5 (March 12, 2012), https://apjjf.org/2012/10/12/john-gittings/3725/article.

▷ Glenn, Russell W., *Achieving Convergence during Humanitarian Assistance and Disaster Relief Operations in the World's Largest Urban Areas: Proceedings of the "Current and Future Operations in Megacities Conference," Tokyo, Japan, July 16-18, 2019*. Fort Eustis, VA: US Army Training and Doctrine Command, October 1, 2019, https://community.apan.org/wg/tradoc-g2/mad-scientist/m/tokyo-megacities-conference-2019/294569.

▷ Glenn, Russell W., *Come Hell or High Fever: Readying the World's Megacities for Disaster*. Canberra, Australia: Australian National University Press, 2023. Available for free download at https://press.anu.edu.au/publications/come-hell-or-high-fever.

▷ Glenn, Russell W., *Counterinsurgency in a Test Tube: Analyzing the Success of the Regional Assistance Mission, Solomon Islands (RAMSI)*. Santa Monica, CA: RAND, 2007.

▷ Glenn, Russell W., "Creating Light at Tunnel's End: Ukraine's Postwar Urban Recovery," *Journal of Strategic Security* 16, no. 4 (2023): 1-14, https://digitalcommons.usf.edu/jss/vol16/iss4/1/.

▷ Glenn, Russell W., et. al, *Evaluation of USAID's Community Stabilization Program (CSP) in Iraq: Effectiveness of the CSP Model as a Non-lethal Tool for Counterinsurgency*. Washington, DC: United States Agency for International Development, 2009, https://pdf.usaid.gov/pdf_docs/PDACN461.pdf.

▷ Glenn, Russell W., "Urban Disaster Wrought by Man: The Battle for Manila, 1945," *Journal of Strategic Security* 16, no. 3 (2023), https://digitalcommons.usf.edu/jss/vol16/iss3/3/.

▷ Godson, Alex, "Nardella: Ambitious proposals to help Ukrainian cities," Euro Cities (August 22, 2022), https://eurocities.eu/latest/nardella-ambitious-proposals-to-help-ukrainian-cities/.

▷ Gourevitch, Philip, "Alms Dealers," *The New Yorker* (October 4, 2010), https://www.newyorker.com/magazine/2010/10/11/alms-dealers.

▷ Green, John, *The Anthropocene Reviewed*. NY: Penguin Random House, 2023.

▷ Greenberg, Lawrence M., *The Hukbalahap Insurrection: A Case Study of a Successful; Anti-Insurgency Operation in the Philippines – 1946-1955*

(Washington, DC: US Army Center for Military History, 1987), https://apps.dtic.mil/sti/tr/pdf/AD1112093.pdf.

▷ Griffiths, Owen, "Need, Greed, and Protest in Japan's Black Market, 1938-1949," *Journal of Social History* 35, no. 4 (Summer 2002): 825-858, http://www.jstor.org/stable/3790613.

▷ Gross, Inge E. Stanneck, *Memories of World War II and Its Aftermath, 1940-1954*, Eastsound, WA: Island in the Sky Publishing, 2005.

▷ Guillian, Robert, *I Saw Tokyo Burning: An Eyewitness Narrative From Pearl Harbor to Hiroshima*. Translated by William Byron. Garden City, NY: Doubleday & Company, 1981.

▷ Gunter, Joel, "Mariupol: Fires, no water, and bodies in the street," *BBC News* (March 6, 2022), https://www.bbc.com/news/world-europe-60637338.

▷ Gunter, Joel, "Ukrainian city of Mariupol 'near to humanitarian catastrophe' after bombardment," *BBC News* (March 2, 2022), https://www.bbc.com/news/world-europe-60585603.

▷ I. Savchuk I. Savchuk, "New Administrative and Territorial Division of Ukraine—New Challenge for National Interest," *National Interest Academic Journal* 1, no. 1 (2020): 37-45.

▷ "Half of the Smokers in BiH buy Cigarettes and Tobacco on the black Market," *Sarajevo Times* (December 10, 2022), https://sarajevotimes.com/half-of-the-smokers-in-bih-buy-cigarettes-and-tobacco-on-the-black-market/.

▷ "Halifax explosion," *Encyclopedia Britannica*, March 7, 2024, https://www.britannica.com/event/Halifax-explosion.

▷ "Halifax Explosion: A List of those that Died," Nova Scotia Archives, April 2024, https://archives.novascotia.ca/remembrance/.

▷ Hall, Robert King, "The Battle of the Mind: American Educational Policy in Germany and Japan," *Columbia Journal of International Affairs* 2, no. 1 (Winter 1948): 59-70.

▷ Harding, Luke, *Invasion: The Inside Story of Russia's Bloody War and Ukraine's Fight for Survival*. NY: Vintage, 2022.

▷ Harding, Luke, "'It's like the USSR': residents on life in Mariupol a year since Russian occupation," *The Guardian*, May 18, 2023, https://www.theguardian.com/world/2023/may/18/its-like-the-ussr-residents-on-life-in-mariupol-a-year-since-russian-occupation.

▷ Harding, Luke, Peter Beaumont, Jon Henley, and Martine Farrer, "Ukraine facing humanitarian crisis amid relentless Russian missile attacks," *The Guardian* (March 2, 2022), https://www.theguardian.com/world/2022/mar/02/ukraine-cities-bombardment-russia-attack-kyiv-kharkiv-russian-war-invasion.

▷ Harshbarger, Sam, "Challenges after Russian Withdrawals in Ukraine," New Lines Institute, (August 10, 2023), https://newlinesinstitute.org/state-resilience-fragility/challenges-after-russian-withdrawals-in-ukraine/.

▷ Hartendorp, A.V.H., "Short History of Industry and Trade in the Philippines: The War Damage and American Aid," in *Journal, American Chamber of Commerce of the Philippines* (1953): 96, https://quod.lib.umich.edu/p/philamer/AAJ0523.1953.001?rgn=main;view=fulltext.

▷ Hasegawa, Junichi, *Replanning the blitzed city centre: A comparative study of Bristol, Coventry and Southampton 1941-1950*. Philadelphia: Open University Press, 1992.

▷ Hasic, Tigran, *Reconstruction Planning in Post-Conflict Zones: Bosnia and Herzegovina and the International Community*, PhD diss. Stockholm: The Royal Institute of Technology, 2004.

▷ Hasic, T, "Sustainable Reconstruction of Post-War Cities: The Case of Sarajevo," *Open House International Journal* 27, no. 4 (2002): 71-82.

▷ Hatsuda, Kosei, and Akito Sakasai, "The Black Market as City: New Research on Alternative Urban Space in Occupied Japan (1945-1952)," summary of presentation, Princeton Mellon Initiative in Architecture, Urbanism & the Humanities (March 7, 2016), https://arc-hum.princeton.edu/black-market.

▷ Hedenskog, Jakob, "The Russian Occupation of Ukraine's Southern Regions," Stockholm Centre for Eastern European Studies report no. 5, June 2, 2022, https://sceeus.se/en/publications/the-russian-occupation-of-ukraines-southern-regions/.

▷ Heeks, Richard, "Understanding success and failure of anti-corruption initiatives," Anti-Corruption Resource Centre U4 Brief, March 2011.

▷ Hein, Carola, "Resilient Tokyo: Disaster and Transformation in the Japanese City," in *The Resilient City: How Modern Cities Recover from Disaster*. Edited by Lawrence J. Vale and Thomas J. Campanella (NY: Oxford, 2005: 213-234).

- Helling, Thomas, *The Great War and the Birth of Modern Medicine: A History*. NY: Pegasus Books, 2022.
- Heslop, Paul (Programme manager - Mine Action, UN Development Programme Ukraine), interview with Russell W. Glenn, March 21, 2024.
- Hewitt, Kenneth, "Proving Grounds of Urbicide: Civil and Urban Perspectives on the Bombing of Capital Cities," *ACME: An International E-Journal for Critical Geographies*, 8, no. 2 (2009): 365-66.
- Higgins, Andrew, "Kharkiv, Ukraine's second-largest city, is a major target of Russia. Here's why," *The New York Times*, February 24, 2022), https://www.nytimes.com/2022/02/24/world/europe/kharkiv-russia.html.
- Hillier, Rick, *A Soldier First: Bullets, Bureaucrats and the Politics of War*. Toronto: HarperCollins, 2009.
- Hinnant, Lori, Vasilisa Stepanenko, Sarah El Deeb, and ElizavetaTilna, "Russia scrubs Mariupol's Ukraine identity, builds on death," Associated Press (December 22, 2022).
- Holbrooke, Richard, *To End a* War. NY: Random House, 1998.
- Hollingworth, Larry, *Aid Memoir*. NY: Refuge Press, 2021.
- "Holodomor," Holocaust and Genocide Studies, College of Liberal Arts, University of Minnesota, 2024, https://cla.umn.edu/chgs/holocaust-genocide-education/resource-guides/holodomor.
- "'The Hope Left Us:' Russia's Siege, Starvation, and Capture of Mariupol City," Global Rights Compliance, June 2024, https://globalrightscompliance.com/wp-content/uploads/2024/06/20240612-Mariupol-ReportENG.pdf.
- Howley, Frank, *Berlin Command*. NY: G. P. Putnam's Sons, 1950.
- Human Rights Watch, "Education under Occupation Forced Russification of the School System in Occupied Ukrainian Territories," June 2024, https://www.hrw.org/report/2024/06/20/education-under-occupation-forced-russification-school-system-occupied-ukrainian.
- Human Rights Watch, "'Our City Was Gone' Russia's Devastation of Mariupol," Ukraine, February 2024, https://www.hrw.org/feature/russia-ukraine-war-mariupol/report.
- Human Rights Watch, "Ukraine: Russian Missile Strike on Lviv a Possible War Crime," July 19, 2023, https://www.hrw.org/news/2023/07/19/ukraine-russian-missile-strike-lviv-possible-war-crime.

▷ Hunder, Max, "Timeline: Russia's siege of the Ukrainian city of Mariupol," Reuters (March 30, 2022), https://www.reuters.com/world/europe/russias-siege-ukrainian-city-mariupol-2022-03-30/.

▷ Hurwitz, Harold, "Comparing American Reform Efforts in Germany: Mass Media and the School System" in *Americans as Proconsuls: United States Military Government in Germany and Japan, 1944-1952*. Edited by Robert Wolfe. Carbondale: Southern Illinois University Press 1984.

▷ Hrytsak, Yaroslav, *Ukraine: The Forging of a Nation*, Translated by Dominique Hoffman. London: Sphere, 2023.

▷ "Hydrostone District National Historic Site of Canada," Parks Canada Agency, undated, https://www.pc.gc.ca/apps/dfhd/page_nhs_eng.aspx?id=788.

▷ "Ice cream in heaven: Ukraine's war orphans," *The Economist* 449, no. 9375 (December 9, 2023): 49.

▷ Ikle, Fred Charles, *Every War Must End*. NY: Colombia University Press, 1971.

▷ Jackson, Julian, *France on Trial: The Case of Marshal Petain*. Cambridge, MA: Belknap, 2023.

▷ Jacobs, Dov, "A Narrative of Justice and the (Re)Writing of History: Lessons Learned from World War II French Trials," in *The Hidden Histories of War Crimes Trials*, Edited by Kevin Jon Heller and Gerry Simpson (Oxford: Oxford University Press, 2013), 122-36, https://academic.oup.com/book/26719/chapter/195545738.

▷ James, Liam, "Russia claims it has seized Kherson as mayor agrees to conditions to keep city running," *Independent* (March 3, 2022), https://www.independent.co.uk/news/world/europe/russia-ukraine-kherson-take-fall-b2027325.html.

▷ "Japanese Attempts at Indoctrination of Youth in Occupied Areas," Research and Analysis Branch, Office of Strategic Services, Current Intelligence Study no. 3, March 23, 1945.

▷ Jenkins, Shirley, "Philippine White Paper," *Far Eastern Survey* 20, no. 1 (January 10, 1951): 1-6.

▷ Jensen, Karl, and Anthony Funkhouser Microsoft Teams interview with Dr. Russell W. Glenn, February 19, 2024.

▷ Jones, Mared Gwyn, "NATO has upped 'vigilance' amid suspected Russian sabotage operations - Stoltenberg," euronews, May 28,

2024, https://www.euronews.com/my-europe/2024/05/28/nato-has-upped-vigilance-amid-suspected-russian-sabotage-operations-stoltenberg.

▷ Jones, Seth E., "Russia's Ill-Fated Invasion of Ukraine: Lessons in Modern Warfare," Center for Strategic and International Studies briefing, June 1, 2022, https://www.csis.org/analysis/russias-ill-fated-invasion-ukraine-lessons-modern-warfare.

▷ Jose, Ricardo Trota, "July 4, 1946: The Philippines gained Independence from the United States," The National WWII Museum, July 2, 2021, https://www.nationalww2museum.org/war/articles/july-4-1946-philippines-independence.

▷ Judt, Tony, *Postwar: A History of Europe Since 1945*. NY: Penguin, 1945.

▷ Kagan, Frederick, Kateryna Stepanenko, and Karolina Hird, "Russian Offensive Campaign Assessment, April 16," Institute for the Study of War (April 16, 2022), https://www.understandingwar.org/backgrounder/russian-offensive-campaign-assessment-april-16.

▷ Kagan, Frederick W., Kateryna Stepanenko, and Karolina Hird, "Russian Offensive Campaign Assessment, April 23," Institute for the Study of War (April 23, 2022), https://www.understandingwar.org/backgrounder/russian-offensive-campaign-assessment-april-23.

▷ Karacas, Cary Lee, "Tokyo From the Fire: War, Occupation, and the Remaking of a Metropolis." PhD diss., University of California, Berkeley, 2006.

▷ Keeney, L. Douglas, *The Lives They Saved: The Untold Story f Medics, Mariners, and the Incredible Boat Lift that Evacuated Nearly 300,000 People From New York City on 9/11*. Guilford, Connecticut: Lyons Press, 2021.

▷ Kessler, Glenn, "Eighty percent of Ukraine-Israel bill will be spent in US or by US military," *The Washington Post*, April 28, 2024, A4.

▷ "Kherson: How is Russia imposing its rule in occupied Ukraine?" BBC (May 11, 2022), https://www.bbc.com/news/world-61338617.

▷ Khurshudyan, Isabelle, "Russia unleashes attacks on Kharkiv border area," *The Washington Post*, May 12, 2024, A10.

▷ Khurshudyan, Isabelle, and Miriam Berger, "Why Kharkiv, a city known for its poets, has become a key battleground in Ukraine," *The Washington* Post, February 28, 2022, https://www.washingtonpost.com/world/2022/02/28/kharkiv-ukraine-russia-war-east/.

▷ Kinstler, Linda, "Architects Plan a City for the Future in Ukraine, While Bombs Still Fall: Irpin was one of the first Ukrainian cities to be destroyed and liberated. Now it's become a laboratory for rebuilding," *The New York Times,* November 7, 2022, updated November 11, 2022), https://www.nytimes.com/2022/11/07/magazine/ukraine-rebuild-irpin.html.

▷ Kirby, Jen, "What Mariupol's fall means for Russia—and Ukraine," Vox, May 17, 2022, https://www.vox.com/2022/5/17/23037687/mariupol-evacuation-ukraine-russia.

▷ Knutson, Jacob, "About 40% of New York 9/11 victims' remains have yet to be identified," Axios, September 11, 2023, https://www.axios.com/2023/09/11/9-11-victims-remains-identification.

▷ Konoplia, Olena, "What Life is Like in the De-Occupied Territories of Ukraine," *Ukraine World* (blog) December 26, 2022, https://ukraineworld.org/en/articles/analysis/de-occupied.

▷ Kortava, David, "In the Filtration Camps," *The New Yorker* (October 3, 2022), https://www.newyorker.com/magazine/2022/10/10/inside-russias-filtration-camps-in-eastern-ukraine.

▷ Kosse, Iryna, "Rebuilding Ukraine's Infrastructure after the War," Vienna Institute for International Economic Studies Policy Notes and Reports 72, July 2023.

▷ Kossov, Igor, "Pro-Russian sympathies make life harder for soldiers, cops in Kupiansk district," *The Kyiv Independent*, August 15, 2023, https://kyivindependent.com/pro-russian-sympathies-make-life-harder-for-soldiers-cops-in-kupiansk-district/.

▷ Kottasová, Ivana, Olga Voitovych, and Svitlana Vlasova, "Russia's war machine is trying to turn Ukrainian teenagers into soldiers," *CNN World* (March 15, 2024), https://www.cnn.com/2024/03/14/europe/ukrainian-teenagers-russian-soldiers-cmd-intl/index.html.

▷ Kozlova, Kateryna, "A Facelift Worth Billions: Urbanist on Why Post-war Restoration of Sarajevo Only Made It Worse," *Bird in Flight*, June, 17 2022, https://birdinflight.com/en/architectura-2/20220617-sarajevo-after-war.html.

▷ Kozlova, Kateryna, "Please, Don't Stop: How Berlin Started the Reconstruction and Has Never Finished," *Bird in Flight* (December 26, 2022), https://birdinflight.com/en/architectura-2/20221226-postwar-berlin.html.

- Kramer, Erik C., telephonic interview with Dr. Russell W. Glenn, February 16, 2024.
- Krasikov, Ivan, "Crimean Canal Key to its Liberation," Institute for War & Peace Reporting, December 1, 2022, https://iwpr.net/global-voices/crimean-canal-key-its-liberation.
- Kravchenko, Volodymyr, "Borderland City: Kharkiv," *East/West Journal of Ukrainian Studies* 8, no. 1 (2020), DOI: https://doi.org/10.21226/ewjus572.
- Kravchenko, Volodymyr, *Kharkov/Kharkiv: a borderland capital*. NY: Berghahn Books, 2023.
- Kyiv International Institute of Sociology, *A Study of Recovery Initiatives in Ukraine*, June 2023.
- Kyiv School of Economics, "The total amount of damage caused to the infrastructure of Ukraine due to the war reaches $151.2 billion — estimate as of September 1, 2023," October 3, 2023, https://kse.ua/about-the-school/news/the-total-amount-of-damage-caused-to-the-infrastructure-of-ukraine-due-to-the-war-reaches-151-2-billion-estimate-as-of-september-1-2023/.
- Labrador, Juan, *A Diary of the Japanese Occupation*. Manila: Santo Tomas University Press, 1989.
- Ladd, Brian "Double Restoration: Rebuilding Berlin after 1945," in *The Resilient City: How Modern Cities Recover from Disaster*. Edited by Lawrence J. Vale and Thomas J. Campanella. (Oxford: Oxford University Press, 2005).
- Landler, Mark, "Allies Pledge Billions for Ukraine's Recovery as Zelensky Stresses Urgency," *The New York Times* (June 21, 2023), https://www.nytimes.com/2023/06/21/world/europe/ukraine-war-recovery.html.
- Lane, Patrick, "A grim day in Russian-occupied Ukraine," The World in Brief, *The Economist* (July 1, 2024), https://espresso.economist.com/706cc8c89430090439d0e3ea6118a8ed.
- Langewiesche, William, *American Ground: Unbuilding the World Trade Center*. NY: North Point Press, 2002.
- "Language Data for Ukraine," Translators without Borders/CLEAR Global Source, map created March 2022 with Datawrapper using 2001 Ukraine census data, https://clearglobal.org/language-data-for-ukraine/.
- "Largest earthquakes in Ukraine on record since 1900—list, stats and map," Volcano Discovery, April 25, 2024, https://www.volcanodiscovery.com/earthquakes/ukraine/largest.html.

- "Lawrence Summers, Philip Zelikow and Robert Zoellick on why Russian reserves should be used to help Ukraine," *The Economist* (July 27, 2023), https://www.economist.com/by-invitation/2023/07/27/lawrence-summers-philip-zelikow-and-robert-zoellick-on-why-russian-reserves-should-be-used-to-help-ukraine.
- "Lessons in Asian resilience," *The Economist* 447, no. 9350 (June 10, 2023): 34.
- Lewis, David, "Life in occupied Ukraine," interview by Scott Detrow, NPR (January 21, 2024), https://www.npr.org/transcripts/1225969992.
- Lewis, Rebecca, *Does the Law Really Matter?: The Role of the Law of Armed Conflict in Contemporary Air Operations* (Canberra: Air Power Development Centre, 2005), 15, https://airpower.airforce.gov.au/sites/default/files/2021-03/FELL29-Does-the-Law-Really-Matter_-The-Role-of-the-Law-of-Armed-Conflict-in-Contemporary-Air-Operations.pdf.
- Lifton, Robert Jay, *Surviving Our Catastrophes: Resilience and Renewal from Hiroshima to the Covid-19 Pandemic*. NY: The New Press, 2023.
- Lippman, Peter, *Surviving the Peace: The Struggle for Postwar Recovery in Bosnia-Herzegovina*. Nashville, TN: Vanderbilt University Press, 2019.
- Ljungkvist, Kristin, "A New Horizon in Urban Warfare in Ukraine?", *Scandinavian Journal of Military Studies* 5, no. 1 (2022): 91—98, https://sjms.nu/articles/10.31374/sjms.165.
- Lodhammar, Pehr, "How Iraq is Changing What We Do: Measuring Clearance in Urban Environments," *The Journal of Conventional Weapons Destruction* 22, no. 2 (August 2018): 30-39.
- Lodhammar, Pehr (former Chief Mine Action Programme Iraq, UN Mine Action Service), interview with Dr. Russell W. Glenn, February 16, 2024.
- Lukiv, Jaroslav, "Germany plans to halve military aid for Ukraine," BBC (July 18, 2024), https://www.bbc.com/news/articles.
- "Lviv: A city embraces innovation, even amidst war," *United Nations Development Programme*, January 18, 2023, https://stories.undp.org/lviv-a-city-embraces-innovation-even-amidst-war.
- "Lviv mayor calls for every Ukrainian region and city to have an EU partner," European Committee of the Regions, October 17, 2023, https://cor.europa.eu/en/news/Pages/WGU-Lviv.aspx.

- MacArthur, Douglas, *Reminiscences*. NY: Crest, 1965.
- MacDonough, Giles, *After the Reich: From the Liberation of Vienna to the Berlin Airlift*. London: John Murray, 2007.
- MacKenzie, Lewis, *Peacekeeper: The Road to Sarajevo*. Toronto: HarperCollins, 1994.
- Malig, Kaela, "'20 Days in Mariupol' Filmmaker on What is Left of the City After the Russian Invasion," Frontline on PBS, November 21, 2023, https://www.pbs.org/wgbh/frontline/article/20-days-in-mariupol-filmmaker-q-and-a/.
- Malo, Sabastien, "The Green Dream to Rebuild a Sustainable Ukraine from the Rubble of War," *Politico* (September 11, 2022), https://www.politico.com/news/magazine/2022/09/11/ukraine-russia-sustainability-00054910.
- Maloletka, Evgeniy, "Upward of 20,000 Ukrainian amputees face trauma on a scale unseen since WWI," Independent (September 4, 2023), https://www.independent.co.uk/news/ap-lviv-europe-rehabilitation-united-states-b2404307.html.
- Martynovych, Nataly, Elina Boichenko, and Maryna Dielini, "Rebuilding of Ukraine After War: Special Restoration Regimes and Stimulation of Sustainable Development of Territories," *International review for spatial planning a sustainable development A: Planning Strategies and Design Concepts*, 11, no. 4 (2023): 54-70, DOI: https://www.jstage.jst.go.jp/article/irspsd/11/4/11_4/_article.
- Mascall, Ben, "Palantir and Ministry of Economy of Ukraine Sign Demining Partnership," April 3, 2024, Palantir [Investor Relations], https://investors.palantir.com/news-details/2024/Palantir-and-Ministry-of-Economy-of-Ukraine-Sign-Demining-Partnership/.
- Masters, Jonathan, "Ukraine: Conflict at the Crossroads of Europe and Russia," Council on Foreign Relations backgrounder, February 14, 2023, https://www.cfr.org/backgrounder/ukraine-conflict-crossroads-europe-and-russia.
- Matthews, Gary (Deputy High Representative, Supervisor for Brcko), "Supervisory Order on the Use of Land in Arizona Market, Office of the High Representative," February 17, 2001, https://www.ohr.int/ohr_archive/supervisory-order-on-the-use-of-land-in-arizona-market-2/?print=pdf.

▷ McCouat, Philip, "Bernardo Bellotto and the Reconstruction of Warsaw," *Journal of Art in Society* (2015), https://www.artinsociety.com/bernardo-bellotto-and-the-reconstruction-of-warsaw.html.

▷ McKay, Sinclair, *Berlin: Life and Loss in the City That Shaped the Century*. London: Viking, 2022.

▷ McMahon, David (Head of Mine Action Project Unit, Peace and Security Cluster, UNOPS Ukraine), interview with Dr. Russell W. Glenn, May 6, 2024.

▷ Medby, Jamison, email to Dr. Russell W. Glenn, Subject: Working weekends, December 25, 2023.

▷ *Médecins Sans Frontières*, "Kunduz Hospital Attack: On 3 October 2015, US airstrikes destroyed our trauma hospital in Kunduz, Afghanistan, killing 42," undated, https://www.msf.org/kunduz-hospital-attack-depth.

▷ Mefford, Brian, "Death of Kharkiv Major Kernes marks end of era," Atlantic Council, December 22, 2020, https://www.atlanticcouncil.org/blogs/ukrainealert/death-of-kharkiv-mayor-kernes-marks-end-of-era/.

▷ Méheut, Constant, "More Drones, Fewer Parks. Ukrainians Urge Spending Shift as War Drags On," *The New York Times,* December 22, 2023), https://www.nytimes.com/2023/12/22/world/europe/ukraine-spending-war-russia.html.

▷ Melvin, Mungo Melvin, *Sevastopol's Wars: Crimea from Potemkin to Putin*. London: Osprey, 2017.

▷ Mezentsev, Kostyantyn and Oleksii Mezentsev, "War and the city: Lessons from urbicide in Ukraine," *Czasopismo Geograficzne* 93, no. 3 (2022): 495—521, https://doi.org/10.12657/czageo-93-20.

▷ Mills, Claire, Philip Brien, and Patrick Butchard, "Post-conflict reconstruction assistance to Ukraine," House of Commons Library research briefing no. 9728, June 15, 2023.

▷ Milton, Giles, *Checkmate in Berlin: The Cold War Showdown that Shaped the Modern World*. NY: Henry Holt, 2021.

▷ Monnery, Neil, *Architect of Prosperity: Sir John Cowperthwaite and the Making of Hong Kong*. London: London Publishing Partnership, 2017.

▷ Moore, Adam, "Localizing Peacebuilding: The Arizona Market and the Evolution of US Military Peacebuilding Priorities in Bosnia," *Journal of Intervention and Statebuilding* (July 2019), 1-18, https://www.tandfonline.com/doi/abs/10.1080/17502977.2019.1610991.

▷ Moorhouse, Roger, *Berlin at War*. NY: Basic Books, 2012.

▷ Müller, Jan-Werner, *Another Country: German Intellectuals, Unification and National Identity*. New Haven: Yale University Press, 2000.

▷ "Multi-agency Donor Coordination Platform for Ukraine," 2024, https://coordinationplatformukraine.com/.

▷ Murphy, Dean E., "Bosnian Swap Meet May Be a Peace Model," *Los Angeles Times* (September 22, 1996).

▷ Murrow, Edward R., *This is London*. NY: Schocken, 1989.

▷ The National Council for the Recovery of Ukraine from the Consequences of the War, Draft Ukraine Recovery Plan: Materials of the "Construction, urban planning, modernization of cities and regions" working group (July 2022), 1, https://www.kmu.gov.ua/storage/app/sites/1/recoveryrada/eng/construction-urban-planning-modernization-of-cities-and-regions-eng.pdf.

▷ National Recovery Council, "Ukraine National Recovery Plan" (July 2022), https://www.urc-international.com/urc2022-recovery-plan.

▷ "A new Marshall Plan?: Donors already wondering how to help Ukraine rebuild," *The Economist* 445 (November 12, 2022), 54-56, https://www.economist.com/international/2022/11/08/donors-are-already-mulling-a-marshall-plan-for-ukraine.

▷ Niksic, Sabina, "Top European court says that Bosnian minorities are treated like 'second-class citizens,'" Associated Press, August 29, 2023, https://apnews.com/article/bosnia-court-ethnic-elections-serbs-croats-dayton-f98eb45e5230a40fe0e4524311ff8e99.

▷ Niland, Paul, "Putin's Mariupol Massacre is one of the 21st century's worst war crimes," Atlantic Council Ukraine Alert (May 24, 2022), https://www.atlanticcouncil.org/blogs/ukrainealert/putins-mariupol-massacre-is-one-the-worst-war-crimes-of-the-21st-century/.

▷ Norman Foster Foundation, undated, https://normanfosterfoundation.org.

▷ Normandin, Henri-Paul, "Ukraine Recovery and Reconstruction: Cities Must Be Part of It," German Marshall Fund (November 14, 2022), https://www.gmfus.org/news/ukraine-recovery-and-reconstruction-cities-must-be-part-it.

▷ "Not Your Grandfather's Mining Industry," Mining Association of Nova Scotia, undated, https://notyourgrandfathersmining.ca/the-hydrostones.

BIBLIOGRAPHY

▷ "#112—A Guide to Fire Department Connection (FDC) Sizes and Threading," Quick Response Fire Supply, June 12, 2018, https://blog.qrfs.com/112-a-guide-to-fire-department-connection-fdc-sizes-and-threading/.

▷ "Number of civilian casualties in Ukraine during Russia's invasion verified by OHCHR from February 24, 2022 to February 15, 2024," Statista Research Department, February 23, 2024, https://www.statista.com/statistics/1293492/ukraine-war-casualties.

▷ Odhiambo, W.A., S.W. Guthua, F.G. Macigo, and M.K. Akama, "Maxillofacial injuries caused by terrorist bomb attack in Nairobi, Kenya," *International Journal of Oral and Maxillofacial Surgery* 31, no. 4 (August 2002): 374-377, available at https://www.sciencedirect.com/science/article/abs/pii/S0901502701901997.

▷ OECD, "The architecture of infrastructure in Ukraine," OECD Policy Responses on the Impacts of the War in Ukraine (July 1, 2022), https://www.oecd-ilibrary.org/governance/the-architecture-of-infrastructure-recovery-in-ukraine_d768a2e4-en.

▷ Office of the Chief Historian, *The First Year of the Occupation: Part One—The Transition from Combat to Military Occupation (8 May—17 July 1945)*, Occupation Forces in Europe Series, 1945-46, Frankfurt-am-Main: Headquarters European Command, United States Army, 1947.

▷ Office of the Chief Historian, *The Second Year of Occupation: Volume III*, Occupation Forces in Europe Series, 1946-47, Frankfurt-am-Main: Headquarters European Command, 1947.

▷ Office of the High Representative, "Brcko Final Award Office," 2015, https://www.ohr.int/ohr_archive_taxonomy/brcko-final-award-office/page/11/.

▷ Office of the High Representative, "Supervisory Order on Arizona Market," November 16, 2000, https://www.ohr.int/ohr_archive/supervisory-order-on-arizona-market.

▷ Office of the Historian, "The Breakup of Yugoslavia, 1990-1992," Foreign Service Institute, US Department of State, undated, https://history.state.gov/milestones/1989-1992/breakup-yugoslavia.

▷ Office of the United Nations High Commissioner for Refugees (UNHCR), "Ukraine Emergency," 2023, https://www.unrefugees.org/emergencies/ukraine/.

▷ O'Hern, Steven K., *The Intelligence Wars: Lessons from Baghdad*. Amherst. NY: Prometheus Books, 2008.

- Ohno, Kenichi, *The History of Japanese Economic Development: Origins of Private Dynamism and Policy Competence*. Milton Park, UK: Routledge, 2018.
- Ong, Susy, "Post-World War II Education Reform in Japan," *Journal of Strategic and Global Studies* 2, no.2 (July 2019): 85-97.
- Onyshchenko, Viktoriia, "Ready, Set, Go: Decolonization! How New Law Changes Public Spaces of Ukraine," Transparency International-Ukraine (July 27, 2023), https://ti-ukraine.org/en/blogs/ready-set-go-decolonization-how-new-law-changes-public-spaces-of-ukraine/.
- Orlean, Susan, *The Library Book*. NY: Simon & Schuster, 2018.
- Osteria, Tristan Miguel Santos, "Building from Within: Indigenous Nation-building and State-making During the Filipino Third Republic, 1946-1957," PhD diss., Texas A&M University, December 2016.
- Owen, David, *Balkan Odyssey*. NY: Harcourt, Brace & Company, 1995.
- Pach, Chester J., *Arming the Free World: The Origins of the United States Military Assistance Program, 1945-1950*. Chapel Hill, NC: University of North Carolina Press, 1991.
- Pancevski, Bojan, "Russian Saboteurs Behind Arson Attack at German Factory," *The Wall Street Journal*, June 23, 2024, https://www.wsj.com/world/europe/russian-saboteurs-behind-arson-attackat-german-factory-c13b4ece.
- Parker, Simon, *Assembled in Japan: Electrical Goods and the Making of the Japanese Consumer*. Berkeley: University of California Press, 1999.
- Pastukh, Marta, Mathias Merforth, Viktor Zabreba, and Armin Wagner, "Anchoring green recovery of urban mobility in Ukraine: Eight building blocks," Transformative Urban Mobility Initiative (TUMI) (October 20, 2022), https://transformative-mobility.org/anchoring-green-recovery-of-urban-mobility-in-ukraine-eight-building-blocks/.
- "The Path to Recovery: How Regions Surviving Russian Occupation are Rebuilding," *Forbes* (December 21, 2023), https://forbes.ua/ru/brandvoice/krok-za-krokom-yak-uzhe-zaraz-tri-vae-vidnovlennya-regioniv-shcho-perezhili-rosiysku-okupatsiyu-21122023-17873.
- Pfeifer, Joseph, *Ordinary Heroes: A Memoir of 9/11*. NY: Portfolio, 2021.

- Picheta, Rob, "Putin should face war crimes probe over 'devastating' assault on Mariupol, HRW report finds," CNN, February 8, 2024, https://www.cnn.com/2024/02/08/europe/mariupol-hrw-report-putin-russia-ukraine-intl/index.html.
- Piplas, Haris, *Non-Aligned City: Urban laboratory of the new Sarajevo*, PhD diss., University of Sarajevo, undated.
- Plapinger, Sam, "Urban Combat Is Changing. The Ukraine War Shows How Four attributes distinguish today's city battles from those that have come before.," *Defense One* (February 3, 2023), https://www.defenseone.com/ideas/2023/02/ukraine-war-shows-how-urban-combat-changing/382561/.
- Polman, Linda, *The Crisis Caravan: What's Wrong with Humanitarian Aid?* NY: Metropolitan Books, 2010.
- "POM-3 Landmine," Collective Awareness to unexploded ordnance, 2024, https://cat-uxo.com/explosive-hazards/landmines/pom-3-landmine.
- "POM-3 (Medallion) Russian Anti-Personnel Mine," US Army Training and Doctrine Command Operational Environment Data Integration Network, undated, https://odin.tradoc.army.mil/WEG/Asset/POM-3_(Medallion)_Russian_Anti-Personnel_Mine.
- Popowycz, Jennifer, "The Allied Responses to the Warsaw Uprising of 1944," (January 18, 2022), https://www.nationalww2museum.org/war/articles/allied-responses-warsaw-uprising-1944.
- "The Prague Charter: Recommendations for Post-war Urban Renewal of Ukraine," Conference on Architecture and Building Culture Policies 2022 summary, March 2023.
- Price, Willard, *Where are you going, Japan?* London: Willian Heinemann, 1938.
- Pritzker, Penny, US Special Representative for Ukraine's Economic Recovery, Remarks to the Chicago Council on Global Affairs, Chicago, Illinois, February 14, 2024, https://www.state.gov/special-representative-pritzkers-remarks-on-ukraines-economic-recovery/.
- "Prospecting for hope: Bosnia," *The Economist* 449, no. 9375 (December 9, 2023): 47. The article appears online as "A mining project revives a dying Bosnian town," https://www.economist.com/europe/2023/12/07/a-mining-project-revives-a-dying-bosnian-town.
- "The race to save Kharkiv," *The Economist* 451, no. 9392 (April 13, 2024): 40-41.

- "Racing against time: Ukraine's electricity supply," *The Economist* 452, No. 9406 (July 20, 2024): 38-39.
- Radio Free Europe/Radio Liberty Ukrainian Service, "Red Cross: Mayor Of Ukrainian City Of Kherson Is In Russian Custody," September 18, 2023, https://www.rferl.org/a/ukraine-kherson-mayor-red-cross-russia-custody/32597782.html.
- Rebuild Ukraine, "Irpin: Digitization of Destroyed Infrastructure (Kyiv region)," undated, 6-7, https://eng.rebuildua.net/irpin.
- *Rebuilding Ukraine by Reinforcing Regional and Municipal Governance*, OECD Multi-level Governance Studies (Paris: OECD Publishing, 2022), DOI: https://doi.org/10.1787/63a6b479-en.
- "Recommendation on the Historic Urban Landscape," United Nations Educational, Scientific, and Cultural Organization, November 10, 2011.
- Reliefweb, "In Ukraine, recovery can't wait: Clearing landmines and rubble makes it safer for displaced families to come home," July 1, 2022, https://reliefweb.int/report/ukraine/ukraine-recovery-cant-wait-clearing-landmines-and-rubble-makes-it-safer-displaced-families-come-home.
- Reliefweb, "The path to recovery: rebuilding hope in Kharkiv," United Nations Office for Project Services press release, December 19, 2023, https://reliefweb.int/report/ukraine/path-recovery-rebuilding-hope-kharkiv.
- RFE/Rl's Crimea Realities, "Ukraine Allows Russia-Related Words to be Written in All Lowercase," Radio Free Europe, September 22, 2023, https://www.rferl.org/a/ukraine-lowercase-russia-related-words-language/32604577.html.
- Robinson, Adam, Erwan Rivault, and Olga Robinson, "The Russians hunting for cheap flats in occupied Mariupol," BBC, August 5, 2023, https://www.bbc.com/news/world-66393949.
- Roblin, Sebastien, "Ukraine says it captured documents revealing that an elite Russian unit lost over 130 tanks in failed attacks on Kharkiv," *Business Insider* (May 20, 2022), https://www.businessinsider.com/captured-documents-say-elite-russian-unit-lost-tanks-kharkiv-ukraine-2022-5.
- Rogoza, Jadwiga, "Ukraine in the face of a demographic catastrophe," Centre for Eastern Studies, July 11, 2023, https://www.osw.waw.pl/en/publikacje/osw-commentary/2023-07-11/ukraine-face-a-demographic-catastrophe.

BIBLIOGRAPHY

▷ Romanova, Valentyna, "Ukraine's resilience to Russia's military invasion in the context of the decentralization reform," ResearchGate (May 2022), DOI: https://www.researchgate.net/publication/360447277_Ukraine's_resilience_to_Russia's_military_invasion_in_the_context_of_the_decentralisation_reform.

▷ Rott, Nathan, Claire Harbage, and Hanna Palamarenko, "As Ukraine seeks to replenish its depleted army, a divide grows among its civilians," NPR (January 31, 2024), https://www.npr.org/2024/01/31/1226251649/ukraine-russia-war-conscription-military.

▷ Roxas, Manuel, "Message of His Excellency Manuel Roxas President of the Philippines Asking the Concurrence of Congress to the Amnesty Proclamation," Government of the Philippines, January 29, 1948, https://www.officialgazette.gov.ph/1948/01/29/message-of-president-roxas-asking-the-concurrence-of-congress-to-the-amnesty-proclamation/.

▷ Ruffner, Kevin Conley, "The Black Market in Postwar Berlin: Colonel Miller and an Army Scandal," *Prologue Magazine* 34, no.3 (Fall 2002), https://www.archives.gov/publications/prologue/2002/fall/berlin-black-market-1.html.

▷ Russell, Alec, "The second battle for Kharkiv: Ukrainian city goes underground to defy Russian missiles," *Financial Times* (October 19, 2023), https://www.ft.com/content/c1719b5c-c30f-4415-a2dd-dc0b4025886b.

▷ "Russia hands out passports in occupied Ukraine cities," BBC (June 11, 2022), https://www.bbc.com/news/world-europe-61770997.

▷ "Russia is poised to take advantage of political splits in Ukraine," *The Economist* 449 no. 9374 (December 2, 2023): 43-44. https://www.economist.com/europe/2023/11/28/russia-is-poised-to-take-advantage-of-political-splits-in-ukraine.

▷ "Russian site recruits 'volunteers' for Ukraine," *BBC News* (March 5, 2014), https://www.bbc.com/news/blogs-trending-26435333.

▷ "Russians are mining the territory of Ukraine with POM-3 "Medallion" landmines," Militarnyi, March 30, 2022, https://mil.in.ua/en/news/russians-are-mining-the-territory-of-ukraine-with-pom-3-medallion-landmines/.

▷ "Russia's Filtration Operations and Forced Relocations," US Department of State, undated, https://www.state.gov/russias-filtration-operations-and-forced-relocations/.

▷ "Russia's FSB Raids Jehovah's Witness Office in Occupied Mariupol," *The Moscow Times* (Jan. 15, 2024), https://www.themoscowtimes.

com/2024/01/15/russias-fsb-raids-jehovahs-witness-office-in-occupied-mariupol-a83726.

▷ "Russia's war on Ukraine's libraries," *Labour Hub* (December 21, 2023), https://labourhub.org.uk/2023/12/21/russias-war-on-ukraines-libraries/.

▷ Sacquety, Troy, "Gen. Lucius D. Clay, a 'brilliant administrator'," United States Army Special Operations Command, January 11, 2019, https://www.army.mil/article/216006/gen_lucius_d_clay_a_brilliant_administrator.

▷ Santora, Marc, "Moscow says babies born in occupied Kherson will automatically get Russian citizenship," *The New York Times,* July 11, 2022), https://www.nytimes.com/2022/06/16/world/europe/ukraine-kherson-babies-russian-citizenship.html.

▷ Santora, Marc, Matthew Mpoke Bigg, and Ivan Nechpurenko, "Brace for Bombs, Fix and Repeat: Ukraine's Grim Efforts to Restore Power," *The New York Times,* December 1, 2022), https://www.nytimes.com/2022/12/01/world/europe/russia-ukraine-war-infrastructure.html.

▷ Schein, Ernest, "War Damage Compensation Through Rehabilitation: The Philippine War Damage Commission," *Law and Contemporary Problems* 16 (1951): 519-542.

▷ Schlitz, Heather, "Customs officials in Philadelphia seize $6.5 million in fake money from Russia," *Business Insider* (October 1, 2021), https://www.businessinsider.com/65-million-fake-counterfeit-money-russia-philadelphia-chicago-2021-10.

▷ Scott, Bruce R., *Capitalism: Its Origins and Evolution as a System of Governance.* NY: Springer, 2011.

▷ Scott, Bruce R., and Edward N. Murphy, "Brcko and the Arizona Market," Harvard Business School paper 9-905-411 (August 14, 2006).

▷ Scott, James M., *Rampage: MacArthur, Yamashita, and the Battle of Manila.* NY: W.W. Norton, 2018.

▷ Sebald, William J., and Russell Brines, *With MacArthur in Japan: A Personal History of the Occupation.* NY: W.W. Norton, 1965.

▷ Seck, Momar D., and David D. Evans, "Major US Cities Using National Standard Fire Hydrants, One Century After the Great Baltimore Fire," Fire Research Division, Building and Fire Research Laboratory, United States Department of Commerce National Institute of Standards and Technology (Gaithersburg, Maryland,

August 2004), https://tsapps.nist.gov/publication/get_pdf.cfm?-pub_id=101300.

▷ Sharpe, George, *Brothers in Blood: A Battalion Surgeon in the South Pacific*. Austin, Texas: Diamond Books, 1989.

▷ Shevchenko, Vitaly, "Ukraine war: Life in Mariupol under Russian occupation," BBC, March 12, 2023, https://www.bbc.com/news/world-europe-64887890.

▷ Slaveski, Filip, *The Soviet Occupation of Germany: Hunger, Mass Violence, and the Struggle for Peace, 1945-1947*. Cambridge, UK: Cambridge University Press, 2013.

▷ "Smoking: An Endemic Problem in Bosnia and Herzegovina," World Bank Group, November 20, 2012, https://www.worldbank.org/en/news/feature/2012/11/20/smoking-an-endemic-problem-in-bosnia-and-herzegovina.

▷ Soguel, Dominique, "As corruption costs lives on the battlefield, Ukrainians demand change," *The Christian Science Monitor* (October 25, 2023), https://www.csmonitor.com/World/Europe/2023/1025/As-corruption-costs-lives-on-battlefield-Ukrainians-demand-change.

▷ Southard, Susan, *Nagasaki: Life After Nuclear War*, NY: Viking, 2015.

▷ "The Spoils of War," *The Economist* (June 22, 2024): 38.

▷ Sredl, Katherine C., Clifford J. Shultz, II, and Ružica Brečić, "The Arizona Market: a Marketing Systems Perspective on Pre- and Post-War Developments in Bosnia, with Implications for Sustainable Peace and Prosperity," *Journal of Macromarketing* 37, no. 3 (2017): 300-316, https://ecommons.luc.edu/business_facpubs/219/.

▷ State of Berlin, "Berlin in Brief: Berlin after 1945," (online article, undated), https://www.berlin.de/en/history/8481782-8619314-berlin-after-1945.en.html.

▷ Statistics Times, "Population of Cities in Ukraine," September 9, 2021, https://statisticstimes.com/demographics/country/ukraine-cities-population.php.

▷ Steege, Paul, *Black Market, Cold War: Everyday Life in Berlin, 1945-1949*. Cambridge: Cambridge University Press, 2007.

▷ Stein, Jeff, "US, allies move to tap interest on frozen Russian assets to aid Ukraine," *The Washington Post*, May 26, 2024, A21.

▷ Steinberg, David Joel, *Philippine Collaboration in World War II*. Ann Arbor, MI: University of Michigan Press, 1967.

- Stepanenko, Kateryna, and Frederick W. Kagan, "Russian Offensive Campaign Assessment, May 13," Institute for the Study of War (May 13, 2022), https://www.understandingwar.org/backgrounder/russian-offensive-campaign-assessment-may-13.
- Stepanenko, Kateryna, and Karolina Hird, "Russian Offensive Campaign Assessment, May 18," Institute for the Study of Warfare (May 18, 2022), https://understandingwar.org/backgrounder/russian-offensive-campaign-assessment-may-18.
- Stepanenko, Kateryna, Karolina Hird, and Frederick W. Kagan, "Russian Offensive Campaign Assessment, May 12," Institute for the Study of War (May 12, 2022), https://www.understandingwar.org/backgrounder/russian-offensive-campaign-assessment-may-12.
- Stepanenko, Kateryna, Karolina Hird, Mason Clark, and George Barros, "Russian Offensive Campaign Assessment, May 23," Institute for the Study of Warfare (May 23, 2022), https://www.understandingwar.org/backgrounder/russian-offensive-campaign-assessment-may-23.
- Stepanenko, Kateryna, Riley Bailey, Grace Mappes, Yekaterina Klepanchuk, and Frederick W. Kagan, "Russian Offensive Campaign Assessment, November 3," Institute for the Study of War, November 3, 2022, https://www.understandingwar.org/backgrounder/russian-offensive-campaign-assessment-november-3.
- Stern, David L., "Heavy destruction of energy network leaves Ukraine fearing winter," *The Washington Post*, May 19, 2024, A16.
- Stern, David L., "Russia destroyed Ukraine's power sector: so it's being rebuilt eco-friendly," *The Washington Post*, July 7, 2024, A16.
- Stivers, William, and Donald A. Carter, *The City Becomes a Symbol: The US Army in the Occupation of Berlin, 1945-1949*. Washington, DC: Center of Military History, 2017.
- Stronger Cities Consortium, "Urban area-based approaches in post-disaster contexts: Guidance Note for Humanitarian Practitioners" (undated), https://www.humanitarianlibrary.org/resource/urban-area-based-approaches-post-disaster-contexts.
- "Supporting Ukraine: A Study on Potential Recovery Strategies for Ukraine," Boston Consulting Group, January 2023.
- Synnott, Hilary, *Bad Days in Basra: My Turbulent Time as Britain's Man in Southern Iraq*. NY: I.B. Tauris, 2008.
- Tabeau, Ewa, Jakub Bijak, and Neda Loncaric, "Death Toll in the Siege of Sarajevo, April 1992 to December 1995: A Study of Mortality

Based on Eight Large Data Sources," Demographic Unit, Office of the Prosecution, International Criminal Tribunal for the Former Yugoslavia, August 18, 2003.

▷ Tabeau, Ewa, Marcin Żółtkowski, and Jakub Bijak, "Population Losses in the 'Siege' of Sarajevo, 10 September 1992 to 10 August 1994," Demographic Unit - LRT research report, May 10, 2002, https://www.icty.org/x/file/About/OTP/War_Demographics/en/galic_sarajevo_020510.pdf.

▷ "A Tale of Five Cities," *The Economist* 449, no. 9377 (December 23, 2023): 11-13 (of the "Holiday specials" section).

▷ Taylor, Adam, Anastacia Galouchka, and Kostiantyn Khudov, "Ukraine dreams of rebuilding but Russian destruction continues," *The Washington Post*, June 21, 2023, https://www.washingtonpost.com/world/2023/06/21/ukraine-recovery-reconstruction-economy-kharkiv/.

▷ Taylor, Harry, and Emily Dugan, "Heavy shelling reported in Kharkiv region after overnight attacks in Kherson—as it happened," *The Guardian* (April 30, 2023), https://www.theguardian.com/world/live/2023/apr/30/russia-ukraine-war-live-russian-soldiers-likely-placed-in-holes-in-the-ground-for-misdemeanours-says-uk.

▷ Thakur, Yoko H., "History Textbook Reform in Allied Occupied Japan, 1945-52," *History of Education Quarterly* 35, no. 3 (Autumn 1995): 261-278.

▷ "Timeline: Key developments in Ukraine's Kherson since invasion," *Aljazeera* (November 9, 2022), https://www.aljazeera.com/news/2022/11/9/timeline-key-developments-in-ukraines-kherson-since-invasion.

▷ "To endure a long war, Ukraine is remaking its army, economy and society," *The Economist* 448, no. 9364 (September 23, 2023): 20, https://www.economist.com/briefing/2023/09/21/to-endure-a-long-war-ukraine-is-remaking-its-army-economy-and-society.

▷ "Tokyo 'Black Markets, 1945," Old Japan website (undated), https://www.oldtokyo.com/tokyo-black-market-1945/.

▷ Trofimov, Yaroslav, *Our Enemies will Vanish: The Russian Invasion and Ukraine's War of Independence*. NY: Penguin, 2024.

▷ Turner, Barry, *The Berlin Airlift: The Relief Operation that Defined the Cold War*. London: Icon, 2017.

- Udovyk, Oksana, Ievgen Kylymnyk, Daniel Cuesta-Delgado, and Guillermo Palau Salvador, "Making Sense of Multi-Level and Multi-actor Governance of Recovery in Ukraine," United National University world Institute for Development Economics Research, (June 2023), https://www.wider.unu.edu/publication/making-sense-multi-level-and-multi-actor-governance-recovery-ukraine.
- "Ukraine," The World Factbook, US Central Intelligence Agency, February 6, 2024, https://www.cia.gov/the-world-factbook/countries/ukraine/.
- "Ukraine: Cluster Munitions Launched Into Kharkiv Neighborhoods: Russian Forces' Indiscriminate Attacks May Amount to War Crimes," *Human Rights Watch* (March 4, 2022), https://www.hrw.org/news/2022/03/04/ukraine-cluster-munitions-launched-kharkiv-neighborhoods.
- "Ukraine: New Laws Criminalize Collaboration with an Aggressor State," Library of Congress, April 4, 2022, https://www.loc.gov/item/global-legal-monitor/2022-04-04/ukraine-new-laws-criminalize-collaboration-with-an-aggressor-state.
- "Ukraine: Russians Pillage Kherson Cultural Institutions: Art and Artifacts Stolen," *Human Rights Watch*, December 20, 2022, https://www.hrw.org/news/2022/12/20/ukraine-russians-pillage-kherson-cultural-institutions.
- "Ukraine says 300,000 people are running out of food in occupied Kherson," Reuters (March 22, 2022), https://www.reuters.com/world/europe/ukraine-says-300000-people-are-running-out-food-occupied-kherson-2022-03-22/.
- "Ukraine Situation Flash Update #67," United Nations Humanitarian Commission for Refugees Regional Bureau of Europe, March 25, 2024, 1, https://reliefweb.int/report/ukraine/ukraine-situation-flash-update-67-25-march-2024.
- UkraineTrek, "Kherson city, Ukraine," November 8, 2023, https://ukrainetrek.com/kherson-city.
- "Ukraine's energy: The battle against General Winter," *The Economist* 449, no. 9366 (October 7, 2023): 45.
- "UN4Kharkiv: Integrated Rehabilitation of Settlements (Territories) in Ukraine with a pilot project in the city of Kharkiv," United Nations Economic Committee for Europe Housing and Land Management, undated, https://unece.org/housing/un4kharkiv-rehabilitation.

▷ "UNESCO Recommendation on the Historic Urban Landscape," United Nations Educational, Scientific, and Cultural Organization, 2024, https://whc.unesco.org/en/hul.

▷ UNESCO World Heritage Convention, 2024, https://whc.unesco.org/en/statesparties/ua.

▷ United Nations Habitat, "Scoping Mission to Ukraine" (October 2-14, 2022), https://unhabitat.org/sites/default/files/2022/11/ukraine_mission_report_oct22_public.pdf.

▷ United States Philippine War Damage Commission, *First Semiannual Report For Period Ending December 31, 1946.* Washington, DC: United States Government Printing Office, 1947.

▷ United States Philippine War Damage Commission, *Seventh Semiannual Report of the United States Philippine War Damage Commission For Period Ending December 31, 1949.* Washington, DC: United States Government Printing Office, 1950.

▷ *The United States Strategic Bombing Survey Summary Report (European War)*, September 30, 1945.

▷ Urban Areas Division, "Effects of Air Attack on Urban Complex Tokyo-Kawasaki-Yokohama," United States Strategic Bombing Survey, June 1947, https://catalog.hathitrust.org/Record/001892321.

▷ Urban Settlements Working Group, "Area-Based Approaches in Urban Settings: Compendium of Case Studies," May 2019, 4, https://reliefweb.int/report/world/area-based-approaches-urban-settings-compendium-case-studies-may-2019-edition.

▷ US Customs and Border Protection, "Philadelphia CBP Officers Seize More than $6.5 Million in Fake Currency from Russia," September 29, 2022, https://www.cbp.gov/newsroom/local-media-release/philadelphia-cbp-officers-seize-more-65-million-fake-currency-russia.

▷ US Secretary of State, "The Philippine Rehabilitation Program Report to the President," Far Eastern Series volume 67, August 31, 1954. Available at https://books.google.com/books/about/The_Philippine_Rehabilitation_Program.html?id=1Z1RD93K6BcC&hl=en&output=html_text.

▷ Vale, Lawrence J., and Thomas J. Campanella, "Conclusion: Axioms of Resilience," in *The Resilient City: How Modern Cities Recover from*

Disaster. Edited by Lawrence J. Vale and Thomas J. Campanella (NY: Oxford, 2005), 335-353.

▷ Vale, Lawrence J., and Thomas J. Campanella, "Warsaw: Reconstruction as Propaganda," in *The Resilient City: How Modern Cities Recover from Disaster*, Edited by Lawrence J. Vale and Thomas J. Campanella (NY: Oxford, 2005), 135-158.

▷ Venter, Lourie (United Nations Mine Action Service, Iraq, November 2016-February 2022), interview with Dr. Russell W. Glenn, March 19, 2024.

▷ Vinacke, Harold M., "Post-War Government and Politics of the Philippines," *The Journal of Politics* 9, no. 4 (November 1947): 717-30.

▷ Voitovych, Olga, Radina Gigova, Svitlana Vlasova, and Christian Edwards, "Zelensky signs law overhauling Ukraine's mobilization rules," CNN (April 16, 2024), https://www.cnn.com/2024/04/16/europe/zelensky-signs-mobilization-law-intl-latam/index.html.

▷ Walzer, Michael, *Just and Unjust Wars: A Moral Argument with Historical Illustrations*. London: Allen Lane, 1978.

▷ Weichert, Brandon J., "Russia Launching Massive 6,600-Pound Glide Bombs at Ukraine," *The National Interest* June 23, 2024, https://nationalinterest.org/blog/buzz/russia-launching-massive-6600-pound-glide-bombs-ukraine-211570.

▷ Weinreb, Alice Autumn, "Matters of Taste: The Politics of Food and Hunger in Divided Germany 1945-1971." PhD diss., University of Michigan, 2009), https://www.academia.edu/85272407/Matters_of_Taste_The_Politics_of_Food_in_Divided_Germany_1945_1971.

▷ Wellerstein, Alex, "Counting the Dead at Hiroshima and Nagasaki," *Bulletin of the Atomic Scientists* (August 4, 2020), https://thebulletin.org/2020/08/counting-the-dead-at-hiroshima-and-nagasaki/.

▷ "What are Tactical Nuclear Weapons?", *Union of Concerned Scientists*, June 1, 2022, https://www.ucsusa.org/resources/tactical-nuclear-weapons.

▷ Wildes, Harry Emerson, *Typhoon in Tokyo: The Occupation and its Aftermath*. London: George Allen & Unwin, 1954.

▷ Williams, Holly Williams, "Russian attacks after occupation ends," *CBS News* (February 26, 2023), https://www.cbsnews.com/news/kherson-ukraine-60-minutes-2023-02-26/.

▷ "Winning the electricity war: How Ukraine tamed Russian missile barrages and kept the lights on," *The Economist* (March 12, 2023), https://www.economist.com/europe/2023/03/12/how-ukraine-tamed-russian-missile-barrages-and-kept-the-lights-on.

▷ "The winter ahead Russia has destroyed half of Ukraine's energy infrastructure. What does that mean for the upcoming heating season," Meduza.io, June 19, 2024, https://meduza.io/en/feature/2024/06/19/the-winter-ahead.

▷ "Within range," *The Economist* 450, no. 9386 (March 2, 2024): 46.

▷ World Bank, "Updated Ukraine Recovery and Reconstruction Needs Assessment Released," February 15, 2024, https://www.worldbank.org/en/news/press-release/2024/02/15/updated-ukraine-recovery-and-reconstruction-needs-assessment-released.

▷ World Bank Group staff, "Relief, Recovery, and Resilient Reconstruction: Supporting Ukraine's Immediate and Medium-Term Economic Needs," Informal approach paper, April 21, 2022.

▷ "The World Factbook: Ukraine—Details," US Central Intelligence Agency, undated, https://www.cia.gov/the-world-factbook/static/maps/UP-map.jpg.

▷ World Health Organization, "Early success in health system recovery in Ukraine, new WHO report highlights," news release (June 21, 2023), https://www.who.int/europe/news/item/21-06-2023-early-success-in-health-system-recovery-in-ukraine--new-who-report-highlights.

▷ World Health Organization European Region, "Case studies of health system recovery in Ukraine: focus on the role of the private sector" (2023), https://www.who.int/europe/publications/i/item/WHO-EURO-2023-7706-47473-69781.

▷ World Population Review, "Sarajevo Population," 2023, https://worldpopulationreview.com/world-cities/sarajevo-population.

▷ "The world this week: Politics," *The Economist* 450, no. 9387 (March 9, 2024): 9.

▷ Wray, Harry, "Education Policy Formation for the Allied Occupation of Japan," *Nanzan Review of American Studies* 18 (1996): 1-25.

▷ Yaffa, Joshua, "The Hunt for Russian Collaborators in Ukraine," *The New Yorker* (January 30, 2023), https://www.newyorker.com/magazine/2023/02/06/the-hunt-for-russian-collaborators-in-ukraine.

- Yorifusa, Ishida, "Japanese Cities and Planning in the Reconstruction Period: 1945-55," in *Rebuilding Urban Japan After 1945*, Edited by Carola Hein, Jeffry M. Diefendorf, and Ishida Yorifusa (NY: Palgrave MacMillan, 2003).
- Yoshikawa, Hiroshi, *Ashes to Awesome: Japan's 6,000-Day Economic Miracle*, Translated by Fred Uleman. Tokyo: Japan Publishing Industry Foundation for Culture, 2021.
- "Your land is my land: Imperialism then and now," *The Economist* 451, no. 9400 (June 8, 2024): 73-74.
- Yovanovitch, Marie, *Lessons from the Edge: A Memoir*. Boston: Mariner Books, 2022.
- Zetter, Roger and George Deikun, "A new strategy for meeting humanitarian challenges in urban areas," *Forced Migration Review* 38 (October 2011): 48-50, https://www.fmreview.org/zetter-deikun/.
- Ziemke, Earl F., *The US Army in the Occupation of Germany, 1944-1946*. Washington, DC: Center of Military History, 1975.
- Zierenberg, Malte, *Berlin's Black Market: 1939-1950*. NY: Palgrave Macmillan, 2015.

INDEX

SYMBOLS

1st Brigade, 1st Armored Division 359
1st Guards Tank Army 128
1949 Public Library Manifesto 103
"bamboo shoot life." 51
"flowers by cable" ploy 68
"How to eat weeds" 49
"kyodatsu condition" 58
"stoplight" chart 333
"Take these seeds," she said, "so sunflowers grow when you die here." 148

A

activists 124, 125, 127
ADM 176
Administrative Court of Appeal 124
adoption 33, 200, 222, 276
Advisory Council of International Experts 133
Afghanistan 165, 187, 237, 242–243, 248, 271, 320, 344
aid distribution 188, 211, 221
aid providers 5, 6, 189-91, 196, 218–219, 221, 238, 368
air raid shelters 42, 67
Alexander II 14
Allied General Headquarters Economics and Science Section 53
Allied Military Marks 70
Allied occupiers 46, 294
al-Mulk, Nizam 372, 389
American Library Association 103

American Revolution 13
ammunition ship 199
amnesty 267, 355
amputation/amputees 216, 217, 222, 239-41
Andreas-Friedrich, Ruth 60, 270–271
Andreas, Peter 100, 113, 347, 355, 368
Andryushchenko, Petro 160, 167-168
Anić, Mijo 360–361
anti-collaboration 266
anti-corruption officials 277
Apteka 911, 193
architects 6, 41, 78, 109,111, 116, 132-33, 166, 174, 181-82, 227, 233, 384, 386
architecture 37, 75-78 111, 115-16, 174-75, 181, 205, 226-27, 317, 386
Arizona Market 348, 357, 359–366, 369, 449–451, 458, 463, 467, 479–480, 482, 487–488
Army of Republika Srpska (VRS) 93, 96
Aron, Raymond 266
artificial intelligence (AI) 255, 341, 389
Artificial Intelligence Platform (AIP) 255
artillery 17, 24, 43, 81, 83, 99, 128–129, 150, 178, 213, 238, 242, 244, 246–247, 290, 325, 387
Asakusa District 42
Australia vi, vii, 198, 218
Avenue of Peace 163
Azovstal steel plant 159, 161, 196
Azov Battalion 157
activists 124, 125, 127
ADM 176

Administrative Court of Appeal   124
adoption   33, 200, 222, 276
Advisory Council of International Experts   133
Afghanistan   165, 187, 237, 242–243, 248, 271, 320, 344
aid distribution   188, 211, 221
aid providers   5, 6, 189-91, 196, 218–219, 221, 238, 368
air raid shelters   42, 67
Alexander II   14
Allied General Headquarters Economics and Science Section   53
Allied Military Marks   70
Allied occupiers   46, 294
al-Mulk, Nizam   372, 389
American Library Association   103
American Revolution   13
ammunition ship   199
amnesty   267, 355
amputation/amputees   216, 217, 222, 239-41
Andreas-Friedrich, Ruth   60, 270–271
Andreas, Peter   100, 113, 347, 355, 368
Andryushchenko, Petro   160, 167-168
Anić, Mijo   360–361
anti-collaboration   266
anti-corruption officials   277
Apteka 911   193
architects   6, 41, 78, 109, 111, 116, 132-33, 166, 174, 181-82, 227, 233, 384, 386
architecture   37, 75-78 111, 115-16, 174-75, 181, 205, 226-27, 317, 386
Arizona Market   348, 357, 359–366, 369, 449–451, 458, 463, 467, 479–480, 482, 487–488
Army of Republika Srpska (VRS)   93, 96

Aron, Raymond   266
artificial intelligence (AI)   255, 341, 389
Artificial Intelligence Platform (AIP)   255
artillery   17, 24, 43, 81, 83, 99, 128–129, 150, 178, 213, 238, 242, 244, 246–247, 290, 325, 387
Asakusa District   42
Australia   198, 218
Avenue of Peace   163
Azovstal steel plant   159, 161, 196
Azov Battalion   157

B

B-29 Superfortress   42, 59, 400(n15)
Bădescu, Gruia   93, 105, 108, 110
banks   50, 87, 202, 234
Barabashovo   124
barcoding   216
barter centers/exchanges/markets   70-73, 259, 351, 407(n122)
barter/trade-in-kind/gray marketing   46, 47, 351
Bastille Day   3
battle for Berlin   59
Battle of Leuthen   302
Belarus   19, 235, 287, 326, 384
Bellotto, Bernardo   78
Belt and Road Initiative   283
Berdiansk   23
Berlin   2, 5, 12, 17, 21–22, 27–28, 30, 38, 42, 58–65, 67–71, 73–79, 90, 96, 98, 101, 111, 114, 129, 136, 150, 165, 170, 199, 211, 227, 231, 235, 246, 270–271, 277–78, 301, 307, 312, 314, 319, 322–24, 343, 347, 349–351, 353, 356, 365, 368-69, 386
Berlin Barter Center   70–73
Berliners   31, 64, 66, 69-70, 73–74, 100, 165, 169, 352

bike lanes/bikeways 4, 34, 342
Black Death 94
black markets 18, 46-51, 53, 67-75, 82, 90, 96-98, 100, 112-14, 211, 264, 270, 313, 336, 347-374
Black Sea 148, 327, 370
blanket pardons 266
body count 329–330
bombing 19, 39, 41–45, 57, 59-61, 78, 80, 216-17, 237, 271, 377, 390
bomb shelters 320
Bondarev, Anton 132
booby traps 83, 175, 240, 243
Bosnia-Herzegovina 93-119, 180-81, 201, 223, 279, 285, 328, 331, 348, 353-69, 386
Bosniak 95-96, 98, 100-02, 109, 112, 114-15, 368, 362
Bosnian Serb 99, 106, 102, 119
Boston 380–381
brain injuries 239
Brandenburg Gate 68
Brave to Rebuild 232
Brcko 96-97, 357-68
bribes 113-14, 187, 277, 281
bridges 77, 82, 197, 248–249, 257, 332-33, 388
British Defence Ministry 315
Bronowsky, I. 39
Brovary 23
Brussels 14, 167
build back better 209
building materials 48, 205, 227–228, 278
building on the cheap 111, 317
building standards 197, 204-05
bureaucracy 205, 253, 260, 275, 320
buying American 273

C

Cambodia 184, 222
Canada (see also Halifax) xv, 191, 381
Canadian Partnership for Local Economic Development and Democratic Governance (PLEDDG) 207-08
canals 77, 148
Career Online High School (COHS) 454
Cargill 176
cash distribution 192, 220-21, 318
casualties 16, 21, 42, 57, 81–82, 99, 128, 215, 216, 255, 269, 314, 330, 401(n15)
casualty estimates 42–43
central business district (CBD) 233
central plan 111
Centre of Humanitarian Demining (CHD) 436
Chicago 33, 236, 313
China 41, 51, 67, 283
chocolate 74
cholera 57
Christian, Patrick 178, 270, 427
Christian Science Monitor 281, 439, 488
cigarettes 70–71, 74, 113, 353, 361, 452, 470
Cities 4 Cities United 4 Ukraine 185, 428, 462
City of Military Glory 163
civil affairs 84, 173, 300, 361
Civil Defense Police 59
civilian casualties 42–43
civilians 4, 21, 54, 60–61, 73, 80–81, 83, 100, 104, 128, 152, 159, 170–171, 179, 181, 201, 242–243, 269, 303, 316, 352
Civil Information and Education Section 296
Clarke, Henry 364
clausewitz 15
Clay, Lucius D. 14, 16, 62, 71-73, 298-300, 341
climate change 25, 191, 197, 228, 327, 342

Clinton, Bill 101
cluster structure 219-21, 224-25, 252
Coca Cola plant 176
coercive measures 169
coherency 29, 115-16
cold 10, 58, 67, 100, 129, 139, 151, 158, 270, 348, 386
Cold War 77, 197, 202, 288-289
collaboration/collaborators 18, 37, 90, 132, 136-47, 154, 164, 168, 180, 195, 263-70, 278, 305, 336
Collective Awareness to UXO 243
Committee on Public Safety 380
communications 136, 151, 153, 158, 184-185, 195, 221, 253, 307, 312, 379, 380
Communists 66, 76, 78, 91, 95, 127, 173, 285, 306, 352
Conant, Even 284
construction 2-3, 7, 27, 29, 48, 52, 55-56, 77, 130, 165, 167, 197, 203, 205, 208, 212, 227, 228, 230, 236, 253, 278, 322, 348, 354, 382, 388
construction codes 228
consumer goods 85
contamination 242-243, 246, 248, 255-256, 259, 332
contracts/contractors 126, 181, 193, 199, 201, 205, 219, 258, 272, 273, 274, 277, 282, 283, 324, 331, 364
contracting regulations 209, 273-77, 335
convertible mark (KM) 364
Cooperative for American Remittances to Europe (CARE) 65-66, 165, 352
corruption 7, 18, 26, 27, 29, 49, 57, 90, 91, 92, 104, 106, 116, 135, 144, 169, 177, 180, 187, 188, 189, 192, 196, 202, 205, 207, 253, 258, 259, 262, 270-83, 313, 317, 322-23, 335-38, 345, 348, 353, 355, 364, 365-66, 370-72, 376, 38

counterproductive measures 329
counter-Russia policies 287, 376
Coventry 2, 30
COVID 32, 250, 290, 389
Crimea 17, 124, 125, 126, 136, 148, 151-52, 157, 289, 305, 311, 327
criminality 49, 70, 113, 176, 199, 278, 355, 364-365, 380
crisis response 186
Croat 95-96, 98, 108-110, 353, 357, 360-362
Croatia 95, 96, 189, 357-358
cross-cluster relationships 221
crowdsourcing 255, 386, 389
cruise missiles 22
crush injuries 238
cultural landmarks 103, 392
curricula 137, 149, 163, 169, 211, 288, 291
Cutts, Mark 114
cybersecurity 185
cybersecurity 185 (n15)

D

Daiichi nuclear reactor failures 381
Danish Refugee Council 194
Dayton Accords 201, 358
DC model 102
deaths 1, 31, 42, 89, 96, 237, 259, 317
debris 58, 78, 247, 315, 322
decentralization 29, 32-33, 91, 147, 162, 207, 232, 375, 376
deminers/demining 182-83, 245-62, 328
demonstrations 110, 124, 150, 375
de-occupied 121, 137, 290, 324
detonation rates 246
die Stunde Null 19, 321
digitization 262
disease 38, 49, 77, 83-85, 140, 182, 195, 199, 237

498

INDEX

disinformation   15, 164, 189, 288, 291
distrust   94, 269, 352
DNA testing   216
Dnieper River   147–148
Dnipro   23, 177, 178
doctors   146, 154, 168, 277, 380, 391
Dodik, Milorad   119
Donbas   17, 19, 124-26, 157, 161, 211, 288
donors   27, 29, 133, 188, 193, 208, 209, 219, 224, 248-49, 260-61, 332, 334–335, 339, 344-46, 354, 372
Dower, John   296, 400 (n7), 402 (n50)
Dresden   60, 64, 230
drones   178, 283, 386
DTEK   5, 276, 321
Dubrovnik   38
dysentery   61

E

earthquake   3, 41-43, 94, 171, 197-98, 199, 229, 236, 381, 382
East Sarajevo (also Istočno Sarajevo)   109, 115
East Timor   194
economic development   196, 206, 207, 318
economies of scale   33, 115
economy   5, 25, 27–28, 45, 47–48, 50–51, 63, 71, 86–87, 131, 167, 182, 191-92, 195, 218, 229, 241–242, 245, 253, 254, 262, 276, 278, 318, 326, 347–348, 351, 354, 371–372, 374
ecosystem   336
education   5, 18, 21, 85, 86–87, 116, 118, 139, 178, 180, 182, 185, 231, 248, 249, 256-57, 267, 288, 290-309, 320, 325, 327, 341, 391, 392, 441 (n236)
Education Policy Guidelines for the Development of New Japan   294

efficiency   115, 173, 188, 191, 197, 207, 224–225, 253, 260, 315
electricity   3, 49, 53, 82, 83, 100–101, 147, 151, 152, 153, 156, 173-74, 210, 213, 234, 238, 248, 262, 326, 379, 394 (n11)
electric vehicles   33–34
emergency evacuation locations   342
employment   18, 34, 45, 84, 88, 131, 137, 161, 165, 180, 185, 196, 206, 226, 318, 344, 347, 349, 362, 365, 374
energy independence   207
Estleman, Loren   355
ethnicization/ethnic conflict   8, 15, 17, 18, 96, 97, 99, 101-19, 126, 132, 138, 145, 147, 180, 201, 226, 228, 235, 273, 283-90, 353, 354-62, 365, 374-76
European Bank for Reconstruction and Development   345
European Commission   344–345
European Green Deal   204
European Investment Bank   345
European Union   26, 29, 31, 134, 145, 166, 189, 207, 288, 344, 370, 391, 397, 466
Exeler, Franziska   145
extradition   270
eye injuries   239, 378

F

Fallujah   11, 332–333, 447
Famine   140, 222, 285
farming   23, 85, 259
farmland   23, 150, 344
Fast Recovery Plan   166
Federal Security Service (FSB)   170
Federation of Bosnia and Herzegovina (see Bosnia-Herzegovina)
Filipino Communist Party   91

filtration/filtration camps/
  filtration centers 150, 158, 159–160, 169, 305
fire 33, 42–43, 55–56, 82, 103, 134, 154, 216, 236, 257, 313, 377–378
firestorms 42, 60, 230
first-first responders 383
First Hague Peace Conference 14
Flemish-speaking community 146
flies 61, 77, 235
floods/flooding 52, 90, 93, 171, 198, 199, 234, 236, 342, 378, 381
Florence 38
Fontenot, Gregory 328, 332, 359, 360, 362, 363, 366
food 5, 41, 45, 47–51, 55, 57, 58, 61, 63-74, 79, 80, 82, 85, 88, 90, 97-98, 101, 112, 129, 148, 150, 151–53, 158, 159, 163, 169, 179, 184, 191–92, 219-22, 242, 257, 264, 278, 281, 318, 339, 341, 348-53, 368–69
food kit 318, 339
food parcel (CARE) 65
Foster, Norman 132–134, 233, 418(n31), 481
Fragebogen 302
France 3, 13, 139, 141, 143–144, 184–185, 266–267
France-Prussian War 13
Frankopan, Peter 195, 234
fraud 188, 189, 191, 204, 340
Frederick the Great 302
Freedom Square 124, 126
fuel 15, 34, 45, 94, 100, 112, 129, 134, 139, 208, 234, 240, 285, 321, 328, 333, 353, 377, 381, 390
Fukushima Daiichi nuclear power plant/disaster 199, 234, 381
funding 7, 24, 27–29, 40, 46, 52, 85, 87, 111, 134, 166–167, 182–183, 187-94, 197–198, 205, 209, 217, 220, 223–224, 231–232, 247, 250, 260, 300, 317, 331, 334, 338, 346, 348, 365, 387, 391

G

G7 countries/nations 344, 391
gangs 47, 96, 347, 350, 371
gas 53, 82, 100-01, 104, 137, 147, 151, 158, 173, 328, 361, 377, 379, 381, 392
Gatow 78
Gaza 6, 11, 254
Gazprom 101
General Framework for Peace in Bosnia and Herzegovina 358
generators 4, 137, 234, 315, 325, 328, 390
Genplans 76
German Democratic Republic 66, 315
German Marshall Fund 27
Germany (see also Berlin) 1, 5, 14, 19, 41, 58–79, 180, 185, 190, 245, 253, 266–267, 291, 296-306, 315, 319, 321, 321, 323, 325, 341, 344, 350, 352-53, 406(n115)
German Youth Activities 303
GI Bill 391
Ginza 48
Global Initiative Against Transnational Organized Crime 365
Global Rights Compliance 170
GONGO 189
government legitimacy 280, 323, 324, 369
government positions 137, 146, 267, 278
Grande, Lise 222
grants 27, 134, 162, 209, 331
Great Britain 13, 63
Greater East Asia Co-Prosperity Sphere 292
Green intiatives/technologices 25, 32, 76, 204, 207, 232–233, 276, 316, 333, 345
green belts 46
Griffiths, Owen 46
Gross, Inge E. Stanneck 59, 66

INDEX

H

Halifax, Nova Scotia 94, 199-201, 210, 215, 236, 239, 376-83
Hamburg 2, 38, 42, 60, 230, 314
harbor pilot 377
Harshbarger, Sam 145
Health care 18, 180, 192-93, 236-39
heating 53, 100, 112, 173, 213, 387
height and weight statistics 50
Heslop, Paul 241, 242, 245-47, 250-51, 255-57, 259, 434
Hillier, Rick 280
Hiroshima 2, 77, 199, 210, 379, 453(n138)
Historic Urban Landscape 327
Hitler 76, 118, 298
Hitlerjugend (see also Hitler Youth) 300, 303
Hitler Youth 298, 300, 303, 305
hoarding 48, 89, 98, 370
homeless 40, 43, 46, 55, 58–59, 82, 168, 210, 378, 381
Hong Kong 214, 236, 279
hospitals 14, 21, 44, 67, 147, 159, 169, 234, 236-239, 249, 325, 329, 332, 333, 390
household goods 348
House of Culture 387
housing 5, 18, 21, 23-24, 25, 44, 48, 52–56, 58, 60, 64–65, 77–78, 89, 103, 107, 117, 166, 178, 180, 181, 187, 196, 202–203, 208, 219-20, 226-36, 238, 269, 285, 302, 319-20, 342–344, 350, 364, 385, 435(n138)
Housing, building, and employment 18, 180, 226
housing privatization 202
hromadas 175, 207
hryvnia 21, 149, 163, 231
Hukbalahap (Huk) insurgency 90–91, 97, 353, 375
humanitarian aid 52, 113, 153, 170, 180-94, 368
Humanitarian Coordination Team (HCT) 221
humanitarian demining 183, 252, 255, 260, 436-37(n158)
Human Rights Watch (HRW) 118, 153, 156, 171, 290, 305
human waste 61
hunger 61, 72, 262, 264, 322, 369
Hurricane Katrina 234, 328, 344
Hurricane Sandy 234
hydrant 33
Hydrostone 382

I

illicit exchanges 73, 277, 356, 369
illicit gains 276, 338
Imo 377–378
imports 86, 370, 410(n164)
indoctrination 291, 298-300, 307–308
industrialization 51, 300
industrial output 45, 49, 130, 157
inflation 29, 48, 50, 52–53, 55, 58, 68, 87–89, 279, 354, 372, 403(n57)
information 10, 15-16, 18, 25, 33, 39, 103, 126, 157, 163–165, 171, 180, 186, 189, 193, 200, 214-15, 217, 220–221, 226, 244, 249, 255, 275, 288, 290-304, 306, 308, 311, 320, 326, 336, 357, 374–376, 392, 436(n158)
information campaign 18, 164–165, 180, 290-304, 376
information operations 374-376
Institute for the Science of Labor 46
insurance 84, 280
intellectual colonization 233
inter-ethnic cooperation 353, 365
intergovernmental organization (IGO) 6, 30, 193, 217, 224–225, 334, 367, 391

501

internally displaced persons (IDP)   23, 34, 106, 156, 186-88, 211, 231, 326, 342, 343
International Committee of the Red Cross (ICRC)   154, 194, 367
International Criminal Court   238, 394(n11)
International Criminal Tribunal for the Former Yugoslavia   104, 413(n36), 489
International Monetary Fund   29, 345
internet   2, 13, 15, 21, 130, 136, 149, 152, 307, 308, 385, 393(n6)
Interregional Centre for Humanitarian Demining and Rapid Response   437(n158)
investors   133, 177, 187, 205, 209, 374
Iraq   5, 11, 113, 137, 182, 187, 194, 225, 241, 243, 251–252, 254, 267, 271, 273, 311, 320, 323, 331–334, 344, 447(n47
Irpin   20, 39, 180-81, 384–388, 414, 454, 475, 484
Ishikawa Hideaki   231
Islamic State of Iraq and Syria (ISIS)   194, 251
Israel Defense Forces (IDF)   11
Istočno Sarajevo (East Sarajevo)   109, 115
Italproject   357, 364
Iwakami Shinichi   49
Izetbegovic, Alija   101
Izyum (also spelled Izium)   137, 140, 146

J

Jackson, Julian   143
James, D. Clayton   265
Japanese forces   80
Jehovah's Witnesses   170
Jewish communities   1, 94, 109, 18, 288
Josip Broz Tito   95
Judt, Tony   135, 141

K

Kalyvas, Stathis   12, 13
Kameo Hideshirô   50, 270
Kamyshin, Oleksandr   177
Kanagawa Prefecture   52
Kazansky, Denys   169
Kernes, Hennadiy Adolfovych   126
Kharkiv   11, 17, 19–20, 22–23, 37–39, 121-147, 153–154, 177, 178, 181, 193, 210–211, 213, 233, 264, 267–268, 283, 386
Kharkiv Oblast   128, 146, 154, 193, 268
Kharkiv School of Architecture   181, 386
Kherson   17, 19–20, 21, 23, 38–39, 121, 146, 147-55, 161, 173, 175, 178, 185, 196, 210, 212, 237, 240, 324
Kherson Art Museum   151
Kherson People's Republic   150
Kherson Regional National Archive   153
Khmer Rouge   222
Kobe   229–230
Kobets, Oleksandr   149
Kolykhayev, Ihor (also spelled Kolyhayev)   148, 149, 154
Kommandatura   302
Koreans   94, 96, 246, 349, 350, 381
Korkhovyi, Igor   3
Kortava, David   160
Kôtô region   55
Kraham, Sherri   273
Kramatorsk   23
Kramer, Erik C.   282-83, 431
Kravchenko, Volodymyr   124-26, 135
Krücke, Georg   319
Kuchma, Leonid   177
Kuindzhi Art Museum   155
Kupiansk   146, 263, 268–269
Kuwait   184

INDEX

Kyiv (includes references to Kyiv as representing the Ukrainian government) 5, 7, 9, 11, 19–20, 22–23, 34–35, 38, 39, 62, 76, 94, 121, 124–125, 127, 131, 145, 147, 149, 157–158, 164, 171, 173, 174, 178–179, 181, 185, 187, 188, 191, 193, 205, 207, 213, 218, 224, 232, 235, 239, 258–259, 262, 268–269, 282–283, 285, 287, 305, 307, 312, 324-5, 338, 371, 374–376, 385, 388, 390, 394(n16)
Kyiv School of Economics KSE Foundation 193

L

labor protests 66
Labour Hub 105
landlords 115, 210, 229-31, 236
landmines (see mines)
language 91, 108, 131, 137, 235, 268, 284, 286–288, 297
language instruction 137
Laurel, Jose P. 264
leadership 5, 18, 27, 95, 98, 99, 102, 126, 150, 180, 210-22, 223, 236
Leipzig Charter 204
Leningrad 22
leprosy 84
lessons learned 318
libraries 82, 93, 103, 105, 263, 287, 294, 387, 391-92, 454(n160)
Lippman, Peter 100, 106, 110-11, 116, 180, 223, 270-01, 278, 331, 412
Ljungkvist, Kristin 11
loans 27, 47, 134, 168, 192, 205, 229, 232, 279, 320
Lodhammar, Pehr 241, 250, 257, 333, 447(n47)
logistics 63, 75, 183, 192, 221, 240, 253, 299, 318, 330
London 19, 38, 42, 134, 178, 271, 279, 301
long-term care 217, 239

looting 61, 105, 114, 151, 153, 271, 323
Los Angeles 229-30, 233, 382, 454(n160)
lowest-bidder award systems 272
Luhova, Halyna 153-54
Lviv 22, 33, 179

M

MacArthur, Douglas 46, 48, 52, 80, 81, 265, 293–294, 349,
Mackay Radio Corporation 68
Maersk 330, 335
mafia 353, 371
Magsaysay, Ramon 91-92
mail 73–74, 100–101, 193
malnutrition 55, 57
management 18, 29–30, 33, 45, 88, 101, 116, 167, 180, 186–94, 205, 209, 210-23, 226, 251, 255, 258, 260, 262, 318, 339, 341, 367
Manila 2, 9, 11, 17, 38, 39, 79–92, 96, 98, 108, 111, 129, 196, 199, 202, 211, 227, 235, 237, 263–264, 278, 312, 322, 324, 343, 347, 349, 352–353, 368, 369, 374-76
Marawi, Philippines 11
Marchenko, Serhiy 177
Mariupol 17, 19–21, 23, 38–39, 77, 121-22, 146, 155-71, 196-97, 250, 285, 289–290, 323-24, 348
Mariupol Museum of Local Lore and History 155
Mariupol Reborn 162, 166–167
Marshall Plan 7, 181, 188, 232
Massachusetts Institute of Technology 111
Masters, Jonathan 288-89
Matthews, Gary 363
McDonald's 176
McMahon, David 182, 209, 253, 258
Médecins Sans Frontières 194, 236–237

503

medical care/services 56, 85, 128–129, 168, 193, 212, 231, 239, 390
medical shortages 148
medical supplies 14, 61, 159
medicines 156, 191, 193, 213, 216, 348
meningitis 57
mental health 25, 380
metrics 247–251, 260, 327–41
Microsoft 185
military demining 183, 252–254
Military Misfortunes 30
Milosevic, Slobodan 95-96, 102, 104
mine action 183, 240-62, 332
Mine Action Centre (MAC) 436(n158)
Mine Action Project Unit (UN) 182
mine clearing 240-62
mines 21, 83, 101, 104, 147, 151–154, 163, 240–62, 328-29, 332–334, 344, 360–361, 436(n142)
Ministry for Communities, Territories Development, and Infrastructure of Ukraine 133
Ministry of Defense 183, 282
Ministry of Energy 261
Ministry of Health 193
misinformation 15, 306, 308
mission command 367
MMK plant 196
modality 220
Monetary Emergency Measures Ordinance 50
monitoring 188, 207, 225, 260, 275, 278, 283, 316, 327, 338
Mont-Blanc 377-79
monuments 105, 115, 126, 127, 163, 179
Moorhouse, Roger 60
mortgages 202, 203

Moscow (also used to refer to Russian government) 11, 22, 37, 62, 64, 66, 122–123, 126, 127, 150, 159, 163–164, 166–167, 285, 287, 289, 375
Moskalkova, Tatyana 289
Mosul, Iraq 11, 113, 194
Multi-agency Donor Coordination Platform for Ukraine 344
munitions 42, 83, 94, 128, 141, 154, 237, 242–243, 246–248, 253, 255, 257–258, 318
Museum of Folk Life 155
museums 82, 103, 105, 111, 151–153, 155, 282, 294, 387, 391

N

Nagasaki 17, 38, 39, 40, 57–58, 77, 216, 376-77, 400(n7), 453(n138)
Nairobi 239
Nairobi's Kenyatta National Referral and Teaching Hospital 239 Nanking 2
National Council for the Recovery of Ukraine from the Consequences of the War 204, 206
National Guard of Ukraine 157
National Health Service of Ukraine 193
National Mine Action Authority (NMAA) 254, 260, 436(n158)
National Police of Ukraine 269
National Recovery Plan 25
National Socialism 300
national standards 33, 184, 205
National Tax Service 336
nationwide standards 33
neo-Nazis 125, 157, 169, 170
NEST 231
Netherlands 141, 185, 293, 345
networks 57, 117, 185, 225-26, 436(n158), 483
New Leipzig Charter 204

INDEX

New York 33, 184, 215–216, 234, 238, 250, 280, 388
Nice, France 3-4
Nicolas II 14
noncombatants 20–21, 80, 129, 242
nongovernmental organizations (NGOs) 6, 30, 113, 131, 133, 179, 182–183, 189, 191, 193-94, 205, 209-10, 217, 219, 221-22, 224–225, 238, 239, 253, 272, 318, 331-32, 334, 339, 367, 389, 391
non-veteran family members 239
Normandin, Henri-Paul 27
Norman Foster Foundation 132, 418(n31)
North Atlantic Treaty Organization (NATO) 103, 163, 288, 289, 359, 361
North Atlantic Treaty Organization Implementation Force (IFOR) 103
North Crimean Canal 148
North Korea 246
Norway 141, 336, 345, 372
Norway's Anti-Corruption Resource Centre 336
Norwegian Refugee Council 194, 219
nuclear reactors 234, 381
nuclear threat 376-383
nuclear weapons 18, 282, 313, 379, 383, 453(n138)

O

oblast 34, 125, 128, 137, 146, 153, 154, 210, 213, 268, 282, 316
occupation marks 68
occupation sectors 62
O'Connell, Arthur 200
O'Connor, Edith 199, 380
Odesa 19, 23, 158, 179, 324
Office of High Representative Supervisor 363
Office of the High Representative (OHR) 201
Okita Saburo 51
Oklahoma City federal building 216
OKNO 231
oligarchs 126, 149, 276, 277, 338
Olympic Museum 103
Operation Desert Storm 315
orchestration 188-94, 195-96, 209, 220, 225-6, 236, 253–254, 301, 341, 343
Organization for Economic Cooperation and Development (OECD) 27
Oriental Institute 103
orphaned elderly 199
orphans 49, 58, 80, 89, 199-200, 349, 369, 382-3
Osteria, Tristan Miguel Santos 91
outcomes 187, 250, 255, 328, 341

P

Palantir 176, 254–255
paper-based methods 215
Paris 13, 38, 105, 204
Paris Agreement 204
passports 150, 152, 160, 168-69, 267, 280, 288, 410(n164), 425(n110)
Pavlohrad 23
payment in-kind 88
pedestrian 3, 33–34, 342
pensioners 137, 149, 217
pesos (Philippine) 85, 88-89, 410(n171)
Pétain, Marshal Philippe 143, 266
Philippine Bureau of Census and Statistics 87
Philippine elite 263
Philippine independence 85–86, 90
Philippine Rehabilitation Act 86

505

Philippines 11, 40, 79-92, 224, 263, 265, 293, 325, 375
Phoenix 33
physical infrastructure 10, 29, 32, 76, 82, 94, 111, 167, 174, 195, 235, 320, 323, 325
Piper, Elizabeth 154
Piplas, Haris 98, 103, 117
plague 38, 94
planning guidance 208
plans 1, 4, 5, 8, 18, 28, 45, 76, 111, 134, 162, 180, 195-210, 214, 231-32, 245, 261, 289, 313, 319, 386-87, 436(n158)
Plavšić, Biljana 99
Poland 185, 322, 345
Poliakova, Valentyna 3
police 49, 59, 66, 67, 70, 74, 94, 103, 114, 125, 136, 139, 140, 141, 154, 168, 175, 188, 218, 240, 243, 251, 253, 269, 280, 334, 338, 343, 351, 353, 354, 363, 364, 365, 381
police headquarters 175, 240
police training 334, 338
polio 57
Poltava 23
POM-3 Medallion mine 243-44
Pomerantsev, Peter 127
Ponakarovski, Andre 281
pool table metaphor 9
pop-up toilets 342
Posavina Working Group 362
post exchanges 71
post-traumatic stress disorder (PTSD) 58, 239
Potemkin, Grigory 22, 153
Prague Charter 24
prefabricated homes 322
prices 47, 49–51, 69, 71, 73, 75, 85, 87, 98, 153, 169, 187, 203, 210, 230, 258, 264, 279, 349, 351, 366, 369–370, 373, 382
prisoners of war 65, 146

Pritzker, Penny 176-77, 187, 427
propaganda 22, 37, 66, 75-6, 94, 149, 152, 156, 164–165, 170, 235, 267, 284–285, 287, 291, 300, 305–307, 376, 384
property lines 76–77
property losses 84, 203
property owners 84, 135, 203, 354, 381
pro-Russian sympathies 126, 128, 137, 263
prostitution 49, 55, 83, 199, 347, 362, 371, 373
protesters 7, 98, 150, 223
psychological injuries 57, 325
PTSD 58, 239
public confidence 356
public health 56, 61, 84-86
public meetings 112, 130
punishments for collaboration 143-44
Pushilin, Denis 161
Putin, Vladimir 22, 122, 132, 149, 153, 156, 163, 167, 317, 326, 375, 379
Putnam, Robert D. 117

Q

quality assurance 209
quality control 209, 331, 339
Quezon, Manuel L. 91
Quisling, Vidkun 140

R

racketeering 264, 351, 369
radiation 57, 216, 234, 379, 380
radioactive contamination 199
ration cards 69–70, 350-51
ration entitlements/standards 64, 65
rats 83, 237, 352, 355
Ravne-Brcko 360, 361

INDEX

Red Army   64, 169
red tape   176
red teaming/teams   205, 222
redundancy   35, 226, 229
re-education   21, 291-304, 307-08, 441(n236)
referendum   95, 149-50, 154, 161
refugees   16, 23, 41, 65, 69, 106, 111, 158, 173, 180, 186–187, 190, 211, 319, 322, 326, 342–343, 391
Regional Assistance Mission to Solomon Islands (RAMSI)   218, 432(n84)
Reichstag   68, 233
religious sites   21
relocating individuals   151, 215
rent/rentals   55, 72, 84, 89, 208, 210, 228–231, 236, 382
repairing rather than demolishing and rebuilding   203, 229, 382
Repair Together   231
report cards for aid providers   194
Republika Srpska   93, 96, 99, 102, 109, 119, 279, 354, 358
residency   55, 96
ReStart Ukraine   25, 232
retroactive crime   266
Return and Reconstruction Task Force   107
returnees   25, 54, 107, 180, 196, 223, 391
rezoning   228
Romans   12
Roosevelt, Franklin D.   5, 103
Roxas, Manuel A.   91, 263–266, 375
Royal Air Force   59
rubble   2–3, 44, 67, 78, 136, 156, 178, 181, 232, 246–247, 252, 257, 271, 314-15, 350, 384–386
Rubin, Eduard   132
ruble   21, 149, 163, 267, 375
Russian annexation   149
Russification   123, 169

S

safety   34, 56, 104, 134, 250, 262, 367
Saint Petersburg (see St. Petersburg)
Saipan   47
Saldo, Volodymyr   149
San Francisco   33, 236
Santo Tomas University prisoner camp   82
Sarajevo   8, 17, 38–39, 93-114, 98–119, 129, 182, 203, 211, 227, 235, 279, 319, 322, 324, 343, 347, 349, 353–358, 362, 367–368, 371
Sarajevo Canton Assembly   118
SCAP (see Supreme Commander for the Allied Powers)
scarlet fever   57, 61
schools   21, 58, 79, 82, 130, 142, 249, 290, 292, 294–295, 298-05, 325, 342, 384, 391
Scott, James M.   83
Second World War [see World War II (WWII)]
Seiko watch factory   43
seized Russian assets   131, 184, 428(n23, n24)
Seoul   12
September 11, 2001   215
Serbs   95–96, 98–100, 101, 102, 103, 106, 108–110, 113, 115, 119, 279, 353, 357-58, 360-62
Serbian Democratic Party (SDS)   98
Serbian Yugoslav People's Army (JNA)   95
sewage/sewerage   32–33, 77, 83, 163, 166, 173, 325, 362
shelters/air raid shelters   42, 45, 55, 67, 80, 84, 89, 107, 111, 129, 130, 157–158, 163, 187, 197, 211, 219, 228, 320, 376-77
Shevchenko, Alexander   232
Shevchenkov   142

507

Shinagawa ward 49
shortages 45, 50, 55, 57, 61, 63, 74, 82, 90, 100, 112, 128, 137, 147–148, 159, 196, 202, 227, 231, 264, 302, 369
shrinkage 356
siblings 201
siege 38-39, 93, 96, 99, 100, 104, 111–114, 118, 156, 227, 353, 355–356
Sierra Leone 222, 344, 368
Sieverodonetsk 23
Simmonds, Ralph 215
Siyasat Nameh or *Book of Politics* 372
Sloviansk 23
smallpox 57
social media 171, 257, 306–308, 389
social networks 57
soft aid 181, 338
soft challenges 135-47
solar farms 321
Southern Front 19
Soviet-era construction 203
Soviets 1, 2, 21, 61-64, 69, 76, 302, 320, 352
Soviet Union 62–63, 74, 123–124, 126, 132, 177, 346
Soviet Zone of Occupation 62–64
SpaceX 185
Spiller, Roger 12–13
Sri Lankan government anti-corruption initiative 337
Stabilization Force (SFOR) 361
Stalin 94, 114, 140, 143, 145, 285
Stalinalle 77, 78
Stalingrad 22
standardization 33
starvation 47, 49, 51, 65, 70, 73, 90, 94, 140, 170, 285, 348–349, 352–353, 356, 369
State Agency for Restoration and Infrastructure Development of Ukraine 324

State Bureau of Investigations 269
State Emergency Service of Ukraine (SES) 436(n158)
State Shintoism 294
State Special Transport Service (SSTS) 254, 437(n158)
statues 75, 127, 136
St. Catherine's Cathedral 153
steel 32, 54, 196, 211, 322
Steglitz 14
STEM subjects 291
step-by-step approach 256
stockpiles 70, 246, 349
stove-piping 221, 226
St. Petersburg 14, 122, 167, 289
Strategic Bombing Survey 39, 41– 42, 44, 45, 60, 377, 400–401(n15)
Strategic Operation for the Destruction of Critically Important Targets (or SODCIT) 315
street names 56, 127
Street Stall Tradesmen's Cooperative Union 47
Strock, Carl 214
student-teacher ratio 302
sub-infrastructures 342
Subotin, Andrii 269
subways 7, 46, 77, 290
suicides 67, 217
Sunak, Rishi 192
Supreme Commander for the Allied Powers (SCAP) 293, 295, 297, 441(n236)
survey teams 256
sustainability 25, 107, 207, 232, 327
sustained levels of funding 346
Swedish Defence University 11
Swiss cheese metaphor 389
synergy 341, 346
Synnott, Hilary 273, 275

INDEX

T

tactical nuclear weapon 379, 383, 453(n138)
Tagalog 91-92
Tate, Andrew 308, 315
tax breaks 202, 259
taxes 50, 259, 262, 280, 357, 359, 362, 373
teachers 50, 58, 137, 139, 142, 149, 153, 168, 268, 270, 288, 290, 292, 295-96, 300-02, 305, 306, 308, 391
Tegel 78
Telegraf 72
Tempelhof 78
temporary structures 202, 236, 316, 344
Teufelsberg (Devil's Mountain) 78
Textbook and Curriculum Branch 297
The City Becomes a Symbol 62
theft 61-62, 69, 88, 90, 153, 192, 272, 287, 322-23, 326, 352, 370
The Kyiv Independent 269
Tiergarten 68
Tokyo 2–3, 5, 9, 17, 27, 38, 40–59, 61, 65, 69, 72, 90, 92, 94, 96, 98, 100, 111, 113, 129, 134, 175, 199, 203, 211, 226–227, 228, 229, 231, 234–235, 270, 278, 307, 312, 314, 319, 322, 323, 324, 342, 343, 347, 349-50, 353, 365–366, 368, 369, 370, 374, 381, 383, 386, 394(n16), 400-01(n15), 401(n27), 441(n236)
Tokyo Metropolitan Government 43
traffic congestion 33, 56, 115
transformers, electical 54, 173, 248
transparency 127, 189, 207
Transparency International-Ukraine 127
transportation 22, 32–34, 55, 57, 72, 109, 117, 125, 151, 195, 254, 269, 331, 379, 390

Trofimov, Yaroslav 38, 142, 156, 210, 240
Trümmerbahnlokomotive 78
Trümmerfrauen 78
tsunami 3, 199, 378, 381
tuberculosis 57, 84
Tuzla canton 363
types of market exchanges 350
typhus 61

U

Ukraine Defense Contact Group 190
Ukraine-Netherlands Urban Network (UNUN) 185
Ukraine's State Agency for Restoration and Infrastructure Development 3
Ukrainian Main Military Intelligence Directorate (GUR) 150
Ukrainian Soviet Socialist Republic 123
Ukrainization 132, 168
Ukroboronprom 281
Ukrposhta (National Postal System) 340
UN4Kharkiv task force 133,
UN 2030 Agenda for Sustainable Development 204
underground (illicit) economy 347-48, 354
underground facilities 3, 76, 130, 157, 197, 290
underhand trade 277, 350
unexploded ordnance (UXO) 2, 18, 23, 104, 153, 163, 180, 226, 241–62, 334, 343, 375
unexploded ordnance disposal 18, 180, 241-62
UN-Habitat 232
UN Humanitarian Coordinator in Yemen 222
Union of Polish Metropolises 166

United National Economic Commission for Europe (UNECE) 133
United Nations (UN) 31, 85, 96, 99–100, 102–103, 112, 114, 182–184, 209, 232, 241, 245, 253, 258, 260, 280-81, 314, 327, 359, 362, 367, 385
United Nations Development Programme (UNDP) 31, 241, 245, 385
United Nations High Commissioner for Human Rights 314
United Nations High Commissioner for Refugees (UNHCR) 184
United Nations Human Rights Commission 99
United Nations Office for Project Services 183, 258
United Nations Protection Force (UNPROFOR) 112
United States 7, 11, 13, 26, 30, 33, 39, 41, 47, 52, 53, 60, 62, 63, 65, 66, 68, 69-75, 81, 84, 85–86, 88-90, 99, 101, 118, 134, 160, 165, 166, 176, 178, 181-82, 184, 187-88, 192, 201, 212, 214, 218, 223, 224, 233–234, 237, 239, 261, 263-65, 267, 271-77, 282-3, 284, 299, 300, 301–303, 312, 326, 334, 344, 346, 351, 359, 369, 377, 380, 406(n115)
United States Agency for International Development (USAID) 166
United States Agency for International Development (USAID) Economic Support for Ukraine Project 166
United States Army (US Army) 56, 59–60, 63, 69, 84, 88, 90, 212, 214, 298, 303, 328, 347, 359, 362, 406(n115)
United States Army Air Force (USAAF) 43, 47, 59
United States Army Corps of Engineers (USACE) 212, 214

United States Forces European Theater 302
University of Santo Tomas prisoner of war camp 352
UN Mine Action in Ukraine 242
unreported cash sales 259
UN Mine Action Project Unit 182
UN Sustainable Development Goals 206-07
urban bias 12
urban planners 132, 174, 182, 197
urban-rural relationship 179
urban transport 34
urbicide 21, 227, 396
US Army (see United States Army)
US Coalition Provisional Authority 273
US Congress 86
US Department of Defense 283, 359
US Department of State 86, 160, 218, 334,
US High Mobility Artillery Rocket System (HIMARS) 387
US Special Representative for Ukraine's Economic Recovery 176
US Strategic Bombing Survey 42, 44, 400-01(n15)
usurped properties 168

V

veterans 11, 25, 58, 190, 201, 217, 239, 322, 323, 375, 391–392
vetting 113, 182, 191, 194–195, 260, 302, 305
Vienna 21, 68
Volkswagen 353–354

W

wage level 85
wages 88, 262, 281, 290
walkways 342

INDEX

Walloons   146
War Damage Corporation   84, 409(n157), 441(n236)
wargaming   205-06, 335
Warsaw   1, 21, 37, 75–76, 78, 281
Wartime Casualties Care Law   216
Washington (used at times to reference US government)   13, 134, 178, 190, 293, 403(n57)
water   32–33, 44, 49, 55–56, 67, 76, 83, 87, 100–101, 129, 136, 147–148, 151–152, 156, 158, 159, 163, 166, 170, 173, 178, 212–214, 234, 248, 262, 325, 342, 369, 377, 379
waterpipes   44
Wehrmacht   70, 74
Weimar Republic   303
Weinreb, Alice   97
Western Allies   62, 301
Western standards   209, 272, 275, 277
Wille, Belkis   153
windows   58, 66-67, 100, 134, 181, 239, 377, 386, 387
Woods, Lebbeus   104
World Bank   29, 184, 189, 192, 245, 320, 345, 347, 371, 435(n138)
World Food Program   184, 219
World Trade Center   215, 217, 238, 323, 343
World War II (WWII)   2, 5, 7, 10, 11, 12, 17, 21, 22, 35, 38, 41, 43, 45, 59, 64, 78, 79, 95, 96, 97, 103, 112, 118, 139, 140, 141, 144, 145, 146, 147, 166, 167, 178, 181, 199, 214, 223, 231, 233, 235, 245, 261, 265, 266, 267, 271, 279, 291–292, 298, 304, 306, 312, 314–315, 319, 323–324, 325, 341, 344, 346, 365, 369, 374, 386, 390, 403(n57)
Wunderlich, Herbert   297

Y

yakuza   47, 92
Yale School of Public Health   316
Yamaguchi Yoshitada   50, 270
Yanukovych, Viktor F.   124, 289
Yarmolenko, Iryna   181, 386
Yokohama   38, 56, 400-01(n15)
Yonosuke Goto   51
Yoshikawa Hiroshi   50
Yovanovitch, Marie   189, 312, 443(n4)
Yugoslavia   95, 99, 104, 141, 355, 364, 413(n36)

Z

zaibatsu   48
Zaporizhzhia (also Zaporizhia)   23, 158
Zelensky, Volodymyr   145, 153, 235, 275, 283, 288, 316, 389, 431(n68)
Zhukov, Gregory   38, 63
Zone of Separation (ZOS)   358-62, 450(n94)
zoning   34, 56, 197

www.ingramcontent.com/pod-product-compliance
Lightning Source LLC
Chambersburg PA
CBHW052027030426
42337CB00027B/4889